# THE LIFE OF
# THE ANCIENT EAST

THE MACMILLAN COMPANY
NEW YORK · BOSTON · CHICAGO · DALLAS
ATLANTA · SAN FRANCISCO

MACMILLAN & CO., Limited
LONDON · BOMBAY · CALCUTTA
MELBOURNE

THE MACMILLAN CO. OF CANADA, Ltd.
TORONTO

PLATE I

HEAD OF TUTANKHAMEN—GRANITE (CAIRO)

# THE LIFE OF
# THE ANCIENT EAST

## BEING SOME CHAPTERS OF THE
## ROMANCE OF MODERN EXCAVATION

BY

REV. JAMES BAIKIE, F.R.A.S.

New York
THE MACMILLAN COMPANY
1923

COPYRIGHT, 1923,

By THE MACMILLAN COMPANY.

Set up and electrotyped. Published October, 1923.

Press of
J. J. Little & Ives Company
New York, U. S. A.

TO

A. St. CLAIR SUTHERLAND, M.A.

WITH THANKFULNESS

FOR

THIRTY-FIVE YEARS

OF

UNCLOUDED FRIENDSHIP

———

ἀδελφέ μου 'Ιωναθάν

# PREFACE

PERHAPS the subject-matter of this volume is too diversified to be completely expressed by its title; but between that and the explanatory note which follows it on the title-page an attempt is made to express, more or less satisfactorily, what the author would be at. The aim of the book is to take certain selected sites of the Ancient East, to recount with reasonable fulness of detail the story of modern excavation on these sites, and to attempt to show, not only what has been accomplished in the actual revelation of relics of antiquity, but also something which is of far more importance, and without which the mere disclosure of ancient buildings, works of art, or weapons and utensils is of little account,—the new knowledge which has come to us by way of excavation of how the great pioneer peoples of the Ancient East lived, thought, believed, and died. After all, this is the true aim of all archæology which really understands its business,—to make the life of the dead past live again before the eyes of the present generation, and for its interest and instruction.

Unless the excavator can do this for us, or, at all events, provide us with the materials which will enable others to do it, his work is merely vanity and vexation of spirit, though wealth and artistry beyond all dreaming should reward his pains; if he can do it, he is a benefactor, though he may have nothing to show for all his labour but a load of broken potsherds. And if these chapters convey to the minds of their readers even a little of the amazing work which modern excavation and the interpretation of its results have accomplished in this direction, they will have fulfilled the purpose for which they were written.

The sites chosen for study have not been taken at random, as might appear on a casual glance. Each one finds its place here because of some special contribution which it made in bygone days to human knowledge and culture, or else because of some special advance of our knowledge of the past which has resulted from its excavation. Thus, to take instances, Babylon has its place, not only because of its ancient greatness, but because of the inestimable value to the human race of its venerable system of law, revealed by the discovery of the Code of Hammurabi; Abydos, not only because it was the chief seat of that form of faith which expressed the Egyptian's invincible yearning for immortality, but also because its excavation has given back to us the centuries which went before the dawn of History in Egypt; and Gezer, because its very obscurity has enabled it to preserve for us, almost unbroken, the evidence of the strange sequence of races which strove for dominion in the most interesting land on earth.

Doubtless the choice might have been infinitely varied or extended; but books, and still more the patience of their readers, must have a limit, and I can only hope that in the main the selection made will justify itself.

The illustrations have been chosen with the view of ex-

hibiting, on the one hand, some of the most notable buildings on the sites dealt with, and, on the other, some of the
most interesting finds which have resulted from excavation.   For the kindness which has enabled me to use some
of them, I am indebted to the Societies and gentlemen who
have given permission, and their names are recorded on the
plates in question.

JAMES BAIKIE.

Torphichen,
July, 1923.

# CONTENTS

# ILLUSTRATIONS

xiii

Sketch map at end of volume.

# THE LIFE OF
# THE ANCIENT EAST

# THE LIFE OF THE ANCIENT EAST

## CHAPTER I

### INTRODUCTORY. THE WORK AND THE METHODS

MODERN times, including in that comparatively vague term the period lasting from the beginning of the nineteenth century to the present day, have witnessed two very remarkable developments of human knowledge. On the one hand, we have seen a wonderful increase of our knowledge of the world on which we live. Man has been rapidly tightening his grasp upon his earthly heritage. Lands that were only imperfectly known and sparsely populated have been brought under control and cultivation; great tracts that were absolutely unknown to our forefathers have become centres of industry and wealth; while the still unknown parts of the world have been steadily shrinking in extent before the daring and persistence of the explorers of all nations. Never, save perhaps in the Elizabethan Period, has the progress of human knowledge with regard to the world been so rapid as during the last century.

Remarkable as this advance has been, however, it is not more so than another which has gone on side by side with it. Man's conquest over the unknown has been steadily paralleled by his reconquest of the once known and forgotten.

Great regions of the earth which were once the centres and sources of civilisation, and from which the light of knowledge and of thought went forth upon its mission of enlightenment, regions which had been inhabited and made splendid by the pioneer races of humanity, had sunk out of human knowledge into oblivion as absolutely as though the earth had opened and swallowed them up.

Here and there scanty fragments of history, strangely distorted, and of legend, so vague in the mists of time as to seem totally fabulous, survived in the great classical writers, to remind us that there had been great men before Agamemnon, and that Babylonia and Mesopotamia and the Nile Valley had once been the seats of great empires, where mighty kings ruled over races skilled in the arts alike of war and of peace, and far advanced in all the material elements of civilisation; where vast cities, like Babylon, with its mountainous walls of burnt brick, or Thebes, with its hundred gates, and its myriads of bronze-clad charioteers, gathered within their circuit glories which the succeeding ages had never been able to emulate; and where great sages had penetrated into the mysteries of the universe deeper than their successors had ever been able to follow them.

Romance (or was it something more than romance?) spoke, too, of another great empire, sea-girt, and supreme in its dominion over the deep, which had been swallowed up at last by the element which it claimed to rule; and the Lost Atlantis flitted across the pages of the greatest philosopher of Greece, a standing temptation to all the mystery-hunters and romance-weavers of subsequent ages.

Scripture, too, contributed its element of reminiscence, and while it recounted solid historical facts about the great empires of the Euphrates and the Nile, mentioned also, in its occasional catalogues of strange and barbaric peoples, the name of an unknown empire recorded by no classical historian. "The Kings of the Hittites" were an unknown quantity, only to be traced, and that dimly, in the records of Israel.

In Egypt, by the very nature of the land, the oblivion that had descended upon the ancient empires which preceded Greece and Rome had not been quite so deep. The vast buildings of the mighty architects and engineers of the Pharaohs were such that nothing short of the absolute destruction of the whole face of the land could obliterate them; and so long as the Pyramids, the Sphinx, the Colossi, and the temples of Karnak and Luxor remained, no man could doubt the fact that there were giants in the days which witnessed the rearing of these huge creations. The piled and carven stones were there to testify to the might of Sesostris or Osymandias, or whatever other strangely distorted name the classical traveller might connect with the great monoliths which excited his wonder. Yet the very mention of Osymandias, with its suggestion of the pious invention of Diodorus, and the fine sonnet which Shelley has built upon it, only reminds us of how little was really known even of Egypt.

The case of Babylonia and Mesopotamia was different, and the ignorance regarding them was yet deeper. The circumstances and characteristics of the land of the

Euphrates and Tigris, and the materials in which its great men wrought their mighty works, alike denied to these the enduring quality of the hewn-stone fabrics of Egypt; and the huge mounds which stood for Nineveh and Asshur, Erech and Ur, hid the memory of these great cities as effectually as they covered the ruins of their greatness. Xenophon's references, vague and inaccurate to a degree, to the great cities of Mesopotamia, past which he and his Ten Thousand marched, and the wild legends of Ninus and Semiramis, suffice to show how entirely the true memory of the empires of Babylonia and Assyria had passed away from the human mind.

As for the Ægean area, Homer's Tale of Troy and its siege by the long-haired Achæans suggested a glorious past, when the men of the Eastern Mediterranean were greater, more highly civilised, more heroic than their successors; but Homer was no historian—a mere romancer, weaving out of his own imagination the beautiful design of a fabric that had never been seen on earth. Nor was there anything in the Scriptural mentions of the Hittites that promised for them any more distinguished destiny than the swift oblivion which has covered their fellows in the same rolls of barbarous and ill-sounding syllables, Hivites, and Perizzites, and Girgashites. A hundred years ago all that was known, or supposed to be known, about the great empires of the Ancient East could have been printed in the thinnest of duodecimos; and even so, the bulk of it would have been either untrue, or so distorted as to be unrecognisable for truth. To-day all that has been entirely changed. Round

these ancient empires, a literature has already grown up
which is almost comparable to that existing about Greece
and Rome, and which is steadily growing in amount and
value year by year. The actual historical outlines of the
fortunes of the better known among them—Egypt, and
the Mesopotamian kingdoms—are becoming more and more
clearly defined; and while there are still great gaps in our
knowledge, and much of the chronology is still uncertain,
the general course of history in these nations can be, and
has been traced with very considerable accuracy. The
buried cities themselves have risen again from their dust.
We can walk along the Procession Street of Babylon, and
tread the great pavement-blocks of red breccia and white
limestone over which Nebuchadnezzar's triumphal chariot
rolled as he went up to give thanks to Marduk in the vast
temple of E-sagila, under the shadow of the actual tower
of Babel, E-temenanki, "the Foundation-Stone of Heaven
and Earth." We can go down into the tomb of Pharaoh,
and see him lying there still, as he was laid in state three
and a half millenniums ago, amid the clash of sistra, and
the loud lament of the myriads of Thebes. We can read
the letters which the king of Babylon wrote to the king of
Egypt a hundred years before Moses was born, and can
hear these mighty potentates wrangling over questions of
tribute or bribe, like bagmen over an order, or horse-copers
over a deal. Europeans of to-day have walked through
halls where Sennacherib "gloried and drank deep," and
have ransacked the library where Sardanapalus, the much-
misunderstood, stored for himself the wisdom of all the

ages that had gone before in Babylon and Assyria; and the worshippers of the God of Israel can tread the Holy of Holies where the prayers of the great Oppressor of Israel were offered. The very graves have given up their dead to show us, so far as the outward form can show it, what manner of men they were who fought and ruled and legislated before Greece or Rome had been dreamed of; and the code by which men's lives were ordered in Babylonia when Abraham was at the start of his great venture can be read to-day in a Paris museum. Above all, the literatures of the greatest among these nations have now become open books. The weird religious legends of Babylonia, and the romances and love-songs of Egypt are the common possession of all who care to read them; and we can follow, in the very words in which they themselves gave utterance to it, the thought about God and the universe of men who died five thousand years ago.

These are the accomplished facts. Less fully realised, but steadily on the way to realisation, are the facts about the great civilisations and empires of the Ægean area and the Anatolian highland. Here we are handicapped by the fact that, while the actual writings of the Minoans and the Hittites are before us in abundance, the scripts are yet, in both cases, undeciphered, so that none can tell what the tablets of Knossos or the inscriptions of Boghaz-Kyoi may contain. Yet even here wonders have been accomplished, and the re-emergence of the ancient sea-kingdom of Crete has been as great a marvel as the whilom disappearance of Atlantis. No doubt, before many years have passed, the key to the mystery of both these scripts will have been found, and the records of the houses of Minos and Shubbiluliuma will be open to all who wish to read them.

Even more remarkable, perhaps, than the reconstruction of historical outlines, has been that of the actual conditions under which life was lived in these ancient days and lands. It is scarcely an exaggeration to say that we are as well informed with regard to life in ancient Egypt or Babylonia in the days of Abraham as we are with regard to life in Britain or France in the Middle Ages; in some respects, our knowledge is much more minute and accurate. In Egypt especially, thanks to the extraordinary skill and patience of the Egyptian sculptors and fresco-painters, the very minutest details, not only of great historical events or of court-life, but of the daily life of the common people, are presented to us with unsurpassable vivacity. In Babylonia and Assyria, the material from this point of view is scantier, for the wonderful reliefs of the palaces are mainly concerned with war, and the doings of kings; but even here, such documents as the Code of Hammurabi, and the contract tablets and accounts of the great business firms, such as Egibi and Murashu, provide abundant detail as to the ordinary life of the citizen. In the other areas, there is not so much to help us in this respect; but the frescoes of the Minoan and the Mycenæan palaces none the less constitute very remarkable and helpful documents for the reconstruction of an outline of life in those lands and times, while some of the details of sanitation and construction in the Cretan palaces and towns are such as to increase very considerably our respect for the civilisation to which these were an essential of daily life.

The outstanding characteristic of the work which has accomplished this remarkable resurrection of the past is that it is entirely a modern work,—modern in the time which it has occupied, and equally modern in the methods by which it has wrought. Practically, in point of date, it begins with the middle of the nineteenth century. Before that, of course, much had been done in the way of general survey and description of the lands and their ruins, so far as these were visible. Napoleon's savants had made their monumental survey of Egypt, and some sporadic and haphazard exploration had been accomplished by Belzoni and others. In the valleys of the Euphrates and Tigris, Rich, Ker Porter, Buckingham and others had done a little in the direction of a superficial examination and description of the mounds which mark the sites of the great cities of Babylonia and Assyria, and had here and there even scratched the surface, and brought back a few inscribed bricks and other relics. Beyond that, the vast field was practically untouched. The whole period which has witnessed the entire transformation of human knowledge with regard to the great empires of the Ancient East, is less than three-quarters of a century.

Even within that time, there has been a radical change in methods of work and in perspective. The early explorers were at first largely guided by, and in fact subservient to, classical authority, and tried to fit their discoveries into the outlines provided by Herodotus, Strabo, Diodorus, Xenophon and others. This was, of course, both natural and necessary; but to-day the proportion of things is reversed. The classical authorities are by no means ignored; but for our ground-work of information we depend, not upon them, but upon the first-hand material provided by excavation in the actual countries concerned; and we correct the errors and the faulty perspective of the ancient historians by the irrefutable data afforded by contemporary documents and relics.

Moreover,—and here the change is even more striking,—as the work has progressed, our ideas of the relative value of the various classes of finds has entirely changed. At first, Mariette, Botta, Layard, and the others looked, naturally enough, for big and striking finds as the fitting rewards of their labours and anxieties. A colossal statue,—a royal palace,—a catacomb with dozens of carcasses of buried beast-gods,—these were the prizes at which they aimed. It was natural, but it was wasteful, and no doubt, much that was of priceless value (in the light of modern methods and ideas) was overlooked and probably lost forever in the process of unearthing the big game of the archæologist. Even Schliemann was far from guiltless in this respect, and in pursuit of his fixed idea destroyed a great deal that his successors would have known how to prize. We cannot blame the early excavators for this. They were at the beginning of things. The science of excavation had to be created by degrees and experience. The knowledge of the importance of everything ancient, from a pyramid to a potsherd, had to be slowly and painfully learned; and many

things suffered in the process by which impatient investigators were at last trained to curb their eagerness, and to
accept the fact that there might be more value in a bit of
broken crockery than in a colossus.

Nowadays that lesson may be said to have been thoroughly learned. When Jim Pinkerton, in Stevenson's
"Wrecker," sent Loudon Dodd to search for opium in the
wreck of the *Flying Scud*, he warned him that he was to
stay by the brig till she was kindling-wood, and to split
that kindling-wood with his penknife, rather than miss
anything in his search. This is precisely the point of view
of the modern explorer, and these are his marching-orders,
for himself and his subordinates. Nothing is too small to
be of value in his eyes; in fact it might almost be said that
the smaller the object is the more likely it is to be of value.
The big spoil, of course, is not despised; it is all in the day's
work; but the first and second and great commandments, on
which hang all the law and the prophets, are to neglect
nothing and to overlook nothing. No matter how un-
promising or how thoroughly worked-over a site may appear,
the true explorer will not leave it until he has got down to
virgin soil, over the whole area if possible, and passed
every spadeful of earth on the site through a fine sieve. It
is slow, it is monotonous, it is almost heart-breaking work;
but it pays.

The public, which reads the occasional accounts of great
discoveries, sandwiched in between the betting-news and
the season's fashions, probably imagines the explorer to be
a man somewhat of the type of Aladdin, spending his time

in wandering through wonderful underground chambers, and lighting in happy moments upon monarchs throned and crowned, and royal palaces, and treasure-chambers, "dis-kivering no end," as the man in "Westward Ho!" puts it. Actually he might be defined, as Dr. Johnson defined the lexicographer, as a "harmless drudge" who lives laborious days toiling at work which a navvy would despise, and is happy if, at the end of many weary weeks, he has found the material,—perhaps a handful of broken potsherds, or a fragment of inscribed stone,—which shall enable him to announce a new fact, or to correct an old one. It is not nearly so romantic as was the old exploration in the fifties of last century; it is infinitely less so than the feats of the dream-explorer of the man in the street, an explorer who never was on sea or land; but the work is done, and the knowledge is secured.

Mr. Weigall, whose right to speak on the subject none can impugn, tells in his own cheerful way the experience which awaits the average digger. "There came to the camp of a certain professor, who was engaged in excavating the ruins of an ancient Egyptian city, a young and faultlessly-attired Englishman, whose thirst for romantic adventure had led him to offer his services as an unpaid assistant digger.

"This immaculate personage had read in novels and tales many an account of the wonders which the spade of the excavator could reveal, and he firmly believed that it was only necessary to set a 'nigger' to dig a little hole in the ground to open the way to the treasuries of the

Pharaohs.  Gold, silver, and precious stones gleamed before him, in his imagination, as he hurried along subterranean passages to the vaults of long-dead kings.  He expected to slide upon the seat of his very well-made breeches down the staircase of the ruined palace which he had entered by way of the skylight, and to find himself at the bottom, in the presence of the bejewelled dead.  In the intervals between such experiences he was of opinion that a little quiet gazelle shooting would agreeably fill in the swiftly passing hours; and at the end of the season's work he pictured himself returning to the bosom of his family with such a tale to tell that every ear would be opened to him.

"On his arrival at the camp he was conducted to the site of his future labours; and his horrified gaze was directed over a large area of mud-pie, knee-deep in which a few bedraggled natives slushed their way downwards.  After three weeks' work on this distressing site, the professor announced that he had managed to trace through the mud the outlines of the palace walls, once the feature of the city, and that the work here might now be regarded as finished.

"He was then conducted to a desolate spot in the desert, and until the day on which he fled back to England he was kept to the monotonous task of superintending a gang of natives whose sole business it was to dig a large hole in the sand, day after day and week after week."

The outsider might suspect that the "certain professor" had been amusing himself at the beginner's expense; but the experience of the skilled excavator is often quite as discouraging.  "Two years ago," says Mr. Weigall again,

"I assisted at an excavation upon a site of my own selection, the net result of which, after six weeks' work, was one mummified cat! To sit over the work day after day, as did the unfortunate promoter of this particular enterprise, with the flies buzzing around his face, and the sun blazing down upon him from a relentless sky, was hardly a pleasurable task; and to watch the clouds of dust go up from the tip-heap, where tons of unprofitable rubbish rolled down the hillside all day long, was an occupation for the damned. Yet that is excavating as it is usually found to be." If the work of the explorer is thus seen to be less romantic, it is also seen to be more heroic than we generally fancy it. Both courage and devotion of the highest type are required; and it is by these, not less than by learning and good fortune, that the results of modern excavation have been achieved.

Occasionally, it is true, there does come a find romantic enough in its circumstances to satisfy even the most hardened devourer of sensational fiction. When Brugsch Pasha was lowered down the shaft at Der-el-Bahri, and found himself face to face with a score of ancient Pharaohs; when Mr. T. M. Davis opened the tomb of Yuaa and Tuau, and found every article of its furniture as fresh as though the tomb had been closed only the day before; when Lord Carnarvon and Mr. Howard Carter gazed through the gap in the wall of Tutankhamen's tomb upon the marvels of art and craftsmanship within; when Schliemann's great pit at Mycenæ revealed the shaft-graves under the great stone circle, with their silent occupants gold-masked and corse-letted; or when the Cup-Bearer at Knossos slowly rose to

view from the soil that had veiled his eyes for three millenniums,—in such moments the romance of exploration is
at its height, and almost touches the level of the cheap
novel.  And these are the moments that live in the mem-
ories of the readers of books on exploration,—not the long
weeks and months of painful and monotonous toil which
produced next to no results, except perhaps a few potsherds
or a fragment of an old inscription.  Yet the broken earthenware or the scrap of lettering may prove in the end to be
more valuable, from the point of view of the archæologist
and historian, than the gold of the Mycenæ graves, or
the exquisite jewellery of Dahshur or the Valley of the
Kings.  A native Egyptian once remarked about Professor
Flinders Petrie, "He has worked five and twenty years
now; he must be very rich."  So he is, no doubt, in the
objects for which he has sought; but as a commercial operation, his excavations can scarcely have been more profit-
able than the search for the Tobermory Galleon.

In fact the whole perspective and ideal of exploration
have gradually changed as time has gone on.  The early
explorers looked for, and made, big and startling finds;
naturally, so far, because the ground was virtually untouched.  To a great extent, also, they had no appreciation
of the value of the smaller materal which lay around them.
We may deplore the fact that much priceless treasure has
thus been over-laid, and has perished; but we have to recognise the fact that pioneer work is always, and necessarily,
more or less wasteful.  That is a condition of its being.  It
is justified if it does genuinely pioneer, and open the way

for others, who, if they have a proper sense of proportion, will not complain unduly of the loss which has been unavoidably entailed by the ruder methods whose success has given them their opportunity.

But to-day the position is different. No longer do we look for the arresting finds,—winged bulls or lions, royal palaces, intact tombs,—by which the earlier explorers justified their work, and drew the public attention and support to their efforts. There may still be the possibility of such discoveries, though in a land like Egypt, for instance, it is steadily growing less. But the explorer's object now is rather the finding of material to link up and connect his already existing knowledge, to correct misconceptions, and to make certain of every step of his ground as he advances. Above all he desires to be able to build his reconstruction of ancient history and life upon first-hand records, and to go straight to the fountainhead for facts. Anything that will help him to do this, however insignificant it may be in itself, is of more value in his eyes than the most imposing monument which adds nothing to what is already known. Thus during the excavations at Babylon, Dr. Koldewey found in the midst of the palace wall a burial which, from the gorgeousness of the robes upon the body, he conjectures to be possibly that of Nabopolassar himself, the founder of the Neo-Babylonian Empire. If that conjecture could be confirmed, it would, no doubt, be very interesting. But supposing that Dr. Koldewey had found Nebuchadnezzar in all his glory, let alone Nabopolassar, the discovery, while of great importance because of the immediate revival of in-

terest in excavation which it would have created, would
not have been one-tenth part as important from a scientific
and historical point of view, as that discovery which was
made, almost by accident, when a fellah woman in Egypt,
digging for phosphates in the rubbish-heaps of Tell-el-
Amarna, came upon a batch of tiny clay tablets inscribed
with the arrow-headed characters of Babylonia. She sold
her interest in the find for a few shillings, and the tablets
would not arrest more than a casual glance from the ordinary curiosity-hunter, for they are neither beautiful nor
imposing. But they are worth infinitely more than their
weight in gold to us now; for they have re-created for us
the whole inner history of one of the most remarkable crises
of the ancient world, and they have given that sense of
reality, that atmosphere, without which all our facts about
the past remain dry, mechanical, and lacking in perspective.
With these little clay oblongs as our guide, it is possible to
make the court intrigues, the plottings and counter-plottings,
the heroisms and treacheries of these ancient days live again,
and display themselves, not in a few dry dates and facts,
but as they actually happened upon the world-stage. We
can hear the very words, we can enter into the hopes and
fears, and sometimes the despairs, of the actors in one of the
great tragedies which determined the destiny of the ancient
world. Alongside a possibility such as this, the most dramatic discovery of buried treasures or royalties seems, and is,
entirely insignificant.

It may seem that when the aims of modern exploration
are thus put in their proper perspective, the romance of

excavation has departed; but this is a total misconception of the case. Even in the old days the thrilling moments were few and brief, compared with the long days of drudgery. At the present time, there are still thrills for the excavator, though perhaps not so many as when the lands were almost untouched. He knows now more or less what to expect, and there is not the breathless awaiting of the unknown, though sometimes it does arise, to confound expectation (notably so in the case of Mr. Howard Carter's 1922 discovery of the funerary furniture of Tutankhamen). But if there is more drudgery and less thrill, that is for the explorer alone. From every other aspect, the outsider, the general reader, has gained. The patient and laborious collection of minute material and detail has made it possible to present a far more brilliant, truthful, and interesting picture of these ancient lands and times than was ever possible before. Take such books as Sir Gaston Maspero's "Histoire Ancienne," or Professor Breasted's "Egypt," and contrast them with what passed for histories of the great lands of antiquity in the days of our grandfathers. It is not only that the facts are more abundant and more accurate, and that instead of a handful of fancies picked from Herodotus, Strabo, or Xenophon, you have the actual truth first-hand from the sculptured stones and inscribed clay of Egypt and Babylonia; it is that the life of these lands and times has been called up again from the grave of the past, and that you see the long procession of kings and armies and peoples passing before you in their habit as they lived.

You can stand in the council-chamber of Sesostris; or

read in the library of Sardanapalus; or, if you prefer it, you can go down to the market-place, and learn how the subjects of these mighty monarchs live, how they are housed, how they transact their daily business, what are their thoughts about life and death. Far from having abolished the romance of the past by his meticulous insistence on the importance of detail, there is no man who has so helped to put flesh and blood upon the dry bones of antiquity, and to breathe the breath of life into its nostrils, as the excavator with his spade and basket, his sieve and his paraffin-wax, and his inexhaustible patience in the pursuit of the very smallest detail which can add to man's knowledge of the days of old.

# CHAPTER II

"In the tomb of the priest Khnemhotp, at Beni Hasan, there
is a great pictured scene which, as the inscription accom-
panying it informs us, represents a voyage made by him in
order *to learn to know the things of Abydos.* His mummy
lies on a vessel under a canopy, and the Sem priest and
Kherheb remain at his side throughout the voyage. In the
sacred town he was placed before the god of the dead as a
new vassal, and also took part in his festival services. Then,
accompanied by wives and children, he returned home once
more to occupy his magnificent tomb at Beni Hasan." These
words of Erman bring before us an outstanding instance of
the persistent Egyptian belief and custom which made of
Abydos, a city by no means important otherwise in Egyptian
history, the Holy City of the land, the place to which every
Egyptian desired to make a pilgrimage either during his life,
or, as in the case of Khnemhotep, after his death; or, if his
circumstances forbade this, at least to have in the sacred
place a votive stone erected, or a funeral offering of pottery
left, to link him with the great god of the resurrection and
the blessings which he bestowed upon his faithful worshippers. There were three places where the devout Egyp-

[ 19 ]

tian hoped to secure for himself after death the blessing of immortality. The first was his own tomb, with its images and offerings, and the services of the tomb-priests; the second was one of the temples where he had worshipped in life, and where, as a special reward from the king, he might be allowed to place a statue of himself, that it might share in the offerings which were made to the god. But these two were essentially for the great and the rich of the land; the third was open to the humblest and the poorest. At Abydos was the tomb of Osiris, the great god of the Under-world,—to be buried near him was infallibly to secure all the blessings which the god could bestow; if your circumstances made such a thing impossible, it was still possible to keep the channel of blessing open by erecting *a stone on the staircase of the great god;* while, if even this was beyond the means of the devout aspirant, he could in the last resort send a piece of votive pottery to be laid as near as possible to the holy place, and so establish the much-coveted link between himself and the lord of eternal life.

Accordingly, from a very early period in Egyptian history, it became the custom for the great and wealthy of the land to have a tomb at Abydos. Often the Holy City was preferred for this purpose even to the capital, where the dead noble might rest beside his king; or, if it was necessary for him to accompany his liege-lord in death as in life, it was still possible for him to erect a cenotaph at Abydos and to furnish it with all that might be needed for his soul when it visited the abode of the great god. During the Middle Kingdom, it was more customary to secure the advantages of Abydos by the erection of a stele or memorial slab; and multitudes of these votive steles are to be found in the museums. But all through, and especially during the earliest period, and again from the XIXth to the XXVIth Dynasty, when there was apparently a great revival of the cult of Osiris, the common folk of the land pinned their faith to the efficacy of the *ex-voto* piece of pottery, laid as near as might be to the sacred site. The result is that Abydos is simply a wilderness of broken pots of all sorts and ages, from the earliest period down to the time of the Saite revival. It is impossible to move about the site of the ancient sepulchres without crushing into yet smaller fragments some of the potsherds which litter the whole ground; and the modern Arab name for the place does no more than justice to its chief characteristic—"*Umm-el-Ga'ab*"—"the Mother of Pots."

The reason for this extraordinary development of devotion lies far back in the religious history of Egypt. In the beginning, Abydos had nothing to do with Osiris, who was essentially a god of the Delta, having his main sanctuary at Tattu or Busiris, where, according to the legend, his backbone was buried, and from which came his emblem, the curious jointed pillar. The original god of Abydos was Khentamenti, "the First of the Westerners," a god of the dead, who was sometimes united with another dog or jackal god, Upuat, the guide of the dead. At a comparatively early date, however, the cult of the Delta god began to find favour at Abydos, and with the growth of the legend that his head was buried at Abydos, after his dismemberment by

Set, his popularity in the southern city was established, and
he was gradually identified with the local Khentamenti as
Osiris-Khentamenti, and took possession of the ancient
temple of the local god, which thenceforth became the most
holy spot in Egypt. Even before the establishment at
Abydos of the one god who could claim universal worship
in Egypt, the site sacred to "the First of the Westerners"
had attracted to it the great kings of the earliest dynasties,
who had left there their tombs or cenotaphs, and whose
example had been followed by their nobles; but from the
time of the Middle Kingdom the vogue of Abydos became
overwhelming, and, as we have seen, "the pious Egyptian
desired no better fortune than to have his corpse carried to
Abydos, there to find its last abode beside the tomb of
Osiris." In the XIXth Dynasty, a great impulse was given
to the cult by the piety of Sety I and Ramses II, who supplemented the ancient sanctuary of the Old and Middle Kingdoms by the erection of their own temples, of which that of
Sety is famous for the beauty and delicacy of its reliefs; and
it seems probable that this revival of interest in the ancient
holy place was due to the discovery of some of the royal
tombs of the early dynasties. The name of one of these
early kings, Zer of Professor Petrie's list, was read by the
antiquaries of the New Empire as Khent, and they evidently
concluded that they had found the actual tomb of Khentamenti, which to their minds was that of Osiris.

Such a discovery, based on a misunderstanding which no
one could correct, was more than sufficient to establish for
the rest of Egyptian history the sacred reputation of the

ancient sanctuary. From this time onwards the mounds in
the neighbourhood of the tomb of the old king who had been
so quaintly metamorphosed into a god were covered with a
continually growing mass of pottery left by pious pilgrims or
sent by devout souls who could not afford the pilgrimage,
so that the place became indeed "the Mother of Pots," and
later a figure of Osiris lying on a granite lion-headed bier
was with all due solemnity placed in the supposed tomb of
the dead god, there to be discovered in the fulness of time
by a French explorer, and solemnly proclaimed by him as
"the Bed of Osiris." Apparently the Egyptians, no less
than M. Amélineau, were often misled in their desire to
find a consecrated site on which to deposit the little brown
offering-cups which were to secure the much-prized blessing
of Osiris, for very often the pots have been placed where
there was nothing beneath, sacred or otherwise. Wherever
there was a mound at Abydos, the Egyptian of the New
Empire evidently concluded that something very sacred
lay beneath, and decorated the hillock with his offerings,
thereby sometimes causing the modern explorer to spend
time and trouble to no purpose. On the whole, however,
the hits were more numerous than the misses, and the presence of pots in large numbers has been often a fairly good
indication of the probability of success in digging.

By the time of the XIIth Dynasty, when the piety of the
great kings of the line of Senusert and Amenemhat erected
a magnificent temple in the Holy City to continue the tradition of the Old Empire, there had been established at
Abydos a kind of Passion-Play, the earliest known drama

in the world, in which the incidents of the myth of Osiris were re-enacted.  The play is, of course, lost; but fortunately a stele of one of the officials of Senusert III, now in the Berlin Museum, gives us at least an outline of the proceedings, from which we may form some idea of how this drama, the father of all dramatic representations, proceeded. The play consisted of eight acts, each of them probably occupying a day, and the king's representative tells us how he took part in each act.  His narrative is as follows: "I celebrated the 'Procession of Upuat,' when he proceeded to champion his father (Osiris)." "I repulsed those who were hostile to the Neshmet barque, and I overthrew the enemies of Osiris." "I celebrated the 'Great Procession,' following the god in his footsteps." "I sailed the divine barque, while Thoth made the voyage." "I equipped the barque 'Shining in Truth,' of the Lord of Abydos, with a chapel; I put on his beautiful regalia when he went forth to the district of Peker." "I led the way of the god to his tomb in Peker." "I championed Unnefer (Osiris) on 'That Day of the Great Battle'; I overthrew all the enemies upon the shore of Nedyt." "I caused him to proceed into the barque 'The Great'; it bore his beauty; I put jubilation in the western highlands, when they saw the beauty of the Neshmet barque.  It landed at Abydos, and they brought Osiris, First of the Westerners, Lord of Abydos, to his palace."

From this summary narrative we can discern the course of the play to have been something like this: On the first day, the ancient god of the dead, Upuat, "the Opener of

the Ways," goes out in procession and scatters the foes of
Osiris, "preparing the way of the Lord." On the second
day, Osiris appears in his sacred barque, accompanied by a
crew of specially favoured pilgrims. The foes of the god,
represented by some of the other pilgrims, beset the barque,
and there is a general *mêlée*, in which the favoured companions of Osiris repel his enemies—a scene which the crowd
no doubt hugely enjoyed and in which each pilgrim would
be able to take his humble part. The death of Osiris is not
mentioned, doubtless as too sacred; but it probably took
place in the third act, for in the fourth Thoth goes out,
probably to find the body of the dead god. In the fifth act
the body of the god was equipped with all the rich funerary
regalia, and he was laid in a mortuary chapel on his barge;
while in the sixth the funeral procession wound out of the
city to lay the sacred body in its tomb in the western desert,
followed by an immense throng of pilgrims and citizens.
In the seventh act, which took place on the river-bank at a
place called Nedyt, there was a great battle, in which the
actors representing Set and the other enemies of Osiris were
triumphantly overthrown by those representing Horus and
his companions. In the eighth and final act, Osiris, restored
to life, enters the temple of Abydos in triumphal procession.

One can readily understand the influence which a great
dramatic spectacle such as this had upon the religious imagination of a simple and comparatively primitive people.
Fifteen hundred years later, Herodotus saw at Papremis a
similar scene, though doubtless on a scale far inferior to the

great celebration at Abydos; and his description shows
what a hold the Passion-Play had on the Egyptian mind
even at such a late date. "A few priests," he says, "are
occupied about the image, but the greater number stand,
with wooden clubs, at the entrance of the temple; while
others, accomplishing their vows, amounting to more than
a thousand men, each armed in like manner, stand in a body
on the opposite side. But the image, placed in a small
wooden temple, gilded all over, they carry out to another
sacred dwelling; then the few who were left about the
image draw a four-wheeled carriage, containing the temple
and the image that is in it. But the priests, who stand at
the entrance, refuse to give them admittance; and the vota-
ries, bringing succour to the god, oppose, and then strike,
whereupon an obstinate conflict with clubs ensues and they
break one another's heads, and, as I conjecture, many die
of their wounds; though the Egyptians deny that anyone
dies."

Perhaps the play was not so deadly to the actors as Herodotus imagined, for the Egyptians, as he himself tells us elsewhere, had good hard heads; but in any case a pilgrim would
no doubt count a broken head, got in the service of Osiris, as
the greatest of honours, while death in such a cause would
infallibly ensure a blessed immortality. The popularity of
the Passion-Play festival is evidenced by the fact that the
pilgrims frequently repeat on their tablets at Abydos the
prayer that after death they may have the privilege of par-
taking in the celebration of the mystery of the death and
resurrection of their god. It was, no doubt, the widespread

vogue of this play which gave to Osiris a place in the affection of the whole nation never held by any other god, not
even by Amen when the fortunes of the Theban dynasties
and their god were at their flood.

Thus, in spite of the fact that Abydos never played in the
history of Egypt a part in any way comparable to that
played by cities like Thebes or Memphis, the Holy City of
Osiris occupied an altogether unique place in the story of
Egyptian Religion and culture, and the massing there for so
long a period of material of all kinds bearing on the religion
and civilisation of the land made it certain that sooner or
later the site would prove to be of the greatest importance
for the study alike of Egyptian origins and of the development of the national faith and art. Abydos was early
recognised as a site which promised results of the highest
value to the student of Egyptian culture; and the promise
has been amply fulfilled, though it is only within the last
quarter of a century that the harvest has been gathered in
with anything like completeness.

The work at the Holy City, as on so many other sites, was
begun by that great pioneer of Egyptian exploration,
Auguste Mariette. In 1859 this great explorer cleared the
temple of Sety I, famous for the wonderful beauty and
delicacy of its sculptures in low relief, which are perhaps
the finest work of their kind left us by the New Empire,
though their slightly morbid grace cannot compare with the
truth and vigour of the Old Kingdom work. Mariette also
excavated at the temple of Ramses II, a little to the north,
and conducted considerable works within the sacred en-

closure of the great temple of Osiris, without, however, any great success. He believed the temple of Sety I to be the Memnonium of Strabo, in which, as subsequent exploration has shown, he was mistaken; and his summary of the prospects of excavation on the site of the Osiris temple reads somewhat strangely in view of the results of Professor Petrie's patient labour in tracing the plans of the various temples which succeeded one another on the site from the Ist to the XXVIth Dynasty. "Unfortunately," he says, "there now remains absolutely nothing of Egypt's most ancient and most venerated sanctuary, nor is there the faintest hope that even the foundations will ever be brought to light by any fresh excavations." Fortune has been kinder than he ventured to hope.

On another point, however, Mariette delivered himself of a more hopeful, and, in the event, a remarkably successful prophecy. Speaking of the mound known as Kom-es-Sultan in the sacred enclosure, he says, "There can be no doubt that the famous tomb of Osiris is not far off. . . . The excavations now being carried on . . . may any day lead to the discovery of the still unknown entrance to the divine tomb, if indeed it were ever a subterranean vault." His prophecy had to wait a good many years for its fulfilment; but it was amply justified, when in 1913-14, M. Naville, and his assistants, following up the work of Professor Petrie and Miss Murray, discovered at the end of a 45-foot sloping passage a great chamber, 100 feet by 60, divided into three sections by two rows of massive granite monolithic pillars, and leading, in its turn, to a smaller chamber, which, from

PLATE II

*Eygpt Exploration Society*

VIEWS OF THE POOL OF OSIRIS-OSIREION, ABYDOS

*Reproduced by permission from the " Journal of Egyptian Archæology "*

its sculptures, was evidently meant as a ceremonial tomb of Osiris.

In Strabo's account of Abydos occurs the following passage: "Abydos, the site of the Memnonium, a wonderful palace of stone, built in the manner of the Labyrinth, only somewhat less elaborate in its complexity. Below the Memnonium is a well reached by passages with low vaults consisting of a single stone and distinguished for their extent and mode of construction." M. Naville finds the old geographer's statement justified in every point. The great chamber was evidently the sacred pool of Osiris. In its centre was a rectangular platform of massive stonework, supporting the granite monoliths which upheld the roof. Around this island platform were the waters of the pool, bordered on all sides by a ledge of stonework at the same level as the platform, from which opened all round the chamber the vaults "consisting of a single stone," of which Strabo speaks. The carvings in the passage are of the time of Merenptah of the XIXth Dynasty, and those in the ceremonial tomb-chamber beyond the pool are also XIXth Dynasty work; but the great chamber of the pool is either a very remarkable imitation of the fine monolithic work of the earliest Dynasties, or actually dates from their time. "The whole building," says M. Naville, "the style of its masonry, the total absence of any decoration reminds one very strongly of the so-called temple of the Sphinx, so that I think that this construction goes back to the age of the pyramids, it may be even older than the temple of the Sphinx." Whether this opinion be justified or not, the discovery is a remarkable confirmation of Mariette's judgment; for, whatever the date of the structure, there can scarcely be any doubt that this great subterranean chamber, with its sacred pool, was the most holy place of the sanctuary of Osiris, and that his ceremonial tomb lay beyond it, renewed perhaps by the kings of the XIXth Dynasty in the same access of piety and devotion to the cult of Osiris which led to the subsequent placing in the tomb of King Zer, assumed to be the real tomb of the dead god, of the granite bier which M. Amélineau discovered.

Apart from the supreme attraction of the Osireion, the main interest of the existing buildings at Abydos lies in the temple of Sety I with its marvellous carvings. The temple is built on a plan quite unusual in Egypt, and due, no doubt, to the fact that it was never meant to be an isolated structure, but to form part of the great complex of sacred buildings associated with the cult of Osiris. Originally it consisted of a pylon and an outer court, now entirely destroyed, a second court, partly preserved, two successive Hypostyle Halls, and a row of seven sanctuaries, instead of the usual single shrine, which are dedicated to Osiris, Isis, Horus, Ra-Harakhte, Amen, and the deified Sety. Behind these lay a western hall with adjoining chambers, and to the south a series of chambers was built at right angles to the axis of the main building, so that the whole building was shaped like a T, with the right arm of the cross-piece wanting. The reliefs on the walls, already mentioned, particularly those in the Second Hypostyle Hall, and the sanctuaries, are of the greatest interest. They have not the vigour and freshness of the great relief work of the Old Kingdom; but the portraits of the king, repeated again and again in the act of adoration, are of very high merit, while Egyptian art has little to show that can surpass for beauty and delicacy the relief in which Osiris is represented sitting on his throne, with the goddesses Maat and Renpet before him, and Isis, Amentet, and Nephthys behind his throne. On the wall of a long corridor of the southern wing is the famous Abydos List of Kings. Sety, bearing a censer, and Ramses II, as crown-prince, reciting hymns from a roll of papyrus, stand before a list of their royal ancestors, the names of seventy-six of whom are recorded, beginning with Mena, the first king of the Ist Dynasty, and extending to the worshipping king himself. The Abydos tablet has been of the greatest importance in the reconstruction of the order of Egyptian history, as representing the knowledge possessed by the XIXth Dynasty, and though it is by no means complete, it remains the most important inscription of its kind existing in Egypt, though of inferior authority, for the early kings, to the Palermo Stone.

Close to the temple of Sety stands all that remains of that of his son Ramses II, once evidently a sumptuous structure built of fine limestone, and adorned with red and black granite and alabaster, but now a melancholy ruin. Some of its relief work is executed, like that of Sety, in fine low relief; but the sunk reliefs in the court and the first hall compare very poorly with the exquisite work of the earlier king.

It is not with the buildings of Abydos, however, interest-

ing and even beautiful though they may be, that its present
importance is chiefly linked, but with the long-forgotten
tombs of the kings of the Ist and IInd Dynasties, which,
after being the objects of reverence during many centuries,
passed for many centuries more into complete oblivion,
but have within our own time yielded up what has survived
of their treasures to enable us to see, albeit dimly, the
picture of an Egypt which was long thought to be only a
matter of romantic and unreliable legend, and have shown
us a civilisation almost incredibly ancient, and organised
even in its earliest stages with a thoroughness and completeness which presupposes many centuries of preparation, going
back to a period so remote that the imagination falters in
the attempt to realise the antiquity of the dawn of culture
in the Nile Valley.   We have now to tell, in brief outline,
the story of the recovery of the fragments of this oldest of
all organised civilisations,—a recovery which has, to some
extent at least, made real to us a race of mighty kings
who a few years ago were but a line of shadowy names in
the list of Manetho or the inscribed tablets of Abydos or
Saqqara, often held to have no more reality than the
shadows of a dream.   The Royal Tombs of Abydos have
neither beauty nor grandeur to attract the attention in comparison with the later temples which grew up on the site
which they had made holy ground; the guide-book which
gives pages to the glories of the temple of Sety dismisses
them with six lines, ending with the remark that "there
is now practically nothing to be seen"; all the same they
have done more for the building up of a true conception of

PLATE III

ROYAL TOMBS OF THE FIRST DYNASTY, ABYDOS

1. ZER        2. KHASEKHEMUI

*Reproduced by permission from "The Royal Tombs of the First Dynasty," by William Petrie*

early Egyptian history and culture than all the temples in the Nile Valley put together.

Up to the nineties of last century, our information with regard to the lines of kings who had reigned in Egypt before the time of the Pyramid-Builders was practically confined to the lists of kings given in the fragments of Manetho's history which have been preserved, and the various king-lists of the temples, the Palermo Stone, and the mishandled fragments of the Turin Papyrus. Of these, Manetho, as reported by his epitomisers, alone attempted to clothe his skeleton of facts, if such they were, with a little flesh and blood; but his praiseworthy efforts rather impaired his credit as an historian than otherwise. It did not conduce to faith in the old writer's trustworthiness to be told that that in the reign of king Neferkheres "the Nile flowed with honey during eleven days," or that king Sesokhris, "was five cubits in height, and his breadth three cubits." Manetho's first three dynasties were looked upon as somewhat more than doubtful quantities, and for all practical purposes Egyptian history began with the Pyramid-Builders of the IVth Dynasty, Khufu, Khafra, and Menkaura, or at earliest with their immediate predecessor, Seneferu.

Within the last thirty years all this has been changed. We now know that the shadowy kings of the first three dynasties were indeed very solid realities, commanding great armies, making conquests which resulted in the unifying of the previously separate kingdoms of the North and South, presiding over a court which even at this incredibly early date was elaborately organised and supplied with a regular bureaucracy, and having at their command the whole resources of a nation already highly skilled in all the arts and crafts. No more extensive or solid contribution to our knowledge of prehistoric times has been made in our day than that which has resulted from the excavations at Abydos, and the related researches at Naqada, El Amrah, and Naga-ed-Der.

We have already seen that as early as the middle of last century Mariette, in describing the results of his own investigations at Abydos, ventured the prediction that antiquities of much more ancient date than those which he had unearthed might yet be discovered on the site, so that it is unjust to the great pioneer to say, as Budge does, that "it is quite clear that he never suspected the real antiquity of the site, nor even suspected the existence there of antiquities belonging to a period earlier than the VIth Dynasty." "The excavations," said Mariette, "may furnish us with valuable tombs which become more and more ancient the further we penetrate into the sides of the mountain, so that it is not unreasonable to hope that in time we may come upon some belonging even to the Ist Dynasty." His prediction began to receive its fulfilment nearly forty years later, when the Mission Amélineau began its work at Abydos in 1895, and was followed by the much more thorough labours of Professor Petrie in 1899 and subsequent years, and those of Messrs. Naville, Hall and Peet in 1909-14.

The site of the Royal Tombs of the earliest Dynasties lies to the south of the ancient temple of Osiris, and nearer

to the hills. "Abydos," says Petrie, "is by its situation one
of the remarkable sites of Egypt. . . . The cliffs, about
800 feet high, come forward and form a bay about four
miles across, which is nowhere more than a couple of miles
deep from the cultivation. Along the edge of this bay
stand the temples and the cemeteries of Abydos; while
back in the circle of the hills lies the great cemetery of the
founders of Egyptian history, the kings of the Ist Dynasty.
The site selected for the royal tombs was on a low spur
from the hills, slightly raised above the plain. . . . The
situation is wild and silent; close round it the hills rise
high on two sides, a ravine running up into the plateau from
the corner where the lines meet. Far away, and below us,
stretches the long green valley of the Nile, beyond which
for dozens of miles the eastern cliffs recede far into the dim
distance."

To this lonely spot came in the winter of 1895-96 M.
Amélineau, and in the course of his first campaign the explorer discovered a number of early graves similar to those
which Petrie had been excavating the previous winter at
Naqada and Ballas, in which the body lay on its side in a
crouching posture, the knees drawn up to the level of the
breast. In these graves was found a quantity of stone
jars and pottery vessels of primitive design and ornamentation. Returning to the attack in the winter of 1896-97,
M. Amélineau discovered a large and important tomb, containing articles of metal, worked flints, and jars of pottery
and alabaster; and this he believed to be of even earlier
date than the primitive graves of the first campaign. What

he believed to be the supreme discovery of his excavations, however, was made in 1897-98, when the diggings disclosed a great tomb belonging to a king whose name the explorer read as Khent.   It seemed to M. Amélineau that a king so named could only be Osiris Khentamenti, who must have actually reigned upon earth; and accordingly he announced the discovery of "the Tomb of Osiris."   The building so named was shaped like an underground house with walls on three sides, and an inner court, and on the fourth side access was given by a staircase, which M. Amélineau held to be that referred to in the Egyptian sacred texts which speak of "the god who is at the top of the staircase."   A little later, on January 2, 1898, his faith was strengthened by the discovery of a skull, which could surely only be that of the dead god whose head was buried at Abydos, and the same day scepticism was finally put to flight by the excavation of a grey granite bier, which was manifestly, in the explorer's eyes, "the Bed of Osiris."   The bier was of the usual lion-headed form familiar in Egyptian funerary scenes.   It had once borne the name of the king who dedicated it, and had this been still legible there would, no doubt, have been no room for controversy; but unfortunately the name had been very carefully erased, and no clue was forthcoming, save such as could be derived from the style of the monument.

The discovery of the dead god and his bier gave rise to a somewhat bitter controversy, but judgment was finally given against the enthusiastic prepossessions of M. Amélineau, and in favour of the less romantic solution of the mystery propounded by the late Sir Gaston Maspero, and already referred to,—namely that the tomb was that, not of a god, but of a king of the Ist or IInd Dynasty, which had been mistaken by the Egyptians of the New Empire, for reasons similar to those which had misled the modern explorer, for the genuine tomb of their god. The bier was a copy of an ancient one, and must have been placed in the tomb by Egyptians of the XXth Dynasty, or later, who believed that they were "restoring," in a manner unfortunately not confined to them, the funerary chapel of the god of the Resurrection. The whole incident is a curious chapter in the history alike of exploration and of religion.

After the great discovery, the work of the Mission Amélineau yielded little of importance, and the site was abandoned by the French excavator in the spring of 1898. Apart from the interest which was aroused by the controversy over the question of the tomb of Osiris, the results to Egyptology were undoubtedly disappointing, and unfortunately the excavations had been conducted with such lack of system and supervision that it is probable that more was lost than gained to archæology by the first attempt to penetrate the secrets of Abydos. Much was destroyed whose value in more careful hands would have been inestimable; and much lost half its value from being torn away from its true historic relationship. When M. Amélineau abandoned his researches, he had no expectation of any further harvest being reaped from the site which had proved so disappointing to him, and his judgment of the royal

cemetery was—"all the fellahs know that it is exhausted."
Fortunately there were other explorers who believed otherwise, and who brought to back their faith, not perhaps
greater energy, but greater persistence and more enlightened
and systematic methods of work.

In 1899, Professor Flinders Petrie, on his fourth application, was permitted to resume the work which had been
abandoned as unlikely to yield further results, and the
fruits of his several campaigns, together with the work of
Reisner, Lythgoe, Mace, and others, at el-Amrah, Naga-ed-
Der and other sites, have been the source of our present
knowledge of the Egypt of the earliest dynastic period,
and its kings. Of course the knowledge is scanty enough,
and will probably never be anything else. Even the order
of the kings whose relics were unearthed is often doubtful,
and there is by no means any unanimity as to the various
identifications which have been proposed. That this would
be the case was only to be expected, when one remembers
that the explorers were dealing with the pitiful fragments
which were all that the lapse of at least six thousand years,
the religious fanaticism of less enlightened ages, the successive robberies of a race to which tomb-robbery is a natural
and praiseworthy trade, and the selfishness of modern explorers have left. The wonder is, not that so much is
wanting, and that there are such gaps in the reconstruction,
but that anything whatever could be made of a site on
which time and vandalism had done their worst.

The Royal Tombs of Abydos whose surviving relics were
recovered for archæology with what Professor Breasted

rightly calls "the most conscientious and arduous devotion," were the natural result of the attempt to provide for royalty a somewhat more stately and dignified version of the simple pit in which the pre-dynastic Egyptian buried his dead. Instead of the pit, with its crouching figure laid on its mat, with its rude equipment of the palette for face-paint, and the jars for food and drink, the king of the earliest dynastic period is provided with what is really an underground house, sometimes of considerable size, thirty to fifty feet in length, and of proportionate breadth. This house is brick-lined, and sometimes provided with an inner panelling of wood, and a wooden floor which looks like an ancient attempt at parquetry. The tomb of King Den, of the Ist Dynasty, revealed the unparalleled splendour of a solid granite floor, the earliest known use of a material of which the Egyptian builder was to make such magnificent use in later days; while the great tomb of King Khasek-hemui of the succeeding dynasty has a central chamber built solidly of limestone blocks—the first piece of masonry work known in the history of man.

Within the central chamber the body of the dead king was no doubt laid to rest, surrounded by a store of articles for his toilet, furniture, personal ornaments, bowls and jars, vases and ewers, in metal or the hard stone which the Egyptian craftsman of this early period worked with such amazing skill. The simple equipment of a few pottery jars for food and wine has now developed into a series of chambers surrounding the central hall of the tomb, in which ample provision is made for the wants of the dead monarch in the shape of a number of huge jars filled with food or wine and sealed with a big cone of Nile mud mixed with straw, and impressed with the royal name, or the name of the vineyard from which the wine came.   Pharaoh's Chief-Butler of those far-back days doubtless little thought, when he used his dead master's signet for the last time on the stoppers of the wine-jars for his tomb, that he was providing the material for the historian of six millenniums ahead; but so it has proved, for these sealings have been of the utmost value in the reconstruction of the outline of the early history of the land.

Remarkably advanced as the state of civilisation in Egypt was at even this early date, the Egyptian of the first dynasties was still sufficiently near to his savage ancestors to require that the king should be accompanied in his tomb by those who had contributed to his pleasure while he lived; and doubtless some of the favourite slaves of his harem, or the dwarf or the jester who had solaced his hours of ennui above ground, were slaughtered by the tomb that they might keep their master company in the shadowy underworld. The custom lingered, as we know, down to the period of the Middle Kingdom, if the interpretation put on the shrines of the priestesses in the Funerary Temple of Mentuhotep at Der-el-Bahri is correct; and we see its quaint survival in the little "ushabti" figures which the kindly mind of the Egyptian devised to take the place of the flesh and blood victims, when enlightenment brought revolt against the idea of human sacrifice.   But time and the plunderer have been too long busy at Abydos for any survival of the actual bodies of those who occupied these great death-chambers, and we shall never see the actual figures of the men who made ancient Egypt in the beginning, as we can see those of their successors. The skeleton arm of a lady of the harem, found in the tomb of King Zer (the tomb of Osiris), with four bracelets of beautiful design and workmanship still clinging round the dry bones; the almost gigantic bones of Sa-Nekht of the IIIrd Dynasty whose discovery by Garstang at Bet-Khallaf, not far away, suggests that old Manetho was perhaps not so far out in his record of the King Sesokhris "whose height was five cubits, and his breadth three cubits,"—there is nothing else remaining of the men who made history in the morning of the world. But it is otherwise with the relics of their magnificence.

Fragmentary as is the condition in which the funerary equipment of these early kings has survived to our time, there is sufficient to allow us to form a picture of the type of civilisation, the surroundings of life, and something of the organisation of society in those far-off days, which, while meagre enough in its details, is yet unquestionably accurate, so far as it goes. History, in the sense of the annals of the period, is represented by ivory and ebony plaques which record the royal victories, the defeats of the people of the North-land, and the bringing of so many thousands of captives to the palace, or which, on the other hand, commemorate the more durable victories of peace, the founding of new temples, the breaking of ground for the cutting of an irrigation canal, or the institution of new

festivals in honour of the gods. The things which surround
the monarch in death are doubtless those in which he took
most delight in life; and so we learn that Pharaoh of 6000
years ago was no rude barbarian, but a man of refined and
cultured taste, who loved to have beautiful things about
him whether for use or for the delight of the eye, who
reclined upon a bed of ivory whose legs were carved into
the shape of the hind-legs of a bull, who sealed his decrees
with a signet of wrought gold, which was kept in an ivory
casket, and who used, for his ablutions, or for mere pleasure
in their beauty, vessels of copper, alabaster, breccia and
diorite, whose grace of shape is equalled by the perfection of
their workmanship.

For the Egyptian craftsman of the early dynastic period
had already, at this remote date, reached a mastery of all
the secrets of his craft which was never surpassed, and
seldom rivalled, by the achievements of any subsequent
period. As yet, the sculptor's work is only on a small scale,
and the skill which was to produce such marvels of portraiture as the diorite Khafra, the Reisner Menkaura, and the
figures of Menkaura with the gods and goddesses of the
nomes, was only finding an outlet in slate reliefs on ceremonial palettes, or in such small statuettes as the wonderful
figurine in ivory of an unknown Ist Dynasty king which
Petrie found at Abydos, though the extraordinary vigour
of the small slate statue of the Kha-Sekhem from Hierakonpolis shows all the promise of the later development;
but the workman who beat the hollow gold balls of the
bracelets of the favourite of King Zer, and soldered them

together, and combined them with amethyst, lazuli, and turquoise, had nothing to learn in the mystery of his craft from the artists of any subsequent age or any country.

Religion was already asserting its place as a permanent factor in the life and the art of the land, and the ebony tablet of Mena gives us the earliest representation of the art in which the Egyptian was to excel almost every other race of the ancient world—the art of architecture. Mena's temple, beneath which the king makes libation "4 times," is rude enough,—a contrast, with its wattle-and-daub, to the stately colonnaded halls of later days; but within a few generations the primitive structure was being superseded by costly stone buildings, as Kha-Sekhem's granite door-jamb at Hierakonpolis testifies. The king, as we have seen from Mena's tablet, was already beginning to assume those priestly functions which later developed into the fiction that all priestly offerings were the king's offerings, only presented by deputy; and another tablet shows us Pharaoh dancing before his god, as David danced before the Ark of the Lord. We may surmise that in archaic Egypt there was no Michal so bold as to mock Pharaoh, in her heart or otherwise, for his piety.

The discoveries at Abydos revealed convincingly how early was the development of the art of writing, whose possession put the ancient Egyptian in the very first rank of the nations of the world. Mena's tablet already contains hieroglyphics which are partly intelligible, though archaic in form; by the middle of the Ist Dynasty, hieroglyphic writing is the regular means of communication; by the end of the dynasty it has become so much a matter of course that the figures are no longer engraved with the minute care which is characteristic of the earlier examples, but begin to show the usual process of degradation due to carelessness and haste.  At a very early date the cursive form of writing known as Hieratic appears, as a substitute in ordinary documents for the more stately and difficult Hieroglyphic, which is reserved more for important matters. The Egyptian had already, at this early stage of his history, discovered the use, not merely of phonetic signs standing for a whole syllable, but also of true alphabetic signs, each standing for one consonant.  He had thus in his hand the key to the modern system of writing, two and a half millenniums at least before it had become known to any other people.  Unfortunately for his own convenience, but perhaps fortunately for the picturesqueness of his records, he was too fast bound in the chains of convention to carry his discovery to its conclusion, and develop a truly alphabetic system, and the syllabic signs remain side by side with the alphabetic in his inscriptions; but there was no reason, save the most rigidly binding one of all—custom—why he should not have been using a regular alphabet by 3500 B. C.

The Egyptian Court of the Early Dynastic Period was fully organised and supplied with a complete staff of high officials.  The Court Chamberlain appears as early as the reign of Narmer.  The Commander of the Inundation, who is mentioned in the reign of Zer, is evidence of the early date at which the Egyptian organised the resources of the state for the purpose of dealing with the life-giving bounty of the Nile. Indeed we may fairly assume that it was the necessity of bridling and controlling an agency like the Inundation, capable of so much good if controlled, and of so much evil if left to itself, which forced the inhabitants of the Nile Valley to organise their resources at a period so early. Similar conditions were producing similar effects in the other great riverine state, and both the Nilotic and the Babylonian civilisations were very really the gifts of their great rivers. A little later in the dynasty comes the Commander of the Elders, while in the reign of King Merneit we have the appearance of a functionary with whom the Bible-stories of our childhood made us familiar,—Pharaoh's Chief-Butler, who figures as the Keeper of the Wine. Still in the Ist Dynasty we have the Royal Seal-Bearer, the Royal Architect, and the Keeper of the King's Vineyards; and the grouping round the king of a regular aristocracy is attested by the names of the Leader of the Peers and the Master of Ceremonies. Evidently Egyptian society in the fourth millennium B. C. had already stiffened into something of the minute ritual of court etiquette which marked it in later days.

The resources of state were kept well in hand, and under complete royal control. There was a regular fiscal administration, as appears from the seals of the fiscal officials found in the royal tombs. "The Provision Office" is one of the state departments mentioned on these seals, and no doubt dealt with the payment of taxes in kind. For purposes of administration the country was at first provided with two treasuries, one for the North, "the Red House,"

and one for the South, "the White House." This was a
relic of the pre-dynastic times, when the two halves of the
land were independent kingdoms, and the fiction of a double
kingdom was perpetuated throughout Egyptian history in
the double crowns, Red and White, which the Pharaoh
wore either together or separately on state occasions. But
in practice the double treasury soon disappeared, and the
White House of the South remained the sole treasury of
the land.

The court circle which had accompanied the Pharaoh in
life accompanied him also in his last resting-place. Not
only were his favourites buried with him, but his courtiers
desired to sleep, when their time came, as near as possible
to the master whom they had served while he lived; and
thus there grew up the custom which prevailed throughout
Egyptian history, to a greater or less extent, of the royal
tomb being surrounded by the tombs of scores or hundreds
of the nobles who had formed the court. Thus the king
passed beyond death into a world peopled with figures and
personalities with which he had been familiar all his life,
and expected the same deference in the shadowy realm of
the West as when he sat on the throne of the Double
Kingdom. Sometimes a touch of the pathos which belongs
in all ages to the thought of love and death creeps in, as in
the case of the tomb of King Mena, before which are two
other graves, one of them apparently that of his daughter—
"Bener-Ab"—"Sweetheart"; and one seems to catch the
faint echo of a royal sorrow which belongs to all time.
"I shall go to her; but she will not return to me."

The Royal Cemetery at Abydos presented none of the imposing features which have made the burial-places of the kings of the IVth and succeeding dynasties the wonder of the world. The idea had not yet entered the mind of Pharaoh to convert his modest grave-mound into a mountain of stone, though we see the dawning of the thought in the two great tombs of Zeser of the IIIrd Dynasty, the Step-Pyramid of Saqqara, and the great mastaba at Bet-Khallaf. "The tombs as they were left by the kings," says Petrie, "seem to have been but slightly heaped up. The roofs of the great tombs were about six or eight feet below the surface, an amount of sand which would be easily carried by the massive beams that were used. . . . But there does not seem to have been any piling up of a mound. . . . On the flat, or almost flat, ground of the cemetery the graves were marked by stone steles set upright in the open air. . . . Each royal grave seems to have had two great steles . . . placed on the east side of the tombs, and on the ground level." So, in forming our idea of this earliest of royal necropoles, we must think, not of the architectural splendours of Gizeh, or the wonders of the Valley of the Kings at Thebes, but rather of something not unlike one of our modern cemeteries, with groups of gaunt headstones rising above the low mounds beneath which lay the mighty dead of the world's childhood,—rather a bleak and disappointing place for the romance of history to find an abode in.

And yet that romance has never, not even in the discoveries which have turned the eyes of the whole world to the Valley of the Kings, and made a comparatively obscure

Pharaoh more famous in death than ever in life, been more convincingly embodied than at Abydos, when the explorer's spade, which is the true modern enchanter's wand, opened for us a whole world of ancient days, new because of its very ancientry, and we saw, emerging from the mists of an immemorial past, Pharaoh of 4000 B. C., no uncultured savage, but a stately, glittering figure, cultured himself, and the cause of culture in others, "girt with many a baron bold," commanding the resources of a mighty nation already far advanced on the path of civilisation, and served by men of genius and of a technical skill which has no cause to blush in the presence of the greatest triumphs of later art. The supreme value of Abydos is this,—not that it has extra-illustrated for us a period already partly known; but that it has held up a light by whose aid we can see, though dimly, far back into the "corridors of time" which hitherto were veiled in darkness. "This," to use Carlyle's phrase, "is precisely a revocation of the edict of Destiny; so that Time shall not utterly, not by several centuries, have dominion over us. A little row of Naptha-lamps, with its line of Naptha-light, burns clear and holy through the dead Night of the Past: they who are gone are still here; though hidden they are revealed, though dead they still speak."

PLATE IV

STELE OF THE SERPENT-KING

Found by Amélineau at Abydos

*After the plate in " Die Plastik der Ägypter," by Hedwig Fechheimer*

# CHAPTER III

AT a point on the Nile about 160 miles above Cairo, and 300 below Thebes, the eastern hills, which in this neighbourhood border the river so closely as to leave no room either for a continuous road or for cultivation, recede, and form a bay whose greatest breadth, from river to cliff, is about 3 miles. Six miles further south, they return to the river bank. The crescent-shaped plain thus enclosed by the cliffs is of clean yellow sand, sloping gently towards the river, which is bordered by a narrow ribbon of cultivated land. Within the crescent are a few Arab villages, Et Till, Hagg Qandil, El Amarieh, Hawata, and Qoser, dating from the settlement in this neighbourhood of the nomad Arab clan of the Beni Amran, in 1737 A. D. On the western bank of the Nile lies a similar but wider plain, bordered by the cliffs which form the escarpment of the western desert. The site, save for the Arab villages, is now deserted, with but few apparent remains to tell of its former history; but it is still one of supreme interest to the student of ancient Egypt, and even the casual tourist has to include it in his itinerary; for this bay in the cliffs is the scene of one of the most remarkable adventures in history, in which a great king and reformer, born out of due time, endeav-

[ 49 ]

oured to realise his religious ideals, and failed because the world was not ready, by many centuries, for the purity and spirituality of the thoughts which had taken shape in his mind. From beneath the sand of the plain excavation has recovered the poor remains of the palace, the temples, and the houses which gave for a short space a local habitation to the reformer's conceptions; on the surrounding cliffs, and scooped into their rocky walls, are the inscriptions in which he described the limits of his City of Dreams, and the splendid tombs which were prepared for his courtiers, but never occupied by them; and here, in a low brick chamber, was found, by a casual fellah-woman, digging for bricks, the correspondence, which, more than any other discovery of our time, has enabled students of ancient history to reconstruct the whole course of one of the turning-points in the story of the Ancient East.

The place is now generally known as Tell-el-Amarna, a name which has no real significance, and is merely a European concoction,—a portmanteau word, made up out of bits of Et Till, El Amarieh, and the Beni Amran. Such as it is, however, the title has passed into such universal use, and gives so convenient a name for the whole district, that it will probably always remain as the modern equivalent for the once famous city of Akhetaten, the home of a lost cause which surely deserved a better fate.

Here, somewhere about the year 1370 B. C., there came down the river from Thebes a stately procession of barges, headed by the Royal Galley of Amenhotep IV, the last direct descendant of the great kings of that XVIIIth

PLATE V

HEAD OF AMENHOTEP IV (AKHENATEN)—LIMESTONE (BERLIN)

*After the plate in "Die Plastik der Ägypter," by Hedwig Fechheimer*

Dynasty which had made Egypt a world-empire, and in some respects, though, unfortunately, not in those which made for the stability of his kingdom, the greatest of them all. Landing from his galley, the king and his retinue camped in the plain beneath the bordering cliffs, till the boundary tablets which should mark out the limits of the new city of which he dreamed should be hewn on the face of the rocky walls which girdled the site. Then, "In year 6, fourth month of the second season, day 13 . . . His Majesty ascended a great chariot of electrum . . . and he started a goodly course (from his camping-ground) to the City of the Horizon. And His Majesty offered a great sacrifice to Aten, of bread, beer, horned bulls, polled bulls, beasts, fowl, wine, incense, frankincense, and all goodly herbs on this day of demarcating the City of the Horizon. . . ." North, south, east, and west the great tablets were hewn into the face of the cliffs, till the whole area, on both sides of the Nile, was fenced off by them, and on the extreme northern and southern steles, the following strange oath was recorded—"I will make the City of the Horizon of Aten for the Aten, my father, in this place. I will not make the city south of it, north of it, west of it, or east of it. I will not pass beyond the southern boundary-stone southward, neither will I pass beyond the northern bound- ary-stone northward to make for him a City of the Horizon there; neither will I make for him a city on the western side. Nay, but I will make the City of the Horizon for the Aten, my father, upon the east side, the place which he did enclose for his own self with cliffs, and made a plain in the midst of it that I might sacrifice to him therein; this is it. I will make for myself the Palace of Pharaoh, and I will make the Palace of the Queen in this place. There shall be made for me a sepulchre in the eastern hills; my burial shall be therein. . . . If I die in any town of the north, south, west, or east, I will be brought here, and my burial shall be in the City of the Horizon."

The city, thus strictly marked off, and planned by one whose word was law, rose like magic from the sandy plain, palace, and temple, mansion and market-place shining in pure white, and glowing with colour under the spotless blue of an Egyptian sky; and there, for perhaps a dozen years or less, the king held his court. Then death came, to take him mercifully from a world which was all unready to receive his gentle teaching, and the beautiful city which he had planned and built swiftly fell into decay and ruin. Twenty-five years from the date of his founding, the City of the Horizon was abandoned to the jackal and the owl, and the gentle dreamer who had reared it as by the stroke of an enchanter's wand was sleeping his long sleep, not, as he had hoped, in the city of his heart, but in a dishonoured tomb in the Thebes which he had hated, and from which he had fled to the virgin splendour of his Holy Place of Dreams.

Since then, the site has never been occupied, save by the paltry villages of wandering Arabs. It remains almost the one instance of a great city whose whole life, from its first foundation to its final desolation, is embraced within a quarter of a century. And now to tell the story of how

PLATE VI

BOUNDARY-STELE OF AKHENATEN, TELL EL-AMARNA

*Reproduced by permission from " The Rock Tombs of El-Amarna," by N. de G. Davies*

so strange a thing as the creation and abandonment of a capital city within the lifetime of a single generation came to pass.

Amenhotep III, the father of the founder of the City of the Horizon, was one of those kings who, like Ashur-bani-pal in Assyria, or Louis XIV in France, seem to sum up in their own persons all the glory of their race, just before it passes away forever. The great warrior-kings of his dynasty, foremost among them Thothmes III, had built up, by ceaseless wars, an Egyptian Empire, stretching from the fourth Cataract of the Nile to the great bend of the Euphrates above Carchemish, and over this great area the terror of the Egyptian arms maintained a profound, if unwilling, peace. The Pharaoh of Egypt was easily the first man in the world. Tribute from Syria, Palestine, and Ethiopia poured into his coffers with perfect regularity, and the vast temples with which he adorned Thebes blazed with gold and jewels, and all the richest products of his tributary states. In his inscriptions, he described himself, in grandiose language, as "A mighty king, whose southern boundary is as far as Karoy, and his northern as far as Naharina." His war-fleets kept the peace of the Mediterranean, and the products of Minoan art, the delicate painted ware, and the damascened bronzes of Knossos and the other Ægean centres became familiar objects in the markets and palaces of Thebes. The mightiest monarchs of the Ancient East courted the friendship and alliance of the Great King, and vied with one another in abject appeals for a share of the prosperity with which the gods had endowed their brother

of Egypt.   In the Tell-el-Amarna correspondence can still
be seen the proof of the proud position which Amenhotep
III held among the rulers of the world.   He is the Great
Jove who "assumes the God, affects to nod, and seems to
shake the spheres."   His land is an enchanted land where
"the peculiar treasure of kings" abounds as nowhere else
on earth.   "Let my brother send gold in very great quantity
without measure, and let him send more gold to me than
to my father.   For in my brother's land gold is as common
as dust."   So writes Dushratta of Mitanni, one of the
greatest potentates of the day, to Amenhotep.   Abimilki
of Tyre absolutely grovels before the mighty dispenser of
benefits.   "To my lord, the king, my gods, my sun; Abimilki, thy servant.   Seven times and seven times at the
feet of my lord I fall.   I am the dust under the sandals of
my lord, the king."   Even the king of Babylon the Great
submits humbly to the refusal of an Egyptian princess
for his wife, and intimates that any beautiful Egyptian
will do instead.   "Who shall say, 'She is not a King's
daughter'?"

Among his other matrimonial adventures, which embraced an alliance with the daughter of the king of Mitanni,
who brought with her a train of three hundred and seventeen maids of honour, Amenhotep had married, early in his
reign, a native Egyptian lady of comparatively humble
origin named Tiy.   She was the daughter of Yuaa, priest
of Min, and his wife Tuau.   The influence of this remarkable woman was completely dominant throughout the reign
of her husband, and though there is no real evidence to show

that she was of North-Syrian descent, as has been claimed, there is no doubt that all her power was exerted in the direction of introducing Syrian customs and habits of thought into the Egyptian court. Particularly was this influence manifested in the direction of religious ideas. At this time the supreme god of the court, and indeed of Egypt, was Amen the great god of Thebes, whose name was borne by the king himself. But the headship of Amen had never been recognised without a grudge, for he was a comparative upstart among the ancient gods of the Egyptian Pantheon. Originally he was only the local god of Thebes, and shared in the insignificance of his city in the early days of Egyptian history. It was only with the rise to power of the Theban princes of the Seventeenth and Eighteenth Dynasties, that the Theban god began to rise to a position of predominance. Gradually, however, as Thebes became supreme, the claims of Amen to a corresponding position among the gods were asserted with growing success; till at last, by the end of the Eighteenth Dynasty, he was unquestionably the first god in the land. His supremacy, none the less, had never been accepted absolutely by the priesthoods and followers of the more ancient divinities. Of these the chief were Ptah, the Creator-God of Memphis, and above all Ra, the Sun-God, the chief seat of whose worship was at Heliopolis. Ra, indeed, represented the nearest approach which the Egyptian mind had yet been able to make to the idea of an universal God, as opposed to the local gods who swarmed in the land. He was, in Egyptian tradition, the father of the gods, and the proudest dignity in the titulary of the Pharaohs was the title "Son of the Sun," whose assumption dated from the Fifth Dynasty. Ra was known by various names. At dawn he was called Khepera, and was represented as a beetle; at noon he was Ra; at evening he was called Atum—a name to be borne in mind; for it is of Syrian origin, corresponding to the Syrian "Adon," "Lord," a title which came to play a great part in the struggle which we have to trace. Near the horizon,—that is at early morning or late evening, Ra was known as Ra-Horakhti, or Ra of the Horizon, another title which came into prominence. It can well be imagined that the representatives of the ancient cult of Ra resented the supremacy of the parvenu god of Thebes who had usurped the position held from of old by their deity, and were ready material lying to the hand of any one who would restore the older god to his pride of place.

Accordingly, when Queen Tiy began to favour a Syrianised form of solar worship, it would not be difficult for the powerful priesthood of Heliopolis to reconcile the new worship of the Aten with their own cult of Ra, who already bore as one of his titles the name Atum, the Egyptian form of the same name. During the later years of the reign of Amenhotep III, this modified form of Ra-worship began to exercise a growing influence upon the court circle, which must have been largely permeated by Syrian elements, arising from the Syrian alliances, matrimonial and otherwise, of the king. We read, for instance, of how the king and Queen Tiy held a water festival at Thebes, sailing on the artificial lake which Amenhotep had made in their barque "Aten-neferu," "Aten-Gleams." Thus the ground was being prepared for the rise of a new faith, which not only had the support of the court, but also was capable of enlisting the sympathy of the still powerful cult of the most ancient god of Egypt.

In the twenty-fifth or twenty-sixth year of their marriage, there was born to Amenhotep and Tiy the son who was destined to carry out to its complete, and as it proved, disastrous fulfilment the new religious idea which had thus been establishing itself in the Egyptian court. The young prince, who was named Amenhotep like his father, grew up under the influence of his mother Tiy; for his father seems, in his later years, to have more and more surrendered himself to the leading of the clever woman who had always been his favourite wife, and, besides, was falling into the ill-health which brought his reign to a close before his fiftieth year. Queen Tiy secured the permanence of Syrian influence in the Egyptian court by the arrangement of a marriage between her young son and the daughter of Dush-ratta, King of Mitanni. The little princess Tadukhipa was brought to Egypt, where she was married to her boy bridegroom, then probably about eleven years old, and renamed Nefertiti. Henceforward the Crown-Prince was bound, by a double link, to the new ideas of which he was to prove so thoroughgoing an exponent. Shortly after the marriage, King Amenhotep III died, and his son, a delicate and abnormal boy of eleven years or so, came to the throne of the greatest empire of the world.

Even when allowance is made for the earlier maturity of

the East, it cannot be imagined that the religious changes which so soon followed upon his accession were the work of the boy-king, acting on his own initiative; and we may probably trace in them the hand of his mother, and her counsellors. But as time went on, it became plain that the king had thoroughly absorbed the conceptions of his instructors, and was determined to carry them to their logical conclusion, no matter what the cost might be. What these conceptions were may be briefly stated, before the story of the religious revolution which followed on their adoption is told.

In one sentence, what Amenhotep IV, or his advisers, designed was nothing less than the supersession of all the old gods of Egypt, and the establishment of a monotheism. The new faith took the form of Sun-worship, but by no means such sun-worship as the Egyptians had long been familiar with. The new deity was not the Sun, but an abstract conception of divinity—the vital power which expresses itself in the Sun and his life-giving light and heat. The word "Aten" was substituted for the old name for god, and the king's new divinity was given a special title, combining the old and the new—"Ra-Horakhti rejoicing in the horizon in his name 'Heat-which-is-in-Aten.'" The old human or semi-human representations of the deity were discarded, and the Aten is represented by a solar disc, from which shoot out, in all directions, rays, each ending in a hand, which grasps the "Ankh" or "Crux Ansata," the symbol of life. The only information which we possess as to the doctrines associated with this god is derived from the Aten Hymns, which are supposed, with some probability, to have been the work of the young king himself.

They tell us that to Amenhotep IV, God was an invisible spiritual being, who was not to be represented by images "graven by art or man's device"; that He was not the God of any one particular city, or even of one people, but of all countries; that He loved all men with an equal love, no matter what their race or colour; and that He was the Creator, Preserver, and merciful Father of all men, and of all living creatures. This Lord, or Aten, he believed to be the invisible and intangible power which creates and sustains all things—an idea, which, in fact, is not very far removed from our own conception of God. "The important dogma in the new faith," says Professor Steindorff, "is that which maintains Aton to be the creator, orderer, and governor of the whole world, and not of Egypt alone. He was the King of the All." It was the first attempt of the human mind to conceive a spiritual divinity—a God who could not be perceived by the senses, who was not clothed with form and substance like a human being, but who was in close touch with mankind, and directly interested in the things which concern all men.

The hymns in which these thoughts are embodied are very remarkable. No such hymns were written in Egypt, before or after, and nothing like them can be found in the literature of any other nation, till the Hebrew Psalmists, centuries later, gave utterance to thoughts which might almost be echoes of the Pharaohs' songs of praise. The parallel, for instance, between the hundred-and-fourth

Psalm and the Hymn to the Aten has often been noticed, and it is so close that one might insert passages from the one hymn in the other without exciting any sense of incongruity. The great Aten Hymn begins with a short introduction, descriptive of the splendour of God:

"Thy dawning is beautiful in the horizon of heaven,
O Living Lord, Beginning of Life!
When thou risest in the eastern horizon of heaven,
Thou fillest every land with thy beauty,
Thou bindest them with thy love.
Though thou art afar, thy rays are on earth,
Though thou art on high, thy footprints are the day."

Then follow instances of the universal beneficence of God, which may be compared with corresponding passages from the Hebrew Psalm.

### THE ATEN HYMN.

"When thou settest in the western horizon of Heaven, the world is in darkness like the dead. Every lion cometh forth from his den. All serpents sting. Darkness reigns. When thou risest in the horizon the darkness is banished. . . . Then in all the land they do their work.

All trees and plants flourish . . . the birds flutter in their nests, their wings uplifted in adoration to thee. All sheep leap upon their feet.

The ships sail up stream and down stream. The fish in the

### PSALM CIV.

"Thou makest darkness, and it is night, wherein all the beasts of the forest do creep forth. The young lions roar after their prey; they seek their meat from God.

The sun riseth, they get them away, and lay them down in their dens. Man goeth forth unto his work and to his labour until the evening.

The trees of the Lord are full of sap, wherein the birds make their nests. The high hills are a refuge for the wild goats.

Yonder is the sea, great and wide, wherein are both small and

PLATE VII

HEAD OF NEFERTITI, WIFE OF AKHENATEN—SANDSTONE (BERLIN)

*After the plate in " Die Plastik der Ägypter," by Hedwig Fechheimer*

river leap up before thee, and thy rays are in the midst of the Great Sea.

How manifold are thy works. Thou didst create all the earth according to thy desire, men, cattle, all that are upon the earth.

Thou hast set a Nile in Heaven, that it may fall for them, making floods upon the mountains, and watering their fields.

The world is in thy hand, even as thou hast made them. When thou hast risen they live; when thou settest they die. By thee man liveth."

great beasts. There go the ships, there is that Leviathan which thou hast made to play therein.

O Lord, how manifold are thy works. In wisdom hast thou made them all. The earth is full of thy creatures.

He watereth the hills from above; the earth is filled with the fruit of thy works. He bringeth forth grass for the cattle, and green herb for the service of man. These wait all upon thee. When thou openest thine hand, they are filled with good. When thou hidest thy face, they are troubled; when thou takest away their breath, they die, and return to their dust."

Quite evidently, the Hymn to the Aten, with a few trifling alterations of names and titles, might be placed in the Psalter, and would be cheerfully accepted as a not unworthy companion to the great Nature-Psalm of the Hebrews. Yet it was written nearly 1400 years before the birth of Christ, and at least 400 years before the earliest of our psalms. No such noble conception of God, so spiritual, so catholic, so wide-reaching in its view of the working of the Almighty, had been reached, or was to be reached for many centuries to come, as this which was embraced and formulated by this young pagan king!

The trouble was that such ideas were in advance of their

time.  Men's minds were far from being ready to receive
them.  Even the priests of Ra, grateful to the king at first,
no doubt, for his re-assertion of the supremacy of the more
ancient god over the upstart Amen, cannot have failed to
see, before long, that the new faith of their Pharaoh was
a very different thing from their own old cult of the Sun.
All the vested interests of the land, which found their
account in the maintenance of the old order and the old
superstitions, would rise in arms against the new faith
which threatened their existence.  But Amenhotep had the
courage of his convictions.  Heretic or not, he was the
supreme power in Egypt, and if the old gods and their
adherents would not tolerate his new ideas, so much the
worse for them—at least so long as his power lasted.

For awhile he attempted to allow the old faiths to exist
side by side with his new conception.  He built a splendid
shrine for the Aten in the immediate neighbourhood of the
great temple of Amen at Karnak, and Thebes saw its
allegiance divided between its old deity and the king's
new god.  But such a state of things could not go on for
long; and it was the new faith which inevitably forced the
issue.  The old faiths were more or less tolerant.  Amen
could endure other gods beside himself.  If he was supreme
in Thebes, Ptah was equally supreme in Memphis, and Ra
in Heliopolis.  But it was not so with the new worship.
As the Aten was the universal, so he was the sole God—
"a jealous God," to use the Hebrew phrase, who could
tolerate no rival.  Therefore a struggle between Amen-

worship and Atenism was bound to come; nor was it long before the battle of the faiths was joined.

In the sixth year of his reign the young king proclaimed the Aten-worship to be the state religion; and a conflict to the bitter end was entered upon. All the subjects of the empire were required to worship the new god, and the opposition of the various priesthoods, and especially of the priests of Amen, forced upon the king the necessity of strong measures. The temples of all the gods were closed throughout the land, and their revenues confiscated. Wherever possible, the statues of the old gods were destroyed, their figures hammered out of the reliefs on the temple walls, their names erased from the inscriptions. Above all, the king endeavoured to destroy every trace of Amen and his worship in the land. The hated name was ruthlessly battered out wherever it was found. No mercy was shown even to the statues of the great kings of the past, and so far did the king carry his consistency, that the inscriptions of his own father were mercilessly mutilated by the erasure of his name. The king's own title, "Amen is content," was in itself an offence to his fanatical desire for the purity of the faith, and so he renounced the name which his fore-fathers had made glorious, and called himself "Akhenaten," "Spirit of the Solar Disc."

A still more radical change followed inevitably from the course of action to which the king had committed himself. Thebes ere long became intolerable to him, for reasons which we can well understand. Everywhere in the great city of Amen he felt himself surrounded and hampered by the ruins of the faith which he had cast down from its pride of place; and no doubt the opposition and hatred of the dispossessed priesthood was none the less bitter and persistent for being driven underground, and may very well have become a source of personal danger to their royal enemy. The vast silent temples, with their mutilated statues and inscriptions, must have been a constant offence to his eyes and a reminder of the instability of even the greatest human power. Accordingly, Akhenaten soon resolved upon the step which we have seen him carrying into execution, and shifted his royal abode and his court, with all the machinery of government, to the unpolluted site of Tell-el-Amarna. There he would build for his god and himself a Holy City on virgin soil, and there he would live, undisturbed by the sight of the desolate temples of Amen, and his scowling priests.

Such an ideal as Akhenaten had in his mind must have taken a considerable time to realise, even though all the resources of the kingdom were devoted to the task; but in two years the city was sufficiently far advanced for the king to take up his residence in it; and in the eighth year of his reign, he left Thebes, never to return, till his dead body was borne back, by the faithful few who still clung to the memory of their young master, and buried hastily and secretly in the tomb in the Valley of the Kings where his loved mother Tiy was sleeping. We can picture the young Pharaoh, only nineteen years old, though already so heavily burdened, with his Queen, Nefertiti, a fair girl of seventeen, and their three daughters, the youngest a mere infant, sailing northward to the City of Dreams, and imagine how eagerly the king watched for the first glimpse of his new home, where strife and sorrow should never come. Alas, that was one of the dreams which come through the ivory gate, for Akhenaten's days in the "Horizon of the Aten" were to be few and evil.

A great palace of brick covered with white stucco had been built for the king's abode. At one end of the building was a huge hall, 426 feet by 234, its roof supported by a forest of 542 pillars and here, no doubt, Akhenaten and his courtiers found shelter and coolness in the burning heats of the Egyptian summer. Everywhere in the various smaller halls and chambers was the evidence of the king's delight in nature and the peaceful life of the country. "In one of the halls which seems to have belonged to the harem," says Maspero, "there is still to be seen distinctly the picture of a rectangular piece of water containing fish and lotus-flowers in full bloom; the edge is adorned with water-plants and flowering shrubs, among which birds fly and calves graze and gambol; on the right and left were depicted rows of stands laden with fruit, while at each end of the room were seen the grinning faces of a gang of negro and Syrian prisoners, separated from each other by gigantic arches. The tone of colouring is bright and cheerful, and the animals are treated with great freedom and facility." The capitals of some of the pillars were inlaid exquisitely with coloured glazes, the curving palm-leaves which formed the capital picked out with alternating colours, and separated from one another by lines of gilding. "A copy," says

Flinders Petrie, "of the favourite cloison work of the Egyptian jewellers, in which minute segments of rich stone were set each in a fitting nest of gold. . . . Here the jeweller's design was boldly carried into architecture on the largest scale, and high capitals gleamed with gold and gem-like glazes." Mr. H. R. Hall has said that compared with the solid splendour of the Minoan Palace of Knossos, "the palaces of Egyptian Pharaohs were but elaborate hovels of painted mud"; but if Akhenaten's palace at Tell-el-Amarna was mainly built of no costlier material than mud-brick, its decoration was such as to glorify the humble material.

Close to the royal palace rose the great temple of Aten, the largest of the many which adorned the city. A high wall enclosed a huge space, nearly half a mile long; but of this vast area, only a small portion was covered by the buildings of the temple proper. Passing through the gate of the temenos-wall, the worshipper was faced by the façade of the first and larger shrine. This consisted of two lofty pylons, each adorned with five tall masts, from whose heads floated long pennons; and between the pylons was the great gate, with its double-leaved door. Beyond the gate was the first court, open to the sun, with its high-altar in the midst; and a series of small chapels or chambers ranged round the wall. From this court one passed through a second gateway into another open court, and thence into a third, from which access was gained to a colonnaded gallery affording grateful shelter from the sun. Then came the fifth, sixth, and seventh courts, all open to the light, the last two having each an altar which stood in the full blaze of the sunlight. The lesser shrine, behind, was fronted by a pillared portico adorned with statues of the king and his wife and daughters. Beyond this screen was a single open court with its altar and surrounding chambers.

The outstanding feature of the Aten-temple was the contrast between its design and that of the normal Egyptian temple. At Karnak, Amen was worshipped in vast dim halls, whose only light came through minute lattices, and where a perpetual twilight imposed a sense of gloom and mystery on the heart of the worshipper, while the actual shrine of the god was enveloped in total darkness. In the Aten-temple, on the contrary, every court, save the one pillared hall, was open to the day, and the act of worship was transacted in the full light of the solar disc to which the worshipper looked as the symbol of his god. There was no concealment, and no mystery; all was simple and straightforward and open. In this, as in other respects, Akhenaten was centuries ahead of his time.

The high priest of the new temple was named Meryra, and on the walls of his tomb in the eastern hills behind the city have been found the pictures which have helped us to see the shrine of Akhenaten's god, and to realise something of the brightness and charm of life in the Holy City of the Sun. In one of these pictures we see the installation of the High-Priest. The king stands with his wife and one of his daughters in a gaily-decorated gallery of the palace. Delicate lotus-shaped pillars support the roof, and gay ribbons flutter from them, while the wall is adorned with wreaths of lotus-flowers and parti-coloured patterns. Be-

neath the gallery is gathered a crowd of courtiers, conspicuous among them Meryra, who has bowed himself before his
royal master.    The king leans from the balcony, and bids
his servant assume the office of High-Priest—"Behold,
I make thee High-Priest of the Aten for me in the Temple
of the Aten in the City of the Horizon of Aten.    I do this
for the love of thee, and I say unto thee: O my servant
who hearkenest to the teaching, my heart is satisfied with
everything which thou hast done."    Meryra is raised
shoulder-high by his brother-courtiers, and the king loads
him with the insignia of his great office and with many
costly gifts, while on the outer edge of the scene his
chariot waits, with fan-bearers and tambourine-women in
attendance, to conduct the man whom the king delights to
honour back to his home.

These pictures, with the many others which have survived
from the tombs of the city and other sources, bring us into
touch with one of the most interesting features of the
spiritual revolution which Akhenaten was trying to accomplish—the temporary transformation of Egyptian art.    For
many centuries, Egyptian art had developed along singularly uniform lines.    It was, indeed, by no means so hide-
bound and stereotyped as is often represented, as even a
comparatively slight study of the portrait-statues of the
Pharaohs will make manifest; and it had elements of
remarkable dignity and force; but the hand of convention
lay heavy upon it, and originality was rendered almost
impossible by a sacred tradition.    From the thraldom which
cramped art, as from that which burdened the spirit, Akhen-

aten's teaching wrought a deliverance, which, if brief, yet produced startling and brilliant results. One of the king's favourite epithets was "Living in Truth,"—his religious ideal was largely a return to simplicity, and the characteristic of the art of his reign is just the natural result of such an outlook. Convention and tradition are discarded, and the Egyptian painter and sculptor, for the first and last time in the history of the national art, seek to represent things and persons, not as tradition said they should be represented, but as they actually saw them.

The king himself, instead of being depicted in one or other of the consecrated attitudes, solemn, majestic, impassive, and uninteresting, is set before us as he really lived and moved. You see him languidly leaning on his staff, while his queen, Nefertiti, with a gesture which can only be described as pert, holds to his nose a lotus-flower, that he may sniff its perfume. Again he is driving in his chariot with Nefertiti beside him. She turns to kiss her husband even while the horses are in full career, while one of the royal daughters leans over the front of the chariot, apparently more interested in the prancing steeds than in the endearments of her parents. Or again you have Akhenaten and Nefertiti seated at table with so dignified a personage as the Great Royal Mother Tiy. Akhenaten is holding in one hand and attacking with his teeth a broiled bone of awe-inspiring size, while his wife makes a gallant onslaught upon a whole chicken. Tiy looks on unmoved by these gastronomic enormities, while three of the royal daughters sit around the thrones, quite unconcerned at the undignified conduct of their parents. Enough, one would think, to make a Pharaoh of the stiff old stock turn in his grave; but human and natural all the same. Practically all the art of the time has the same characteristics of naturalism and veracity, and while the result has not the monumental dignity of the normal Egyptian work, it has often a freshness and charm entirely wanting in the older art.

The one unpleasant feature of the art of the reign is the abnormal structure of the abdomen and thighs as represented in almost every instance. Whether this is the result of a diseased development of the body of the sickly king, which was accentuated by the courtly artists, and perhaps adopted by the courtiers as a fashion in order to flatter their young ruler, or not, the fact reveals something abnormal in an art which otherwise is natural and pleasing, and suggests an element of unhealthiness and unreality in the movement which Akhenaten was pressing with such vigour.

The fact is that the whole structure of the king's religious reformation rested upon a radically unsound foundation. Akhenaten was trying to impose his ideas, pure and lofty though they were, upon a reluctant and unprepared nation, simply by his own fiat; and to ensure the success of such an attempt, he would have needed to be prepared for the use of the whole force of his empire. This, however, was the last thing of which he dreamed. His whole ideal was pacific, and for a religion of peace, and an empire which depended on the might of ideas, and not upon armed force, the world was quite unready. Akhenaten was born out of due time and it was not long before the hard facts demonstrated how fatal may be the gift to a kingdom of a ruler who is too far ahead of the standard of his world to be able to meet his opponents with the only argument which they understand. Within a few years the great empire which his ancestors had gained and kept by the strong hand had crumbled into ruin, and the king was left to die brokenhearted amidst the wreck of all his beautiful hopes.

How the story of the downfall of Akhenaten's dream-empire of righteousness, peace, and joy came to light, is one of the romances, not indeed of exploration, for scholarship came rather poorly out of it, but of almost incredible chance. In 1887, a peasant woman, grubbing, like her neighbours, among the ruins of the Holy City, came upon a small chamber where were stored hundreds of clay tablets, inscribed with cuneiform characters. "The tablets," says Professor Flinders Petrie, "were all grubbed out by the fellahin, many were broken, or ground to pieces, during transit on donkey-back; the authorities to whom the things were shown, despised them; and it was very fortunate that the whole discovery was not irrevocably lost. What is saved is but a portion—perhaps not half—of what might have been preserved with proper care." The story is sufficiently deplorable in itself; but all the more so when we realise what these tablets, thus summarily despised by those whose work it was to care for such things, turned out to be. For, when at last the poor remains of the find had found homes in the British and Berlin Museums and other collections, and the decipherment of them began, it was seen at once that no such illuminating discovery had been made for many years.

The chamber was "The place of the Records of the palace of the King," the archive-room, in fact of Akhenaten's Foreign-Office, and the tablets were the Foreign-Office correspondence of his reign and that of his father. From them it is possible to reconstruct the story of how the king's noble ideals came to naught, and the Empire fell to pieces while Akhenaten was writing hymns and superintending ceremonies in his City of Dreams. We learn that two disruptive movements were going on within the Syrian provinces of the Empire from an early stage of the reign. In the North, the Hittite power, strong and ambitious, was pressing down upon the loyal adherents of the Egyptian Crown, aided in the aggression, till such time as it had succeeded so far that the Hittites were able to turn upon their helpers and eat them up, by a couple of Amorite traitors, vassals of Egypt, Abdashirta, and his son Aziru.

In Southern Palestine, the Egyptian dominion was threatened by the incursion of a race of Aramæan Semites, the Habiri, who are supposed by some to be the Hebrews pressing in out of the desert where they had been wandering, to the conquest of their Land of Promise.

The Tell-el-Amarna Tablets tell us the story from the point of view of the loyal vassals of Egypt, who were striving, with insufficient resources, and with little help or none from their suzerain, to make head against the double tide which threatened to overwhelm them; and their tale, even after so many centuries, is infinitely pathetic. The

northern vassals are represented chiefly by Ribadda, governor of Byblos, and Abimilki of Tyre, the southern by
Abd-khiba of Jerusalem, who have to deal respectively
with the Hittites and their allies Abdashirta and Aziru, and
the Habiri. From both north and south, the tale is the
same. At the beginning the situation is serious, indeed,
but by no means desperate. If the King will only listen
to his faithful servants, and send troops or ships, the loyal
governors are quite confident of their ability to defeat the
invaders. The merest handful of Egyptian troops—a score
or so,—would change the whole situation, and the sight of
the Egyptian banners in the field would mean everything.
But troops and ships were the last things that Akhenaten
thought of meddling with; he was much more concerned
with the installation of his new high-priest, or the regulation of the worship in the new temple at Akhetaten. So
things go steadily from bad to worse, and the tone of the
letters grows more and more despairing. Here is one of
the later letters from Jerusalem. "As long as ships were
on the sea (i.e., as long as Egypt had "a fleet in being"),
the king occupied the land of Naharina and the land of
Kash. Now the Habiri occupy the cities. Not one prince
remains, all are ruined. . . . If there are no troops in this
year, let the King send his officer to fetch me and my
brothers, that we may die with our Lord the King." Then
the heavy-laden man thinks that he has not yet said enough,
and he adds a postscript addressed to the Foreign-Office
scribe who translated the cuneiform correspondence: "To
the scribe of my Lord the King, thy servant. Bring these

words plainly before my Lord the King. 'The whole land of My Lord the King is going to ruin.' " Abd-khiba was a loyal subject, but a poor courtier, and no doubt Akhenaten's cuneiform scribe told his master just as much or as little of the governor's straits as he thought would conduce to his own personal interests.

One letter is from a loyal northern town, and has its own pathetic appeal even after those who sent it, and waited in vain with sick hearts for the answer, have been dust for so many centuries. "And now Tunip, thy city, weeps, and her tears are flowing, and there is no help for us. For twenty years we have been sending to our Lord the King, the King of Egypt; but there has not come a word to us, no, not one." Ribadda in the north was in the same straits as Abd-khiba in Jerusalem, and his letters grow more and more gloomy and indignant as hope after hope fails, and he is left to face the result of his vain loyalty to a power which would not or could not be loyal to her true servants. "If the King does not send troops, Byblos will fall into Abdashirta's hands, and all the King's lands as far as Egypt will fall into the hands of the Habiri. Behold Byblos is not like other towns, Byblos is the faithful city." His story closes with a bitter letter addressed, not to the king, but to some official who had held out delusive promises of help. "Why was Ribadda told to send messengers to receive men and chariots from Egypt? He did so, but the messenger returned alone. And Beyrut has fallen to the enemy, though troops were there. And the enemy do not depart from the gate of Byblos." Poor Ribadda closes his record with that sombre sentence. His fate is unknown; but no doubt he fell in the storm of his faithful city, the victim of his loyalty to an idealist who could not grasp the practical needs of a crisis. In a few years the whole of Syria was either overrun by the Hittites and Habiri, or had deserted to what was manifestly the winning side, and the Empire of Thothmes III had ceased to be.

Such were the dispatches which came from the provinces to trouble the peace of Akhenaten's dreams. Fanatically devoted as he was to his ideals, such news cannot have failed to force upon him at last the consciousness that he had failed in his attempt to establish a faith of universal brotherhood and peace. No doubt at home things were not going much better than in Syria. The poisonous hatred of the priesthood of Amen was continually active, and the intrigues of these deadly enemies were aided by the disastrous news which every messenger brought from the north. "That criminal of Akhetaten," the priests called him, and they could point to lost provinces and ruined cities as proof of how Amen was revenging himself upon the madman who had cast off the god who made Egypt glorious. The army which, so far as we know, he had never used, would grow more and more sullen and discontented with every message of the disaster which it had not been permitted to avert; while the common folk, who may have been drawn to Akhenaten's pleasant faith readily enough at first, would speedily forsake it when they became conscious that somehow things were going wrong.

Self-interest would hold his more immediate circle of

courtiers to him as long as they believed that loyalty was safe; but one may doubt if there was much true devotion, even in the court circle, to a faith so new and strange, when its star was no longer in the ascendant. Not least among his troubles was the fact that though he had six daughters, he had no son to succeed him, and he can scarcely have regarded the marriages of the princesses to powerful nobles as much of a make-weight against this fatal handicap.

Altogether, between disaster abroad and discontent at home, one can scarcely wonder that the sickly king found the burden too heavy for him. How the end came, we do not know; but less than twelve years from the time when he joyfully entered the gates of his Holy City he died, at the age, Professor Elliot Smith tells us, of not more than 28. Medical men have suggested that his death was due to a stroke or fit, perhaps a sufficiently natural suggestion; but when one remembers what he had attempted, and how he had failed, a simpler explanation suggests itself—a broken heart! One way or another, the young reformer laid down a task which had become too heavy for him, and passed to his rest out of a world which was not ready for his teaching.

The body of the dead king was wrapped in thin flexible sheets of pure gold, and placed in a splendid coffin shaped to the recumbent figure, and brilliantly inlaid with rare stones and coloured glass. Down the front of the coffin ran an inlaid inscription. "The beautiful Prince, the Chosen One of Ra, the King of Upper and Lower Egypt, living in Truth, Lord of the Two Lands, Akhenaten, the beautiful child of the Living Aten, whose name shall live for ever and ever." So he was borne to his burial in the tomb in the eastern cliffs of Tell-el-Amarna which he had prepared for himself; but he was not destined, even in death, to find repose in the City of his Dreams. He was succeeded on the tottering throne of Egypt by Smenkhara, one of his great nobles, who had married the eldest daughter of the dead king—Merytaten. Smenkhara's reign, however, was brief. Within a year he died or was deposed, and another noble, Tutankhaten, who had married Ankhsen-paaten, another of the royal princesses, succeeded him. The new king soon found himself obliged to bow to the reaction which was setting in in favour of the old religion. The priests of Amen were by far the strongest force in the realm, now that their enemy was gone, and Tutankhaten was forced to renounce whatever allegiance he still held to the ideas of his late master, and submit to their behests. Little more than a year after his accession, he removed the seat of government to Thebes again, and the City of the Horizon was left practically deserted. For a short time, no doubt, its manufactures of coloured glass and faïence kept it alive; and then even these decayed, as the manufacturers found the need of going to where there was a readier market for their wares, and Akhenaten's City of Dreams was left to the jackal and the owl, and gradually passed away from the memory of men, as if itself had been no more than a dream.

In the year 1907, an American explorer, Mr. Theodore M. Davis of New York, whose remarkable combination of patience and good fortune had already been rewarded by the discovery of the untouched tomb of Yuaa and Tuau, the father and mother of that Queen Tiy of whom we heard so much, laid bare, in the Valley of the Kings at Thebes, the entrance of a tomb which appeared to be that of some royal personage of the XVIIIth Dynasty. The entrance passage was partly blocked by one of the sides of a large funeral shrine of gilded cedar-wood past which the explorers had some difficulty in wriggling. In the funeral chamber, they found the other portions of this shrine, and a magnificent coffin, shaped like a recumbent figure, and inlaid with brilliant stones and coloured glass. The lion-legged bier on which the coffin had lain had collapsed, and the coffin had fallen to the ground, so that part of the lid had been thrust aside, revealing the skull of the body, crowned with a golden vulture. The body was wrapped in thin sheets of gold, and the inscription on the coffin gave the titles of Akhenaten, "the beautiful Child of the Sun"; but, on the other hand, the inscription on the gilded shrine stated that King Akhenaten made it for his mother Queen Tiy. The beautiful Canopic jars which accompanied the burial had lids carved in the likeness of a very remarkable human face, which might have been either male or female, though the wig worn by the heads was a male one, and bore the royal uræus; while the toilet utensils found in the tomb were certainly for a woman's use. Accordingly it seemed most natural to believe that the body was that of Queen Tiy, buried here in royal state by her unfortunate son, whose own burial could scarcely have been expected in the neighborhood of the hated Thebes; and it was announced

that the tomb and mummy of Queen Tiy had been discovered.

The greatest surprise of the discovery was, however, still
to come. The bones, soaked in wax, were sent by Mr.
Weigall of the Department of Antiquities to Professor
Elliot Smith for expert examination. He wrote back—
"Are you sure that the bones you sent me are those which
were found in the tomb? Instead of the bones of an old
woman, you have sent me those of a young man. Surely
there is some mistake." There had been no mistake. In
spite of the inscription on the shrine, and the character
of the funeral utensils, the witness of the coffin was true,
and contrary to all probability the body was that of Akhenaten himself, and bore evidence that the "beautiful
Child of the Sun" was not more than twenty-eight when he
died.

Gradually the probable explanation suggested itself.
The king was buried, as we have said, in his tomb at the
City of the Horizon; but when the city was deserted, and
the court returned to Thebes, some of his followers, still
loyal to the memory of their dead master, carried him away
from the lonely tomb in the eastern cliffs, and laid him to
rest in his mother's tomb, since none other was prepared for
him in Thebes. But as the reaction grew fiercer and more
triumphant, the priests of Amen could not endure even to
let the body of their dead enemy rest in honour beside the
mother whom he had loved. They opened the tomb, cut
the hated name of Akhenaten out of the gold-foil
around the body and left their dead foe nameless in the

tomb, thereby, as they thought, sending him an outcast through the spirit-world. Queen Tiy could no longer be permitted to rest in a tomb polluted by the presence of "that criminal," and her coffin was carried elsewhere, perhaps to the tomb of Amenhotep III. Akhenaten was left, in solitude and shame, till more than 3000 years later his resting-place was revealed to a generation perhaps a little better fitted to understand and appreciate the nobility of his ideals.

Yet even to-day controversy is keen over the dead king, and if he has been somewhat fantastically praised by his admirers, he has been as bitterly blamed by some who can see in him nothing but a fanatical doctrinaire, who deserted his faithful servants in the interests of a sickly and morbid religiosity. "In an age of superstition," says Weigall, "and in a land where the grossest polytheism reigned absolutely supreme, Akhnaton evolved a monotheistic religion second only to Christianity itself in purity of tone. He was the first human being to understand rightly the meaning of divinity. When the world reverberated with the noise of war, he preached the first known doctrine of peace; when the glory of martial pomp swelled the hearts of his subjects, he deliberately turned his back upon heroics. He was the first man to preach simplicity, honesty, frankness, and sincerity; and he preached it from a throne. He was the first Pharaoh to be a humanitarian; the first man in whose heart there was no trace of barbarism." Breasted's praise is scarcely less high. "There died with him such a spirit as the world had never seen before,—a brave soul, undauntedly facing the momentum of immemorial tradition, and thereby stepping out from the long line of conventional and colourless Pharaohs, that he might disseminate ideas far beyond and above the capacity of his age to understand. Among the Hebrews, 7 or 800 years later, we look for such men; but the modern world has yet adequately to value or even acquaint itself with this man, who in an age so remote and under conditions so adverse, became the world's first idealist and the world's first *individual.*"

Budge may be taken as representative of the other side. "That he was a fond husband and father is likely enough; but the spectacle of the king spending his time in heated disputes with the priests of Amen on a point of doctrine, and living in luxury among artistic surroundings of every kind, whilst his empire was falling to pieces, and his too loyal servant Abi-Milki was sitting shivering with cold and hunger upon the rocks of Tyre, or writing piteous appeals for help to protect his master's interests, is not edifying. That such a man ever sat upon the throne of the Amenemhats and Usertsens is a fine example of the irony of fate."

Possibly the truth may lie somewhere between the extremes of extravagant laudation and somewhat purblind condemnation. At all events, the young idealist of Akhetaten has fairly earned a distinction to which few men, and those generally of the very first rank, have attained—that of being able to force men of learning, after so many centuries, to take sides concerning him as hotly, and with as keen an interest, as though he were a politician of to-day. Not many men live in the minds of the thinking world after they have been dead for three thousand three hundred years; but within the last forty years Akhenaten has stepped into a foremost place among these few immortals, whose force and originality keeps their memory green long after the whole order with which their names were identified has crumbled into dust. He failed in his day, and it has taken the world thirty centuries to waken up to the truth and freshness of his master-ideas; perhaps that is only the measure of the real greatness of the man.

# CHAPTER IV

OF all the lands of the Ancient East, Egypt is by far the richest in relics of the great past; so much so, that all the antiquities of all the other lands would scarcely, if put together, equal in mass or interest those which have sometimes been gathered from one single Egyptian site; but, in the irony of fate, Egypt is also the land of which it is quite impossible to tell the story of exploration as a single connected narrative. The Mycenæan Age and district found one explorer, who, however rash his methods may sometimes have been, was imbued with a devout reverence for the material with which he was dealing, and who was followed at once by the school of scientific exploration which had been growing up, largely as the fruit of the interest excited by his success. Minoan Crete reaped the full fruit of the lessons which had been learned by the earlier workers, and the excavations at Knossos, Phaistos, and the other Cretan sites have been models of what such work should be. Even in Mesopotamia and Babylonia, though there the earlier part of the story is disfigured by international rivalries, and lack of funds, and the necessary inexperience of pioneers led to wasteful methods of working, it is possible to give a clear narrative of the main progress of excavation;

while Palestine, still remaining largely a subject for future work, has yet furnished, in such explorations as those of Dr. Macalister at Gezer, an example of thoroughness and care which can leave nothing to be desired. But the story of early work in Egypt!

There is no story, for there was no work, in the true sense of the word. Many men worked in their own interests, or in those of others who employed them to carry on what was in reality only a shameless rifling of the nation's treasures; many men intrigued over the question of who, or which nation, should become the possessor of a statue, a sarcophagus, or an obelisk, with an energy, not to say a ferocity, worthy of a better cause; many men, let us say "conveyed," the plunder of Ancient Egypt to various European capitals with such energy, that over a good deal of the material which is the pride of some of the greatest museums there might be written with perfect truth "stolen goods"; but of real exploration as we understand it, in the interests of the general sum of knowledge, you will look in vain, in the generally sordid story of the early nineteenth century scramble for Egyptian antiquities.

To read the pathetic preface which the late Sir Gaston Maspero set at the beginning of the Guide to the Cairo Museum is to realise, with a good deal of shame, how infinite may be the loss, and how great the hindrance put in the way of real study, by methods such as were adopted, without the least regard either to science or the rights of the land concerned, by the men who wrangled like shrews, cheated like horse-copers, and fought like brigands over mummies, papyri, statues and inscribed stones, when the nineteenth century was young.

It was, of course, Napoleon's great expedition of 1798-99, with its wonderful gathering of savants as camp-followers, which first really opened the eyes of the nominally civilised world to the treasures which lay in Egypt for the picking up. Denon's great volumes turned all eyes to the Land of the Nile. Herodotus grew from an old romancer into an inspired guide to a magic Tom Tiddler's ground, where treasures, or what might be turned into treasure, lay about everywhere; and all the eagles, or rather cormorants, were gathered together to where the body was.

No doubt, MM. Drovetti, Passalacqua, Belzoni, and the rest of them, were in ordinary life most estimable members of society; but put them in the presence of an interesting mummy or statue, and forthwith morality fell from them like an outworn garment, and they lied, cheated, and stole, not to put too fine a point upon it, like a gang of thieves. "Twenty collections were formed in this fashion," says Maspero with an honest Egyptologist's natural indignation, "the Salt Collection, the Drovetti Collection, the Passalacqua Collection, the Anastasi, the Athanasy, the Thedenat du Vent, the Belzoni Collections, which, sold into Europe, became there the nucleus of the principal State Museums, at Leyden, at London, at Paris, at Turin, at Berlin. It was an unbridled pillage which lasted more than thirty years, and against which the learned did not fail to protest." Protests, however, even though it was Champollion who protested, went for nothing, in view of the hard cash which

was to be made out of the nefarious business, and it was
not till Mariette attained influence with the Khedive that
the evil was even partially checked.  What perished in
those thirty years—material that would have been priceless
to-day, and can never be replaced, we can only conjecture
and mourn over!  Of these robbers, using the term in its
Pickwickian sense, the most preferred to remain mute, as
they certainly were inglorious, and you can trace them only
in yellow pamphlets which the librarians of our great libraries, with groans, extract from recesses where even librarians do not often penetrate—Catalogues of the Collection Passalacqua, and the like.  Fortunately, however, one of
them, and he the most engaging, was vocal, and his "Narrative of the Recent Operations and Recent Discoveries within
the Pyramids, Temples, Tombs, and Excavations, of
**EGYPT** and **NUBIA**" is well worth the few pence which
the second-hand book-seller charges for it.

Belzoni, as I have said, is an engaging character, and his
utter lack of any sense of the enormity of the crimes which
he was committing, his humble consciousness of his own
supreme importance, and his quiet assurance that he was
always and unalterably right, and his opponents always and
unalterably wrong, make his Narrative most amusing reading,—which, perhaps, was scarcely what he intended it to
be.  The misguided man was so innocent of any evil intent
that he even dared to take his wife with him on his campaign
of spoliation, and Mrs. Belzoni adds to the gratitude of the
reader by contributing to the book what she humbly calls
(rightly or wrongly I shall not say) "A Trifling Account of

the Women of Egypt, Nubia, and Syria"—a title which the unkind printer has abbreviated on its title-page to "Mrs. Belzoni's Trifling Account."

A faint far-off savour of Benvenuto Cellini comes from the pages of Belzoni, though far be it from me to suggest any comparison in criminality between the much-aggrieved agent of the British Consul in Egypt, and the most delightful rascal of the Renaissance. Yet there is somewhat of the same conviction of being quite the finest fellow in all the world, and the same confidence that whatever the writer does is sanctified by the fact that it is he who does it, which make Cellini's memoirs so delightful. One has heard, even in modern times, that jealousies between explorers are still not quite unknown; but surely they never reach such proportions as those which led to the blood-curdling results described in Belzoni's chapter, "Assaulted by a band of Arabs, led on by two Piedmontese in Mr. Drovetti's employ"—Mr. Drovetti being the French Consul in Egypt. Double-barrelled guns and pistols pointed at his breast, curses and threats that now he should pay for having stolen the obelisk from Philæ, and so robbed his assailants of the profit which they should have had from the stealing of it —such were the difficulties under which Belzoni laboured in his efforts to enrich our museums, to say nothing of himself, with the results of this nefarious traffic. Let us be thankful that the little amenities of exploration in 1817 no longer exist.

Occasionally Mr. Belzoni earns our gratitude by rising into the sublime, almost as successfully as Mr. Robert

Hichens does in similar circumstances; but he contrives to close with a decided advantage over Mr. Hichens which may best be exhibited by quotation. "The sanctuary, wholly formed of fine red granite" (he is speaking of the ruins of Karnak), "with the various obelisks standing before it, proclaiming to the distant passenger, 'Here is the seat of holiness'; the high portals, seen at a distance from the openings to this vast labyrinth of edifices; the various groups of ruins of the other temples within sight; these altogether had such an effect upon my soul, as to separate me in imagination from the rest of mortals, exalt me on high over all, and cause me to forget altogether the trifles and follies of life. I was happy for a whole day, which escaped like a flash of lightning; but the obscurity of the night caused me to stumble over one large block of stone, and to break my nose against another, which, dissolving the enchantment, brought me to my senses again." Visitors to the British Museum who wonder at the colossal granite statues of Thothmes III and Ramses II, should not forget that Mr. Belzoni shed his blood to bring them to their resting-place,—even if it was only from his nose!

Belzoni's work, however, haphazard and unscientific as it may have been, is by no means to be merely dismissed with a laugh, in spite of the merits of his style as a narrator. We owe to him, not only the statues already mentioned, and others, only less important and imposing, but the opening of the Second Pyramid, and the discovery of what is by far the finest of the tombs of the Theban Pharaohs of the New Empire—that of Sety I. To this day the donkey-boys call

Sety's tomb "Belzoni-Tomb," and his narrative, with all its ridiculous pomposity, was to many who afterwards took a deep interest in Egypt their first introduction to the wonders of that ancient land. Yet the imagination almost boggles at the thought of what he must have had under his hand, and failed to recognise the importance of. To read his description of his doings among the tombs on the west bank of the Nile at Thebes must seem like a nightmare to the modern explorer with his meticulous carefulness that no fragment of antiquity shall escape his scrutiny. If there is an Inferno for bad explorers, to what circle of it should he be consigned who was guilty of the enormities which he calmly describes in the following passage? "After getting through these passages, some of them two or three hundred yards long," he says, describing one of his mummy-raids, "you generally find a more commodious place, perhaps high enough to sit. But what a place of rest! surrounded by bodies, by heaps of mummies in all directions; which, previous to my being accustomed to the sight, impressed me with horror. . . . After the exertion of entering into such a place, through a passage of fifty, a hundred, three hundred, or perhaps six hundred yards, nearly overcome, I sought a resting-place, found one, and contrived to sit; but when my weight bore on the body of an Egyptian, it crushed it like a band-box. I naturally had recourse to my hands to sustain my weight, but they found no better support; so that I sank altogether among the broken mummies, with a crash of bones, rags, and wooden cases, which raised such a dust as kept me motionless for a quarter of an hour, waiting till it subsided again.  I could not remove from the place, however, without increasing it, and every step I took I crushed a mummy in some part or other.  Once I was conducted from such a place to another resembling it, through a passage of about twenty feet in length, and no wider than a body could be forced through.  It was choked with mummies, and I could not pass without putting my face in contact with that of some decayed Egyptian; but as the passage inclined downwards, my own weight helped me on: however, I could not avoid being covered with bones, legs, arms, and heads rolling from above.  Thus I proceeded from one cave to another, all full of mummies piled up in various ways, some standing, some lying, and some on their heads.  The purpose of my researches was to rob the Egyptians of their papyri; of which I found a few hidden in their breasts, under their arms, in the space above the knees, or on the legs, and covered by the numerous folds of cloth that envelop the mummy."

One imagines Mr. Belzoni in the Egyptian Underworld, forever pursued by the ghosts of the indignant Egyptians on whose bodies he had sat, and the wrathful Egyptologists of a later age whose success he had fatally discounted—the only fitting punishment for such a crime!  His narrative sufficiently explains why it is quite impossible to tell the story of Egyptian Exploration.  Multiply Belzoni by a score or a hundred and you have the story—not of exploration, but of the raids of a horde of thievish ghouls, scuffling among themselves over their gruesome plunder.  Mariette's large and wasteful methods have been often, and justly, criticised; but Mariette was an angel of light, and a model of scientific method, compared with his predecessors, who, in pursuit of their own sordid ends, wasted and destroyed a mass of priceless material, for which the modern Egyptologist would almost be ready to sell his soul. Let it not be forgotten, either, that it was to Mariette's patient and persistent efforts, persevered in under such difficulties as Maspero has feelingly described in his Preface, that we owe the creation of the great Museum of Cairo—that unrivalled treasure-house of the world's greatest historic past, and the establishment on a sound footing of the Service of Antiquities, which, in spite of all mistakes, and of the unconquerable propensity of the modern Egyptian to make a trade out of the remains of his dead ancestors, has done so much for the study of Ancient Egypt.

We cannot therefore tell the tale of the exploration of the great city, which for practically the whole period of Egypt's existence as a world-power was the glittering focus of her dominion. We can only try to describe something of the remains of her ancient glories, and tell, incidentally, how modern explorers, with higher aims and better methods, have rescued for science and history a little of what might have been ours but for the ravages of ignorant cupidity.

Thebes only became the capital of United Egypt at a comparatively late date in the history of the land. The Old Kingdom found its centre near the head of the Delta, in and around Memphis—that is to say, in the neighbourhood of the modern Cairo. Towards the close of this period, the national centre of gravity began to shift further south, and the weaker Pharaohs of the IXth and Xth Dynasties held their court at Henen-Suten, better known by its Greek name of Herakleopolis, a little over 70 miles south of Cairo. They were maintained in power, however, only by the exertions of their powerful vassals, the princes of Siut, and when these wearied, or found themselves no longer capable of upholding the throne against the pressure of the rival princes of Thebes, the Double Crown passed to the Antefs and Mentuhoteps of the XIth Dynasty, whose most notable relic is the terraced temple of Mentuhotep Neb-hapet-Ra, which stands at Der-el-Bahri, side by side with the later and larger temple of Queen Hatshepsut, to which it gave the inspiration.

Their dominion lasted, roughly, for 160 years, say till 2000 B. C., and they were succeeded by another Theban line, that of the XIIth Dynasty—the dynasty of the Amen-emhats and Senuserts, whose period, that of the Middle Kingdom, has of late come to be regarded as the most brilliant period of Egyptian History, the true Golden Age of the Nile Valley. The XIIth Dynasty monarchs, however, though Thebans, held their court, no doubt for politic reasons, and with a view to overawe the restless North, more often in the neighbourhood of the Fayum, where Amenemhat III, perhaps the greatest of them all, con-structed the first great barrage of a type with which we have grown familiar in Modern Egypt, creating the Lake Mœris, which seemed a wonder of the world to Herodotus, and the vast Labyrinth, a building which the old Greek historian describes as surpassing even the Pyramids. What

it was designed for, Temple, as Petrie holds, or Adminis-
trative-Building, as Breasted suggests, is not determined;
but its poor remains, traced by Petrie, show that it was by
far the largest building ever reared by the Egyptians, surpassing even Karnak. "The whole area of the building,"
says Petrie, "is about 1000 feet long, and 800 feet broad,
or enough to include all the temples of Karnak and of
Luxor."

With the waning of the Middle Kingdom, and the coming
of the Hyksos, we have another shift of the capital, which
in the time of these Semitic usurpers was probably mainly at
Tanis in the Delta; but when Seqenen-Ra and Aahmes, the
Theban princes, had brought the War of Independence to a
successful close, and the XVIIIth Dynasty had begun with
Aahmes I, the great southern city came to its own, and rose
to a pre-eminence among the cities of Egypt which was to
endure through all the period of Egypt's world-dominion,
say from 1580 to the death of the last great Egyptian soldier
Pharaoh, Ramses III, in 1170 or 1167 B. C., and which
has made Thebes the typical representative of Egyptian
glory and pride. "Art thou better than No-Amon," says
the prophet Nahum, denouncing judgment on Nineveh,
"that was situate among the rivers, that had the waters
round about it, whose rampart was the sea, and her wall
was from the sea? Ethiopia and Egypt were her strength,
and it was infinite. . . . Yet was she carried away, she went
into captivity."

Nahum's amazement at the fall of Thebes gives you the
measure of the awe which the great city inspired in the mind

of the ancient world. If Thebes fell, what city was secure! Homer's casual reference, in the speech of Achilles, in the IXth Iliad, bears witness to the same feeling, almost of reverence, though by his time, as by Nahum's, Thebes had fallen far below her ancient glories.

> "The world's great empress on th' Egyptian plain,
> (That spreads her conquests o'er a thousand states,
> And pours her heroes through a hundred gates,
> Two hundred horsemen and two hundred cars
> From each wide portal issuing to the wars";)

This, of course, is poetic license—and on a gigantic scale. The Egyptian army under Ramses II at the battle of Kadesh, one of the great critical battles of the nation's history, mustered something like 25,000 men, all told,—a little more than the cavalry alone of Thebes, according to Homer; but the exaggeration only helps to show more clearly the impression which the imperial city had made upon the mind of the ancient world.

After the death of Ramses III, the glory of the great city rapidly declined under the feeble Ramessides with whom the XXth Dynasty dribbled to an inglorious close. The XXIst Dynasty had its capital at Tanis, the old Hyksos seat, the XXIInd and XXIIIrd held their court at Bubastis, while the Ethiopians of the XXVth bore the Double Crown in savage Nubia. It was under Tanutamen, the successor of Taharqa, that the crowning disaster fell upon Thebes. His attempt to assert himself as Pharaoh of all Egypt brought down upon him the terrible Ashurbanipal with the whole power of Assyria. Beaten in Lower Egypt, Tanutamen fled to Thebes, and when the remorseless Assyrian pursued him there, escaped to Ethiopia, leaving the capital to its fate. What that fate was we learn from Ashurbanipal's Cylinder. "I went to Thebes, the strong city; the approach of my powerful army he [Tanutamen] saw, and Thebes he abandoned, and fled to Kip-kip. That city [Thebes] the whole of it, in the service of Assur and Ishtar my hands took; silver, gold, precious stones, the furniture of the palace, all there was; garments costly and beautiful, great horses, people male and female, two lofty obelisks covered with beautiful carving, 2500 talents their weight, set up before the gate of a temple, with them I removed, and brought to Assyria. Its spoils unnumbered I carried off."

From what we know of Assyrian practice in warfare, we may be sure that the sack was a thorough one. Prince Mentuemhat, the governor of the city under the Ethiopian Pharaohs, did his best to restore the damage that had been done by the ruthless conquerors; but in any case he could only prolong for a little what was inevitable. Gradually Thebes sank into comparative insignificance, as first Sais, and then Alexander's new capital rose to supremacy. Her great temples were still honoured, and it was to claim sonship with the God of Thebes that Alexander journeyed to the Oasis of Ammon; but the great city of Thothmes and Amenhotep got its death-wound when Ashurbanipal's brutal soldiery stormed its walls in 661 B. C.

In the hey-day of its splendour under the New Empire, Thebes must have been one of the most imposing cities of the ancient world—"a worthy seat of empire, the first monumental city of antiquity," as Breasted calls it. Nebu-chadnezzar's Babylon, even if we divide by four the vast circuit of fifty-three miles assigned by Herodotus to its walls, as we probably should do, may have exceeded it in mere size; but not even the splendours of the Ishtar Gate, and the Procession Street, the Royal Palace, and the great Temple of Marduk, can have presented a more gorgeous spectacle than the City of Amen, when Amenhotep III had completed his work upon it, and Sety I and Ramses II had added their contribution to the glories which their fore-runner had left. A great white city filled all the plain between the river and the eastern hills, the royal palace with its gardens occupying a huge area in the centre of the crowded town, and the mansions of the nobles clustering around, the vast bulks of the Temples of Karnak and Luxor towering above everything else, with their gigantic pylons, their lofty obelisks and flagstaves, and their gates of bronze and gold, with the broad Nile sweeping past, its quays thronged with the shipping of the whole land, mingled with the vessels of Phœnicia and the Ægean. On the western plain, beyond the river, lay the silent city of the dead, where temples, only less great than Karnak and Luxor, crowded one another from Qurneh on the north to Medinet-Habu, and the western Palace of Amenhotep III on the south. The ancient world had nothing to show which could surpass the solid and enduring magnificence of the seat of empire of those great kings to whom the proudest monarchs of the east wrote—"Seven times and seven times at the feet of my Lord I fall. I am the dust under the sandals of my Lord, the King."

"The general effect," writes Breasted, describing Thebes as Amenhotep III left it, "must have been imposing in the extreme; the brilliant hues of the polychrome architecture, with columns and gates overwrought in gold and floors overlaid with silver, the whole dominated by towering obelisks clothed in glittering metal, rising high above the rich green of the nodding palms and tropical foliage which framed the mass,—all this must have produced an impression both of gorgeous detail and overwhelming grandeur, of which the sombre ruins of the same buildings, impressive as they are, offer little hint at the present day."

Of all this great city, so far as the dwelling-places of its inhabitants are concerned, scarcely a trace is left. The palaces of kings and nobles were built, not of the enduring materials which they used for the temples of the gods, but of crude brick stuccoed and painted, and, even in the climate of Upper Egypt, such buildings quickly fell into decay and ere long became mere mounds of earth. What remains of Thebes is not any abode either of king or commoner. It is "the eternal habitation," as the Egyptian called it, the house of his god, or of his deified dead. Thebes to-day is the City of Temples and Tombs,—temples of the great gods who ruled forever, and of "the good gods" who ruled for awhile as kings, and then were adored, only a little more than when they were on earth, in the stately houses which they had built for their glory,—tombs such as no other race has ever fashioned, because no other race has ever been possessed by such an universal passion for immortal endurance.

Our task then, is to tell first of the Temples, which needed no discovery because their ruins were, unlike those of Babylon and Nineveh, impossible to hide; but which yet, during the century which has elapsed since Napoleon's expedition blazoned abroad the wonder of them, have been studied, till now the story of their growth and decay is fairly well understood; and then of the Tombs, from which, for the last half-century, patient exploration and research have been drawing treasures of the arts and crafts of Ancient Egypt, and documents for the study of her history and her religion, precious in themselves, but priceless as materials for the reconstruction of the history and the faith and life of one of the most interesting of races.

Of the Temples, Karnak, of course, comes first, claiming precedence as the oldest, the greatest, and the most important of Theban sanctuaries, and as the hugest ruin in the world. It is almost impossible to realise by how much Karnak is the hugest of ruins. To say that the actual temple building is about 1200 feet in length, by about 330 in breadth, while the sacred enclosure measures about 1500 feet by 1500, is merely to convey an impression of considerable size; while to put it in another fashion, and say that the area of the actual building is roughly close upon 400,000 square feet, and that of the enclosure 2,250,000 square feet, is to convey no impression at all, save one of bewilderment. Comparisons may help us a little. St. Peter's, Rome, Milan, and Notre Dame, Paris, are three

of the most familiar and imposing of European cathedrals
—the whole three put together just about equal in area the
actual temple building of Karnak. Into the sacred enclosure, you could pack St. Peter's, Milan, Seville, Florence,
St. Paul's, Cologne, York, Amiens, and Antwerp; while
Notre Dame would go comfortably into one of the halls of
Karnak, and that not the largest, though the most complete and imposing.

We are thus dealing with by far the largest complex of
religious building in the world, though the famous Labyrinth of the XIIth Dynasty Pharaoh, Amenemhat III, now
almost totally destroyed, was still larger in its day. The
sacred enclosure of Etemenanki, the Tower of Babel, as
traced by Dr. Koldewey, comes close to that of Karnak in
area; but the Tower of Babel, massive as its remains are,
was a trifle compared with the halls and pylons of Karnak,
and none of the other buildings of the temenos of Babylon
are to be mentioned in the same breath with the vast courts
of the Egyptian temple.

Karnak is by no means one of the most ancient of Egyptian sacred buildings. Doubtless there were on the site
originally far more ancient buildings than any now
remaining; but the temple, as we know it now, was founded
by the great Pharaohs of the XIIth Dynasty; and even of
their work little now survives, and that surrounded and
smothered by the larger and more imposing structures of
the XVIIIth and XIXth Dynasty monarchs. The ruins
which to-day fill the mind of the tourist with amazement
do not date further back than 1580 B. C., which is

comparatively modern as things go in Egypt, though it is a thousand years older than Nebuchadnezzar's great Temple-tower at Babylon; and most of the courts and pylons are of even later date.

It was with the rise of the XVIIIth Dynasty to power after the expulsion of the Hyksos that the glory of Karnak began. The long War of Independence had created a new consciousness of power and a new spirit of adventure in the normally quiet and peace-loving Egyptian; and this is the period when Egypt made her only real bid for world-empire. It was now that she produced the one really great soldier-king of her long history, and though Thothmes III was the solitary flower of her century-plant in this respect, there were other kings of his race who were, as Alan Breck Stewart puts it, "most respectable persons on the field of war." Of all the spoils and the tribute which Thothmes gathered as the fruit of his seventeen campaigns in Syria and Naharina, and his predecessors and successors in their wars in the north and in Ethiopia, no small portion went to glorify the sanctuary of the god who had given strength to their arms in the day of battle.

Thothmes I, who by his conquests in Syria showed the way to the greater soldier who was to follow him, began the work by building to the west of the old Middle Kingdom sanctuary a fine hall adorned with Osiride statues, and a great pylon (the present Vth). Later he added another pylon (the present IVth), and, between the two great gates, he erected a colonnaded hall. Then, in honour of his thirtieth anniversary, he sent his architect, Ineni, up the

PLATE VIII

KARNAK, THE GREAT HALL, WITH OBELISKS OF HATSHEPSUT AND THOTHMES I.

Nile to Aswan to bring down two red granite monoliths, to be set up as obelisks before the western pylon. Ineni carried out his task with complete success and has left us his own record of how he brought the two huge stones down the Nile in "an august boat" of 120 cubits in length by 40 in breadth; while he enlarges on how the great doorway named "Amen-Mighty-in-Wealth" was fitted with its "huge door of Asiatic bronze," first-fruit of the conquered lands, "whereon was the Divine Shadow inlaid with gold"—a prefiguring of the greater splendours which were to follow. The achievement of Thothmes I did not long retain its pride of place at Karnak. He was succeeded, whether peaceably or not is doubtful, by his daughter, the famous Queen Hatshepsut, and she showed how much or how little reverence she had for the memory of her father by the extraordinary position which she chose for the noble monuments which still keep alive her memory at Thebes. As the time for her jubilee drew nigh, she, too, sent her architect and vizier, the famous Senmut, to Aswan to bring down two more shafts of red granite for the adornment of Amen's House; and when the gigantic stones, 97½ feet in height, arrived, she unroofed part of the colonnaded hall of her father, thus rendering it useless for any ceremonial purpose, and set up her obelisks in the ruined chamber. Curiously enough, one obelisk of the father and one of the daughter still stands; and though that of Thothmes is a noble monolith, it is completely overshadowed by that of his undutiful daughter. Indeed Hatshepsut's obelisk is the tallest now standing in Egypt, and is only second to that of her equally undutiful successor Thothmes III, which now stands in front of St. John Lateran at Rome, and which measures 105½ feet. Hatshepsut has left us her account of how she was prompted to erect the obelisks—"I was sitting in my palace, I was thinking of my Creator, when my heart urged me to make for him two obelisks of electrum [gold-silver alloy, with which the obelisks were either overlaid, or at least tipped], whose points reach unto the sky." It is a pretty touch of piety,—if only she had been a little more regardful of filial piety as well.

The inscription goes on to say that the time occupied in the work was seven months, either "from the ordering of it in the quarry," or "making seven months of exaction in the mountain." If the first reading is correct, and the whole work of quarrying, transit, hewing, sculpturing, and erecting the great 300-ton blocks was finished in such a time, it is nothing short of a marvel; and even if the seven months refers only to the quarrying of the blocks, such expedition is sufficiently remarkable. Thothmes III, carrying on the amiable family tradition which Hatshepsut had established, sheathed the lower part of the great queen's obelisks in masonry, so that her inscriptions should not be seen. In so doing he has unwittingly contributed to their preservation; his sheathing has now fallen down, and the inscription can be read probably all the more clearly for being protected so long.

The fate of the obelisks of Thothmes III himself is sufficiently curious. He reared them all over Egypt; but not one solitary shaft remains where he placed it. One of the finest of them, as we have seen, is in Rome; one of the pair which stood before the temple at Heliopolis now adorns the Thames Embankment, and is known as "Cleopatra's Needle" to millions of Londoners to whom the far greater personage who actually reared it is not even a name; while its twin is in Central Park, New York. What is perhaps the most interesting of them all is the stunted shaft, 61 feet in height, and 199 tons in weight, which stands in the centre of the ancient Hippodrome at Constantinople, near to the famous Serpent Column, on which are recorded the names of the Greek cities and tribes which fought against Persia at Platæa. Manifestly this is only the fragment of a far larger shaft, and Professor Flinders Petrie has shown that though it is said to have come from Heliopolis, its size, were it complete to the length which its proportions require, and the fact that it is dedicated, not to the Sun-God of Heliopolis, but to Amen of Thebes, make it probable that this is a piece of one of the two gigantic obelisks, 185 feet in height, which as we know from an inscription in the temple at Der-el-Bahri, Thothmes erected before Queen Hatshepsut's beautiful "paradise of Amen." If this is the case, then the Constantinople obelisk, when complete, must have weighed about 800 tons, and must have been by far the largest, though not the heaviest stone ever dealt with by human hands. Hatshepsut thought it necessary to swear a great oath that her two $97\frac{1}{2}$ feet shafts were each "of one block of enduring granite, without seam or joining"; but they were very small affairs beside these monsters of her successor. Captain Engelbach has recently calculated

(Ancient Egypt, IV, 1922) the strain on an obelisk of the dimensions mentioned, and finds it to be 5120 pounds per square inch—an impossible figure, as granite breaks at 1500 pounds per square inch. An obelisk of 100 cubits high (or 172 feet), would need to be 36 feet square at the base, and 19 at the tip, and would weigh 11,000 tons! Some other explanation must therefore, as Professor Petrie indicates, be found for the still greater height ascribed to the obelisks —108 cubits.*

Karnak owed many of its finest chambers to the piety with which Thothmes attributed his unvarying success as a soldier to Amen. At the east end of the temple he built a great Festal Hall, 144 feet by 52, whose columns have the peculiarity, more curious than beautiful, of tapering downwards, instead of upwards, while their capitals follow the same inverted rule, and appear like bells standing on their mouths. The idea of the downward taper may have been borrowed from Minoan practice, where, of course, it was general. Minoan influence, as we learn from the tombs of Hatshepsut's factotum Senmut, and Thothmes' vizier, Rekh-ma-ra, was never stronger than during the last half century before its eclipse by the sack of Knossos, and perhaps Thothmes got his idea from the "Men from the Back of Beyond." The feature, however, did not commend itself to Egyptian taste and was never repeated. Besides

* Capt. Engelbach explains (Ancient Egypt, Part II, 1923, p. 62) that by a slip in his calculation the amount of the stress is exactly double what it should be—i.e., the actual stress is 2560 pounds per square inch, instead of 5120. This of course correspondingly reduces the dimensions of the obelisk necessary to sustain the stress, but still leaves these beyond the bounds of reasonable size.

PLATE IX

NAVE OF THE GREAT HALL, KARNAK, AND OBELISK OF THOTHMES I.

the Festal Hall, Thothmes erected a Mortuary Hall for the worship of his ancestors, on the walls of which he engraved the famous Karnak Table of Kings, now in the Bibliothèque Nationale at Paris, several new pylons, and a number of other chambers. Behind the VIth Pylon, which he thrust in to the east of that of Thothmes I, he erected a Hall of Records, whose roof was once supported by the two beautiful granite pillars, bearing the Lily of Upper Egypt, and the Papyrus of Lower Egypt, which still attract the admiration of all visitors.

Amenhotep III, the Super-Solomon of Egyptian history, added a huge gateway in front of that of Thothmes I; it is now known as Pylon III; but with his death came a temporary eclipse of all the glories of Thebes, due to the fanaticism of his son Akhenaten. The death of "that criminal of Akhetaten," however, brought a renewed outburst of zeal for the worship of the Theban God, and it is to Sety I, and Ramses II of the XIXth Dynasty, that Karnak owes her greatest splendours, and above all the famous Pillared Hall. This vast building measures 338 feet by 170, and its area is about 50,000 square feet. That is to say it could comfortably accommodate Durham Cathedral, leaving about 5000 square feet to spare. It is divided into a nave and two side aisles. The pillars of the nave, six on each side, are each as large as Trajan's Column at Rome, and on their open-flower capitals, on each of which 100 men could stand, are laid the huge architraves, ranging from 60 to 100 tons in weight, which supported the roofing-blocks. Had the hall been completed in the same dignified

style, it would have been one of the wonders of the world
for majesty, as it is now is for size; but in the aisles the effect
is frittered away by the forest of 122 columns, which
absolutely seem to jostle one another, and effectually
destroy the feeling of space which so great a building should
convey.   Even as it is, the Pillared Hall is a marvel; but
it might have been so much more!

Karnak, as the XIXth Dynasty left it, was completed
by the Pylon of Ramses I, which formed its West Front,—
a front over 330 feet in breadth, or almost twice that of
St. Paul's, London.   Ramses III, conscious of the folly of
trying to rival the work of his predecessors, confined his
attention to the erection of a small temple to the west of
the façade, and at right angles to the main axis of the
temple; but the Bubastite Pharaohs of the XXIInd Dynasty
were not so modest, and beyond the Pylon of Ramses I they
planned a court which was to be still larger than the Hall
of Sety and Ramses II, measuring over 314 feet by 269.
Their ambitions were greater than their resources, however,
and the Court of the Bubastites was never finished, though
the Ethiopian Taharqa carried on the work, and has left one
fine open-flower pillar as a memorial of his grandiose
design.   Sheshanq, the most powerful of the Bubastites,
planned a noble river-front to the temple, in the shape of
a vast pylon, 357 feet in breadth, 150 feet in height, and
over 36 feet in thickness; but neither he nor the Ptolemies,
who took up the gigantic task, ever came within sight of its
completion, and the river-front of Karnak remains unfinished to this day.

Such was the main structure of Karnak,—the most amazing complex of religious building (if we except the XIIth Dynasty Labyrinth, as being possibly a religious building) that the world has ever known. But beyond the main building lay a crowd of other structures, pylons, temples to Mut and Khonsu, the other members of the Theban Divine Triad, sacred lakes for purposes of ceremonial ablution and procession; enough, in fact, to make Karnak a great religious city rather than a temple. The history of all this amazing tangle of buildings, temple upon and within temple, has been slowly wrought out by patient investigation, while the great building itself has gradually been put into a condition of greater security by the efforts of the Service of Antiquities; and now it is possible, as we have seen, to form some idea of how the whole stupendous structure grew to its present shape, and to hope that it may endure for as long as it has lasted already, spite of careless builders, the hazards of war, and the depredations of ancient and modern relic-hunters.

From the Portal of Ptolemy Euergetes I, before the Temple of Khonsu, there stretched southward for over a mile and a half one of the most imposing features of ancient Thebes—the western avenue of ram-headed Sphinxes, reared by Amenhotep III of the XVIIIth Dynasty, and bearing each a portrait statue of the king between its forepaws. Of this grand avenue, only a fragment now remains; but it is sufficient to enable one to realise the dignity of this approach to the glories of Karnak. Following the avenue, and the road which has taken its place, we reach the other great temple of the Eastern City, Luxor. Luxor is second only to Karnak among Egyptian temples, and had it not been overshadowed by its greater neighbour, would have been accounted a wonder. As we see it, it owes almost all its fabric to two Pharaohs, famous in history, Amenhotep III and Ramses II. We shall not go far wrong if we say that it owes all its beauty to the first of these; for the work of Ramses here is of a clumsiness and coarseness which only serves as a foil to the graceful and dignified work of the earlier monarch.

As in the case of Karnak, Amenhotep was building on a site which had already been occupied by his predecessors; but his beautiful courts entirely superseded the earlier sanctuary. At the southern end of the temple he built a group of chambers around the old holy place, in one of which can still be seen the relief picturing the divine birth of the king. Before the sanctuary rose a vestibule, its roof borne by 32 clustered papyrus columns; and in front of this the forecourt, which is still, with its shapely papyrus-bud columns, one of the most graceful specimens of the Egyptian architecture of the New Empire. North of this again, the king had planned to build a great Pillared Hall, which, had it been finished on the scale on which it was begun, would have almost rivalled the great Hall of Karnak in size, and certainly surpassed it in beauty. The design, however, was never carried beyond its opening stage, for the religious revolution of Akhenaten put a stop to all building in honour of Amen, and when the kings of the XIXth Dynasty began to build again in honour of the Theban god,

PLATE X

they were more concerned with their own work than with the finishing of Amenhotep's. The nave is all of the hall that was even partially carried out; but its seven couples of great open-flower columns, each 52 feet high, make a very impressive picture. In front of the unfinished nave, Ramses II added his contribution to Luxor, with a change of axis, due to difficulties of the site. His 74 columns are of the papyrus-bud type, like those of the forecourt of Amenhotep; but with a difference! The difference between art, at its summit, and art in its decadence, could scarcely be better illustrated than by a comparison of the design of the columns of Amenhotep, and those of Ramses.

The main front of the temple was also built by Ramses. The pylon was adorned with six colossal statues of himself, two sitting and four standing, of which only the sitting figures and the westernmost of the standing ones remain. In front of the statues rose two great 80-feet obelisks of red granite, of which one is still in its original position, while the other was removed in 1836 to Paris, where it now adorns the Place de la Concorde. Luxor as Ramses left it was second only to Karnak in size, measuring 850 feet in length. The whole building which we see was practically completed within 200 years,—a very unusual thing for a great Egyptian temple. Karnak, for instance, was building for a matter of 1700 years, from the XIIth Dynasty to the time of the Ptolemies! We wonder at the time which some of our great mediæval cathedrals took to build; but Karnak was longer in building than any one of them has been standing—more than twice as long, in point of fact!

# CHAPTER V

THE two great temples, with the numerous subsidiary ones around Karnak, make up the main interest on the east bank of the Nile at Thebes; but on the western side of the river there lay another city, scarcely less gorgeous, certainly more populous, and, to the modern student, almost of greater interest than the capital of the Thothmes and the Amenhoteps. This was the City of the Dead, with its silent lines of tombs innumerable, its stately temples, and its memorial statues. To an Egyptian our soldier's phrase in the late war—"going west"—would have seemed the natural one to express the fact of death; for all good Egyptians went west when they died. The hills along the western bank of the Nile are honeycombed for hundreds of miles by the tombs of many centuries, and in the neighbourhood of a great city like Thebes the number of tombs, as Belzoni's narrative sufficiently shows, must have been immense. It is from the treasures of art and literature and the articles of domestic use unearthed from the tombs of the land that most of our knowledge of the life and history of the people of Egypt has been derived; and nowhere has this search been rewarded with richer results, or have the circumstances attending on exploration been more interesting or dramatic

than on the western bank of the Nile at Thebes, and above
all in the Valley of the Kings, where for centuries the greatest kings of Egypt were buried.

In the wild, sun-scorched valley, the Biban-el-Moluk, as
it is called, there was room only for the wonderful rock-
hewn tombs to which we shall presently be introduced.
Consequently, place had to be found elsewhere for the
funerary chapels which were necessary for the funeral rites
and the worship of "the good God," when his earthly reign
had closed, and he had joined the company of the gods in
the Egyptian Elysian Fields, the "Sekhet-Aaru." Thus
there grew up, along the narrow plain between the river and
the western cliffs, a series of Temples, the lineal descendants of the tomb-chapels and Pyramid-Temples of earlier
days, but on a scale far greater and more gorgeous. Of
these, there still remain, more or less perfectly preserved,
such notable buildings as the Temple of Sety I at Qurneh,
the temples of Mentuhotep and Hatshepsut at Der-el-Bahri,
the Ramesseum, the beautiful little Ptolemaic temple of
Der-el-Medinet, and the great temple of Ramses III at Medinet-Habu. But these are only a remnant of the crowd of
splendid buildings which almost elbowed one another over
all the space, two miles long by almost one and a half broad,
between the Nile and the hills opposite Thebes. Two
temples of Thothmes III, the temple of Amenhotep II, of
Amenhotep III, of Merenptah, of Thothmes IV, of Siptah,
of Tausert, to say nothing of others, have vanished almost
entirely, leaving only pitiful fragments of foundation, painfully traced out by the modern explorer, to show where

they once stood, or a few broken blocks and fragments of statues from which something of their glory and beauty may be inferred. In spite of the ruin, largely wrought, not so much by enemies or ignorant relic-hunters, as by the irreverent hands of successive Pharaohs, who had no taste for ancient history, and found the temples of their ancestors most convenient quarries, whence they could draw blocks of stone ready-hewn, and statues which needed only the altering of a cartouche to make them proclaim the glory of the reigning Pharaoh as they had proclaimed that of his deified ancestor, the work of the last half-century has done wonders in the way of enabling us to reconstruct in imagination, from the actual remains, and from the graven descriptions of the monarchs who built them, the vanished splendours of Western Thebes.

Probably our greatest loss has been that of the Funerary Temple of Amenhotep III, the most glittering, though perhaps by no means the greatest, of the kings of the Theban Empire. The two gigantic relics of it which remain are probably the most salient objects on the western plain. After the Pyramids, and the mighty mass of ruin at Karnak, there is nothing which so impresses the mind in Egypt as the two Memnon Colossi, sitting in gaunt and scarred majesty and loneliness, with hands on knees, staring eternally across the river to the sunrise. Battered and mutilated as they are, their mere mass is yet sufficient to suggest something of the huge building of which they were but the guardians of the gate. They stand, or rather sit, 65 feet in height even now; when the vanished crown was upon their heads, they must have been almost 70 feet high. They are hewn each out of a single block of quartzose sandstone conglomerate, weighing 700 tons, and the labour of bringing them 70 miles down the river from the quarries beyond Edfu, where this stone is found, and setting them up in their place, must have been immense. Perhaps they are even more impressive in their present loneliness than they were in the days when they were only part of the decoration of an over-whelming whole. But you have to try to imagine them as they were 3300 years ago. A long avenue of couchant jackals, each bearing between its forepaws a portrait statue of the king, leads up from the quay on the river-bank, and is terminated by a pair of towering red granite obelisks, which stand in front of the colossi. Behind the two great figures rises the vast mass of the pylon, with its two frown-ing towers, and its stately gateway closed by great cedar doors, overlaid with bronze, inlaid with gold-silver alloy, while in front of each tower a group of tall flagstaves flaunts its gaily coloured banners. Entering between the towers, you find yourself in a spacious open court, surrounded by a graceful colonnade, and adorned with numerous royal statues. In the centre of the court rises a stele of sand-stone, thirty feet high, and encrusted with gold and precious stones, which marks the "Station of the King," where he stands when engaged in his priestly function; against the wall in one of the loggias stands a fine black granite slab, engraved with the record of all the magnificence of the temple, while it is balanced by another in white limestone, which tells the tale of the king's prowess as a warrior, and

of his triumphs in the field.  The floors of the various courts
and chambers are overlaid with gold and silver, and the
whole building, despite its massive solidity, is like a dream
of splendour from the Arabian Nights.  "Behold!" says the
king, in the inscription on the black granite stele, "the
heart of His Majesty was satisfied with making a very
great monument; never has happened the like since the
beginning . . . an august temple on the west of Thebes,
an eternal, everlasting fortress of white sandstone, wrought
with gold throughout; its floor is adorned with silver, all
its portals with electrum [gold-silver alloy].  It is numerous
with Royal statues of Elephantine granite, of costly gritstone, of every splendid costly stone, established as everlasting works."  "It is made very wide and large, and
established forever," says Amenhotep, with, one can imagine, a sigh of satisfaction, as he looks upon the "holy
and beautiful house" which he has built to the glory of
Amen and himself.  But human "forevers" are a doubtful
quantity; and King Amenhotep's lasted not much more than
a century and a half.

By that time Merenptah of the XIXth Dynasty was
thinking of his own needs, and realising that with a
dwindling empire, and an ebbing treasury, it was not so
easy as it once had been to send to Aswan and Edfu for
costly stones of granite and gritstone; so he took who had
the power, and the indignant shade of the greater monarch
had to endure the spoliation which he could not prevent.
"The temple of Merenptah," says Petrie, who excavated it
along with five other temples, in 1896, ". . . was entirely

formed from the plundering of Amenhotep's temple. The avenue of jackals with statues of the king between the paws, the inscribed bases on which they stood, the colossi, the sphinxes, the steles, the sculptured blocks, and even the bricks, were all plundered and destroyed for the sake of materials." Beside this wholesale robbery, the feats of the early nineteenth century spoilers, recorded a little ago, seem negligible, almost laudable. Merenptah, of course, had learned thievery in a good school, for his father, Ramses II, was the record thief of other men's monuments in all Egypt's long history. Wherever, throughout the land, an extra fine block of stone, statue or obelisk, column or lintel, is to be seen with the cartouche of Ramses II upon it, the chances are perhaps about ten to one that the stone belonged originally to another and better man. "What became of the lower part," says Petrie, speaking of the Constantinople obelisk of Thothmes III, "we may guess when we see the multitude of obelisks erected by Ramessu II." Even royal thieves get found out at last.

Fortunately the black granite stele which has been mentioned was recovered by Petrie, along with the white limestone one, from the ruins of Merenptah's temple, and is now in the Museum at Cairo. On the back of it, the robber had engraved that Triumph Inscription in which occurs the first known mention of Israel on any Egyptian monument— a mention which instead of proving a light to a dark place of history, has only made the darkness more visible.

Behind the ruined temple of Amenhotep, and to the northeast of the temples of Merenptah and Thothmes IV, stands the Ramesseum, the huge funerary temple of Ramses II, which he built from the first to the eighth year of his reign, and which has been thoroughly explored and published in recent years by Mr. J. E. Quibell. Why a young king should make his first great work the building of his funerary temple is not apparent at first sight; the reason, however, is simple, and quite in accordance with his character. His father, Sety I, from the record an honourable man and a good king, had built at Qurneh for his father, Ramses I, the temple which now bears the names of both Ramses I and Sety. He had then begun to build his own temple— the present Ramesseum; but it was only partly completed when he died, and his loving son, so early beginning to display his rooted objection to all personal property except his own, immediately stole the unfinished temple and packed his father's memory and his priests off to the smaller temple at Qurneh, to share it with his grandfather! Such was filial piety in the year 1300 B. C.! When some of our modern purists make a great to-do over the certainly lamentable necessity which has sacrificed the beautiful (but comparatively modern) ruins of Philæ to the needs of a few millions of living men and women, it is in place to remind them that the greatest destroyers of the most interesting relics of Egypt's history and art have not been the engineers who have given new life to the land, but the most notorious and grandiose of the Pharaoh's, over whose (mostly stolen) works they are quite willing to go into raptures.

The Ramesseum, however, stolen or not, is a splendid and

PLATE XI

THE RAMESSEUM, THEBES, WITH FRAGMENTS OF COLOSSUS OF RAMSES II.

impressive building—on a scale worthy of its builder's (or appropriator's) opinion of himself. Its ruined pylon measures 220 feet across the face, and from the gate to the wall of the chambers behind the sanctuary the great structure measures over 520 feet. Thus it is about 7 feet longer than York Minster, and almost exactly the same length as Ely Cathedral; in breadth, of course, it more than doubles either of them. It originally consisted of three great halls preceding the sanctuary; but of the first practically nothing is left, and of the second only a few pillars of Osiride form. The third, or Hypostyle hall, is fairly preserved, and though not comparable to that of either Karnak or Luxor in point of size, is yet a noble chamber, with a nave of six pairs of open-flower columns, each 36 feet in height, and aisles with bud-columns of 25 feet. In the first hall stood the huge red granite sitting statue of the king, whose great fragments now strew the ground beside the Osiride pillars of the second court.

With the possible exception of its standing brother colossus at Tanis, of which Petrie discovered the fragments in 1894, this is the largest block of stone which was ever handled by Egyptian stone workers, or indeed by any stone-workers in the world. A few figures may help to give some idea of its monstrous greatness. The breadth of the shoulders was 22⅓ feet, the length of the ear, 3½ feet, that of the index-finger, 3¼ feet, while the breadth of the foot across the toes was 4½ feet. The weight of the vast mass was probably close upon 1000 tons—a sufficiently mighty monument, one would think, to the vainglory of one

man, not by any means in the first rank of Pharaohs except
in his overweening consciousness of his own deserts.  It is
perhaps only poetic justice that the great usurper of other
men's monuments should have had his own two greatest
statues overthrown and smashed by later Pharaohs with a
patient industry which has left them mere battered fragments; but we have thereby been robbed of the chance of
seeing the vastest work of art, if these monstrous statues
can be called works of art, ever wrought by the hands of
man.  The Ramesseum is adorned with reliefs of the battles
of Ramses, including, of course, the Battle of Kadesh,
which afforded an opportunity of glorifying the valour
of the king, though indeed he should rather have been
ashamed of the bad generalship which made the valour
necessary.  The reliefs of Ramses, however, here, and in
most other places, are comparatively poor and coarse
work, and not to be mentioned along with those of his
father, Sety.

North of the Ramesseum, in a great bay of the cliffs
behind which lies the Biban-el-Moluk, is Der-el-Bahri,
"The Convent of the North," so called because the Copts
usurped part of the site for one of their monastic buildings,
and along with it no small part of the materials of the two
great temples which they found there.  Of these, the larger
and later, that of Queen Hatshepsut, was first made known
to the scholars of Europe by MM. Jollois and Devilliers,
two members of the French Expedition.  Along with
their description they gave a plan, fairly accurate in what
it shows, though a great deal of the building was then

hidden in the sand. They were followed by various explorers, chief of them Mariette, who succeeding in laying
bare enough of the building to show how remarkable, and,
as was then thought, unique a specimen of Egyptian architectural work it was. Finally the complete excavation of
the temple was undertaken by the Egypt Exploration Fund,
whose operations were directed in 1894 and subsequent
years by M. Edouard Naville. The seven volumes of the
Fund's Report on Der-el-Bahri with their superb plates,
form one of the finest records of such work ever published,
just as the temple with which they deal is itself the finest
memoir ever published of a voyage of exploration.

Hatshepsut has left on the walls of her temple an account
of the inception of the expedition to Punt or Somaliland
which preceded, and was the necessary condition of the
founding of the temple. As in the case of the erection of her
Karnak obelisks, she ascribes the beginning of the work to
a direct divine inspiration. Amen himself, she says, commanded her, "to establish for him a Punt in his house, to
plant the trees of God's Land beside his temple, in his
garden," and to this end, "a command was heard from the
great throne, an oracle of the god himself, that the ways
to Punt should be searched out, that the highways to the
Myrrh-terraces should be penetrated." In obedience to
this divine behest, the queen got ready five ships of her fleet,
and the little squadron found its way down the Red Sea,
reaching it apparently by a canal from the Nile, as there is
no record of transshipment of cargo, and finally arrived at
the land which the Egyptians called God's Land, or the

Divine Land, which was always to them a land of Romance, and from which they seem to have had some idea that their own ruling race had originally come. It may have been the country which we now know as Somaliland.

Arrived at their destination, they amicably accomplished all that was desired in the way of trade with the natives, buying great heaps of the green gum which the Egyptians prized for the making of incense, numbers of the gum-bearing trees themselves, ebony, ivory, gold-dust, apes, dogs, panther-skins, and even some of the natives and their children. "Never," says the inscription, "was brought the like of this for any king who has been since the beginning." The return voyage was safely accomplished, and the voyagers had a gala reception at Thebes, with a guard of honour of soldiers to meet them, while the treasures which they had brought were measured and carefully stored in the treasure-house of Amen. Meanwhile the temple had been preparing, and when at last all was completed, the incense-gum duly offered to Amen, and the incense-trees planted on the terraces of his new and beautiful house, the queen proudly records her satisfaction at the completion of the great work, —"I have made for him a Punt in his garden, just as he commanded me, for Thebes. It is large enough for him to walk abroad in."

The great temple on whose walls the whole story of the expedition is portrayed in a series of the finest reliefs which Egyptian art ever produced, is itself a sufficiently remarkable building. It was planned by Hatshepsut's famous architect and vizier, Senmut, and while deriving, as we

shall see, its first inspiration from the older and smaller
XIth Dynasty temple which stood close beside it, it was far
superior to the older building both in size and beauty.  Only
in one point did the XVIIIth Dynasty workers fall below
their predecessors—in the quality of their masonry.  That
of Hatshepsut's temple is of fairly good quality; but it is
not to be compared to the fine work of the masons who
worked for Mentuhotep Neb-hapet-Ra.  With this one
qualification, it may safely be said that it is scarcely possible
to imagine a more satisfactory solution of the problem with
which Senmut was confronted—of placing in a great bay
of the desert, backed by towering red cliffs, a building
which should neither be dwarfed by its surroundings nor
seem to compete vainly with them.  The old architect's
design is in the most perfect harmony with its environment.
"In a series of three terraces," says Breasted, "the temple
rose from the plain to the level of an elevated court, flanked
by the massive yellow cliffs, into which the holy of holies
was cut.  In front of the terraces were ranged fine colonnades, which, when seen from a distance, to this day exhibit
such an exquisite sense of proportion and of proper grouping
as to quite disprove the common assertion that the Greeks
were the first to understand the art of adjusting external
colonnades, and that the Egyptians understood only the
employment of the column in interiors."  This high praise
is thoroughly well deserved.  Der-el-Bahri remains a model
to all architects of the perfect understanding of the true
relation between a noble building and a noble site.  Mr.
Robert Hichens may be somewhat over-fanciful and precious

in his description of Hatshepsut's beautiful creation—"The temple at Deir-el-Bahari," he says, "came upon me like a delicate woman, perfumed and arranged, clothed in a creation of white and blue and orange, standing—ever so knowingly—against a background of orange and pink, of red and of brown-red, a smiling coquette of the mountain." It does sound a little like an extract from somebody's Fashion Magazine; but it has caught the essential note of the grace with which the temple is fitted into its environment— beauty under the shadowing protection of majesty.

When M. Naville had finished his long work at Hatshepsut's temple, and given us back as much of its beauty and historic interest as the hatred of Thothmes III, the fanaticism of Akhenaten, and the stupid materialism of the Copts had left comparatively intact, he, along with Mr. H. R. Hall, of the British Museum, began operations on the site immediately south of the XVIIIth Dynasty building, where there was some evidence of the existence of an XIth Dynasty necropolis, and where Mariette, as long ago as 1879, had suggested that a temple of one of the Mentuhoteps of that Dynasty might be found. The great explorer's anticipation was almost immediately justified. Soon there came to light an inclined ramp, like that of Hatshepsut's temple, running parallel to the boundary-wall of the later building, and leading up to a square platform. This platform had been surrounded by a double colonnade, the pillars of the upper part of which were octagonal on plan—"proto-Doric" in fact, like those of the north colonnade of Hatshepsut's temple. This colonnade had enclosed a square mass in the

centre of the platform, which proved to have been the base
of a small pyramid, which rose above the hall; and behind
the pyramid an open court, surrounded by octagonal pillars,
led to a second colonnaded hall, driven back into the solid
cliff, beneath which a rock-hewn passageway descended to a
subterranean sanctuary.

The temple proved, as Mariette had suggested, to belong
to Mentuhotep-Neb-hapet-Ra, of the XIth Dynasty, and is
therefore one of the very earliest fairly complete specimens
of Egyptian temple-architecture, and of inestimable importance. Within the hall which surrounds the pyramid
were found six shrines of princesses, probably members of
the king's harem, while in the southern court of the temple
were found six statues in grey granite of one of the most
famous of Egyptian Pharaohs, Senusert III, the true Sesostris of later tradition. They were a revelation of the power
of Egyptian sculpture at this period, and the strong, harsh,
truculent features are thoroughly in keeping with what we
know from other sources of the character of this great conqueror. One of the great artistic finds of the exploration—
indeed one of the great finds in the whole story of the re-
discovery of Egyptian art, was that of a very beautiful
XVIIIth Dynasty shrine of Hathor which had been intruded
into the north corner of the temple. Within the shrine
stood a statue of the goddess herself in the shape of a cow
sculptured in sandstone. With the possible exceptions of
the granite lions of Amenhotep III and Tutankhamen, now
in the British Museum, this is by far the finest piece of
Egyptian animal sculpture which has survived. "Neither

Greece nor Rome," says Maspero, "has left us anything that can be compared with it; we must go to the great sculptors of animals of our own day to find an equally realistic piece of work."

One result of the new excavations at Der-el-Bahri was, of course, to destroy the claim to originality which had been advanced on behalf of the architect of Hatshepsut's temple.   Manifestly Senmut found his inspiration in the earlier work which was before his eyes when he began his task; but he was a sufficiently great man to make his borrowings his own by the brilliant use to which he put them, and the result is ample justification for his plagiarism, if one can use so harsh a name for what is really only a very skilful adaptation of a simple motive.   The two temples, ancient and modern, with about six centuries between them, must have made a wonderful pair, when both were standing complete in all their splendour, with their solemn environment of cliff and desert; and even now, after so many centuries of ruin and desolation, they form one of the most remarkable pictures that Egypt has to show.

From Der-el-Bahri we turn to the last of the temples of Thebes which we can notice before we visit the Biban-el-Moluk, and tell of some of the wonders which have been revealed there, and the romance of their discovery.   The huge memorial temple of Ramses III, at Medinet-Habu, has many claims on our attention.   It is, to begin with, the almost intact work (in the sense of not having been usurped and altered by another monarch) of one of the greatest of Egyptian Pharaohs—the last of Egypt's great soldier-kings,

PLATE XII

TEMPLE OF RAMSES III., MEDINET HABU

and a man who deserved far better of his country than the other Ramses who generally goes by the name of "The Great." Moreover, Medinet-Habu is by far the most perfectly preserved of any of the Egyptian temples dating from before the Ptolemaic period; and in addition, its battle-reliefs, with their careful studies of the racial types against which Ramses was warring, and in particular its picture of his naval victory over the fleet of the Sea-Peoples (the first picture extant of a sea-fight), are invaluable to the student of ancient history. Even artistically, some of the reliefs, such as that of Ramses hunting the wild bull, are far from despicable. But having said so much, one has said all that can be said in favour of Medinet-Habu. It is a thousand pities, as Professor Breasted has pointed out, that the completest temple of genuinely ancient Egyptian work should be, as Medinet-Habu is, a temple of the decadence, when art had lost even the slightly mannered and morbid grace which marked it even as late as the XIXth Dynasty, and had sunk into the gross and heavy tastelessness which characterised the XXth Dynasty work in general. "The Medinet-Habu temple," says Breasted, "is therefore unique, and we must intensely regret that it was a Twentieth rather than an Eighteenth Dynasty temple which survived." In spite of this fact, sufficiently obvious to any serious student of Egyptian architecture, one finds Medinet-Habu selected by one of the most brilliant critics of architecture as the typical Egyptian temple, and therefore a fitting platform from which to pour the vials of his scorn upon Egyptian architecture generally. The author of "The Works of Man" is perfectly right in talking of the columns of Medinet-Habu as "gigantic sausages," but just as perfectly wrong in taking them as in the least degree typical of true Egyptian architecture.  One might as well judge Greek sculpture, not by the Parthenon Frieze or the Hermes of Praxiteles, but by the grossness of the Farnese Hercules, or the ignoble brutality of the Boxer in the Terme Museum.  The real value of Medinet-Habu is not artistic, but historic and ethnological, and consists in the record of the wars of Ramses III against the Libyans, and the Confederation of the Sea-Peoples, whose invasion of the Egyptian Empire followed upon the break-up of the Minoan power after the sack of Knossos.

And now we must leave the temples of Thebes, and turn to its tombs, which are scarcely less remarkable in their own way, and the story of whose exploration makes the nearest approach to the Romance of Excavation, as the general public conceives it, that the record of Egyptian discovery has to show.  Indeed, there have been few more thrilling moments in any explorer's life than when, on the fifth July, 1881, Emile Brugsch was lowered into the *cache* at Der-el-Bahri, and found himself in the presence of Thothmes III, Sety I, Ramses II, and a score of other less distinguished Egyptian royalties, or when the American explorer, Theodore M. Davis, with A. E. P. Weigall and a few others, found, in January, 1907, in the tomb of Queen Tiy, in the Valley of the Kings, a mummy wrapped in thin sheets of gold, which they at first took for that of the great queen, but which bore the name, written in costly stones, of "Akhenaten, the beautiful child of the living Aten, whose name shall live for ever and ever," and which has indeed proved to be that of the "heretic king" himself—first of all religious reformers.

The Valley of the Kings is entered by a winding gorge called El-Wadiyen, which runs from Drah Abu'l Negga, to the northeast of Sety's temple at Qurneh, and winds round westwards into a rugged and barren hollow behind the cliffs which rise above the temples of Der-el-Bahri. In the time of Strabo, there were 40 tombs known to the priests and recorded by him as being worthy of a visit; but by the date of Napoleon's Expedition the number known was only 11, and when Belzoni started his search in October, 1817, he tells us, "I could distinguish only ten or eleven that could be honoured with the name of tombs of kings, nor do I suppose when Strabo was told by the Egyptian priests that there were forty-seven tombs of the kings of Egypt, they meant to say, these tombs were all in the place now named Beban-el-Moluk." The information of the priests has, however, proved to be more accurate than Belzoni imagined, for at present more than 50 tombs are known, and no doubt further discoveries will yet raise the number.

Belzoni, to whom we owe the discovery of what is still the finest of the royal tombs in the valley, began his work on October 6, 1817. On the ninth he discovered his first tomb, which though unfinished, contained some fine paintings. On the eleventh, he discovered a second, and on the sixteenth he hit upon the spot which he calls justly, "the fortunate spot, which has paid me for all the trouble I took in my researches." A short extract may be given from the passage in which he lovingly pats himself on the back over his discovery—a discovery on which he had every right to plume himself. The whole passage is thoroughly characteristic, in its naïve pride and pomposity, of the pioneer. "I may call this a fortunate day," he says, "one of the best perhaps of my life; I do not mean to say, that fortune has made me rich, for I do not consider all rich men fortunate; but she has given me that satisfaction, that extreme pleasure, which wealth cannot purchase; the pleasure of discovering what has been long sought in vain, and of presenting the world with a new and perfect monument of Egyptian antiquity, which can be recorded as superior to any other in point of grandeur, style, and preservation, appearing as if just finished on the day we entered it; and what I found in it will show its great superiority to all others." After all, Belzoni was not so far out in his self-gratulation; for though many tombs have been since found far richer in many respects than the tomb of Sety I, it still remains unrivalled in the Valley of the Kings for the beauty and splendour of its decoration.

Two days' work brought the diggers to the actual entrance to the great tomb, and then the next day, the 19th October, was spent by the lucky explorer in wandering through what seemed to him a sort of subterranean fairyland, passing through chamber after chamber, fancifully named by him "the Drawing-Room," "the Room of Beauties," "the Hall of Mysteries," and so forth, until at last in "the Apis' Room," he found the sarcophagus of the famous king, and

went into ecstasies. "But the description of what we found
in the centre of the saloon, and which I have reserved till
this place, merits the most particular attention, not having
its equal in the world, and being such as we had no idea
could exist. It is a sarcophagus of the finest oriental alabaster, nine feet five inches long, and three feet seven inches
wide. Its thickness is only two inches; and it is transparent,
when a light is placed in the inside of it. It is minutely
sculptured within and without with several hundred figures,
which do not exceed two inches in height, and represent,
as I suppose, the whole of the funeral procession and ceremonies relating to the deceased, united with several
emblems, etc. I cannot give an adequate idea of this
beautiful and invaluable piece of antiquity, and can only
say, that nothing has been brought into Europe from Egypt
that can be compared with it." The explorer's pride was
thoroughly justified, as any one who has seen the great sarcophagus, now in the Soane Museum, London, or read
Bonomi's elaborate description and facsimile of it, "The
Sarcophagus of Oimenepthah," will realise. The great
tomb is 328 feet in length, and contains 14 corridors and
chambers, hewn out of the rock, of which the sarcophagus
chamber, for instance, measures $43\frac{1}{3}$ feet by $17\frac{1}{2}$, and
its walls are adorned with illustrations and extracts from
the funerary literature which was popular in the XIXth
Dynasty, "The Praising of Ra," "The Book of Him Who
Is in the Underworld," and "The Book of the Gates."

It was perhaps fortunate, when one remembers what
Belzoni has himself told us of his manner of handling

mummies, that the mummy of Sety was not in the magnificent sarcophagus which had been made for it. Otherwise we should never, in all probability, have had the chance of seeing how kingly and dignified a Pharaoh of early Bible times could look. By the time that the explorer found his way into Sety's pictured resting-place, the mummy of the great king had been lying for nearly 3000 years in an obscure pit at Der-el-Bahri, and another half-century and more was to pass before it was brought to the light of day. And our next chapter of the romance of exploration takes us out of the Valley of the Kings to the hiding-place in which the priests of the XXIst Dynasty concealed from the tomb-robbers of 1100 B. C. the bodies of the most famous kings of Egypt which they could no longer protect in their original rock-hewn sepulchres. Sir Gaston Maspero has told the whole story of a veritable resurrection of Pharaohs, and it forms one of the most curious, and not the least interesting chapters of the tale of Egyptian exploration.

It was in the year 1876 that the first indication of a great discovery began to appear in the shape of a ritual papyrus of the Priest-King Pinezem of the XXIst Dynasty, which was bought by General Campbell. Then followed the purchase by the Louvre of the latter part of a Book of the Dead which had belonged to the mother of the Pharaoh Her-hor, and the presentation to the museum at Boulak of two papyri of the same period. Mariette realised that some fellah had discovered a store of antiquities of great value, and at once took steps to find out the fortunate robber. Suspicion fell upon a certain Mohammed Abd-er-Rassoul of Sheikh Abd-el-Qurneh, and finally M. Maspero arrested with his own hand another member of the family, Abd-er-Rassoul Ahmed, and handed him over to the Mudir of Keneh for inquiry to be made into his misdeeds. "The Mudir, Daoud Pacha," says Maspero quietly, "conducted the investigation with his customary severity"—words which are no doubt significant of a good deal; but the only result for a time was to produce a crop of testimonies to the entire respectability and virtue of Abd-er-Rassoul Ahmed which would have convinced any one who did not know his Egyptians thoroughly. The suspect had to be released; but his two months of imprisonment, and what Maspero delicately calls "the vigour with which the investigation had been conducted by Daoud Pacha," had made him see, if not the error, at least the danger of his ways, and after a month of discussions and quarrels among the five Abd-er-Rassoul brothers, Mohammed, the eldest of them, came to the Mudir, and made a full confession, offering to guide an official of the Cairo Museum to the scene of his find.

On the 5th July, 1881, Emile Brugsch, representing the Museum, and accompanied by two other officials of the same service, was led by the repentant or terrified thief to a spot a little west of the temples of Der-el-Bahri, where a spur juts out from the cliffs. Here the Princess Astemkheb of the XXIst Dynasty had begun the preparation of a tomb for herself, and had caused a shaft to be dug, about 40 feet in depth, from the foot of which a gallery ran at right angles to the well for 200 feet, ending in a roughly hewn and undecorated chamber. Down this shaft Brugsch was lowered, and what he found at the end of his perilous descent may best be told by Maspero. "The first object which met the eyes of Emile Brugsch when he landed at the foot of the well was a white coffin bearing the name of Nebseni. It lay across the gallery about two feet from the entrance; a little further on lay a second coffin, whose form recalled the style of the XVIIth Dynasty, then the queen Hent-taui, then Sety I. Boxes for funerary statuettes strewed the ground on every side, Canopic vases, and libation vases in bronze; and in the angle which the gallery makes as it turns towards the north, the funeral canopy of the queen Astemkheb, crumpled and tattered like a worthless object which a priest in a hurry to depart had thrown carelessly into a corner. All along the great gallery, the same kind of impediment; it was necessary to grope one's way forward, without knowing where one's hands or feet were being placed. The coffins and the mummies, glimpsed hastily by the light of a candle, revealed historic names on every side. Amenhotep I, Thothmes II, in the niche near the stair, Aahmes I, and his son Siamen, Seqenenra, the queen Aah-hotep II, Aahmes Nefertari, and others. In the end chamber, the disorder was at its height, but even at the first glance the predominance of the style of the XXth Dynasty could be recognised; the fellahs had unearthed a catacomb crammed with Pharaohs."

Egypt in her long history must have witnessed many strange scenes; but surely few stranger than that presented when on the 11th July the steamboat of the Museum arrived at Thebes, and Thothmes III, Sety I, Ramses II, Ramses

III, and a score of less notable royalties made their first, and what we may hope will be their last voyage by steamer down the river to Cairo, accompanied all the way by the wailing of the fellah women on the banks, and the rifle-shots of the men. It was not till the month of May, 1886, that the unwrapping and measuring of the royal mummies took place, some of the most famous being unwrapped in the presence of a distinguished gathering of celebrities. Sir Gaston Maspero has published the results of the investigation in "Les Momies Royales de Deir-el-Bahari," and some of the notable figures, Sety I, and Ramses II, are now almost as familiar by their photographs as any of our living royalties; but while the gain to our historical knowledge through the discovery has been very great, it may be questioned whether, so far as the mummies are concerned, they might not have been safer in their dark pit below the cliffs than in the great Cairo Museum. "The last century," says Professor Flinders Petrie, "has seen Napoleon's raids on artistic wealth, thefts from at least three national museums, the attempted burning of one great museum, the destruction of the gold in two provincial museums, and the entire wreck of everything in another important museum. . . . Such are the chances that valuables suffer when known. The printed description distributed in all the libraries of the world will last far longer than most of the objects themselves." Already the royal mummies show signs of deterioration in their new abode, and as Maspero remarks, "One foresees the day when they will disappear." Brugsch's haul of royalties was supplemented in 1898 by Loret's discovery, in the Valley of the Kings, of the almost complete tomb of Amenhotep II, the son of Thothmes III. Tomb-robbers had indeed entered the chambers, and had done some damage to the funerary furniture, and to some of the mummies; but the body of Amenhotep still lay in its sarcophagus, and beside it lay the famous bow of which he boasted that none could bend it but himself, and which bore the inscription—"Smiter of the Cave-Dwellers, overthrower of Kush, hacking up their cities . . . the great wall of Egypt, protector of his soldiers." In the same tomb lay the mummies of another batch of Egyptian royalties—Ramses IV, Siphtah, Sety II, Amenhotep III, Thothmes IV, Setnekht, Ramses V, Ramses VI, and Merenptah. M. Loret was instructed to leave Amenhotep II to rest in his own tomb; one had almost said to rest peacefully, but that is precisely the wrong word. He has been left to become a raree-show to gaping tourists. "The royal body," says Mr. H. R. Hall, "now lies there for all to see. The tomb is lighted with electricity, as are all the principal tombs of the kings. At the head of the sarcophagus is a single lamp, and when the party of visitors is collected in silence around the place of death, all the lights are turned out and then the single light is switched on, showing the royal head illuminated against the surrounding blackness." "The effect," he adds, with singular simplicity, "is indescribably weird and impressive." Who was responsible in the beginning for this piece of indescribable vulgarity is not stated; perhaps as well for him, lest the dishonoured shade of the great soldier with his redoubtable bow should get upon

PLATE XIII

AMENHOTEP II. IN HIS COFFIN, VALLEY OF THE KINGS, THEBES

Photograph from the "National Geographic Magazine," International Copyright, 1923

his track. Even M. Maspero seems to have had his doubts as to the taste of the outrage. "And yet," he says, "I sometimes ask myself if these tombs, now so brilliantly illuminated, may not lose some small part of their attractiveness." The question is needless, in this case, at all events. To light empty tombs with electricity in order to show their reliefs and paintings without the smoke and soot of the candles whose use was rapidly destroying their beauty, is perfectly legitimate; but to make a show, with the most vulgar sensationalism, of a dead king, even though he died 3300 years ago, is a piece of bad taste unworthy even of a decent showman.

It was in 1903 that the American explorer Theodore M. Davis began in the Valley of the Kings the researches which have been crowned with perhaps the most remarkable series of successes which has rewarded any modern excavator. In the nine years from 1903 to 1912, he discovered the tombs of Queen Hatshepsut, of Thothmes IV, of Siptah-Menephtah, and of Horemheb, besides the two greater finds which have been of supreme importance to our knowledge, first of Egyptian arts and crafts, and next of the close of the life of the most interesting figure of Egyptian history.

It was on the 13th of February, 1905, that Mr. Davis discovered a roughly hewn and comparatively undistinguished tomb, without a trace of the carved or painted decoration in which most Egyptian tombs of any importance abound. This inconspicuous sepulchre, however, was to prove one of the richest storehouses of Egyptian art and

manufacture which has ever been opened.  It proved to be
the tomb of Yuaa and his wife Tuau, the parents of the
famous queen Tiy, the wife of the magnificent Amenhotep
III, and the mother of Akhenaten, and in all probability the
prime moving force in the great religious revolution which
her son set on foot, and which convulsed the whole Egyptian
Empire.

Mr. Davis has published in sumptuous form the authoritative account of his finds, and the student of Egyptian
art and craftsmanship must always turn to his splendid
plates for first-hand information; but for the dramatic
aspect of the discovery we turn to Mr. A. E. P. B. Weigall,
who was present at the opening of the tomb as representative of the Service of Antiquities, and who has given us
in his "Treasury of Ancient Egypt," a picture of the scene,
drawn with the hand of a born romancer,—only in this
case a romancer dealing with the truth which is sometimes,
though not often, stranger than fiction.

"Imagine entering a town house which has been closed
for the summer," he says: "imagine the stuffy room, the
stiff, silent appearance of the furniture, the feeling that some
ghostly occupants of the vacant chairs have just been disturbed, the desire to throw open the windows to let life into
the room once more.  That was perhaps the first sensation as
we stood, really dumfounded, and stared around at the
relics of the life of over three thousand years ago, all of
which were as new almost as when they graced the palace
of Prince Yuaa.  Three arm-chairs were perhaps the first
objects to attract the attention; beautiful carved wooden

chairs, decorated with gold. Belonging to one of these was a pillow made of down and covered with linen. It was so perfectly preserved that one might have sat upon it or tossed it from this chair to that without doing it injury. Here were fine alabaster vases, and in one of these we were startled to find a liquid, like honey or syrup, still unsolidified by time. Boxes of exquisite workmanship stood in various parts of the room, some resting on delicately wrought legs. Now the eye was directed to a wicker trunk filled with trays and partitions, and ventilated with little apertures, since the scents were doubtless strong. Two most comfortable beds were to be observed, fitted with springy string mattresses and decorated with charming designs in gold. There in the far corner, placed upon the top of a number of large white jars, stood the light chariot which Yuaa had owned in his lifetime. In all directions stood objects gleaming with gold undulled by a speck of dust, and one looked from one article to another with the feeling that the entire human conception of Time was wrong. These were the things of yesterday, of a year or so ago."

One is almost ashamed to disturb the picture by Mr. Davis's candid confession that the thing they imagined to be honey proved to be not honey but natron; but in all else it remains perfectly true to the facts, and no description of the articles found can exaggerate their actual beauty. In such discoveries, the romance of exploration reaches its height, and as we stand with Mr. Weigall and Professor Schiaparelli before the sealed door of another tomb, and listen to the echoes reverberating through the long silent

passages, we can sympathise with the writer's feeling—
"One felt that the mummy, in the darkness beyond, might
well think that his resurrection call had come.  One almost
expected him to rise, like the dead knights of Kildare in
the Irish legend, and to ask, 'Is it time?' for the three
thousand years which his religion had told him was the
duration of his life in the tomb was already long past."

In the tomb of Yuaa and Tuau were found the mummies
of these two old world dignitaries,—a matter of the greatest
interest to the student of Egyptian history.  For in the
attempt to account for the strange religious development
which marked the reign of their grandson Akhenaten, all
sorts of theories had been woven around them, attributing
to them a North Syrian or Mitannian origin.  So far as the
evidence of the tomb and the mummies goes, all these
theories proved to be baseless.  "If Yuaa was a foreigner,
as has been thought," says Mr. Quibell, "it must be admitted that he had a very orthodox Egyptian funeral"; and the
mummies of both husband and wife exhibit no particular
characteristics pointing to a foreign origin, though Mr.
Weigall suggests that Yuaa's hooked nose may be of the
Syrian type—a remark which would apply just as forcibly
to the beak of Sety I.  The explorers were deeply impressed
with the dignity of the two silent figures.  Mr. Davis speaks
with a feeling of reverence of the calm majesty of Tuau,
and Yuaa seems to have made an equally deep impression
on Mr. Weigall.  "The stern features of the old man commanded one's attention, and again and again our gaze was
turned from this mass of wealth to this sleeping figure in

PLATE XIV

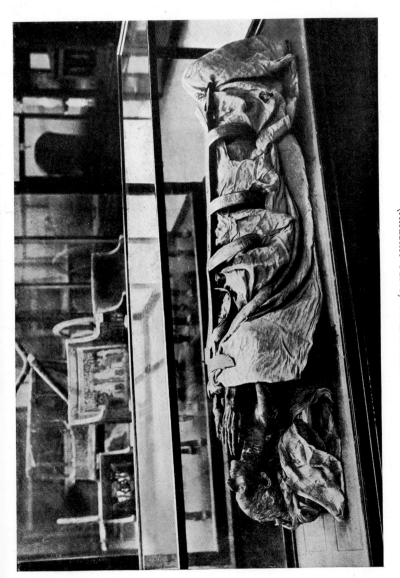

PRINCE YUAA (CAIRO MUSEUM)

*Photograph from the "National Geographic Magazine." International Copyright, 1923*

whose honour it had been placed here." "He was a personage of commanding presence, whose powerful character showed itself in his face. One must picture him now as a tall man, with a fine shock of white hair; a great hooked nose, like that of a Syrian; full strong lips; and a prominent determined jaw. He has the face of an ecclesiastic, and there is something about his mouth which reminds one of the late Pope, Leo XIII. One feels, in looking at his well-preserved features, that here perhaps may be found the originator of the great religious movement which his daughter and grandson carried into execution." Be that as it may, no more interesting discovery has been made since that of the *cache* of Der-el-Bahri, unless it be that which we have next to recount.

It was in January, 1907, that Mr. Davis made the find which was the complement to his discovery of Yuaa and Tuau, and the crown of his wonderfully successful work. At that time he was digging on a site close to the tomb of Ramses X, of the XXth Dynasty, at the corner of the ravine which leads to that of Sety I. The site was completely covered with gravel and loose stones, with nothing about to indicate that there was a tomb below. Mr. Davis, however, persevered, and after several days of hard work there came to light the square mouth of a pit, then a staircase closed by a door at its lower end, then a passage, with a wall of stonework and beaten earth at its end. On this the seals affixed by the priests 3000 years before were still unbroken. On January 6, the seals were broken by the explorer, and he, with Mr. Weigall and others, entered into that greatest of rarities, an untouched tomb.  Across the passage lay a heap of fallen stones, and on the top was the gilded panel of a large funeral shrine, which almost entirely blocked the entrance.  With considerable difficulty the explorers succeeded in wriggling past between the panel and the roof of the passage, and found themselves at last in a chamber, where, besides the rest of the gilded shrine, lay the remains of a splendid coffin inlaid with rare stones and coloured glass.  "A wire connected with the generating station that supplied light to the royal syringes had been brought into the tomb, and, at the first ray that shone forth, reflections of sparkling gold responded in every direction.  Mr. Davis might have thought himself transported to one of the marvellous treasure caves of the *Arabian Nights*.  Gold shone on the ground, gold on the walls, gold in the furthest corner where the coffin leant up against the side, gold bright and polished as if it had just come freshly from the goldsmith's hands, gold half-veiled by, and striving to free itself from the dust of time.  It seemed as if all the gold of ancient Egypt glittered and gleamed in that narrow space."  The news of the marvellous discovery quickly spread, passed by the two native workmen who had witnessed the opening of the chamber to their companions, and, of course, the rumour grew as it flew from mouth to mouth.  "The ingots of gold multiplied, the urns overflowed with heavy coins, and the plaques and the vases, the arms and the massive statues had reached such alarming numbers by nightfall, that it was necessary to give notice to the police to prevent danger of an assault."

All this treasure, of course, was only rainbow-gold. The splendour which had gleamed before the astonished eyes of the explorers, proved, on a closer inspection, to consist chiefly of heavy gold-foil wrapped round a mummy which lay in a gilded coffin adorned with coloured stones and glass. In almost all other respects the tomb was singularly devoid of articles of interest, such as those which made the tomb of Yuaa so remarkable. In a recess close to the coffin stood four alabaster Canopic jars, exquisitely sculptured into the likeness of a very remarkable human head; but beyond that there was little to reward the searchers, save the coffin with its silent tenant. Here, however, was a find more precious than all the gold with which the imagination of the fellahs had crammed the tomb, and its importance increased as the full facts came gradually to light.

Within its golden sheath, the mummy was little more than a heap of disconnected bones, with a little dried flesh clinging to them. The dry skull was enclosed in a wrapping of gold-foil, cut in the shape of a vulture with outspread wings, bearing in its talons the seal of eternity; but so careless had the attendants been when they adjusted its last head-dress to the head, that the head of the vulture was turned to the back of the skull, and its tail to the forehead. The inscription on the coffin, wrought in coloured stones, gave the titles of Akhenaten, "the beautiful child of the Sun"; but on the funeral shrine was another inscription which stated that Akhenaten had made this shrine for his mother Queen Tiy. The explorers therefore concluded that the burial was that of Tiy, as the probabilities were that

Akhenaten would not be buried at Thebes, but in his own City of the Horizon at Tell-el-Amarna. When the bones were sent to Professor Elliot Smith for examination, however, they proved to be not those of a woman, but of a young man; and there can be little doubt, that, as we heard in the story of Tell-el-Amarna, they are those of the most remarkable figure of ancient Egyptian history. How they may have come to be in the Valley of the Kings, near to the hated city of Amen, and not in the place which Akhenaten had prepared for himself and to which he had vowed himself in life and in death, is suggested in the story of his great attempt and its failure.

Such are some of the most notable discoveries which have been made in the Valley of the Kings. But the tombs of the ancient royalties of Thebes are by no means the only ones which make the remains of the City of the Dead at Thebes as important as the City of the Living. Some of the private tombs of the Theban grandees are quite as imposing and quite as finely decorated as those of the Pharaohs. One tomb, indeed, that of Pedu-amen-apt, at El-Assasif, is far larger than any of the royal tombs, measuring 870 feet in length, as against the 328 of the tomb of Sety I, and some of the other private tombs are of great interest because of their elaborate decoration. The construction and decoration of these rock-tombs must have been one of the most thriving businesses in Thebes, employing architects, masons, sculptors and painters; and the Egyptian's craving to be surrounded in his eternal habitation by the scenes of life in which he had delighted on earth has been of the utmost value to the student of Ancient Egypt, presenting us with series upon series of brilliant pictures of the manners and customs of the Empire.

Where sculpture was possible in these tombs, it was used because of its permanency, and the scenes are depicted in low relief and painted. But owing to the poor quality of the rock in which the tombs were hewn, and also, of course, to the expensive nature of the work, painting is often substituted for sculpture. A layer of plaster was spread over the rough walls of the rock-chambers, and on this the set of pictures ordered for the tomb was sketched out and executed, often with the greatest vivacity, the amount of work done, and the quality of it, varying in proportion to the length of purse of the family of the dead man, or perhaps to the regard which they had to his memory. As a matter of custom, the artists of the tombs had two or three sets of themes which were in regular demand, and on these they played variations of greater or less importance, seldom, however, departing much from the standard motives. "The first series comprised scenes from the private or public life of the dead man, as well as the representation of the crafts needed to keep up a great house; the second showed the funeral rites from the time the corpse became a mummy until the moment when the gods of the other world, Anubis the jackal and Amentit the mistress of the west, took possession of the mummy wreathed in flowers." Other pictures represented the ceremonies which enabled the statue of the dead man to receive the funeral offerings, or to become the habitation of the soul; while a further series pictured the destiny of the deceased in the Underworld, his travels through the realm of darkness, his voyaging in the Boat of Ra, his peaceful enjoyments in the Fields of the Blessed, or his encounters with the demons who sought to bar his passage to these delectable regions. No small part of our knowledge of how the Egyptian lived, what he believed, what he hoped for hereafter, has come from these pictured tombs, or from the papyri inscribed with the chapters of the so-called "Book of the Dead," and its vignettes, which, from the time of the Theban Empire and onwards, became the popular furniture of the dead man's coffin, instead of the "Pyramid Texts," which had been the provision for the needs of the soul in the Old Kingdom, or the "Coffin Texts," which had served the same purpose under the Middle Kingdom.

Among these private tombs, one of the most striking is that of Nekht, a Theban gentleman of the early XVIIIth Dynasty. It contains two chambers, of which only the first is decorated, the paintings being in wonderfully good preservation. They represent, with remarkable vivacity, scenes from the daily life of Nekht and his wife, with all the operations of the farm and the vineyard in the different seasons, and the pleasures of spearing fish and fowling. Nekht's tomb is perhaps the most familiar of all Theban tombs, having been reproduced again and again both in photography and in colour. In less perfect preservation, but of even superior interest, is the tomb of Rekh-ma-Ra, vizier of the Empire under Thothmes III, and Amenhotep II. Unfortunately the pictures, which represent the vizier receiving gifts and tribute from various foreign peoples, have been subjected, as Mr. H. R. Hall observes, "to a century of inspection with naked candles and pawing with greasy hands," and are consequently much defaced; but their supreme interest is in the representation of the ambassadors of the Keftiu, "the Men from the Back of Beyond," whom we can now recognise as the Minoans of Knossos. They are the complement of the frescoes which Sir Arthur Evans discovered in the Palace of Minos. "It is evident," says Mr. Hall again, "that the first three ambassadors are faithfully depicted, as the portraits are marked. The procession advances from left to right. The first man, 'the Great Chief of the Kefti and the Isles of the Green Sea,' is young, and has a remarkably small mouth with an amiable expression. His complexion is fair rather than dark, but his hair is dark brown. His lieutenant, the next in order, is of a different type,—elderly, with a most forbidding visage, Roman nose, and nutcracker jaws. Most of the others are very much alike,—young, dark in complexion, and with long black hair hanging below their waists and twisted up into fantastic knots and curls on the tops of their heads. . . . Any one of these gift-bearers might have sat for the portrait of the Knossian Cupbearer, the fresco discovered by Mr. Evans in the palace-temple of Minos; he has the same ruddy-brown complexion, the same long black hair dressed in the same fashion, the same parti-coloured kilt, and he bears his vase in much the same way. We have only to allow for the difference of Egyptian and Mycenæan ways of drawing. There is no doubt whatever that these Keftiu of the Egyptians were Cretans of the Minoan Age."

One of the assured results of modern investigation has been the destruction of the old idea of Egypt as a sort of hermit-nation nursing its own marvellous civilisation jealously within its own narrow limits, and the substitution for it of the picture of an ancient world in which there was far more intercourse between the nations than we had dreamed of,—an intercourse in which Egypt played its full part; and now that the discoveries in Crete have come to supplement those of similar bearing in Egypt, we are able to interpret much that was obscure before, and these tomb-frescoes take their true place as evidence linking together two of the great antique civilisations—the Nilotic and the Ægean. Further evidence in the same direction is given by the pictures in the tomb of one of the most interesting Egyptians of the Empire,—Senmut, the famous architect and vizier of Queen Hatshepsut, and tutor of the Princess Neferura. Senmut, a notable example of the self-made man, for he states on his statue at Berlin that his "ancestors were not found in writing," hewed his tomb in a very fitting site—at the top of the hill at Abd-el-Qurneh, and overlooking Der-el-Bahri, where his spirit might rejoice in the sight of his greatest work, the colonnaded temple of the great queen. The tomb was known in the early days of Egyptology, as is evidenced by the copies of its paintings made by Prisse d'Avennes. Then for many years it was lost to memory, and had to be rediscovered by Mr. Newberry and Professor Steindorff. It is in a very ruinous condition; but there is no question as to what its frescoes are meant to represent. "From right to left, walking in procession, we see the Minoan gift-bearers from Crete carrying in their hands and on their shoulders great cups of gold and silver, in shape like the famous gold cups found at Vaphio in Lakonia, but much larger, also a ewer of gold and silver exactly like one of bronze discovered by Mr. Evans two years ago at Knossos, and a huge copper jug with four ring-handles round the sides. . . . The bearers wear the usual Mycenæan costume, high boots and a gaily ornamented kilt, and little else, just as we see it depicted in the fresco of the Cupbearer at Knossos and in other Greek representations." So the Palace at Knossos and the tombs of Thebes supplement one another, and just as the Tell-el-Amarna letters reveal the closeness of intercourse between the civilisation of the Nile Valley and that of Mesopotamia, so the tombs of Rekh-ma-Ra and Senmut show us the meeting of the Nilotic with the Ægean culture.

No account of the City of Temples and Tombs would be complete without some reference to what has for more than three millenniums been one of the most thriving trades of the inhabitants of ancient and modern Thebes,—tomb robbery. We have seen that the great find of Pharaohs at Der-el-Bahri was due directly to the efforts of two sets of tomb-robbers between whose evil deeds lay a space of 3000 years,—the plunderers of the XXIst Dynasty from whom the priests, despairing of being able to guard their charges, hid the mummies in the tomb of Astemkheb, and the Abd-er-Rassoul family of the nineteenth century, whose trade in

dead Pharaohs was spoiled by the gentle repression of the
Service of Antiquities.  But the trade of tomb-robbery goes
further back than even the XXIst Dynasty,—indeed it
goes back almost to the very beginning of things in Egypt.
The classical case is the record of the law-suits in the reign
of Ramses IX of the XXth Dynasty, in which the Mayor
of Thebes, Paser, brought charges against those who had
charge of the City of the Dead on the Western bank of
having robbed the tombs entrusted to their care, or allowed
them to be robbed by others.  Paser, who evidently had a
grudge against his colleague, Pewero, who was in charge
on the Western bank, was unable at first to substantiate his
charges, and further let himself into a false position by his
unguarded words to a riotous deputation of necropolis
workmen, who made a demonstration before his house on
the breakdown of his first charges; but gradually it came out
that the charge of carelessness or worse on the part of the
guardians of the necropolis was only too well-grounded, and
that robberies of the dead were common to a most dis-
creditable extent.  The proceedings are recorded in the
Abbott and Amherst Papyri, and the documents are full of
interest not only for the facts which they disclose as to the
robberies, but for their revelations as to Egyptian judicial
procedure, which apparently had not changed a great deal
in the interval of 3000 years between the time when the
vizier Khæmuas, the king's butler Nesu-amen, and their
colleagues "examined" their culprits "by beating with a
double rod, smiting their feet and their hands," and the
year 1881 A. D. when Daoud Pasha "conducted the ex-

PLATE XV

ENTRANCE TO THE VALLEY OF THE KINGS

amination" of the Abd-er-Rassoul family "with his customary severity."

A specimen of the confessions extracted by these gentle
means gives the story of the robbery of the tomb of King
Sebek-em-saf, of the XIIIth Dynasty, and his wife, Queen
Nubkhas. "We opened their coffins and their coverings in
which they were. We found the august mummy of this
king. There was a numerous list of amulets and ornaments of gold at its throat; its head had a mask of gold
upon it; the august mummy of this king was overlaid with
gold throughout. Its coverings were wrought with gold and
with silver, within and without; inlaid with every splendid
costly stone. We stripped off the gold, which we found on
the august mummy of this god, and its amulets and ornaments which were at its throat, and the coverings wherein
it rested. We found the King's-Wife likewise; we stripped
off all that we found on her likewise. We set fire to their
coverings. We stole their furniture which we found with
them, being vases of gold, silver, and bronze. We divided,
and made the gold which we found on these two gods, on
their mummies, and the amulets, ornaments, and coverings,
into eight parts." Nobles and commoners had fared no better than royalties at the hands of these sacrilegious rascals.
The Commission of Investigation thus reports on this aspect
of the case. "The tombs and sepulchres in which the nobles,
the Theban singing women, and the people of the land rest,
on the west of the city; it was found that the thieves had
broken into them all, that they had pulled out their
occupants from their coverings and coffins, they (the

occupants) being thrown upon the ground; and that they had stolen their articles of house-furniture, which had been given them, together with the gold, the silver, and the ornaments which were in their coverings."

Altogether this gruesome trade must have been quite a thriving one. One of the rogues concerned, evidently a luxurious as well as a light-fingered gentleman, did well enough out of it to set up a double establishment, and we read of "the lady Taruru, and the lady Tasuey, his other second wife." We may be sure that all was not done without the connivance of high officials, and that probably Paser was not far out in his charges against his colleague of the Western bank, though it took time for the truth to leak out. Indeed Mr. Engelbach, in his account of the finding of the Jewellery Tomb at Riqqeh, states that the majority of the tombs there were plundered either contemporarily or within a generation of the last burial in each tomb, and that the robbery was generally the work of the sextons, who knew exactly what to look for in each tomb, and possessed maps of the cemetery to guide them. In this tomb, from which came some fine gold and jewellery work, Mr. Engelbach had dramatic evidence of how the career of one of these rascals came to a sudden and lamentable close. The roof of the tomb had collapsed in ancient times, and examination showed how the collapse had occurred with the most exact timing, just when the interests of justice could be most righteously served by the disaster. "The coffin, which had been crushed flat, had been laid in the centre of the chamber. . . . Over what had been the foot of the coffin, and across it, with the head to the east, there could easily be traced the remains of a skeleton which appeared to be male, and again over this were the arm-bones of another body, the remaining bones of which were in a heap about two feet north of the chest of the first body; it appeared as if it had been suddenly crushed while in a standing, or at least a crouching position when the fall occurred." Mr. Engelbach's explanation is that the upper skeleton is that of a tomb-robber, who had got the mummy out of its coffin, and was proceeding to unwind the bandages in search of the jewellery which he knew to be there, when the roof fell in, and crushed him and the body of his victim together. The robber's accomplices, seeing the dreadful fate which had overtaken their colleague, "filled in the tomb-shaft so that their doings would never come to light, and they never had a chance to reach the jewels again." And so the tomb, with its grim evidence of ancient roguery, was left to be discovered 4000 years later, and to tell us that the ancient Egyptian was much the same as his modern descendant,—at least in his attitude to the property of dead men.

Every modern Theban believes that treasure, "beyond the dreams of avarice," is buried somewhere in one of the tombs with which he is surrounded, and he can see no sense in the laws which make searching for it a misdemeanour. "As a matter of fact," says Mr. Weigall, who has a romancer's sympathy with any searcher for hidden treasure, "they are no more thieves than you or I. It is as natural for them to scratch in the sand for antiquities as it is for us to pick flowers by the roadside; antiquities, like flowers, are the product of the soil, and it is largely because the one is more rare than the other that its promiscuous appropriation has been constituted an offence." Whether there is justification for this light-hearted attitude towards the rascals who greeted Mr. Weigall himself at the entrance to a tomb at Abydos with the courteous remark—"Go away, mister. We have all got guns," following up their greeting with a rifle shot, is another matter. It may be regrettable that the Theban should be restrained from his pursuit of what he regards as his legitimate perquisite; but perhaps in the interests of science it is better that investigation should be conducted by more satisfactory methods than either those of Belzoni, with whom our chapter opened, or those of the fellah with whose report of his search for hidden treasure at Nag Hamadi it closes. "Having reached the spot indicated the man started to blow the stones by means of the Denamits. Also he slaught a lamb, thinking that there is a treasure, and that when the lamb being slaught he will discover it at once." The methods of our modern investigators may not be so picturesque as those of this gentleman who combines modern dynamite and ancient sacrifice,—in vain; but perhaps on the whole they are less risky, and more likely to add to the store of human knowledge.

# CHAPTER VI

## TUTANKHAMEN IN ALL HIS GLORY

### THE ROMANCE OF AN EGYPTIAN ROYAL TOMB

THE ink was scarcely dry on the preceding description of the work of modern exploration in the Valley of the Kings, when one of those incidents occurred to which reference was made in a sentence of our introductory chapter. "He knows," it was said there, referring to the modern explorer, "more or less what to expect, and there is not the breathless awaiting of the unknown, *though sometimes it does arise, to confound expectation."* Never, surely, was expectation more thoroughly confounded than when, on November 29, 1922, there came a runner to Luxor from the Valley of the Kings, with the news that Mr. Howard Carter, carrying on excavations in conjunction with Lord Carnarvon, had discovered, beneath the well-known tomb of Ramses VI, a tomb which appeared to belong to the comparatively obscure Pharaoh Tutankhamen, and to contain a wealth of splendid funerary furniture such as no other tomb had ever yielded. From that moment, "Tutankhamen's Tomb" became the sensation of the day. The Valley of the Kings was thronged, day after day, with crowds of eager tourists, whose persistent interest became a somewhat serious hindrance to the legitimate work of the explorers, and who seemed to con-

sider it a personal grievance if the articles removed from
the tomb on any particular day were not sufficiently rich
and splendid to gratify their excited imaginations.  All over
the civilised world the interest and excitement grew to
fever-pitch.  Tutankhamen's somewhat rugged name grew
familiar on lips which had never pronounced the name of a
Pharaoh before, and which wrought strange "sea-changes"
on the unfamiliar syllables.  The movements of great nations seemed small things in comparison with the movement
of the old arm-chairs and couches of a king who had been
dead for more than three thousand years; and even that consecrated drudge of British conversation, the weather, was
given for awhile rest from its labours.  It may be questioned
if even the Der-el-Bahri find of 1881, widespread as was
the interest which it excited, created anything like the same
enthusiasm as was aroused by the new discovery.

As a discovery, it had been thoroughly well earned.  There
have been instances where newcomers to the field of exploration have carried off, almost at their first attempt, the
prizes for which more experienced workers had been
labouring in vain for years; but the lucky finders of Tutankhamen's tomb had toiled long and hard for their reward.
Mr. Howard Carter's name is well-known to every student
of Egyptology, and the best part of his life has been devoted
to Ancient Egypt, and the interpretation of its treasures;
while Lord Carnarvon's collection of Egyptian antiquities is
rich in objects of interest.  For sixteen years these two had
been associated in work on the western bank of the Nile opposite Thebes, and for nine of these years they had been

working in the Valley of the Kings. On the whole their efforts had been singularly unfruitful. "Beyond the finding of some alabaster vases and a few minor and mostly broken objects," said Lord Carnarvon, "nothing had rewarded our efforts until this autumn." When Mr. Theodore M. Davis closed, in 1914, the work which had been so amazingly successful, he did so with the remark,—"I fear that the Valley of the Tombs is now exhausted"; and all the early course of the later explorers' work seemed to confirm the idea that his prophecy was justified. They proceeded on a different system from the American excavator, who had made his remarkable series of finds chiefly by means of "sondages" or trial-pits, sunk in promising places. Mr. Carter and Lord Carnarvon preferred to work over a certain area, clearing it absolutely down to bed-rock; and in this laborious process they had removed from 150,000 to 200,000 tons of rubbish with little result save that of providing steady work and wages to their native diggers. But the bed-rock system, laborious as it is, has at least this advantage, that if there is anything of interest in your selected area, and if your patience, or your life lasts long enough, you are pretty certain to get it in the long-run, even though the run be long.

So it proved with the British explorers. On November 5, 1922, Mr. Carter came upon a rock-cut step in the area below the tomb of Ramses VI. For a day or two he continued clearing step after step, and finally came upon a wall covered with cement, on which the seal of the Royal Necropolis, with its nine captives and jackal couchant, was discernible. Realising that he was on the verge of an important discovery, he covered up the steps, and, cabling to Lord Carnarvon to come out to Egypt, waited till his partner should arrive. On his arrival the door was again uncovered, and the cartouche of Tutankhamen was traced upon it; while evidence was found that the door had been penetrated in ancient days by a tomb-robber. Precautions were taken to secure the spot against the attacks of any modern successors of the ancient spoiler, and a guard of soldiers and police, with the headmen of the excavating party, kept watch night and day. Clearing out the passage, about eight metres long, which led away from this first door, the explorers came to a second door, sealed as the first had been. A few stones were taken out of the wall which blocked it, so that Mr. Carter was able to get his head into the hole, and catch a glimpse, by the light of a candle, of what was inside. Behind him the rest of the party waited, in scarcely suppressed excitement, till at last Lord Carnarvon anxiously put the question—"Well, what is it?" Mr. Carter's answer was guarded, but sufficient—"There are some marvellous objects here," he said. At first all that could be seen in the dim light was the glitter of gold, as in the tomb of Tiy. Then gradually there loomed up colossal gilt couches with awesome heads, stools, boxes of all sorts and sizes,—such a profusion of funerary furniture as had never before been seen in any tomb.

In a little while the hole was enlarged so that the explorers could enter the chamber, and the bringing in of electric light enabled them to appreciate more fully the

PLATE XVI

*Rev. J. Laidlaw, B.D.*

A ROYAL TOMB IN THE VALLEY OF THE KINGS (TOMB AND
SARCOPHAGUS OF RAMSES IV.)

wonders of their discovery. Standing against one wall
were two life-sized statues of the king in bituminized wood
and gold. The floor was crowded with beds, chariots, boxes,
vases of alabaster of the most elaborate shape, walking-
sticks gorgeously adorned, inlaid coffers, cases innumerable
of provisions for the dead king's sustenance in the spirit-
world. The most remarkable object was a throne of wood
overlaid with gold, on the back panel of which the king and
queen were portrayed in inlay of precious and semi-precious
stones, coloured glaze, and painting overlaid with crystal.
The royal figures were represented with the rays of the
Aten, each ending in a hand, shining down upon them, so
that the throne was evidently a relic of the earlier days of
Tutankhamen's reign, when his court was at Tell-el-Amarna,
and the Aten faith was still in the ascendant. No trace
could be seen of any coffin or sarcophagus; but ere long it
became apparent that the reason for the absence of any
such thing was that this was simply the ante-chamber of
the tomb, and there were still other rooms waiting to be
explored. Beneath one of the state couches, a small opening
was found giving access to another chamber. It proved
utterly impossible to enter this second room; for it was
packed almost solid, to a height of five feet, with chairs,
beds, coffers, vases, and all sorts of other objects. Further,
between the two statues of the king it appeared that a piece
of the rock-wall of the tomb had once been pierced for a
doorway, and then walled up. The wall was covered with
seal-impressions; but near the floor, in the centre of the
space, there were traces that a breach, sufficient to admit

a small man, had once been made. This had afterwards
been re-sealed by the royal tomb-inspectors. The explorers
had no doubt in their minds that beyond this wall there
existed another chamber, and that they might find the body
of the king resting in its nest of coffins, beneath the royal
funerary canopy, when an entry was made.

In the meantime, however, this was impossible. The
outer chamber, and the annexe to it, were crowded with costly and rare articles to such an extent that movement in them
was difficult. It was manifest that many of the objects
were of a character and delicacy which would require the
utmost care to be exercised in their removal, and the use of
all sorts of preservatives to secure the endurance of the
fragile fabrics. To attempt the opening up of another
chamber was plainly to risk the damage, and perhaps the
total destruction, of the articles which were already under
the explorer's hands. Therefore, though the temptation
must have been strong to break the wall, and penetrate the
secret of the tomb, any further advance was postponed until
the great mass of precious treasures should have been
removed from the two chambers to a place of safety, and
secured from the risk of unfavourable atmospheric conditions. This was accordingly done; and for days the Valley
of the Kings was busier than it had ever before been in its
long history. Each day brought its fresh crowd of tourists
from Luxor, impatient to see some new wonder of ancient
Egyptian art and craftsmanship; and each day witnessed an
unending procession of glittering wonders from the chambers to the empty tomb of Sety II, which was used as a

storehouse and laboratory. At last the clearance had advanced sufficiently far to enable the excavators to proceed further in their task without risk to what they had already discovered; and on February 16, the seals of the inner chamber were broken in the presence of a distinguished company, and the wonders of the actual sarcophagus chamber revealed, though the formal opening, at which the Queen of the Belgians was present, did not take place till two days later.

Expectation had been high, and the possibility of bitter disappointment was correspondingly great; but for once at least in the story of excavation, expectation was completely outrun by reality. The first glance into the interior of the inner chamber revealed one of the most marvellous objects which has ever greeted the eye of any explorer. The funeral canopy of a Pharaoh was not an unknown thing; part of that of Queen Astemkheb, in embossed leather and gold, had been found in the great *cache* at Der-el-Bahri, and a panel of the shrine of Queen Tiy had been found in her tomb by Davis, along with the coffin of her ill-fated son; but the funeral canopy of Tutankhamen, which glittered before the eyes of the astonished spectators as they peered through the opening into the inner chamber of the tomb, infinitely surpassed in splendour and beauty all that had ever been imagined.

The chamber itself was in no wise conspicuous in comparison with the chambers of some of the royal tombs. It was some 20 feet in length, and its decoration, so far as could be estimated by eyes which were completely dazzled by the glories of the shrine, was comparatively poor, both in design and execution. But the shrine itself more than atoned for any deficiency in its surroundings. It was a great tabernacle of wood, overlaid with gold, and adorned with blue enamelled tiles, and with golden pillars of Osiris, and buckles of Isis. Its length was about 16 feet, and its height 12, so that it almost entirely filled the room, leaving only a narrow space between itself and the wall all round. It was finished at the top with the usual Egyptian gorge cornice and moulding, supporting a coved roof; and at its eastern end were two great folding doors, closed and secured with bronze bolts. On the floor of the chamber lay the oars of the funeral barque, for Tutankhamen's use on the canals of the Sekhet Aalu. When the doors of the outer shrine were opened, there appeared a second canopy, covered with a pall which had rosettes of gold upon it, and between the two canopies lay a collection of jewels and amulets, including a number of beautiful scarabs in red, blue, and bluish-green glaze.

Towards the further end of the eastern wall of the canopy chamber, a door, which had never been closed, led into an annexe, which appeared to have been a kind of storeroom for the objects which could find no room in the larger chamber. At the entrance to this store-room the figure of the Jackal God, Anubis Upuat, in black and gold, stood upon his shrine, which rested upon the sledge on which it had been dragged to its place. Behind Anubis, the floor of the chamber was covered with boxes, shrines, chariots, and one special tier of ivory and wooden coffers, studded with gold

PLATE XVII

THE RESURRECTION OF OSIRIS (RELIEF FROM ABYDOS)

and inlaid with faïence. But the great treasure of the store-chamber was the exquisite shrine, surmounted by a cornice of uræi, and guarded by protecting figures of Isis and Nephthys, their outstretched arms enveloping the shrine, while their lovely faces were turned with a pathetic expression of reproach towards the intruders who had broken the solitude of thirty-three centuries. This shrine, in all probability, was the coffer for holding the Canopic Jars which contain the viscera of the dead. This, however, is not certain, as no detailed examination of the two inner chambers was possible.

The season was advancing, and the heat in the narrow Valley of the Kings was already beginning to be intense. To expose the rich and delicate fabrics of the tomb to the risks of the hot season was considered to be inadvisable, and despite the eagerness alike of the explorers and of the public to reach the heart of the mysteries of the tomb, it was decided to close the operations, and to resume them in the autumn of 1923. Accordingly the door was carefully barricaded, the workmen who had excavated the entrance so short a time before were set to fill it up again, and by the end of February Tutankhamen was left to sleep for a little longer in the tomb where he had lain for 3300 years. In one way the break in the work is exasperating and disappointing. So many questions have been raised which will be discussed with vigour during the next few months, but which cannot be answered with anything approaching to certainty until we know all that the tomb has to reveal; so many things have been left in a half-light by which we

can only get glimpses of tantalising possibilities of revolu-
tionary changes in our ideas as to the culmination of Egyptian history and art, that patience is apt to fail in the
presence of a delay of such length.  Discussion of the significance of the finds there must and will be; yet always at
the back of it all will lie the possibility that the first result
of the renewed operations may be to render all the theories
of the experts a mockery.  In such circumstances the study
of what we have so far been told of the contents of the tomb
must manifestly be of a tentative and carefully qualified
character, and it will be wisdom to dogmatize as little as
may be; but perhaps it is better that impatience should be
curbed for awhile, rather than that the raw haste which is
half-sister to delay should risk the permanent loss of the
priceless materials to which we are looking anxiously for
the extension of our knowledge of Egyptian history and
culture in one of its most interesting periods.  Before we
turn to the provisional description and discussion of some
of the most important objects found in the tomb, let us
summarise as briefly as may be the story of Tutankhamen's
reign, and endeavour to place him in his proper setting and
perspective.  Fortunately the foundations of our survey
have already been laid in our discussion of the latter part
of the reign of Akhenaten, in the chapter on Tell-el-Amarna,
so that our historical summary can be as brief as was apparently the reign with which it deals.  When Akhenaten died
amidst the collapse of his foreign empire, and the breakdown of his religious ideals, he was succeeded by one of his
nobles,—Smenkhara, who had married his eldest daughter

Merytaten. The reign of Smenkhara, however, was of the briefest, perhaps only to be reckoned in months; and as Akhenaten's second daughter, Maktaten, had died before her father, the succession fell to Tutankhaten, who was married to the third daughter, Ankh.s.en.pa.aten. Accordingly he ascended the throne, and for a time maintained his court at his father-in-law's capital, Akhetaten, or Tell-el-Amarna. His own origin is doubtful. In his inscription on one of the Gebel Barkal lions in the British Museum (originally dedicated by Amenhotep III), he claims that most gorgeous of the Pharaohs as his father; and on this account it has been supposed that he was indeed the son of Amenhotep III by a secondary wife. The words, however, do not necessarily imply more than the honourable acknowledgement of his forerunner in the kingship, and we must be content to leave the question to be settled with fuller knowledge than we now possess. Ere long the young king and his wife found themselves helpless against the reaction which was drawing back all Egypt to the worship of the old gods once more; and the court was removed to Thebes. The king, in sign of his return to the faith of the fathers, changed his name to Tutankhamen (Living Image of Amen), while that of his wife was changed to Ankh.s.en.-Amen. At Thebes he did some building work, though neither in quantity nor in quality was it very conspicuous. Apparently he made some effort to regain something out of the wreck of the foreign empire which Akhenaten had left; for in the tomb of Huy, one of the nobles of the reign, there is record of tribute both from Syria and from

Ethiopia; and Horemheb, the general, who after the ephemeral reign of Ay usurped the throne, states in one of the inscriptions in his pre-regal tomb that he was "Companion of the feet of his lord upon the battlefield on that day of slaying the Asiatics," and this lord can scarcely have been other than Tutankhamen. But beyond these brief and obscure references, there is no evidence as to the events of the reign, which in any case must have been brief—probably not longer than nine years. It has been supposed that some of the indications in the tomb point to his having died very young—in fact almost before reaching manhood according to western standards; but such conclusions are premature, though he cannot have been past early middle-age at the utmost when he died.

It is evident, then, that we have to do with a Pharaoh whose reign, so far as our knowledge of it previously extended, was comparatively unimportant. The evidence extant up to the time of the discovery of his tomb would place Tutankhamen in a very humble position on the long roll of Pharaohs. No one would ever have dreamed of naming him in the same breath with any of the great soldier Pharaohs of his dynasty, Thothmes I, or Thothmes III, or even with Amenhotep II. Even the dimmer glories of the XIXth Dynasty have left a far profounder imprint upon history than anything which we know of Tutankhamen's achievement; and his reign, like that of his predecessor or of his successor, has always been reckoned as a brief and somewhat inglorious interlude between the sombre tragedy of Akhenaten's noble failure and the gallant attempt of Sety I and Ramses II to recover the lost empire. Yet we find this obscure and unimportant Pharaoh buried with a splendour surpassing anything that the wildest fancy could have imagined. Of course Tutankhamen's is the one royal tomb which has been found practically unrifled, and it is possible that, had we been able to find, say, the intact tomb of Amenhotep III, with that great king sleeping in the midst of all his splendours, instead of finding the bare walls of his sepulchre, and, well-nigh a century later, his mummy hidden in another tomb, we might have seen something which would have made even the glories of Tutankhamen seem shabby; but it is difficult to believe that even the greatest of Egyptian monarchs had ever a more gorgeous burial than that which has astonished the civilised world to-day. Are we to conclude then, that our estimate of the man and his achievement has been all wrong, and that this chapter of Egyptian history must be rewritten, with a glittering conqueror in the place of the ineffective stop-gap whom all histories pictured, and a nation girding itself heroically to its gigantic task of regeneration, and rising in the effort to heights of art hitherto unsuspected?

The question is one which, no doubt, will exercise the minds of students of Egyptian history and culture for many a day, and which will only be answered conclusively when the tomb in the Valley of the Kings has given up its last secrets, should it have any to yield which will give us the evidence required. Meanwhile it is only possible to state summarily and cautiously the reasons which seem to render it unlikely that so drastic a revision of our reading of

Egyptian history will be necessary; and the necessary preliminary to such a statement is the consideration of the
articles which seem to be the most important and significant
of those found in the tomb. We may find that some of
these have their own suggestiveness as to the reasons which
made the burial of Tutankhamen so unusually rich.

Of the articles found in the outer chamber of the tomb,
the one which, by common consent of all who saw it, was
the most brilliant and wonderful, was the royal throne, of
which Professor Breasted said,—"It is one of the wonders
of the world." Its material is wood, overlaid with a thin
plating of gold, and adorned with carvings of lions' heads.
Beneath the arms of the throne are uræi, partly in glaze,
with the crown of Egypt in silver. On the back panel the
King and Queen are portrayed. He is sitting in a natural
attitude, with crossed legs, and gives his hand to the Queen,
who stands beside him. The work, which in the faces and
the other parts of the flesh exposed appears to be executed
in a reddish glaze, is of very high quality, the modelling of
the figures being finely carried out. The King's dress was at
first thought to be in inlay, but was found to be of painting
overlaid with crystal. The Queen's dress is wrought in
silver, and beside her is the bouquet of flowers which the
Egyptian was never long without. Its colour scheme is
carried out in inlay of semi-precious stones; and the seat of
the throne is patterned in squares of gold, blue, and white
mosaic, arranged in diagonal lines.

Obviously, if the published descriptions are to be relied
upon, we have here a very notable work of art, the details

of which are very suggestive. The parallel which at once occurs to the mind is with the King's Gaming-Board from the palace of Knossos, with its blaze of gold and ivory, crystal and blue glaze; and it is interesting to speculate on the possibility of the Egyptian artist having been influenced by the work of Minoan craftsmen. The two objects are not very widely different in date, and we know how close was the intercourse between Crete and Egypt during the XVIIIth Dynasty; but in the meantime, and until coloured reproductions are available, the idea must remain only a speculation. The description of the attitude of the king, quite unconventional, and realistic, recalls the famous Berlin slab with its relief of Akhenaten leaning on his staff, while Queen Nefertiti holds out a lotus bloom for him to sniff. The design of the throne appears to belong to the same type of art, in which the Tell-el-Amarna artists were discarding the old conventions, and reaching out towards a greater realism in the representation of the human figure. That the throne belongs to the Tell-el-Amarna period is evidenced by one interesting detail. The royal cartouches wrought in the gold plating of the throne have been carefully altered, to correspond with the king's change of faith, and give his name as Tutankhamen; but the cartouche at the side of the arms, which is inlaid in semi-precious stones and glass, retains the old title, Tutankhaten. Plainly it was more difficult to carry out the alteration in the inlay than in the gold; and we are left with the plain proof of two things,—first, that the throne was made during the early days of the reign, and, second, that Egyptian royalty, in the midst of all its splendours, had yet, like Mrs. Gilpin, "a frugal mind," which saw no sense in scrapping a fine piece of furniture, though it bore heretical emblems. One is reminded of the chair of the Princess Sat-Amen found in the tomb of Yuaa and Tuau, which had been patched, when the original string seat wore out, with a piece of board painted yellow, exactly in the same humble way as a modern householder would have a useful chair repaired to-day. We may find in Tutankhamen's tomb other evidences of the care with which pieces of furniture of an ancient date were treasured up, and handed down in the royal palace; and the fact has its own bearing on the question of the extraordinary accumulation of treasures in the tomb.

Nothing in the find excited greater interest than the coffers containing the royal robes. It is to be hoped that the preservation of these delicate fabrics may be possible; but it has to be remembered that stuffs over three thousand years old are of the last degree of fragility, and it is not unlikely that the dress-designers who have been looking to the coffers of Tutankhamen and his queen for new inspirations may find their hopes disappointed, and have to call in imagination to supply the place of reality. It may be doubted, in any case, whether robes designed for the climate and the taste of an Oriental court of 1350 B. C. would be found either practicable or comfortable for our less generous climate, and our less tolerant taste. Thus the wonderful robes of diaphanous bead fabric, of which reports have been given, and which carry us back to the ancient legend of Seneferu of the IIIrd Dynasty and his barge crew of twenty pretty girls "clad in fishing-nets," would probably go beyond the limits of the most daring taste of the present time. The Egyptian had his own conceptions of what was proper and decent, and they are not ours, though it does not follow that he was a worse man than his successor of to-day.

Among the robes was a so-called corselet, which would seem to be of remarkable interest, not only because of its beauty, but because it would appear to be the one surviving specimen of the ceremonial coat of mail which is represented in several tomb-pictures of the empire, and which apparently was an essential part of the funerary equipment of an Egyptian royalty. The corselet is made of pear-shaped links of faïence laid on gold over the supporting fabric. In appearance it somewhat resembles chain, or rather scale-armour, and beneath the collar there is wrought a splendid design which extends across the chest, and represents Tutankhamen being introduced by Horus to the presence of Amen. It was, no doubt, such a corselet as this which was the cause of the great tournament held in the Delta, at Nebesheh, about 700 B. C. Ka.amenhotep, prince of Mendes, we are told in the Rainer Papyrus, had stolen the funerary corselet of Eiorhoreru, prince of Heliopolis, without which the obsequies of the dead prince could not be completed. His son, Pimay, complained to Pedubast, overlord of the Delta, and the latter appointed that the destiny of the corselet should be determined by a combat of champions, and the mêlée resulted in the victory of the aggrieved Pimay's side, and the return of the bone of contention. The Tutankhamen corselet, of course, belongs to a period more than six centuries earlier; but doubtless its significance was the same.

Among the minor articles found in the tomb, none was of greater or more curious interest than the little bronze candlesticks, shaped in the form of the Ankh, and provided with metal bands for attaching the linen wicks soaked in oil. No such objects have hitherto been found, and while we need not imagine that these small stands were representative of the sole lighting of the Egyptian palaces, they yet give us an idea of the inconveniences which went along with the splendours of life in Ancient Egypt; for the light which such devices can have given must have been of the most inefficient and unstable sort.

After the throne, perhaps the most significant objects were the great state couches, with lion, Hathor, and hippopotamus heads. The importance of these does not lie in their beauty, for they are frankly hideous, but just in the fact that their ugliness is of a type which is quite un-Egyptian. The Egyptian craftsman, when he liked, could design a sufficiently fearsome object, witness his representations of the Goddess Taurt; but he never, in our previous knowledge of him, was guilty of such monstrous abortions as the nightmares which must surely have made sleep an impossibility on these state couches of Tutankhamen. The word which any one seeing them in any other environment than that of an Egyptian tomb would infallibly use with regard to them is "barbaric." How, then, do they come to be among the funerary furniture of an Egyptian Pharaoh of the XVIIIth Dynasty, when the taste of the native craftsman was capable of such work as the throne and the hunting-casket which were found beside them? Professor Petrie has suggested an explanation which seems not only natural, but is of the highest interest, because, if it be confirmed, it helps us to a solution of the mystery of Tutankhamen's tomb and its unparalleled richness. He maintains that the decoration of these couches, with trefoil ornament, is not Egyptian, but Babylonian; and further, that the structure of the couches is of a type unknown to the Egyptian craftsman. They are made in sections, with bronze joints, so that they can be dismantled for transport, and reassembled; and the suggestion made is that this form of construction was used because the pieces had in fact a long distance to travel before they reached Thebes. There exists in the series of the Tell-el-Amarna letters, a letter to Amenhotep III from Kadashman-Enlil, king of Babylon, in which he states that he has sent as a present to the Egyptian king "a couch of *ushu* wood, ivory, and gold, and three couches and six thrones of *ushu* and gold." The nightmare couches of Tutankhamen's tomb are in Professor Petrie's opinion the identical couches to which the Babylonian king refers,—heirlooms handed down from Amenhotep to Akhenaten, and from him to his son-in-law. They would be about forty years old when they were buried.

They were, however, by no means the oldest objects in the tomb. The footstool with the inlaid figures of Asiatics, placed there so that Pharaoh might every day trample on his foes, is, in Petrie's opinion, undoubtedly the same as that which is figured in a representation of Amenhotep II, and is therefore another heirloom, of considerably more ancient date, as Amenhotep II reigned almost a century before Tut-ankhamen. We have already seen evidence of the frugal Egyptian respect for good work, even though it might be out of date or unorthodox, and the footstool points in the same direction as the preservation of the throne, with its heretical emblems, and that of the little chair of Sat-Amen with its patched seat.

Among the objects which were either unique or conspic-uous by their rarity, none attracted more attention than the much-discussed "mannikin." This was a half-length wooden figure of the king without arms, manifestly a careful study of the person whom it was intended to represent. The idea that it was a portrait of the king was early questioned, and it was argued that it rather represented the queen. From this fancy, which can scarcely persist in face of an actual study of the figure, opinion veered round to the idea that the figure was a dummy used for the purpose of trying on the royal robes before they were worn in public. Its armless condition might be thus accounted for; but it is difficult to see why, in a land where royalty wore long flow-ing robes, a half-length figure should be deemed sufficient to test the fit of robes which would reach to the feet. The opinion of Professor Petrie is that it may be either the equivalent of the head-portrait of Old Kingdom tombs, or perhaps part of the core on which a statue of beaten copper,—like the famous one of King Pepy,—might be built up. In the absence of positive indications as to the use to which the statue was put, any judgment is more or less speculative and perhaps we shall never get such indications; but in the meantime the figure is evidently a clever piece of portrait sculpture, and conveys the idea that it must have been a good likeness of the king.

Some of the objects found, however, were of types quite familiar to us from previous examples but were conspicuous because of the fineness of their materials, or of the skill with which their ornamentation was executed. Of these we may take as a specimen the comparatively small coffer with representations of the king hunting on the sides, and with his cartouches at the ends, between figures of Tutankhamen as a human-headed lion, trampling his enemies underfoot. This is an object of a class perfectly familiar, the whole design of the coffer being almost identical with that of the small cabinet of wood and blue enamel, with inlay of semi-precious stones, which was found in the tomb of Yuaa and Tuau, the only difference being that the earlier casket stands higher than the Tutankhamen one. The design of the decoration is also of familiar type, and the figure of the Pharaoh shooting from his chariot is one of the commonest motives of Egyptian art, though his targets are generally human enemies; while the lion figure of the king is of con-secrated antiquity, and can be found at least as far back as the Vth Dynasty. The value of the Tutankhamen find in this case is in the skill of the workmanship, and the clever way in which designs which have nothing in them but the commonest and most threadbare of motives are yet so adapted to their purpose as to make this small coffer one of the most charming and effective pieces of work removed

from the tomb, so far as can be judged from the black and
white reproductions which have appeared.  Some of the
objects possessed neither beauty of design and execution, nor
costliness of material, but drew the attention by reason of
a certain suggestion of pathos attaching to them—their
very commonness and unpretentiousness lending to them
that touch of nature which makes the whole world kin.
Such were the shrivelled glove of linen, and the child's
hood and tippet in linen with gold sequin adornment.  It
has been conjectured that these, and especially the smallness of the glove, point in the direction of the extreme youth
of the king at the time of his death; but such conjectures
belong rather to the realm of romantic fancy than to that
of sober fact.  We know just as much and as little about
the question of who wore the glove and the tippet as we
know about the wearer of the false front and plait of
false hair which Petrie found in the tomb of King Zer of
the Ist Dynasty at Abydos.  The false hair tells us that
feminine human nature was much the same in the dawn
of history as it is to-day.  The glove and the tippet may be
the evidence of some ancient story of love and loss of which
we shall never know anything more.  That is all. . . .

And now we turn, in conclusion, to the question,
already suggested, of what change, if any, is to be wrought
in our reading of the history of Egypt at this period by
this disclosure of the splendour with which the last Pharaoh
in the direct line of the XVIIIth Dynasty was laid to rest.
The nature of the problem has already been stated in our
summary of the reign of Tutankhamen, as known to us

before the discovery of his tomb. Here is the statement of
the new theory as to the actual history of the reign, as it
was conceived by an enthusiastic witness of the wonders
of the tomb in the Valley of the Kings. "It seems certain
that under Tutankhamen Egypt made a wonderful last
attempt, not merely to restore her prestige, but to emblazon
her imperial crown with diadems from other states. It
seems to have been a supreme and sublime effort to triumph
over tremendous difficulties; it seems to have been the soul
of a nation striving to rise by sheer force of personality,
backed with many strong right arms and dauntless courage
over enemies hurling themselves at her Imperial throat; it
seems to have been an emotional period, a period when
spiritual ardour fired her people to tremendous efforts, when
emotional waves of enthusiasm carried a nation exultingly
to the crest of victory. That national effort recaptured for
Egyptians their highest inspirations, and in that brief but
glorious span those impulses led her army and her priests,
her artists and her sculptors to deeds and works which
deserve to be immortalised, and which this discovery will
immortalise. . . . That is the first lesson which this discovery teaches; it cannot be too strongly emphasised. This
is Egypt's golden age in the height of its lustre."

It seems almost a pity to add anything which will dim
the splendour of such sonorous periods, which seem to have
caught a little of the gorgeousness of the tomb itself. But
unfortunately we have to deal with facts, and not with
fancies; and the single fact that one obscure Pharaoh
had an unusually gorgeous burial seems a somewhat

shaky foundation on which to rear an entirely new theory of the course of Egyptian history in the end of the XVIIIth Dynasty. Outside the tomb the sole evidences of Tutankhamen's reign are a few fragments of comparatively unimportant building at Thebes, the record of the burial of an Apis at Memphis, the inscription in the tomb of Huy, and that in the pre-regal tomb of Horemheb, and a few trifling objects which have been found at Tell-el-Amarna, Gurob, and elsewhere. It is frankly inconceivable that if the reign had been marked by such a national renaissance as has been suggested, the only traces of it, apart from these pitiful scraps, should be the treasures of the tomb. No matter how short the duration of the renaissance, it was bound to have left traces, far other than those which exist, of its passage.

Of course it is possible, though perhaps highly improbable, that the opening of the royal shrine may reveal records of historical importance which may claim a higher place for Tutankhamen than historians have hitherto allowed him. Even then one would hesitate to accept as gospel the unsupported claims of a royal inscription, in face of all the evidence which shows us that immediately before his reign the Egyptian empire was in an alarming condition of decay and danger from external enemies, and that almost immediately after it the soldier Pharaohs, Sety I, and Ramses II, had to do all over again the work which we are now invited to believe that Tutankhamen had done. We need not suppose, and it has never been supposed, that all Egypt's Syrian possessions were absolutely lost to her by the misfortunes of the latter days of the reign of Akhenaten; the record of Syrian tribute in the inscription of Huy forbids such a supposition, though we are not necessarily to take it at its face value.   There has never been any evidence that the Ethiopian part of the empire was lost at this time, and again Huy's record tells us of the continuity of Egyptian suzerainty there.   But that is all that we can safely affirm; and to suggest that, on the evidence of a mass of tomb furniture, however gorgeous, we are to scrap all previous conceptions of the history, based on such indisputable facts as the Tell-el-Amarna letters before the reign, the absence of any relics of great accomplishment during the reign, and the state of affairs to which the XIXth Dynasty shortly succeeded, is to invite us to convert serious history into romantic fancy.

Further, it is difficult to believe, on the evidence before us, that there was such a culmination of art in the reign of Tutankhamen as we are asked to accept as a proved fact. Unquestionably some of the articles found in the tomb are of very high artistic quality; but the best of them, so far as we have seen, are of a type already familiar, and it is only in quantity and richness that they excel those previously known.   Indeed some of the objects to which greatest attention has been drawn seem to an unprejudiced eye to be the products, not of art at its highest point, but rather of art which has already passed its culmination, and is now on the down grade.   Notable instances of this are the famous alabaster vases, carved all in one piece with their stands, and wreathed round with carved Nile plants, which have been claimed to be "the most beautiful alabaster vases in the world." It may be said without fear of question that if these had been found anywhere else than in the midst of such a collection of marvels, they would have been unhesitatingly pronounced bad art,—radically bad in their over-complication of design, however fine their execution, —characteristic products, in fact, of decadent art. The Egyptian vase designer, at his best, could do infinitely better work than this. They show us, in short, exactly what one would have expected from the decline of a period of naturalism in art such as was characteristic of the reign of Akhenaten,—the clumsy and cumbrous attempt to adapt naturalistic motives to conventional objects where they are entirely out of place, with the resultant over-complication and over-elaboration which are always the marks of such bad design. Besides, if such a revival of art existed in the reign of Tutankhamen, where are the other evidences of its existence? Surely they were not all buried in the royal tomb. The XVIIIth Dynasty, we already knew, was a period when art, both in design and execution, reached a very high level. It may be that we may be obliged by the evidence of this tomb to place its height a few years later than we had been in the habit of doing; but this is as yet quite uncertain. It seems more likely that we may find another explanation of the presence of so many wonders among the funerary furniture of Tutankhamen, and that the old conception of his reign as one marked by gradual decline, both in world-power and in art, on the part of Egypt, is still valid.

We have already seen reason for believing that certain of the articles found in the collection of funerary furniture do not belong to the reign with whose close they have been associated. Thus the hideous state couches are probably Babylonian work of nearly half a century earlier date, and the footstool is probably Egyptian work of the time of Amenhotep II,—a century old when it was buried with its last user. No doubt when the contents of the tomb are subjected to close and thorough examination by experts there will be more identifications of different national styles and periods, with a great resultant increase in our knowledge of ancient art between 1500 and 1300 B. C. Meanwhile it seems natural to assume that what we see is not the product of one marvellously prolific and equally marvellously eclectic period of art, but a collection of the art of various periods, and even of different nations,—in short a collection of the palace heirlooms gathered by Pharaoh after Pharaoh over a considerable period.

For the burial of such a collection in the tomb of Tutankhamen we can see a very valid reason. Whether he was the son of Amenhotep III or not, Tutankhamen was at least, by his marriage with the daughter of Akhenaten, in the direct line of succession, according to Egyptian custom. His marriage with Ankh.s.en.Amen was childless, and the other daughters of Akhenaten were apparently married to foreigners, and therefore incapable of succeeding to the throne. Tutankhamen was therefore the last of the great line of the XVIIIth Dynasty which had made Egypt a world-empire. We know, from a letter of the Hittite King Mursil

II, recently deciphered by Professor Sayce, that Ankh.s.en.-Amen made an attempt to secure that the succession should not be interrupted. She wrote to the Hittite King Shubbiluliuma, suggesting a match between herself and one of the Hittite princes, and the negotiations proceeded so far that she had selected the prince whom she desired to wed. But apparently some obstacle hindered the carrying out of her purpose. There was never much love lost between the Egyptians and the Hittites, till the hatred between the two races was patched over by the marriage of Ramses II with a Hittite princess; and perhaps the Egyptians indicated that they would not have a Hittite to reign over them. In any case, poor Ankh.s.en.Amen's scheme failed, and we know that the succession fell, first for a short time, to an obscure priest "The Divine Father Ay," and then to a soldier, Horemheb, who usurped the throne.

From these facts it is not difficult to construct a picture of the situation which is probably not far from the truth. Queen Ankh.s.en.Amen finds herself left in a hopeless situation by the death of her husband. Doubtless she knows that the priests of Amen still regard her as suspect because of her descent from "that criminal of Akhetaten," as they always called her father. Had it been otherwise, it is possible, though scarcely probable, that she might herself have taken the crown, as Hatshepsut did, and given Egypt another woman sovereign; but, as it was, that was impossible, and, as a matter of fact, she vanishes from the page of history on the failure of her attempt to secure the succession by the Hittite match. What more likely than that she made up her mind that so long as she had the power she would see to it that the treasured heirlooms of her ancestors, gathered in the palace by successive generations of mighty Pharaohs, should be kept safe from the greedy hands of those who were already snatching at the crown and sceptre? They had been used by the conquerors of Syria, the creators of Egyptian fame and glory; they should not be profaned by the touch of a nobody like the common priest whose hand was almost on the sceptre already, or the rough soldier who was erelong to shake the usurper from his unstable throne and usurp it in turn himself. The surest way to secure the treasures from profanation was to bury them with the dead Pharaoh, where even the hatred of the priests would scarcely venture to disturb the rest of one, who if he began his reign as a heretic, yet restored the worship of the old gods, and died in the odour of orthodox sanctity.

So it may well be that what we have seen and may yet see of the splendours of the tomb of Tutankhamen is not, as some have imagined, the evidence of the rebirth of a great nation, waking after its enchanted slumber, and its dreams of a God of Love who should unite all the nations, to the stern realities of a struggle for life and power, and rising in the struggle to heights which it had never previously reached; but rather the evidence, not less interesting, and far more touching, of a widowed woman, the unconscious picture of the widowed Egypt which like her had lost the last of the great line which had been its strength, well aware of the fact that for her, and perhaps for her land, there was no future to match the glories of the past, and burying in the tomb of her dead husband the splendours of the great days of old which she was too proud to see used by lesser men.

# CHAPTER VII

## LAGASH: THE TYPICAL CITY-STATE OF EARLY BABYLONIA

THE land which we now know as Babylonia, from the great
city which was its head and centre during many centuries, is,
like the Delta of Egypt, almost entirely an alluvial land,
formed by the deposits brought down by its two great rivers,
the Euphrates and the Tigris, and continually enlarged in
extent by the same process which created it in the beginning.
At present, the coast line at the mouth of the Shatt-el-Arab,
by which the united rivers pour their waters into the Persian
Gulf, advances about 72 feet in a year, or a mile and a half
in a century, and the advance must have been even more
rapid in ancient days.  We know that Spasinus Charax, the
modern Mohammerah, was situated on the coast-line in the
time of Alexander the Great; it is now some 47 miles inland,
so that the land must have gained on the sea since his time
at a rate of about 115 feet yearly.  The ancient coast-line
of Babylonia is marked by the present Abu Shahrain, which
represents the ancient city of Eridu; and this point is now
at a distance of more than 120 miles from the sea, so that
the land in the period with which we have to do was materially smaller than it is at present.  To-day the plain of
Babylonia embraces an area of about 30,000 square miles;

but in the time of its earliest civilisation it cannot have been more than about 23,000 square miles in extent.

The alluvial plain extends from a line drawn from a point a little below the present Samarra on the Tigris to Hit on the Euphrates. North of this point the undulating plain gradually rises to the more elevated lands of the true Mesopotamia, where the Assyrian colonists founded their kingdom. Towards the east, the Babylonian plain stretches for a distance of from 30 to 50 miles, till it meets the mountains of the ancient Elam, where dwelt the traditional enemies of the inhabitants of the plain; on the west it merges imperceptibly into the desert at a distance of from 20 to 30 miles. In ancient days this area, small in itself, was subdivided into two regions, a northern and a southern. The northern division was known as Akkad, and the chief centres of civilisation in it were the cities of Akkad, Sippar, Kish, Opis, Cutha, Babylon, and Borsippa; while the southern section was called Sumer, and its chief cities were Lagash, Erech, Ur, Larsa, Umma, Isin, and Eridu. Between the two groups, and rather nearer to the southern than to the northern, lay the sacred city of Nippur, the abode of the god Enlil, whose excavation during the years from 1888 onwards by the Expedition of the University of Pennsylvania has yielded such a wealth of information as to the civilisation and the religion of early Babylonia. Originally Nippur seems to have formed a part of Sumer; but gradually it came to occupy an intermediate position as a sort of central shrine, held sacred by both divisions of the land.

It was the southern or Sumerian portion of the land which gave its name to the whole type of civilisation which is found in this region at the earliest period of which we have any record; and the language which was used by the inhabitants, and which, though superseded in general use by the Semitic speech of the later conquerors, yet formed the basis of the system of writing which we know as cuneiform, and continued in use as the sacred language, was Sumerian, the language of these pioneers of culture. There has been much conjecture as to the origin of the Sumerians, and the region from which they came into the plain of the two rivers. The fact that their first settlements seem to have been near the mouths of the rivers has led to the idea that they came by sea, and that we have here perhaps the origin of the strange legend recorded by Berosus of the gift of letters and religion by the fish-man Oannes, who came up from the Gulf. On the other hand their development of the *Ziggurat* or Temple-tower, "built like a mountain," and the fact that the Sumerian language employs the same ideogram for "mountain" and for "land," have led others to suggest that they must have originally been a race of mountaineers. It is not improbable that they did originally descend on the fertile plain from the mountain lands on the east, as so many waves of immigration have since done; but beyond that possibility, speculation is vain.

Research into the earliest development of the human race in Sumer and Akkad is met at once with a marked difference between the conditions prevailing here and those which obtain in the other great sphere of such work,—the Nile

Valley.  In ancient Egypt the graves of Neolithic man,
shallow and unprotected as they are, have remained practically undisturbed during all the centuries, and on the upper
plateau the traces of Palæolithic man, in the shape of his
flint implements, still strew the surface of the desert sand.
But in Sumer and Akkad, such traces of early development
are almost entirely wanting.  The reason of this difference
is, of course, the difference in climate and in the character
of the soil.  The natural causes of the annual floods, the
comparatively damp nature of the soil, and the steady
growth of the alluvium, sufficiently account for the disappearance of the traces of pre-historic man.  The same
absence of such traces is to be noted in Egypt itself in the
Delta, where the conditions prevailing are not dissimilar
to those in Babylonia.  It is not till the advent of the
Sumerian, with his prudent practice of building his cities
upon great artificial mounds, thus raising them above the
action of the flood, as well as making them more easy of
defence in war, that we find ourselves in possession of satisfactory evidence as to the development of early civilisation
in this region.

At what point are we to place the earliest evidences of
Sumerian culture known to us?  The question is one which
has been the subject of infinite debate; but it would appear
that controversy is now more or less at an end, and that the
authorities are coming in the main to agreement on a system
of chronology which contemplates a much shorter period
of development than was formerly held to be necessary, and
indeed to be proved by historical evidence.  Till within

the last twenty-five years, all estimates of early Babylonian and Sumerian chronology were based on the statement in the cylinder of Nabonidus, the last king of Babylon (now in the British Museum), that 3200 years elapsed between the burial at Sippar of the foundation-deposit of Naram-Sin, one of the early kings of Akkad, and the discovery of it by himself during his restoration of the temple in which the memorial had been placed. This would place Naram-Sin about 3750 B. C., and his father, the famous Sargon I, about 3800; and consequently the numerous earlier rulers of Sumer and Akkad must have still more remote dates assigned to them. Working on this basis, the beginnings of Sumerian history have been assigned to an antiquity even more hoary than the corresponding developments in Egypt. Hilprecht formerly assigned to the foundation of the temple of Enlil at Nippur, and the first settlements there, a date somewhere between 6000 and 7000 B. C., "possibly even earlier"; and Goodspeed's chronology (1903) gives as its first item— "By 5000 B. C. City-states flourish in South Babylonia." Of late years, however, there has been a reaction against these early dates. Various lines of evidence, which it is impossible here to review in detail, have led to the conviction that the vast gulf of years between Naram-Sin and Nabonidus is partly a pious invention of the latter king, due to his desire to make the antiquity of the realm as venerable as possible, and partly an honest mistake on the part of his scribes, who have reckoned as consecutive several dynasties which were really contemporaneous. With the discussion we need not concern ourselves; it is sufficient to give the result,—with the proviso and caution that it involves the very serious step of scrapping a positive statement made by a king who stood nearly 2500 years nearer than we do to the events which he was dating, and whose scribes had doubtless access to documents which carried them back very much further still. At all events, the position which is at present accepted by the bulk of expert opinion is that we must place the earliest rulers of Sumer of whom there is any trace somewhat more than a thousand years later than the dates formerly assigned to them. Thus the beginnings of government as known to us would fall somewhere between 3000 and 4000 B. C., the reign of Ur-Nina, the earliest king of Lagash who is more than a name, would fall about 3000 B. C., and Sargon I and Naram-Sin, instead of rejoicing in the venerable antiquity of 3800 and 3750 B. C., would be reduced to the humiliating position of being mere kings of the day before yesterday, so to speak, and would date from 2650 and 2600 B. C.

Probably the change does not make a great difference to them; nor need it make much to the ordinary reader. The rulers and the culture with which we have to do are still quite ancient enough for all practical purposes, with a gap of nearly 5000 years between them and the men who have disinterred the relics of their ancient splendour. For purposes of comparison, it may be noted that on the short Berlin system of Egyptian chronology, Mena, the founder of the Egyptian monarchy, dates from 3400 B. C., and thus antedates Ur-Nina of Lagash by a mere four hundred years, —a trifle when one is dealing with millenniums. On the longer system, however, which shifts all these early Egyptian dates back by a whole Sothic period, the date of Mena would fall about 5510 B. C., and even Ur-Nina would seem modern in comparison with the hoary age of the Egyptian monarch. In any case the advantage in point of age, even on the shortest system of Egyptian dating, lies with the civilisation of the Nile Valley; but is, comparatively speaking, so small as to justify us in speaking of the beginning of civilisation in the two lands as being contemporaneous. With them we may equate the beginnings of Minoan civilisation in Crete, Early Minoan I dating probably from about 3000 B. C.

We take, then, as our typical city-state of Sumer, the city of Lagash; and the reason for choosing it in preference to other cities such as Nippur, Erech, or Ur, is simply that Lagash remained from its rise to its destruction a purely Sumerian city. It began with the very dawn of civilisation in Sumer, and it was destroyed at a period certainly not later than the rise of the First Babylonian Dynasty, say, about 2225 B. C. From that time it lay deserted and forgotten until it was re-occupied for a time by the Parthians in the second century B. C. Other sites, such as Nippur, were occupied for a much longer period, and consequently their ruins and their records contain elements of different races and types; but the work carried on at Lagash, ruling out the Parthian element, which is easily distinguished, has revealed nothing which does not belong to the first civilisation of the land. Lagash, from first to last, is purely Sumerian, and there is thus a unity in its story which makes it desirable that it should be chosen as our representative of the early Babylonian city-state. Moreover the results of excavation on this ancient site have been published with a fulness and an orderliness which leave little to be desired, and which enable the story of Lagash to be told as we can tell that of no other of the city-states of Sumer and Akkad.

The ruins of Lagash are situated at the mounds now known as Tellô, "in a district which is half the year a desert and the other half a swamp." The mounds lie about eight miles from the little town of Shatra, and form a rough oval which runs north and south, and is about 2½ miles long, by 1¼ broad. There are three principal elevations, varying from 50 to 56 feet in height above the plain. Tellô was already beginning to be recognised as a site likely to repay excavation, from the discoveries of inscribed cones and bricks, which had been made there by Arab diggers, when, in the early spring of 1877, M. Ernest de Sarzec, the newly appointed Vice-consul of France at Basra, had his attention directed to it by J. Asfar, a native Christian of the district. De Sarzec at once entered into negotiations with Nasir Pasha, the semi-independent chief of the Muntefik, whose goodwill was far more necessary for the prosecution of the work than any Turkish firman; and at his very first visit to the mounds he was fortunate enough to find a large fragment of a great dolerite statue lying at the foot of one of the slopes, and inferred that the statue must have occupied a place in some large building from which it had rolled down to its present position. This was in January, 1877, and, spurred on by the success of his preliminary investigation, by March he was busily engaged in the excavations, which, lasting with intervals from 1877 to 1900, have resulted in the restoration of much of the story of Lagash, and in the revelation of the high state of civilisation and art which had been reached by the earliest Sumerian inhabitants of Babylonia, and have established his own fame as the worthy successor of Botta, the explorer of Khorsabad.

Roughly, de Sarzec's work falls into three divisions. In 1877 and 1878, he was employed in determining the character of the whole mass of ruin by means of trial trenches; in 1880-1881, after an interval spent largely in France in the work of enlisting the sympathy and support of the home authorities, he returned to Tellô, and proceeded with the excavation of the Parthian palace which had been reared over the remains of the buildings of the earlier Sumerian rulers, and had incorporated in its fabric a great deal of their material. In this campaign he was accompanied by his young wife, and was successful, not only in the unearthing of the large building, and the discrimination of the different periods to which its materials belonged, but also in the gathering of a fine collection of ancient Sumerian works of art, particularly a notable set of statues from the principal mound, which have placed our conception of the art of this remote period on an entirely new footing. Finally, in campaigns carried on in 1888-89, 1893-95, 1898, and 1900, he revealed sculptures and inscriptions of still earlier date in another of the Tellô mounds. The death of de Sarzec in 1901 brought the excavations to a sudden close; but they were resumed in January, 1903, by Captain Gaston Cros, whose chief discovery was the massive city wall built by Gudea, one of the most famous *patesis*, or priest-kings of the city (2450 B. C.). This formidable fortification proved to be about 32½ feet in thickness, and was still in position at some points to a height of 26 feet.

One of the most fortunate features of the long and devoted work of de Sarzec was his association with M. Léon Heuzey, the Curator of the Department of Oriental Antiquities at the Louvre, whose profound knowledge of Babylonia enabled him to carry on the interpretation of the material which de Sarzec's untiring labours supplied, and whose name is coupled with that of the great explorer in the monumental work, "Découvertes en Chaldée," which embodies the fruits of so much toil. The most remarkable results of the excavations were the two great terra-cotta cylinders of Gudea, two feet long by a foot in diameter, inscribed with about 2000 lines of early cuneiform writing, and forming the longest inscriptions of the period yet known, the famous Stele of the Vultures, on which are depicted with rude force the victories of the early king Eannatum of Lagash, and which forms an invaluable source of information with regard to the war-like equipment and the burial customs of the ancient Sumerians, the numerous fine dolerite statues of Gudea, the beautiful silver votive vase of Entemena, second in descent from Eannatum of the Vulture Stele, many thousands of inscribed tablets, and, not least, the solitary tablet, belonging to no official collection, in which some broken-hearted citizen of Lagash, probably a priest, bewails the wreck of his city wrought by the neighbouring city of Umma, and calls upon just heaven to visit on the head of the *patesi* of Umma and his goddess the ruin which they had brought upon an innocent town and king.

"Since the discovery of Nineveh," said Oppert, in his opening speech at the Fifth International Congress of Orientalists at Berlin, "no discovery has been made which compares in importance with the recent excavation in Chaldea." To a casual observer, this estimate may at first seem exaggerated. No comparison seems possible between the stately winged lions and bulls, the endless slabs of sculptured alabaster covered with masterly scenes of warfare, feasting, and hunting, and the headless and cumbrous dolerite statues and pitiful shattered fragments of the Vulture Stele which form the most spectacular result of de Sarzec's labours. But a closer examination leads to a revision of such a judgment. Even from the artistic point of view, the Gudea statues, though immeasurably inferior to the living work, such as the great diorite Khafra, which Egyptian craftsmen had been doing centuries before, are yet infinitely superior to any other Mesopotamian work in the round. The famous statue of Ashur-natsir-pal in the British Museum, for instance, is clumsy stone-hewer's work compared with the seated figure of Gudea designing the temple of Ningirsu. The same cannot be said with regard to the reliefs which have been found at Lagash, for in this department the Assyrian artist was supreme. But though the Lagash reliefs are crude and primitive as works of art, to say nothing of their fragmentary condition, they have an intrinsic interest far exceeding that of the most finished work of the Assyrian schools.  For they reveal to us the appearance, the dress, the equipment, the organisation, and much of the habit of life of a race which was already old before the Assyrian was thought of, and whose culture was the basis on which the Babylonian reared that civilisation which the Assyrian took over with him into his northern home, and to which he added little or nothing.  The Sumerians of Lagash and the other cities must be recognised as one of the great seminal peoples of the world's history, whose long-forgotten work, only now beginning to be partly understood, laid the foundations of all that we now know as human culture; and the results of de Sarzec's labours at Tellô give us the picture, not only of a race which has done for the world far more than the Assyrian, with all his brutal splendour, ever did, but also of an ideal of society which at one time seemed to be the not unequal rival of the ideal of the great centralised empire, and which, in the fulness of time, came to its splendid flower in the city-states of Greece, with Athens as its supreme expression.

For the characteristic feature of the early civilisation of Babylonia is that the city, and not the kingdom, is the unit.  The city, of course, is ruled by one individual, who may call himself either "King," or more modestly "Patesi," but who in either case unites in his own person the functions of ruler and high-priest of the City-God of whom he and all the citizens were the servants; but the community is bounded by the circle of the cultivated fields and the pasture-lands around the city wall, and within that limit is complete and self-sufficient. Let us try, then, to trace the fortunes of one such unit in Lagash.

"In their origin," says the late Dr. L. W. King, "the great cities of Babylonia were little more than collections of rude huts constructed at first of reeds cut in the marshes, and gradually giving place to more substantial buildings of clay and sun-dried brick. From the very beginning it would appear that the shrine of the local god played an important part in the foundation and subsequent development of each centre of population." We may imagine a little community gathering on the banks of the branch of the Euphrates whose former existence is evidenced by the dry channel whose course can still be traced, rearing their rude shrine of wattle and mud to their god Ningirsu, and planting round the temple their poor huts, with a somewhat larger one for the man who looks after the shrine, and who, being in the counsel of the god, is deferred to in matters of dispute. A very short experience teaches the citizens of the little town that houses of wattle and daub built on the swampy Babylonian plain are not only unhealthy, but are likely to have the shortest of short lives in face of the regular floods of the river. So before long there follow the two first steps for the raising of the community in a double sense, material and spiritual. The population has to unite for the formation of a large platform which will place their houses beyond the reach of the floods; and it has to organise its labour in a still more elaborate fashion for the creation and maintenance of a system of irrigation canals,

which shall bridle the overflow of the river, and transform
it from a constant danger into a source of fertility and
wealth. We need not look much further for the reason
which brought it about that the earliest civilisations which
we know were both developed in lands subject to annual
inundation, but capable, once this inundation was controlled, of the highest fertility. It was simple necessity,
which, alike in the Nile Valley and in Babylonia, forced
early man to subordinate his selfish individuality and to
organise; and the same cause which makes one of the first
Egyptian officials named to be "the Commander of the
Inundation," makes also each early ruler of a Sumerian
city first and foremost a digger and maintainer of canals.

Having got the little city raised on its platform, the next
stage is to secure that the buildings for the service of the
city-god are made of more permanent materials than the
crude brick, which in a variable climate has an unpleasant
habit of dissolving into its original elements; and consequently we find structures of kiln-burnt bricks, with elaborate double walls to protect their contents from damp and
heat, being built as storehouses for the various offerings
which would be brought to the god, while the walls are
still further protected by verandahs of cedar wood, whose
pillars rest on brick bases. The desire for beauty as well as
usefulness is already showing itself, and we have a rude
relief of a votary, crowned with palm-branches, and raising
one hand in adoration before two colossal votive maces.
The archaic inscription appears to record a list of offerings
to Ningirsu, who is already established as the permanent

god of the city, and whose temple is named by the same name,—E-ninnu,—which it bears all through the history of the city. This may be about 3000 B. C., or somewhat earlier; but obviously the existence of such buildings, and of such an attempt at art, crude though it may be, pre-supposes a development of centuries previous, of which we have no record, and never shall have any. When we first meet the Sumerian in Lagash, he is already advanced to a considerable extent in civilisation, using metal, though only in the form of copper, capable of the execution of designs of considerable complexity, as evidenced by the pattern of lions on the mace-head of Mesilim of Kish, found at Tellô, in possession of a regular system of writing, and accustomed to regulate his business affairs by a settled code, which embraces a system of land-tenure recognised all over Sumer and Akkad.

The mention of the mace-head of Mesilim of Kish intro-duces us to a curious evidence of the advanced character of Sumerian civilisation in one particular which we are accus-tomed to regard as a growth of our own time; for the first appearance of this king in connection with Lagash is in the matter of a dispute about the boundary-line between the territory of Lagash and that of the neighbouring city of Umma. Mesilim, who appears to have exercised a kind of suzerainty, certainly over Lagash, and possibly over Umma also, was called in to act as arbitrator, and executed the first frontier delimitation of which we have any record. The account of the treaty which he negotiated is peculiar be-cause it gives us a glimpse of the fashion in which the

respective city-gods of the communities were regarded as the
real representatives of their people. The ruling *patesis*
of Lagash and Umma are not so much as named in the document. The dispute is adjusted, at the command of Enlil,
the generally recognised god of Sumer, by Ningirsu, the
god of Lagash, and the city-god of Umma. Even Mesilim,
though he acts as arbitrator, is named only as acting at the
command of his own goddess Kadi, and his functions are
limited to the recording of the treaty which the gods had
drawn up. Theocracy was a very real thing in those days.

The names of several of the early *patesis* of Lagash have
survived,—Lugal-shag-engur, Badu, Enkhegal;—but they
are no more than names, and we know nothing of them,
save that Lugal-shag-engur was *patesi* at the time of Mesilim of Kish. But with Ur-nina we enter on a period which
has left us some important evidence of the state and the life
of the growing city about 3000 B. C. Since the time of
Mesilim's arbitration, Lagash must have been steadily increasing in power, and had probably been able to assert its
independence of any outside suzerain, for Ur-nina no longer
calls himself *patesi*, but has assumed the title of king,
which he invariably uses. He was not of royal descent; but
we have no record of how he secured the throne. Whether
he was an usurper or not, however, his reign was both
peaceful and prosperous. There is no record of any war-
like achievement; the victories of Ur-nina are peaceful
ones, and his inscriptions tell us of the building of temples,
and the cutting of canals. He rebuilt the temple of Ningirsu, E-ninnu, sending an embassy to the god Enki of

Eridu, who as the Chief Diviner was implored to use his pure reed, the wand of divination, to secure the success of the work, and he records that in the construction of the building he employed wood from the mountains, which may mean cedar from Lebanon. He also cut the canal Asukhur, afterwards famous in the history of the city, and evidently by his activity in such work he greatly added to the prosperity of his city, for we have the record of many storehouses and granaries which he built. His reign seems to have been regarded as a kind of Golden Age, for his descendants always speak of him with reverence, and for several generations offerings were made in connection with his statue. Fortunately this peaceful king has left us several representations of himself and his family, in the shape of limestone plaques carved in low relief. On one of these the king is depicted, clad in the scalloped kilt which was apparently the Sumerian costume, and bearing on his head a basket, while his sons and ministers of state stand before him. The inscription on the plaque records that he has built the temple of Ningirsu, the great laver for its service, and the temple of Nina, and the relief probably depicts him as a labourer bringing material for his building. On another smaller plaque he also commemorates the building of Ningirsu's temple, and is represented as standing before the god with hands folded on his breast in an attitude of adoration, with his sons and his cupbearer Anita behind him. On all these plaques the figures conform to one type. They are all clean-shaven, the head as well as the chin being shaven. They have all prominent noses, but of a type quite un-Semitic, almond eyes, and strongly marked features, and all are nude to the waist, wearing only the heavy woollen scalloped kilt.    Later we shall see their equipment in time of war.

About 3000 B. C., then, we are to imagine the little city-state as fully organised.    In the centre of the town stands the great temple of Ningirsu, with its tower, and its magazines grouped around it.    The palace of the king is another prominent building, and there are several lesser temples to the other gods of the pantheon of Lagash, the goddess Nina, her daughter Ninmar, and her intercessor Gatumdug.    These buildings rise high on platforms of brick, as, indeed, does the whole town, though its foundations are on a lower level than those of the temples. Around the whole city runs a strong wall of brick, many feet high and thick, with towers at intervals, and strong gates, which are shut at sunset, and opened at sunrise, to allow the men of the city to go out to their labours in the fields which surround their homes, and which are as yet the only empire to which Lagash lays claim.    As the city grows in population and in power, the ring of cultivation and pasture naturally extends, to supply the needs of the increasing numbers within the walls.    And with this extension of territory there comes inevitably and automatically the threat of war.    Erelong the circle, as it grows, touches the circle of cultivation which is spreading in a similar manner from the next city-state, whose temple-tower may perhaps be seen from the tower of Ningirsu.    The cultivators, or the herdsmen, for it would be the pastures

which would first meet, quarrel over the question of which
city shall have the right to certain lands; fighting begins,
and a man or two is killed on this side or on that. Then
the men of the city which thinks itself aggrieved take
down their spears and helmets, and raid the lands of the
other city; and war has definitely begun, and threatens to
become chronic. Already, long before the time of Ur-nina,
we have seen that Mesilim of Kish had to be called in as
arbitrator between Lagash and its neighbour Umma; and
we shall see that war between these two towns was almost
as normal a feature of their life as the sowing and harvest.
Lagash was in possession, in particular, of a specially desirable bit of land, the plain Gu-edin, to which the men of
Umma conceived they had some right, or on which they cast
envious eyes, and the whole history of the towns is punc-
tuated, at frequent intervals, by raid and counter-raid,
designed to put one city or the other in permanent possession
of this Naboth's vineyard. During the reign of Ur-nina,
Lagash was apparently too strong to be meddled with by
its envious rival; but in the time of Eannatum, the grandson
of Ur-nina, the old sore broke out again, and Umma had
to be taught a sharp lesson.

The record of the first of these neighbourly bickerings,—
war is much too dignified a title to apply to such parochial
squabbles,—is preserved on the famous Stele of the Vultures,
one of the finest trophies of de Sarzec's labours at Tellô. In
the sixth column of the inscription on this priceless document, Eannatum tells us that the *patesi* of Umma, whom
he does not name, but whom we know from another inscrip-

tion to have been called Ush, was commanded by his own city-god to plunder Gu-edin, the territory beloved of Ningirsu. You will notice again the polite theocratic fiction which ascribes all the mischief to the gods of the two cities, as it had previously ascribed the treaty of peace to them also. On learning of this wanton aggression on the divine territory, Eannatum, like a wise soldier, did not allow himself to be hurried by his wrath into a hasty and ineffectual pursuit. Umma was too near to Lagash for any chance of overtaking the raiders before they had reached the shelter of their own walls. So the *patesi* quietly gathered his own army, and got it ready for the field; then, repairing to the temple of Ningirsu, he laid his grievance before the god, and lying flat on the ground, awaited the divine answer. It came in the form of a dream, in which Ningirsu came forth and stood by the head of his servant. He promised victory, and said that when Eannatum went forth to battle, the Sun-god, Babbar, who makes the city bright, would go with him, and ensure his triumph. Thus encouraged, Eannatum led his army out to avenge the slight which had been put upon Ningirsu. The men of Umma, on their part, already apparently held the sound military doctrine that the worst place in which to make war is your own territory. They did not await the attack of Eannatum, but came out to meet him, and the battle was joined probably on the disputed ground.

The result was a splendid triumph for the arms of Lagash. Eannatum completely defeated his rival, and pursued him to the shelter of his city walls with great slaughter. He put the number of the slain at 3600, or according to a possible reading, 36,000 men. We may rest assured that the larger of these figures is a wild exaggeration, and that probably even the smaller requires to have the two last figures struck off to bring it into anything like correspondence with reality. There is not the slightest evidence that these little city-states held a population which would have made such a loss as 36,000 men a possibility; even a loss of 3600 would probably have meant almost the depopulation of the city; and moreover, we know that in his victory over the ancient enemy the later *patesi*, Entemena, only claims to have slain 60 of the men of Umma. It is not obvious why there should be so great a discrepancy between the two battles as to require us to accept in Eannatum's case a slaughter which is sixty times as great as that in the case of Entemena's victory.

In any case, the result of the battle was so decisive as to take the heart completely out of the men of Umma. When Eannatum pressed on to the assault of the rival city, he found little opposition, and, as he tells us, he swept over the city "like an evil storm." Ush, the unlucky *patesi* whose devotion to his god had so misled him, disappears from the scene, whether slain in the battle, or got rid of otherwise, we do not know, and the subsequent treaty of peace was signed by a new ruler, Enakalli. It restored to Lagash the disputed territory of Gu-edin, ordered that to prevent disputes in future a deep frontier-ditch should be dug between the lands of the two cities, provided for the re-erection of the previous frontier-stele of Mesilim, which the men of Umma had very naturally knocked down in their raid, and for the erection of a new one of Eannatum on which the text of the treaty should be engraved. Then Eannatum returned to the duty of burying the slain of his own army, over whom he heaped, as he tells us, twenty burial mounds. As for the slain of his vanquished foe, they were left where they fell, to have their bones picked clean by the birds of the air and the beasts of the field; and the Vulture Stele derives its name from the picture which it gives of a part of this gruesome banquet, in which vultures are represented swooping down on the dead and carrying off heads and limbs. The burial of the heroes of Lagash is carefully depicted, with an amusing lack of perspective.

But the most interesting portion of the great stele is that in which we see Eannatum leading out his phalanx to the battle. He himself marches in front of them, wearing a conical helmet with ear-pieces, and a long cloak of woollen material, perhaps quilted, and carrying a spear and a throwing-stick. Behind him comes the close array of his infantry. The front rank is made up of men armed with battle-axes, and carrying huge bucklers, which cover them from their shoulders to their feet. Behind this shield-wall come the spearmen, each carrying in both hands a long pike, which projects beyond the bucklers of the front rank. It is a regular Macedonian phalanx, and one can imagine that its impact must have been hard to resist. Doubtless the opposing army was armed and drawn up in a similarly cumbrous fashion, and when phalanx met phalanx, it was a case of stiff pushing and endurance, until at last the stronger men broke through. Then the shield-bearers would throw away their cumbrous bucklers, and pursue the broken enemy with their axes, and it was doubtless then that the slaughter, on whatever scale it may have been, took place. It is difficult to see how there could be much bloodshed in the actual shock of the phalanxes, pushing at one another from behind their shield-wall. No doubt, as Mr. H. R. Hall says, Eannatum's phalanx represents "a highly developed military machine, which had clearly been evolved by long years of constant civil war"; but one can scarcely follow him in his suggestion that "the bow-and-arrow and hatchet fighting of the contemporary Egyptians was by no means so efficient." One would rather imagine that a captain capable of using good archers to advantage would have made hay of the slow and cumbrous Sumerian phalanx, which could have been cut up without ever being allowed to come to close quarters.

One point, which, though merely curious, has its own interest, is the extraordinary resemblance which these spearmen of Eannatum present to the knights of William the Conqueror, as depicted on the Bayeux Tapestry. One of Eannatum's men would look quite in place among the Conqueror's peaked-helmeted knights; which goes to show, not any connection, but the fact that early developments in arms and armour, as doubtless in many other forms of tool, may follow similar lines in lands and periods widely separated, and that there is no need, as there may often be no possibility, of supposing that direct influence is to be inferred in every case of similarity between the products and utensils of even contemporary civilisations.

The treaty of peace was sanctioned by the swearing of oaths by Eannatum and Enakalli, and in the Vulture Stele inscription Eannatum refers to these oaths, and calls down curses on the men of Umma should they violate their compact. "On the men of Umma, have I, Eannatum, cast the great net of Enlil! I have sworn the oath, and the men of Umma have sworn the oath to Eannatum. . . . Who from among the men of Umma will go back upon the word, and will dispute it in the days to come? If at some future time they shall alter this word, may the great net of Enlil, by whom they have sworn the oath, strike Umma down!" Eannatum then turns to Ninkharsag, to Enki, to Enzu, Babbar, and Ninki, appealing to each god that if the men of Umma shall violate the treaty the offended god may cast his net over them. What is meant by the god casting his net over the men of Umma is seen from another scene on the Vulture Stele, where the god Ningirsu is depicted, bearded as all the gods of the clean-shaven Sumerians always are. He holds in his left hand the ancient cognisance of Lagash, the Eagle clutching in its talons two lions, and from his hand there hangs a net, in whose meshes the foes of Lagash writhe and struggle. One of them has succeeded in getting his head out of the net, and Ningirsu is gently clubbing him with a mace which he holds in his right hand. Such, no doubt, was the fate which Eannatum foresaw for the men of Umma in the event of their breach of the treaty.

Eannatum's victory over Umma was by no means his only triumph, though it may have been the one in which he took most pride. He claims to have conquered Kish, the city of the former suzerain of Lagash, Mesilim, and to have also vanquished Opis and to have repulsed Elam, the secular enemy of Babylonia. "By Eannatum was Elam broken in the head, Elam was driven back to his own land; Kish was broken in the head, and the king of Opis was driven back to his own land." It will be noticed that in these claims of victory the rôle of Lagash is not that of an aggressive power, but rather that of a state attacked by invaders, and successfully defending itself. Perhaps we may see a relic of the former days, when the terror of Kish was over all the land, in an early inscription of Eannatum on a votive mortar of black basalt, now in the British Museum, in which the *patesi*, in dedicating the mortar to the goddess Nina, prays that no man may damage it or carry it away, and adds the petition, "May the King of Kish not seize it!" Before the end of Eannatum's reign, the boot was apparently on the other leg, and it was the king of Kish who had to do the praying.

Evidently this was the period when the power and influence of the little city-state was at its height, and we shall probably not be far wrong if we picture Lagash as exercising a kind of supremacy over the whole of Sumer, and a part of Akkad. But Eannatum, though so successful as a soldier, was by no means neglectful of his duties to the town which was the centre of his dominion. He records how he enlarged and beautified the temples of the gods in the city, and how when his victories had given peace to the land, he attended to what was always a Sumerian ruler's first duty towards the prosperity of his land, and dug new canals for irrigation purposes. "In that day Eannatum . . . when his might had borne fruit, dug a new canal for Ningirsu, and he named it Lummadimdug." The frontier-ditch which was dug after the war with Umma was also made to serve as an irrigation-canal for the territory of Gu-edin which had been the bone of contention between the two cities. It was given the appalling name of Lummagirnuntashagazaggipadda, a title sufficient in itself, one would think, to prevent the men of Umma from meddling with it.

Altogether one gathers from Eannatum's inscriptions and sculptures a picture of the state over which he ruled which is pleasant and prosperous enough. War had brought security in its train, and with security had come increase of wealth and consequent abundance in the land. No doubt there was a seamy side to all the outward prosperity, as we shall see from the records of Urukagina; but on the whole it seems that Lagash never was happier or more prosperous than in the days of Eannatum, and that the claim of his well inscription is justified—"In those days did Ningirsu love Eannatum."

Darker days, however, were ahead of the little state, though they were to be lit with an occasional gleam of victory. When the great *patesi* passed away, and was succeeded by his brother Enannatum I, the men of Umma apparently thought that the time was ripe for risking the net of Ningirsu, and all the other curses of the treaty. Enakalli, who had sworn to it, was either dead or deposed, and Urlumma, who had succeeded, had perhaps less of a wholesome dread of the might of Lagash. Anyhow he invaded Gu-edin, and, not content with removing Eannatum's frontier stele, as Ush had removed that of Mesilim, he broke it to pieces by casting it into the fire, while he also levelled to the ground the frontier-chapels to the gods who had been invoked to guard the treaty. Then he sat down with his army on the disputed territory, and waited for Enannatum to give him battle. Enannatum was nowise loth, and the later king Urukagina records that he was victorious. His own son Entemena, however, in telling of the incident, says nothing as to which side triumphed, so that we may probably conclude that the battle was indecisive. At all events Urlumma continued to be a thorn in the flesh of Lagash till he was finally taken in hand and disposed of by Entemena himself.

Entemena's succession was the signal for a fresh raid on the part of Urlumma, who evidently relied upon such changes as working in his favour. On this occasion, however, he found that he had tried the trick once too often. Entemena met him at the frontier-canal, with the alarming name, Lummagirnunta—and the rest of it, and inflicted on him a complete defeat. The men of Umma were utterly routed and fled, leaving sixty of their number dead on the field. Entemena followed up his victory, as Eannatum had done two generations before, and, like his grandfather, succeeded in capturing the hostile city, and bringing it

under the sway of Lagash. The office of *patesi* in the conquered city was entrusted to Ili, one of the Lagash officials.
Urlumma, the source of all the mischief, was slain in the
battle. The fact that Entemena's victory was won, and
the city captured in consequence of a slaughter so small, is
sufficient to discredit the high figures which the Vulture
Stele gives for the victory of Eannatum. If the loss of 60
men so disheartened or weakened Umma as to render its
capture easy, there is no reason to suppose that on the
former occasion it took the loss of 36,000 or even of 3600,
to accomplish the same result. Entemena caused the record
of his victory to be engraved on a great limestone stele,
which was set up on the frontier as a memorial, and a
warning to the men of Umma. Fortunately, he did not only
entrust the record to the large copy of it engraved on stone,
but buried copies of the same inscription as foundation-
deposits, in the shape of small inscribed clay cones. The
great stele has perished totally; but one of the little clay
cones has survived, and is our authority for this chapter
in the history of his city.

Apart from this record, Entemena's chief memorial is
the magnificent silver votive vase mounted on a copper
stand, which was found at Tellô, and is now in the Louvre.
Its decoration consists of two bands of incised ornament.
The upper one, directly below the neck of the vase,
gives representations of reclining cattle; the lower and
more important shows Imgig, the lion-headed eagle of
Lagash, grasping in his talons the two lions. The workmanship of this beautiful vase is such as to inspire all

respect for the skill of the metal-workers of Sumer of 2850 B. C.

Behind Entemena, there comes a string of *patesis* in Lagash of whom we know little more than the names, Enannatum II, Enetarzi, Enlitarzi, and Lugal-anda. And then comes the man who may fairly claim to be the most interesting of all the rulers of the Babylonian city-state, and who occupies in the realm of practical statesmanship in Babylonia a position somewhat resembling that which is occupied in the realm of religious affairs by Akhenaten in Egypt, though of course his sphere of influence is much more limited than that of the unfortunate Egyptian king. Both were visionaries, or rather, perhaps, both were far-seeing men who had the ill-luck to be born before the world was ripe for their teaching, and to whom the possession of a throne as a theatre for their experiments proved in the end a dire misfortune.

Urukagina, who may fairly claim to have been the first social reformer, and a royal one at that, was apparently an usurper of the throne of Lagash. At all events he states that Ningirsu had given him the kingdom, and had established his might, which is a convenient theocratic formula for cloaking an unauthorised succession. The trouble was that Ningirsu had not established his servant's might quite strongly enough for all the strains which his reforms were to put upon it. For a year, or more, after his accession, Urukagina adhered to the old title of *patesi* which had been borne by Eannatum and Entemena; then he changed it for the more ambitious one of King, and thereafter began the course of reform which has made him conspicuous in history, but which was so disastrous to his city. He appears to have conceived the idea, very strange to the minds of those days, however natural it may appear to us, that government was a matter which ought to be organised in the interests, not of the governor, but of the governed. When he came to the throne, he tells us, he found that all the splendours of his predecessors, splendours which had no doubt grown under the rule of the conquerors, rested upon a basis of injustice and oppression. The common people were taxed almost out of existence to supply the funds for the great building works and other enterprises of their rulers; or as Urukagina quaintly puts it, in a phrase which indirectly shows how much the territory of the little state had been extending, "Within the limits of the territory of Ningirsu, there were inspectors down to the sea." Besides the heavy weight of taxation, the people had to bear the load of unjust administration. The *patesi* had been in the habit of appropriating to his own use the revenues of much of the sacred land of the temples, and where he led the way in injustice, it was not likely that his officials would be far behind. Extortion and oppression prevailed in every part of the state. It may be sufficient to give a single instance, —that of the burial fees. In the case of an ordinary burial it was the custom for the priest to ask as his fee for officiating seven urns of wine, 420 loaves of bread, 120 measures of corn, a garment, a kid, a bed, and a seat. From this astounding list it is quite obvious that about the most expensive thing that you could do in Lagash was to die.

PLATE XVIII

STELE OF THE VULTURES, LOUVRE

*Reproduced by permission from "Découvertes en Chaldée," Vol. 2, Plate III,
by E. de Sarzac*

Urukagina reduced this charge to three urns of wine, 80 loaves of bread, a bed and a kid, and people doubtless felt that now one could almost afford to die when living had become otherwise inconvenient, though the charges for the privilege seem still rather high to modern ideas. In every department of state the king introduced the same sweeping system of reform, and always in favour of the poorer classes; and he showed the absolute sincerity of his position by abolishing the charges which had been a perquisite of the ruler himself. Thus in the case of every one who wished to consult the oracles of the gods by way of divination, a fee had not only to be paid to the diviner, but no fewer than five shekels, five times the diviner's fee, had to be paid to the *patesi*, and a further fee of one shekel to the vizier as well. Urukagina not only abolished the one shekel fees of the diviner and the vizier, holding, no doubt, that as both were salaried officials they had no need of perquisites, but gave up also his right to the much larger fee of the crown, so that, as he tells us, after his accession, "the *patesi*, the vizier, and the diviner took money no more." Not many reformers have had the courage of their convictions to such a practical extent as this first of the breed. Unfortunately in this imperfect world it is not always possible to carry out even the most desirable reforms, or to put into practice the noblest ideals, without causing considerable dislocation in the body politic, and giving many people a grievance which seems to them greater than the grievances which the reformer is trying to abolish. So Urukagina found in the administrative sphere, as Akhenaten, after him, found in the

spiritual one. One can imagine the indignation of the
ruling families of the state, who found half of the offices on
which they had depended for the support of their younger
sons abolished by the stroke of Urukagina's stylus, the
disaffection of the army of tax-gatherers who found their
occupation gone, the disgust of the priestly robbers who
could no longer claim half the estate of a man in return for
the mumbling over his dead body of a few prayers, the
spite of the diviners who found themselves obliged to live
on their salaries, and the general conviction of the bureaucracy that things would never be right until this upsetting
usurper was got out of the way. There were others, as we
shall see, who thought differently, and appreciated what the
king had been doing for the poor and the helpless, and
fortunately one of these was vocal, and has left us the evidence of what he thought of Urukagina; but we must imagine all the influential classes in the state of Lagash as
violently opposed to the unheard-of doctrines and practices
of their new king.

Not far off, the old enemy Umma was watching its
opportunity, under a new and vigorous ruler who was
troubled by no such scruples as vexed Urukagina. Lugal-
zaggisi, the *patesi* of Umma, took advantage of the dis-
organisation and disaffection of his old rival, swept over
the territory of Lagash with fire and sword, and carried the
city by storm, giving it up to all the horrors of a sack.
What became of the reforming king, whose goodness of
heart was so ill-repaid by a hard world, we have no means
of knowing; but the mention of his name in the strange

document from which we must now quote seems to con-
template him as still living, though perhaps it would have
been more in accordance with poetic fitness if he had perished
in the storm which swept away all the fruit of his ideals.

The document in question is a tablet which was found
by Captain Cros to the north of the mound which covered
the most ancient remains at Tellô. It came apparently
from no official source, no other tablets were found beside
it,—in short it bore all the marks of being the production
of a private individual, probably a priest, and a supporter
of the reforming king. After the storm and the sack of
the city, he had apparently found consolation in reciting
all the enormities of which the invaders had been guilty,
and in calling down curses upon their heads in connection
with each individual transgression. Without preface or
explanation he plunges into his recital of the wicked deeds
of the men of Umma. Out of a heart full and overflowing
with grief and indignation he pours the flood of his
denunciation, and at last appeals to the gods above to
avenge the wrongs which human strength had been powerless to avert.

"The men of Umma," he writes, "have set fire to the Eki-
kala; they have set fire to the Antasurra; they have carried
away the silver and the precious stones! They have shed
blood in the palace of Tirash; they have shed blood in the
Abzu-banda; they have shed blood in the shrine of Enlil
and in the shrine of the Sun-god; they have shed blood in
the Akhush; they have carried away the silver and the
precious stones! They have shed blood in E-babbar; they

have carried away the silver and the precious stones!" So
the dark recital runs on through line after line, naming
every sanctuary in the ruined city, never varying in the
wording of its accusation, and growing strangely impressive
at last by its very monotony. Then it ends with an appeal
to divine power to avenge the insult to divinity and righteousness, and with the assertion of complete innocence on
the part of the king whose throne had gone down in the
ruin of the city. "The men of Umma, by the despoiling of
Lagash, have committed a sin against the god Ningirsu!
The power that is come unto them, from them shall be taken
away! Of sin on the part of Urukagina, king of Girsu,
there is none. But as for Lugal-zaggisi, *patesi* of Umma,
may his goddess Nidaba bear this sin upon her head!"

So ends this strange document, surely the most human of
any that have come down to us from ancient Sumer.
Whether the high gods listened to the appeal of the unknown writer, who shall say? Lugal-zaggisi, at all events,
bore lightly the curse which had been laid upon him; for
his conquest of Lagash was the prelude to further triumphs
which ended in his claiming for himself the proud title of
"the minister of the gods." While his star was rising to its
culmination, that of Lagash had set, apparently, for ever,
and for long the city lay desolate. In course of time she
rose again from her ruins, and was rebuilt in even greater
splendour by her later *patesis;* but it may be questioned if
she ever regained the position of supremacy among the
states of Sumer which she lost when her power was overthrown by Lugal-zaggisi.

For the next three centuries and a half Lagash remains under the mist. Further north the conditions of empire were changing, and the Dynasty of Akkad, of Semitic origin, was asserting its supremacy, and under great kings like Shargani-sharri and Naram-sin was establishing a real kingdom as distinguished from the loose organisation of the city-states, with their temporary suzerainty over one another. From this period we have the names of a number of *patesis* of Lagash,—Engilsa, Urukagina II, Lugal-ushumgal, Ur-babbar, Ur-E, Lugal-bur, Basha-mama, and Ug-me; but again these are little more than names, and we have comparatively little evidence of the state of the city. Towards the end of the period, however, it becomes evident that the power of the Semitic rulers of Akkad, the "Kings of the Four Quarters of the World," as they proudly called themselves, is weakening, and that the city-states are in process of a temporary revival of power and of prosperity. We must now turn to the surviving records of this revival.

The first *patesi* who has left us any considerable proof of this renaissance in Lagash is Ur-bau, of whom we have a small diorite standing statue, headless like almost all such figures found at Tellô. He tells us that he rebuilt on a larger scale the temple of Ningirsu, and part of one of his walls has been found still standing. Further, he built temples in honour of Ninkharsag, Geshtin-anna, and Enki, and various shrines to other deities. There is no record of any expansion of the power of Lagash during his reign, and we may conclude that his activities were confined to the restoration of the city, and the consolidation of its resources,

—a process of which his successors, and especially Gudea, the greatest of them, reaped the fruits.

With Gudea, however (c. 2450 B. C.), we find a distinct advance of the old city-state, not only in internal prosperity and splendour, but in external influence. Obviously the decline in power of the Semitic kingdom of Akkad was now leaving the Sumerian cities in a position of greater freedom, and in Gudea Lagash found a ruler capable of taking full advantage of the opportunity. Indeed it seems probable that the period of his rule was that in which Lagash reached its highest level in point of size and magnificence, and enjoyed a material prosperity such as it had never before attained. At the same time, though the city may have been absolutely greater than at any previous period in its history, its relative importance was not what it had been in the days of Eannatum and Entemena. The orientation of the political world in Babylonia was changing, and the day of the small state, exercising a petty hegemony over a few other small communities, was all but over; and though circumstances conspired to give the city-state a short respite at this time, the period of renaissance was to be but brief, and the growth of the more ambitious kingdoms was soon to be resumed. Meanwhile, for a time, Gudea had his chance, and he made good use of it.

His reign was not a warlike one. He tells us, indeed, that he smote with his weapons the town of Anshan in Elam, and dedicated its spoil to Ningirsu; but this is the solitary reference to warfare in his inscriptions, and its chief importance is the proof which it affords that he was sufficiently independent to be able to levy war on his own account. Like those of the first great ruler of Lagash, Ur-nina, the victories of the last great ruler of the city were victories of peace. Chiefly he was a mighty builder before the Lord, and his contributions to the architectural splendours of Lagash and to the glory of the city-gods were many and important. Luckily, he was not a builder alone, but a man who was sufficiently interested in himself and his work to record all his doings in a series of picturesque narratives, full of detail, and of the greatest importance as records of the ways of thinking, and the religious customs of Babylonia and the Babylonians at this early date.

His longest narratives are those inscribed on the two great cylinders of baked clay which were found by de Sarzec in 1877. They are both concerned with the great triumph of Gudea's life, the rebuilding of E-ninnu, the temple of the city-god Ningirsu; and the one supplements the other, the first giving the account of how the temple was rebuilt, and the second of the installation of the god within his restored shrine. The prelude to the story of the building is in the shape of a very vivacious narrative of what had been happening in heaven before the gods communicated to their representative on earth their will as to his duty.

The occasion of the conference of the gods was a drought which had been devastating Sumer. On the day "on which the destinies were fixed in heaven and on earth," Enlil, chief of the gods, and Ningirsu, the god of Lagash, held high converse. Enlil turned to Ningirsu, and said, "In my city that which is fitting is not done. The stream doth not rise. The stream of Enlil doth not rise. The high waters shine not, neither do they show their splendour. The stream of Enlil bringeth not good water like the Tigris. Let the King [Ningirsu] therefore proclaim the temple. Let the decree of the temple E-ninnu be made illustrious in heaven and upon earth!" In consequence of this command of Enlil, there came to Gudea a dream. He beheld a man whose stature was so great that it equalled the heavens and the earth. On his head was a crown, and Gudea knew that he was a god. By his side was the eagle Imgig, the badge of Lagash, his feet were upon the whirlwind, and a lion crouched at his right hand and another at his left. The figure spoke to Gudea, but in words which he could not understand. Then the sun rose, and the *patesi* beheld a woman holding a pure reed, and carrying a tablet on which was a star of the heavens. While Gudea beheld, he saw a second man, whose likeness was that of a warrior; he carried a slab of lapis-lazuli, on which he drew the plan of a temple. Before Gudea there was placed a fair cushion, and on the cushion a mould, and within the mould was the brick of destiny. And at his right hand Gudea saw an ass which lay upon the ground.

Gudea was troubled at the vision for which he could find no interpretation, and he sought the goddess Gatumdug, and besought her that she would interpret the dream to him. The goddess heard his prayer, and told him the meaning of what he had seen. The man of great stature was her brother Ningirsu, and the words which he spoke were

PLATE XIX

*Photo by W. A. Mansell & Co.*

DOLERITE STATUE OF GUDEA, LAGASH

his command to Gudea to build the temple E-ninnu. The sun which rose was the god Ningishzida, who goes forth like the sun from the earth. The woman who held the reed and the tablet with the star, was the goddess Nidaba, and the star was the pure star of the temple's construction. The warrior with the plan was the god Nindub, and the plan was that of E-ninnu. The brick was the sacred brick of E-ninnu. As for the ass which lay on the ground, that, said the goddess, perhaps with unconscious irony, was Gudea himself.

Having thus received his commission, Gudea tells us how he proceeded to carry it out. The record of the resources on which he drew for the erection of the splendid building is of the greatest interest as revealing to us, not only the extent of the power of even a small city-state like Lagash, but also the manner in which trade had been developed, and the transport of articles of great weight and value arranged over a vast extent of territory. It would appear as if the trade-routes from Babylonia to Syria and Arabia were better organised and safer in the middle of the third millennium B. C. than they have ever been since.

Gudea tells us that he fetched cedar-wood from Mount Amanus, the mountain of cedars, the beams measuring 50 and 60 cubits in length. From Basalla, a mountain of Amurru, he brought great blocks of stone, from which he made steles, and set them up in the courts of E-ninnu. From Tidanu, also in Amurru, he got marble, and from Kagalad a mountain in Kimash, he mined copper, which he used for a great mace-head. For *ushu*-wood he went to the mountains of Melukhkha, and gold-dust he fetched from the mountain of Khakku, and therewith gilded a mace-head carved with the heads of three lions. He felled *khuluppu* trees in Gubin, the mountain of *khuluppu*-wood; he drew asphalt from Magda, and used it for the platform of E-ninnu; and he brought down from the mountain of Barsib blocks of *nalua* stone, which were brought down the river in great boats to Lagash, and used to strengthen the base of the temple. Altogether a remarkable picture of architectural sumptuousness, and commercial enterprise; and all the more remarkable because all these costly materials are not, as in the case of the great works of the Assyrian monarchs, mainly the spoil of war. Gudea's materials come to him by the peaceful avenues of trade; and it seems that at this period we must conceive of an Oriental world more at peace, happier, and more in the way of legitimate expansion by mutual intercourse and commerce, than it ever was again in ancient days, or, for the matter of that, is still.

It was not only commodities that were exchanged between states in those days; there was international interchange of skill and craftsmanship on occasions which called for such a thing. Gudea tells us that for the work of his temple the Elamite came from Elam, and the man of Susa from Susa, just as, more than 1400 years later, Solomon got his craftsmen from Phœnicia for the building of Jehovah's holy and beautiful house in Jerusalem. For the material for his votive statues which adorned the court of E-ninnu, and now rest in the Louvre, he had recourse to diorite, or rather dolerite, from Magan. He journeyed, he says, in search of building material, from the lower country to the upper country, and Ningirsu, his beloved king, opened the ways for him from the Upper to the Lower Sea, i.e. from the Mediterranean to the Persian Gulf.

The great temple thus splendidly provided for was duly completed, and consecrated with elaborate ceremonial. Perhaps the most interesting passage in the description of the inaugural solemnities is one which shows that something of the spirit of the long-dead and unfortunate Uru-kagina survived in his more happily-starred successor. For seven days Gudea tells us, he feasted with his people after the consecration of E-ninnu, and during this time the maid was the equal of her mistress, and master and slave consorted together as friends; "the powerful and the humble man lay down side by side, and in place of evil speech only propitious words were heard; the laws of Nina and Ningirsu were observed, and the rich man did not wrong the orphan, nor did the strong man oppress the widow." It is, no doubt, an idyllic picture of what Gudea was aiming at, rather than an accurate representation of what he actually succeeded in realising in practice; nor are we to imagine that conditions which may have prevailed, even imperfectly, during a short period of special rejoicing are to be taken as in any way representative of the normal social conditions in Lagash. Had it been so, then, indeed, the days of Gudea's rule would have been the Golden Age, not only of Lagash, but of the world's history. But at least it may be said of the *patesi* as it was said of another Oriental ruler whose dreams were higher than his accomplishments,—"Thou didst well that it was in thine heart."

So with this pretty picture of piety and lovingkindness, of which latter there is never too much in the ancient history of Mesopotamia, we may leave the story of Lagash. After the bright days of Gudea's rule the gleam soon faded, and the days of the city-state were few and evil. Erelong the rise of the last great dynasty of Sumerian rulers, the dynasty of Ur, with Ur-engur and Dungi at its head, absorbed the little semi-independent communities, which still lingered on with the forms of their old governments, but without any real power. Ur was succeeded by Isin in the supremacy; and by the time that the dynasty of Isin had worn itself out, the giant shadow of Babylon the Great was falling across the land, and the stage was being cleared for the great Semite lawgiver Hammurabi.

# CHAPTER VIII

## BABYLON: THE FOUNTAIN OF LAW

OF all the cities of the ancient world, there is none which has left such a deep impress upon the mind of man, or indeed upon the history of the race, as Babylon. Nineveh may appear to rival her for a moment; but it is only for a moment. The Assyrian capital is a mere upstart compared with the hoary splendour of her great competitor; her period of power gives to the world nothing that can for a moment be compared with the solid and enduring contribution which Babylon has made to the civilisation of mankind; and long after Nineveh had fallen never to rise again, the old Queen of the Euphrates was renewing her youth, and starting, under her New Empire, on a fresh career of glory and dominion. Rome may exercise over our minds her own marvellous fascination, in which the material and the spiritual are so wonderfully mingled; but Rome too is a thing of yesterday compared with Babylon, and though her great contribution to the development of the race is on the same lines as that of her more ancient rival, Rome's gift of law cannot be equalled with that of Babylon, for Rome was only treading a well-marked path, while Babylon was a pioneer. The supremacy of the first of great world-cities is sufficiently marked by the fact that it is her name, and not that of any of her rivals, which we use to this day to express the greatness, above all the material greatness, of the mightiest cities of our time.   Just as the writer of the Apocalypse could find no term so suitable as "Babylon" to express the might, the sinister charm, and the wickedness of the Rome of the Cæsars, so to-day we sum up all these things, in the London, New York or Paris of our own time, in the same word.

The reason for this wonderful fascination is complex. On the one hand the glowing descriptions of the classical historians, Herodotus, Diodorus, Ktesias and others, have impressed themselves indelibly on the imagination of mankind.   Herodotus, in particular, has painted such a picture of a mighty city, with its vast walls, 53 miles in circumference, and so broad that a four-horse chariot could turn upon them, its hundred brazen gates, its vast temple of Bel, its river-front with its quays and gates, that when we think of the typical great city of the ancient world, it is his Babylon that we cannot help seeing in fancy.   We may know that there is more romance than truth in his story, that his figures have to be divided by four at least to bring them anywhere near the reality, and that all his grave accounts of Semiramis and Nitokris, and his circumstantial narrative of the capture of the great city by Cyrus are sheer fable.   It does not matter; the spell of the old romancer is too strong for us, and we still see Babylon as he wished us to see it.   On the other hand, the power of the great city over our imagination derives in no small degree from its association with Old Testament Scripture.   Daniel has left us a picture as vivid in its own way as that of Herodotus. Nebuchadnezzar looking abroad over the great city which owed its second life to him—"Is not this great Babylon which I have built?" Belshazzar feasting, while the weird fingers write upon the wall the doom of his kingdom, and the Persian is at the gate,—these are all pictures more vivid to our minds than many of the things that we have actually seen.

Cyrus succeeds to the empire which Hammurabi had established and Nebuchadnezzar restored, and for two hundred years the great city lies under the Persian yoke. And then the last chapter of its ancient romance tells how Alexander came to Babylon to celebrate there the magnificent obsequies of his favourite Hephæstion, and how the hand of death touched the great conqueror in the city which has seen so many mighty kings pass across its stage. The great king lies dying in the palace of Nebuchadnezzar, his generals and Companion Cavalry filing in speechless sorrow past his bed, and catching the last feeble accents in which he bequeathes his kingdom "to the strongest." With his last breath the romance of the mighty city closes, and her glory gradually dwindles, as newer rivals arise. By the end of the first Christian century Babylon was in ruins and deserted; but the memory of her former greatness was too firmly impressed upon the minds of men to allow of such utter oblivion descending upon her as was the case with her ancient rivals. The very site of Nineveh might be so forgotten that Layard might think that he was excavating Nineveh, when he was actually dealing with Kalah; but the place and name of Babylon never altogether perished from the earth, and persistent tradition has always linked the name of Babel with the great mounds from beneath which modern exploration has recovered at least some traces of the splendour of Nebuchadnezzar's capital.

"Babil," which is the modern equivalent for the ancient "Bab-ili," "the Gate of the Gods," is still the local name for one of the mounds, while the Arabs call the chief mound "Kasr," "palace" or "castle," following therein a true tradition, for it was beneath this mound that the German explorers discovered the great palace of Nebuchadnezzar. When the wandering Jewish physician, Benjamin of Tudela, visited Baghdad in the twelfth century, he was told by his fellow-countrymen in the city that in the neighbourhood of Hillah, not far off, it was possible to see the palace of Nebuchadnezzar, and beside it the fiery furnace into which Shadrach, Meshach and Abed-nego were thrown. Benjamin remarks that the ruins are "to men inaccessible, on account of the various and malignant kinds of serpents and scorpions living there"; and there is no evidence that he took any risks in the matter. In the sixteenth century, John Eldred, an English traveller, made three journeys to Baghdad, or New Babylon, as he calls it, passing on his way the ruins of the greater city. "In this place which we crossed over," he says, "stood the olde mightie city of Babylon, many olde ruins whereof are easily to be seene by daylight, which I, John Eldred, have often beheld at my good leasure. . . . Here are also yet standing the ruines of the olde tower of Babel, which being upon a plaine grounde

PLATE XX

1. CYLINDER OF NEBUCHADNEZZAR    2. CYLINDER OF CYRUS

From the original clay cylinders in the British Museum

1. Gives account of Nebuchadnezzar's building operations at Babylon.    2. Inscribed with account of conquest of Babylon.

seemeth a farre off very great, but the nerer you come to it, the lesser and lesser it appeareth,"—like a great many other less famous wonders.

Towards the end of 1616, the famous traveller Pietro della Valle visited the mound of Babil, and brought thence a few inscribed bricks, probably the first which ever reached Europe. The mound, as he saw it, was a huge rectangular tower, with its angles pointing to the cardinal points. He noted that the mass of the building consisted of sun-dried bricks, though here and there, especially at places which served as supports, the bricks were baked. He was followed, in the end of the eighteenth century, by the Abbé de Beauchamp, who was the first to give to the public a clear idea of the vast extent of the ruins of Babylon; and one result of the interest excited by his visit was that the East India Company secured through their agent in Basra a case of Babylonian antiquities, which afterwards proved of considerable importance in the decipherment of the cuneiform inscriptions.

The more modern period of exploration begins with the visit of Carsten Niebuhr in 1765; but before we enter upon the results of modern explorers, we may glance at the site, and the various mounds which occupy it. The ruins of Babylon lie on the eastern bank of the river Euphrates. South-west, on the other side of the river, rises the mound of Birs-Nimrûd, believed by many of the earlier explorers to have been part of the great city, but now known to cover the ruins of Borsippa, while due east lies El-Ohêmir, also accepted for a time by those who believed implicitly in the huge figures of Herodotus, as coming within the circuit of the city walls, but now believed to mark the site of the ancient city of Kish. The area of ground now recognised as having certainly come within the enclosure of the city, contains five important mounds. On the north of the site lies Babil, the mound which has kept the ancient name; Kasr, the Citadel, occupies the centre, and Amran-ibn-Ali, the southern extremity of the site; while to the east lies Homera, and a little east of the line between Kasr and Amran, is Merkes. North of Amran, and between it and Merkes, lies a small plain, known as Sachn, "the Pan," which has proved of great importance. The names of these mounds are important in connection with the various phases of investigation.

Carsten Niebuhr, on his visit in 1765, indicated the Kasr, rightly as it has turned out, as the Citadel of Babylon, and the probable site of the Hanging Gardens. Under the spell of the figures of Herodotus, he regarded the mound of Birs-Nimrûd, with its fragments of a temple-tower, as the site of the tower of Babylon, the "Temple of Belus" of the Greek historian. Claudius James Rich, in 1811, varied the identifications somewhat. He believed Babil to be the site of the Hanging Gardens; but agreed with Niebuhr in placing the citadel at the Kasr. Here, in his time, there was apparent a very remarkable ruin, "which, being uncovered, and in part detached from the rubbish, is visible from a considerable distance." It consisted of walls and piers, eight feet thick, built of fine burnt brick, laid in lime-cement, and was, in fact, the Palace of Nebuchadnezzar, the scene of the death of Alexander the Great. Rich was also fortunate enough to secure a barrel-cylinder with Nebuchadnezzar's account of his work on the Canal Libil-Khegal, and a number of contract-tablets and account-lists. He, like so many of the early explorers, identified Birs-Nimrûd with the Temple of Belus. Forty years after Rich, Layard visited the site; but his work here was comparatively slight in character, and unimportant in results, though he uncovered at Babil piers and buttresses bearing the name of Nebuchadnezzar, and secured a few enamelled bricks from the Kaṣr. Nor was the expedition of Fresnel and Oppert, in 1852, productive of any very important results. Oppert placed the Hanging Gardens in Amran, and carried his conviction of the gigantic size of Babylon to the point of including not only Birs, but El-Ohêmir also within the circuit of the city walls.

The last explorer to work upon the site before the beginning of systematic exploration by the German Expedition, was Hormuzd Rassam, Layard's former assistant in Assyria. During his work at Babylon, which lasted from 1879 to 1882, he unearthed at Babil four remarkable wells of red granite, which he concluded to be part of the equipment of the inevitable Hanging Gardens, an opinion shared by Hilprecht. To the south of Amran, in the mound known as Jumjuma, he discovered thousands of inscribed tablets, chiefly business documents of the great Babylonian banking house of Egibi, which flourished in the time of Nabopolassar and Nebuchadnezzar. These tablets have been of supreme importance in the reconstruction of Babylonian life and civilisation as they existed in the New Empire.  A further find of great interest made by Rassam here was the cylinder on which Cyrus has inscribed his own account of the capture of Babylon,—an account which relegates the narrative of Herodotus to the realm of fiction.

Such was the state of our knowledge, or rather our ignorance, with regard to the ruins of Babylon, when in March, 1899, the expedition of the German Orient Society, under Dr. Koldewey, began its operations.  With the exception of the work of Rassam, nothing of real importance had even been attempted, and a good deal of energy had been wasted in chasing a will-o'-the-wisp, under the amiable guidance of Herodotus.  All that has now been changed, and our knowledge of the Babylon of the New Empire, the Babylon on which the Jewish exiles of the Captivity looked, and which Cyrus conquered, while admittedly incomplete, at least rests on a sure foundation.  When Dr. Koldewey published, in 1912, a provisional account of the results of his explorations, he estimated that after fourteen years' work, with from 200 to 250 workmen, about half of his task had been accomplished; and it is not likely that he has under-estimated the work still to be done.  Further, the fruits of the expedition have been disappointing in this respect, that practically the whole of the remains found, with but small exceptions, belongs to one single period, and that the latest, of the native glories of the great city.  The claim of Nebuchadnezzar to have been the builder of "Great Babylon" has proved to be well founded, so far as the existing ruins go, and the destruction of the ancient city by Sennacherib was evidently so thorough as to leave him a free hand. Only in one place, the mound Merkes, which appears to have been the business quarter of the city, was anything more ancient than the period of the Neo-Babylonian Empire discovered. In another respect the results of the work at Babylon were somewhat disappointing. The amount of artistic work found on the site was extremely small. Evidence that such work had once existed was not lacking; but the spoilers of later ages had done their work thoroughly.

With these qualifications, however, the German work at Babylon, incomplete as it is, has yet been of surpassing interest, and has enabled us to form some idea of the glory of the greatest city of the Ancient East, when that glory was at its height,—at least materially. The interest of the excavations largely centres on three points,—the great walls which defended the city, the huge palace-citadel which lay beneath the mound Kasr, and the temple of Marduk, or Bel, —"E-sagila," "the House of Heaven and Earth," with its gigantic temple-tower, "E-temen-an-ki," "the House of the Foundation of Heaven and Earth,"—the true Tower of Babel. The account which Herodotus gives of the walls of Babylon is sufficiently imposing. "In the first place," he says, "a moat, deep, wide, full of water, runs entirely round it; next there is a wall, 50 royal cubits in breadth, and in height 200. . . . On the top of the wall, at the edges, they built houses of one storey, fronting each other, and they left a space between these dwellings sufficient for turning a chariot with four horses. In the circumference of the wall there were a hundred gates, all of brass, as also are the posts and lintels. . . . In this manner Babylon was encompassed with a wall." "The wall on either bank of the Euphrates," he goes on to say, "has an elbow carried down to the river; from thence along the curvatures of each bank of the river runs a wall of baked bricks. . . . At the end of each street a little gate is formed in the wall along the river-side, in number equal to the streets; and they are all made of brass, and lead down to the edge of the river. This outer wall then is the chief defence, but another wall runs round within, not much inferior to the other in strength, though narrower." Amazing as the old historian's description sounds, the excavations have shown that he was not drawing the long-bow unduly. The circuit of 53 miles which he assigns to the walls is, of course, exaggerated,—in fact it looks as though in this and other instances the ancient writers had mistaken the measurement of the whole circuit for that of one of its sides. Divided thus by four, most of the measures would work out fairly well. But the boundary wall of Babylon was formidable enough in all conscience. The fosse was faced on its inner side with a wall of burnt brick, 3.3 metres in thickness. Then came the main outer wall, also of burnt brick, and 7.8 metres thick,—then an interval of 12 metres, and then an inner wall of crude brick, 7 metres thick. The space of 12 metres between the two walls was filled in with brick rubble, so that the whole formed one tremendous structure over 26 metres, or nearly 85 feet, in thickness. The only ancient walls which can compare with this are the Cyclopean fortifications of the little Mycenæan hill-fortress of Tiryns. Excavation revealed also that the inner section of this vast enceinte had cavalier towers upon it, which would show a single storey above the outer wall, just as Herodotus says; and the broad surface of the top quite bears out what he says about the chariot. The height of the wall, of course, remains unknown, as only its lower courses survive; and the measure of Herodotus is no doubt exaggerated; but, on any estimate, the fortifications of Babylon must have been stupendous and imposing structures. Between the southern citadel and the ancient bed of the Euphrates, the explorers laid bare the remains of successive fortified walls, which represent, not unworthily, the river walls of Herodotus.

From north to south, there ran through the city a noble street, "the Procession Street" or Sacred Way of Babylon, whose remains, with those of the great Gate of Ishtar, which crossed it at the approach to the Southern Citadel, give the clearest surviving evidence of the splendour of Nebuchadnezzar's capital. The middle section of this grand highway was formed of fine white limestone blocks, each 1.05 metres square, while the sidewalks were paved with blocks of red breccia, veined with white, each block measuring 66 centimetres square. Each slab bore on its edge an inscription, invisible, of course, once the stone was laid in place, "Nebuchadnezzar, King of Babylon, son of Nabopolassar, King of Babylon, am I. The Babel Street I paved with blocks of limestone (or breccia), for the procession of the great Lord, Marduk. Marduk, Lord, grant eternal life!" These blocks were laid upon a bed of brick, covered with asphalt, so that one can scarcely conceive of a piece of road-making more sumptuous or more durable. On either side of the street rose high defensive walls, 7 metres in thickness, which linked up the northern fortifications with the walls of the Southern Citadel. Thus this great artery of the city, far from being a weakness to the defence, was an added strength, for an enemy, gaining access to it, would find himself in a veritable death-trap, through which he would be obliged to struggle under a hail of missiles from the defenders who manned the walls on either hand. "The impression of peril and horror was heightened for the enemy, and also for peaceful travellers, by the impressive decoration of long rows of lions, advancing one behind the other, with which the walls were adorned in low relief and with brilliant enamels."

At the point where this magnificent street meets the defence walls of the Southern Citadel, it was crossed by the Ishtar Gate, the most imposing relic now remaining of Babylon's former splendour. The two eastern towers of this wonderful gate are still standing to a height of twelve metres, and are the most striking, and the best preserved, of any Mesopotamian buildings. The gate-way was double, and consisted of an outer and an inner gate-house, each with a double door. These gate-ways are connected by short walls bounding the passage on either side, and thus forming a court between the gates, in which, as in the Procession Street, an enemy who had breached the first gate would find himself trapped, and helplessly exposed to the arrows of the defenders. The decoration of this great gate is

PLATE XXI

THE TWO EASTERN TOWERS OF THE ISHTAR GATE

*Reproduced by permission from " Excavations at Babylon," by Robert Koldewey*
*(Macmillan & Co.)*

remarkable. The whole surface of the walls was adorned with figures of bulls and dragons in brick relief, enamelled in brilliant colours, chiefly white and yellow upon a bright blue background. The figures are so arranged that to any one entering the gate they would appear as though coming to meet him. There were at least 575 of these creatures on the walls of the gate-towers and court, and the whole structure must have been a blaze of brilliant colour. One can imagine the impression produced on the mind of a stranger, entering the city for the first time, as he passed along the magnificent Procession Street, guarded on either side by figures of menacing lions, and was finally confronted by the Ishtar Gate, with its lofty towers and curtain walls covered with the figures of the sacred bull and dragon.

On the left hand of the gate, as one approaches from the north, stood the small temple E-makh, dedicated to the goddess Nin-makh, "the Great Mother," and on the right rose the great fortified mass of the Southern Citadel, with its palaces. Entering the citadel by the Beltis Gate from the Procession Street, one finds a great courtyard surrounded by houses which open on the court, and probably formed the offices of the administration. In the opinion of the excavators, this section of the palace occupies the site of the very earliest settlement, Babilu, or Babilani, "the Gate of the Gods." North of this first court, stands the building which the excavators believe to represent the famous Hanging Gardens. It is a group of fourteen cells roofed with barrel-vaulting, and partly built of stone. In one of the cells is a well with a triple shaft, adapted to secure a continuous flow of water, and the theory is that the gardens were raised upon this vaulting, and watered from the well. If so, our ideas of their size and splendour must undergo a considerable diminution. Strabo and Diodorus both assert that the quadrangle of the gardens measured four plethra,—about 120 metres,—on each side. The actual measurement is exactly one-fourth of this,—30 metres a side. The Hanging Gardens, if this building represents them, were no very inconceivable thing after all.

Passing westwards through a smaller court, we enter the main courtyard of the palace, a noble oblong of 55 by 60 metres. On its southern side the throne-room, the stateliest chamber found in Babylon, 52 metres by 17, opens by three doors on the court. It is decorated in a striking and taste-ful manner with a conventional design in enamelled brick-work, representing yellow columns with light-blue capitals upon a background of dark blue. A recessed niche opposite the main doorway no doubt once held the throne, so that the king could be seen by his subjects gathered in the court. In this stately hall, almost unquestionably, we may lay the scene of that last great revel, when "Belshazzar the king made a great feast to a thousand of his lords, and drank wine before the thousand," and when "in the same hour came forth fingers of a man's hand, and wrote over against the candlestick upon the plaister of the wall of the king's palace; and the king saw the part of the hand that wrote. Then the king's countenance was changed, and his thoughts troubled him, so that the joints of his loins were loosed, and his knees smote one against another." Nebuchadnezzar himself has described for us the splendid palace whose ruins have thus been brought to light after more than 2000 years of desolation and darkness. "In those days," he says in the Grotefend Cylinder, "I built the palace, the seat of my kingdom, the bond of the vast assemblage of all mankind, the dwelling-place of joy and gladness, where I made the gifts, in Babylon anew, laid its foundations on Earth's wide breast with bitumen and brick, mighty cedar-trunks I brought from Lebanon, the bright forest, for its roofing, I caused it to be surrounded with a mighty wall of bitumen and brick, the royal command, the lordly injunction I caused to go forth from it." So much glory and power; and now a heap of tumbled brickwork, and a few enamelled tiles, are all that is left to witness to the might of the Great King!

West of Nebuchadnezzar's palace lies that of his father Nabopolassar, among whose ruins was found the burial of a man, evidently of high rank, who had been laid to rest clothed in gold-spangled garments, and decked with golden ornaments. The explorers suggest that the burial may be that of Nabopolassar himself, thus interred with honour by his son, in the house which he had reared for himself. Nabopolassar's palace is bounded to the west by the former bank of the Euphrates, and guarded on this side by the river-walls which Herodotus has described.

Most interesting of all, perhaps, were the results attained by the excavations in the hollow known as "Sachn," "the pan," south of the palace area. Here there was revealed a huge enclosing wall of crude brick, forming an almost perfect square of enormous dimensions—409 metres on the side. This wall is double, the intervening space being occupied by chambers. In the southwest angle of this great square stood a vast tower, whose core still remains, with a great stairway or ramp leading up to it on the south side. The eastern gate of the enclosure is bordered by two large buildings with open courtyards, which may have been the temple storehouses, while on the south the boundary wall is lined with a range of large buildings which must have been the homes of the priests. South of the enclosing wall, again, stands the ruin of a great temple, a solid imposing mass of building 79.3 metres by 85.8, with a central court of 31.3 metres by 37.1.

We turn at once to the indispensable Herodotus. "The precinct of Jupiter Belus," says the old historian, "was still in existence in my time, a square building of two stades on every side. In the midst of this precinct is built a solid tower of one stade both in length and breadth, and on this tower rose another, and another on that, to the number of eight. And an ascent to these is outside, running spirally round all the towers. And in the uppermost tower stands a spacious temple, and in this temple is placed, handsomely furnished, a large couch, and by its side a table of gold. . . . There is also another temple below, within the precinct at Babylon; in it is a large statue of Jupiter seated, and near it is placed a large table of gold; the throne and the step also are of gold."

Nowhere has the credit of the old historian been more thoroughly vindicated than in the excavation of the temple enclosure of Babylon. Golden statues, and tables, of course, need not be looked for, though no doubt they were there once, as Herodotus says. There have been too many plunderers at Babylon for any of the precious metal to be left; but in all other respects the facts tally point for point with the description. The great tower is his eight-staged temple, or all that is left of it, and the temple south of the wall is his "temple below."

But the discovery of these buildings has an interest greater than that of the vindication of the credit of Herodotus. They are, to begin with, the relics of the temple of the supreme god of Babylon, Marduk, or Bel, the conqueror of Tiamat, or Chaos, in the old Babylonian Creation-Legend. The tower is the famous E-temen-an-ki, "the House of the foundation of Heaven and Earth," and the lower temple is E-sagila, "the House of Heaven and Earth." These identifications are made certain by the discovery of bricks of the Assyrian kings Esarhaddon and Ashur-bani-pal, and of Nebuchadnezzar himself, naming the buildings. Here then, we have the central shrine of Babylonian faith, and the great Ziggurat or temple-tower is the tower of which the sacred historian speaks. "And they said, Go to, let us build us a city, and a tower whose top may reach unto heaven; and let us make us a name, lest we be scattered abroad upon the face of the whole earth"— the true Tower of Babel. Rebuilt again and again, as it fell into disrepair, in the fashion of all brick buildings, it appears always to have occupied the same site, and its latest restorer describes his achievement in terms almost identical with those in which Scripture tells of the presumption of its first builders. "To raise up the top of E-temen-an-ki that it may rival Heaven, I laid to my hand." So says Nebuchadnezzar. The height of the tower is, of course, unknown, as only its lowest stage survives; but in all probability, it must have been at least 300 feet. The explorers believe the summit to have been used for purposes of astronomical observation, height being required to lift the observers above the thick atmosphere of the plain. "The greatly renowned clearness of the Babylonian sky," says Dr. Koldewey, "is largely a fiction of European travellers, who are rarely accustomed to observe the night sky of Europe without the intervention of city lights." So, even as he rescues for us one romance of our childhood, the explorer ruthlessly destroys another; and we may no longer think of the wise men of the East looking up to skies of dazzling splendour, but rather as peering through mist and dust-clouds for the faint gleam of the herald-star!

One apparent disappointment in the excavations led the explorers to an interesting link with Alexander the Great. They were struck during the work at E-temen-an-ki by the absence of debris around the base of the great tower, and when they came to work upon the mound Homera, to the northeast of the tower, they were disappointed to find that it covered no buildings whatever, and consisted only of a tremendous mass of debris, mainly broken brickwork, with the stamp of Nebuchadnezzar, and a few Greek terra-cottas. The meeting of these two facts,—at the tower, a huge building practically without debris,—at Homera, a

mass of debris without any trace of a building, recalled the
statement of Strabo that Alexander intended to rebuild the
tower, which had fallen in his time, and spent 600,000 day's
rations in having the rubbish removed, but left the task
unfinished. To have found Alexander's rubbish-dump is
not a great achievement; but the incident has its own interest as an illustration of how not only facts, but the absence
of facts may be suggestive, and may lead to additions to our
knowledge.

The buildings which have been dealt with so far, have
been exclusively of the late Assyrian and Neo-Babylonian
periods. At one point, however, the mound called Merkes,
the explorers gradually worked their way down through
Parthian, Greek, Persian, and Neo-Babylonian remains,
till they reached a level where the houses contained tablets
of the reign of Merodach-Baladan I, and Enlil-nadin-shum
(1300-1400 B. C.). In the lowest stratum of all, contract
tablets of the First Dynasty were discovered, bearing date
formulæ of Samsu-iluna, Ammi-ditana, and Samsu-ditana,
the successors of Hammurabi. Here we get back as far as
we are ever likely to get back towards the beginnings of
Babylonian history, and the fact that the city of those early
days was evidently destroyed by fire confirms the account
of the disaster which overwhelmed the First Babylonian
Dynasty, and prepared the way for the rise of the Kassite
Dynasty. This destruction was probably the work of the
Hittites, whose great raid took place in the reign of Samsu-
ditana.

The houses of this earliest Babylon were crowded pretty

closely together, but the streets were laid out with fair regularity. The main arteries run north and south, parallel to the Procession Street, and are crossed by others at right angles. In fact the Babylon of the First Dynasty presents one of the very earliest attempts at town-planning on a scientific basis, with island-plots approximately rectangular. Ancient Babylon is thus seen to have been the representative of order and system in this, as in other respects.

Such are the results of excavation on the site of the city of Hammurabi and Nebuchadnezzar, so far as the work has progressed. At present, not more than half of the area has been dealt with, and it may be that many years will elapse before the work is completed. But enough has been done to show us that the traditional greatness and glory of the first world-capital were but little exaggerated in the writings even of those who have often been regarded rather as romancers than as sober historians, and that the Queen-City of the Ancient East was not unworthy to exercise the spell which she has cast over the minds of men for forty centuries. In the hey-day of her splendour under the New Empire, when the Jews of the Exile first beheld her, the city must have appeared a miracle of glory and beauty. Her explorer permits himself few superlatives in writing of what he has discovered; but even his style warms as he speaks of the wonders of the vast temple of Marduk. "The colossal mass of the tower which the Jews of the Old Testament regarded as the essence of human presumption, amidst the proud palaces of the priests, the spacious treasuries, the innumerable lodgings for strangers,—white walls, bronze doors, mighty fortification walls set round with lofty portals and a forest of 1000 towers,—the whole must have conveyed an overwhelming sense of greatness, power, and wealth, such as could rarely have been found elsewhere in the great Babylonian kingdom." Dr. Koldewey speaks of one temple.  When you add to the picture the many others, only less glorious than the mighty house of Marduk, the glittering palaces, the many coloured splendours of the great Procession Street and the Ishtar Gate, the frowning might of the vast ramparts, with their gates of gleaming bronze, and people the whole with the thronging rainbow-hued crowds of an Eastern city, and the flashing bravery of an unconquered army, you can understand something of the pride with which the great king said, as he walked in the palace of the Kingdom of Babylon, "Is not this great Babylon, that I have built for the house of the kingdom, by the might of my power, and for the honour of my majesty?"

Remarkable, however, as the results of excavation in Babylon itself have been, no small part of our information with regard to the land and its early conditions, its literature, its religion, and, above all, the system of law by which Babylon is so honourably distinguished, has come to us from explorations conducted in many other places, some of them far enough from the great city.  Thus the great source of information with regard to the literature of Babylonia has hitherto been the store of clay tablets discovered during his second expedition by Layard at the mound of Kouyunjik, the ancient Nineveh.  Here in the palace of

Ashur-bani-pal, the last of the great Assyrian kings, Layard discovered two rooms filled with tablets, which turned out to be part of the Royal Library gathered by the king, who had formed the design, not only of preserving the records of his own reign and glory, but of establishing a collection of Babylonian literature in the true sense. Holding, as he did, dominion over Babylonia as well as Assyria, the great king was able to command access to the temple archives of the more ancient land, and his scribes made copies of the original texts from these, and especially of writings from Babylon and Borsippa. Layard's find was supplemented by a further discovery made by Rassam, and altogether the remains of the library which we owe to the literary and archæological tastes of King Ashur-bani-pal, now gathered in the British Museum, amount to about 30,000 tablets—probably the most precious collection of ancient literature in existence. Foremost in interest in this collection were the myths and legends recording Babylonian ideas as to the Creation, the conquest of Chaos, and the Deluge, with the Epic recounting the feats of the national hero Gilgamesh. These legends have been of the greatest importance for purposes of comparison with the corresponding Hebrew literature, to which they present remarkable resemblances, and divergences not less remarkable. The largest section of the collection was composed of manuals of divination, astrological handbooks, and collections of dreams and omens. Connected with these were the tablets relating to magic and incantation, with quasi-medical texts giving prescriptions for driving out demons of disease, and counteracting the evil influences of witches and sorcerers. Besides these there were found many genuine medical texts, presenting a fairly complete idea of the state of medical science in Babylonia, and a large number of sacred texts, prayers, hymns and penitential rituals, while not less important were the language text-books, giving sign-lists, grammatical rules, and exercises, commentaries on various texts, and school editions of literary productions. Altogether the library of Ashur-bani-pal gives an insight into the mental outlook of the Babylonian race such as is paralleled by the literature of no other ancient race.

The library of Nineveh has been supplemented by the large finds of tablets made at Nippur by the American Expedition under Peters, Haynes and Hilprecht. The value of this great collection of more than 20,000 tablets has been mainly in the direction of the enlargement of our knowledge of Babylonian Sacred Literature; but there are also hundreds of texts relating to the language, and a large number of business documents, chiefly relating to the operations of the great banking firm of Murashu, which conducted business at Nippur in the fifth century B. C. These give a useful parallel to the records of the great firm of Egibi, of Babylon, which was established before the time of Sennacherib, and which in the period of the Neo-Babylonian Empire and the Persian rule, became the Rothschilds of the ancient world, lending money to the State as well as to private individuals. The firm of Egibi comes comparatively late in the history of Babylon, but the multitudes of Contract-Tablets found in the mound of Merkes by the German

Expedition, and elsewhere by earlier explorers, show that at least as early as the days of Hammurabi (c. 2123-2081, B. C.), business in Babylon was as thoroughly organised as at the present time, and that the Semite of that early date had already developed that remarkable business instinct which has characterised his descendants ever since.

Again, it has been from the wonderful discoveries of de Sarzec and Gaston Cros at Tellô, the ancient Lagash, and not from Babylon, that the course of development of the early City-States in Babylonia has been revealed,—a subject which has been dealt with elsewhere.

But the discovery of supreme importance with regard to the place of Babylon in the history of human development, especially in connection with her greatest claim to be the leader of the race as the Fountain of Law, was made far to the East, beyond the bounds of Babylonia, in the land of Babylon's ancient rival, Elam. There stood the city of Susa, the ancient Persepolis, the "Shushan the Palace" of the Book of Esther, and at one time the capital of the Elamite kingdom. At Susa, M. J. de Morgan, excavating for the French Ministry of Instruction, found in December, 1901, and January, 1902, three large pieces of black diorite which, when fitted together, formed a complete monolith stele, about 88 inches in height, and tapering upwards from about 73 inches in circumference at the base to about 65 near the top. The stone now stands in the Louvre at Paris. At the top of the stele stands, carved in low relief, a figure of the great king Hammurabi, receiving his laws from the Sun-God Shamash, who was regarded in Babylonia as the

PLATE XXII

W. A. Mansell & Co.

HAMMURABI WORSHIPPING THE SUN GOD

From the Stele with the law code in the Louvre

supreme judge, whose attendants were Misharu and Kit-taru, "Rectitude and Right." Below this carving is the inscription, written in Semitic Babylonian and arranged in parallel narrow columns. The writing goes from left to right, but each column goes across the stele, so that the reader has to turn his head sideways to read the inscription. The front of the stone contains sixteen columns, with traces of five more which have been erased. On the back are 28 columns, perfectly preserved, save for faults in the stone. The whole inscription originally contained 49 columns, 4000 lines and about 8000 words.

The erasure on the front was probably the work of the Elamite conqueror Shutruk-Nakhunde, who carried the stele, along with other Babylonian monuments, to Susa, in the twelfth century B. C., as a trophy of his conquests, and no doubt intended to fill in the cleared space with the record of his achievements, but left his purpose unaccomplished. Had he completed his bit of vandalism, the value of the ·historical record might have somewhat reconciled us to the loss of part of the original inscription,—a loss which other records only partly enable us to get over. The existence of fragments of other copies, found at Susa and at Nippur, shows that the Code was executed in several copies, which were probably set up in the chief cities of the kingdom; while fragments found, in Assyrian, in the library of Ashur-bani-pal, show that the knowledge of the code was widespread.

The text begins with a prologue in which the great deeds of its author are recorded in magniloquent language.

"When the lofty Anu, king of the Annunaki, and Bel, lord of heaven and earth, he who determines the destiny of the land, committed the rule of all mankind to Marduk, the chief son of Ea, . . . when they pronounced the lofty name of Babylon; when they made it famous among the quarters of the world, and in its midst established an everlasting kingdom whose foundations were firm as heaven and earth, —at that time, Anu and Bel called me, Hammurabi, the exalted prince, the worshipper of the gods, to cause justice to prevail in the land, to destroy the wicked and the evil, to prevent the strong from oppressing the weak, to go forth like the Sun over the Black-Head Race, to enlighten the land and to further the welfare of the people. Hammurabi, the governor, named by Bel am I, who brought about welfare and abundance . . . the exalted one, who makes supplication to the great gods, the descendant of Sumu-lailu, the powerful son of Sinmuballit, the ancient seed of royalty, the powerful king, the Sun of Babylon, who caused the light to go forth over the lands of Sumer and Akkad; the king who caused the four quarters of the world to render obedience; the favourite of Nana am I. When Marduk sent me to rule the people and to bring help to the country, I established law and justice in the land and promoted the welfare of the people." Though we need not take all these swelling words at their face value (for much of this prologue is the common form of every king of Ancient Mesopotamia no matter how paltry his royalty may be), and though we need not regard Hammurabi as the original author of all the laws recorded in his code, yet in substance

his claims seem to have been justified, and his glory, even
as the codifier of already existing enactments, is not small,
as the Code itself amply proves.  The prologue is followed
by 282 sections, which deal with almost every conceivable
aspect of business life, whether agricultural or commercial,
with navigation, with the relations of master and slave, of
patient and surgeon or physician, of borrower and lender,
of landlord and tenant, with family life and crimes against
its sanctity, with the regulation of irrigation and cultivation, and with the supervision of certain trades which were
peculiarly liable to abuse.  And then the Code closes with
an epilogue as grandiloquent as the prologue, in which the
king commends his laws to the observance of his successors,
and calls down the judgment of the gods on those who
despise his "weighty words."  "In the days that are yet to
come, for all future time, may the king who is in the land
observe the words of righteousness which I have written
upon my monument! . . . If that man pay attention
to my words which I have written upon my monument, do
not efface my judgments, do not overrule my words, and do
not alter my statutes, then will Shamash prolong that man's
reign as he has mine, who am King of Righteousness, that
he may rule his people in righteousness.  If that man do not
pay attention to my words which I have written upon my
monument; if he forget my curse and do not fear the curse
of God; if he abolish the judgments which I have formulated, overrule my words, alter my statutes, efface my name
written thereon and write his own name; or, on account of
these curses, commission another to do so,—as for that man,

be he king or lord, or priest-king or commoner, whoever he may be, may the great God, the father of the gods, who has ordained my reign, take from him the glory of his sovereignty, may he break his sceptre, and curse his fate!" Thus the code of Hammurabi contains, not only the earliest extant collection of laws, but also the first claim of copyright on record,—a claim which carries that venerable bone of contention back to 2000 B. C., and already at that early date, contemplates ways and means by which the literary robber might dodge the statute!

The state of society revealed by the laws is remarkable. We are no longer dealing with a primitive community, but with a highly organised State, from which the tribal system has vanished, and where even the city-states of early Babylonia are absorbed in the national life. Local government exists, but the royal judges are over the local courts, as in our own social order, with appeal from the lower court to the higher, and ultimately to the King himself. The family is the unit, with rights in the family estates, handing over its rights to individual members as they form new branches of the stock, but always retaining rights of reversion, on the lines of entail. The population is largely engaged in agriculture, holding land on one or other of various forms of tenure, feudal, implying military service, religious, by payment of tithe and temple-dues, or "metayer," the landlord finding cattle, implements, and seed, and being repaid by a fixed portion of the return. There are many industries, which are in the hands of trade guilds, resembling those of the Middle Ages, whose membership is largely hereditary, but into which entrance may be gained by adoption or apprenticeship. The amount of attention paid to the relations of borrower and lender shows that the business of banking was already highly developed, and that the dealings of the money-lender with his needy clients required then, as now, careful watching, generally, though not altogether, in the interests of the weaker party. Thus, if a business man borrowed a sum of money and afterwards repudiated the loan, he was obliged, on his liability being proved, to restore the amount borrowed three-fold; but if the lender made a false claim for the repayment of money which had been already repaid, he got much harder measure on proof of his sharp practice. "If a merchant lend to an agent, and the agent return to the merchant whatever the merchant had given him; and if the merchant deny receiving what the agent has given to him, that agent shall call the merchant to account in the presence of god and witnesses, and the merchant, because he has had a dispute with his agent, shall give to him *sixfold* the amount which he obtained." The predecessors of Messrs. Egibi and Murashu were evidently not allowed to have it all their own way in Babylonia when Hammurabi was king.

The medical profession was as carefully legislated for as the banking, and some of the provisions of the Code would no doubt be welcomed by modern doctors as giving them some legal security for their fees; while other regulations would doubtless be somewhat unwelcome. Fees were strictly appointed by law, with corresponding security for their payment; but penalties for erroneous or unskilful practice were also exacted—and the penalties were on a somewhat higher scale than the fees. "If a doctor operate on a man for a severe wound with a bronze lancet, and save the man's life; or if he open an abscess in the eye of a man with a bronze lancet, and save that man's eye, he shall receive ten shekels of silver." This was for a patrician; the operation on a plebeian only carried a fee of five shekels, and in the case of a slave, only of two. The penalties for unskilful practice were another story. "If a doctor operate on a man for a severe wound with a bronze lancet, and cause the man's death; or open an abscess in the eye of a man with a bronze lancet, and destroy the man's eye, they shall cut off his fingers." No more bungled operations from that practitioner! "If a doctor operate on a slave of a freeman for a severe wound with a bronze lancet, and cause his death, he shall restore a slave of equal value." Probably the profession was not overcrowded in Babylon in the days of Hammurabi!

Money-lenders and doctors were not the only classes whose evil or careless propensities were sternly restrained by law. The jerry-builder had a poor time of it in Hammurabi's Babylon. "If a builder build a house for a man, and do not make its construction firm, and the house which he has built collapse and cause the death of the owner of the house, that builder shall be put to death. If it cause the death of a son of the owner of the house, they shall put to death a son of that builder. If it cause the death of a slave of the owner of the house, he shall give to the owner

of the house a slave of equal value." Babylonia was not a
"Dry" state; but the trade of the drink-seller was held in
no very high repute, and the laws regarding it were such
as to discourage, more or less mildly, the desire to make a
modest competence by the weakness or vice of one's fellow-
citizens. Wine-sellers were apparently always women, and
the great lawgiver evidently had no very high opinion of
either their character or their loyalty. "If a wine-seller do
not receive grain as the price of drink, but if she receive
money by the great stone" (an opulent phrase which
quaintly recalls Dr. Johnson's remark at the sale of Thrale's
brewery, "We are here to sell the potentiality of growing
rich beyond the dreams of avarice,") "or if she make the
measure for drink smaller than the measure for corn, they
shall call that wine-seller to account, and they shall throw
her into the water." "If outlaws collect in the house of a
wine-seller, and she do not arrest these outlaws and bring
them to the palace, that wine-seller shall be put to death."
Obviously saloon-keeping in Babylon 4000 years ago had its
exciting moments and "the trade" of to-day scarcely realises
how little it has to suffer, even from the most drastic modern
legislation, compared with the stern methods of Babylonian
temperance reform!

The connection between drink and the church has always
been the subject of more or less irreverent and ill-natured
jesting; but in Hammurabi's Babylon it was no joke. It
was discouraged, to put it mildly, in a fashion which probably acted as a fairly effective deterrent. "If a priestess
who is not living in the sacred precincts, open a wine-shop,

or enter a wine-shop for a drink, they shall burn that woman!" The provisions which have been quoted are perhaps the quaintest, and in some respects among the most primitive of the great code, savouring a good deal of the "Eye for an eye and tooth for a tooth" idea which is characteristic of all primitive law; and indeed there is a considerable stratum of this most ancient form of justice in the Code,—even literally. "If a man destroy the eye of another man, they shall destroy his eye." "If one break a man's bone, they shall break his bone." "If a man knock out the tooth of a man of his own rank, they shall knock out his tooth." But side by side with this application of the primitive *lex talionis*, we have land and irrigation laws of the most just and enlightened character, with careful provision against the possibility of land going out of cultivation because of the slackness of the occupier, and equally careful provision against the oppression of the unlucky cultivator in years of drought or flood; while a curiously advanced section provides for the cultivator acquiring an owner's interest in part of his holding by diligent cultivation. "If a man give a field to a gardener to plant as an orchard, and the gardener plant the orchard and care for the orchard four years, in the fifth year the owner of the orchard and the gardener shall share equally; the owner of the orchard shall mark off his portion and take it." The laws regarding family life are of considerable strictness, especially those intended to preserve the sanctity of family relations and the purity of descent. On such points early law recognised, as later law has also had to recognise, that offences which may vitiate the succession in a family are of peculiar significance, and must be visited with special severity. But, on the other hand, the rights of women are owned and safeguarded with minute care, the weak, the widow, and the orphan are fully protected, and "women are placed in a position of freedom and independence of their husbands, such as they have only enjoyed in Britain since the Married Women's Property Acts."

Not that the poor husband's interests were altogether neglected, as the following section shows: "If a woman have not been a carefull mistress, have gadded about, have neglected her house, and have belittled her husband, they shall throw that woman into the water." One is tempted to speculate as to how many deaths by drowning would take place in an average modern community were Hammurabi's legislation suddenly to come into force; but perhaps even in Babylon gossip was irrepressible, no matter how severe the law!

The Code reveals to us that in Babylonia in the time of the First Dynasty there were three classes recognised in the social order. Highest came the "Amelu," who was the man of the predominant class, probably one of the conquering race, an Amorite by descent, or else one who had been admitted, by intermarriage, or by adoption, to the ruling caste. The King himself is the head of the caste, and is regarded as the First Gentleman of Babylonia. The Amelu is often, but not necessarily, an official of the government, and the title is used, like our "Sir," or "Esquire," to mark a certain social status. The Amelu might be a poor gentleman; but, even so, he was always on a higher footing than even a wealthy member of the class below him. His title might be best rendered by "Patrician," and his status was very much that of the Norman in England or Sicily.

The class next in rank was the "Mushkenu," who was a freeman, but essentially a commoner. He lived in a special quarter of his city, the "Mushkenutu," and was probably the backbone of the business community, having no pretensions to a share in the sweets of officialdom. He was not necessarily poor, for he might hold property and slaves, and no doubt he existed in all grades, as in our own social order. His title has had a curious history. It passed into Hebrew as "Misken," and thence into modern languages, as the Italian "Meschino," the Portuguese "Mesquinho," and the French "Mesquin," with varying shades of meaning, but always with the suggestion of inferiority. Originally he may be defined as the Plebeian.

Lowest of all came the "Wardu," or slave, who was a mere chattel of his master. He could be sold or pledged, branded or fettered at his owner's will, while if he was injured, the compensation for his injuries went to his master. On the other hand, he seems to have been, on the whole, well treated, as a valuable piece of property, and was even allowed to engage in business on his own account, though his master claimed a share of the profits. He could marry a free woman, and often did so; and if he was successful in business, he could buy his own freedom. Slavery in Babylonia was as merciful as such an institution can ever be, and doubtless the lot of a clever slave, under a kind master, was often much better than that of a poor Amelu or Mushkenu.

Justice in Babylonia had no regard to the principle which we hold to be at the foundation of all just law. It was essentially a respecter of persons; but this, in the main, in no unworthy sense. On the contrary, Hammurabi held the view that "Noblesse oblige," for when a patrician commits a crime, his punishment is heavier than that of a plebeian. Thus the Amelu who strikes a man of his own rank has to pay a fine of one mina of silver, while the Mushkenu who is guilty of the same assault on a plebeian is only fined ten shekels of silver. The patrician's medical fees, as we have seen, were also higher than those of the plebeian. A plebeian, however, who strikes a man of superior rank, is sentenced to 60 strokes with an ox-tail whip, administered in public, and while a patrician pays with the loss of his own eye or tooth for having destroyed the eye or tooth of a fellow-patrician, he is only fined for a similar outrage on the person of a plebeian, the fine in the one case being one mina, in the other one-third of a mina of silver. On the whole, given the distinction of class as a fundamental condition of society, there is little to find fault with in the Babylonian view of justice as between class and class.

Such then is the Code of Hammurabi, the earliest known body of law in the world. The influence of such a code, instituted at such an early date, can scarcely be overestimated. It formed the basis of all subsequent legislation in the Semitic East, and the Mosaic code shows obvious traces of a study of the earlier body of law, as Dr. C. H. W. Johns has shown, though along with remarkable likenesses there are apparent also decided contrasts, as was to be expected, having regard to the different conditions for which Hammurabi and Moses were legislating. Viewed as a whole, its existence affords ample justification to the claim of Babylon to a glory far greater than that of conquest or material splendour,—that of having been, to the world of four milleniums ago, the Fountain of Law.

# CHAPTER IX

## NINEVEH AND ITS ROBBER-KINGS

"NINEVEH, that great city," shares with its older and longer-lived rival Babylon the distinction of having made upon the imagination of mankind an impression more deep and lasting than that made by any other city in the history of the world, with the exception, perhaps, of Rome. The traditions that were handed down of her greatness and her splendour were even wilder and more unreliable than those which lingered around the greater name of Babylon; but the monstrous exaggeration of the figures of Diodorus, and the statement of the Book of Jonah that Nineveh was "an exceeding great city of three days journey," themselves reveal the extraordinary mark which the city of Sennacherib and Sardanapalus had made upon the ancient world. The fact of such an impression is all the more striking when we remember for how short a time the last capital of the Assyrian Empire actually occupied her royal position as Queen of the Ancient East. Babylon, her inveterate enemy, had already passed through many centuries of alternate glory and decay before Nineveh began to rise from the position of an obscure provincial town to that of the capital of a world-empire; and long after the glories of Nineveh

were laid forever low in the dust, Babylon went on adding
new glories to her ancient splendours.

The old centres of Assyrian power were Asshur, Kalah,
and Khorsabad.  It was only with the reign of the mighty
Sennacherib that Nineveh, which he found a "wretched
poor place," began to enter upon the brief summer of her
splendour, and within a century of the time when the great
conqueror reared her mighty walls, her glory had faded and
passed away, never to be renewed.  There is no record of
any other city which, in so brief a time, inscribed its name so
deep upon the tablets of the human mind.

The reason, of course, is that Nineveh offered to the
world the crystallisation of the genius and power of the
Assyrian Empire, precisely at the time when that empire
was making its vastest bid for world-supremacy.  Asshur
might be the most ancient seat of Assyrian power, Kalah
might hold the records of a far more brilliant career of
conquest, Khorsabad might be the monument of a monarch
(Sargon), infinitely greater in reality than the men whose
names are associated with Nineveh; but it was Sennacherib
of Nineveh whose figure bestrode the Ancient East as the
typical world-conqueror, who threatened even the ancient
empire of the Pharaohs, and humbled, forever, as he vainly
imagined, the pride of Babylon; and it was Ashur-bani-pal,
the Sardanapalus of Greek story, who completed what his
grandfather had begun, and, by the capture of Thebes, laid
low in the dust the power of the great empire of the Nile.

The splendour of Nineveh came at a time when all the
ancient world was trembling before the revelation of the

grim and terrible meaning of World Power. The present
generation in Europe, which has passed all its days under
the blighting shadow of an arrogant and aggressive mil-
itarism, can realise something of the feeling with which
the smaller nations of the Ancient East beheld the colossus
of Mesopotamia straddling over the world, strangling all
independence in his blood-stained hands, and crushing down
with the most barbarous cruelty all opposition to his will.
The great Hebrew poet and statesman Isaiah has left us a
vivid picture of the Assyrian as he saw himself, and as he
appeared to the terrified nations around him, in the days
when Sennacherib was making Nineveh the centre of his
brutal dominion over the world. "By the strength of my
hand I have done it, and by my wisdom, for I am prudent;
and I have removed the bounds of the people, and have
robbed their treasuries, and I have put down the inhabitants
like a valiant man: and my hand hath found as a nest, the
riches of the people; and as one gathereth eggs that are
forsaken, have I gathered all the earth; and there was none
that moved the wing, or opened the mouth, or chirped."
Helpless under the heel of the conqueror, the world quivered
beneath his brutal cruelty, and hated, and feared. And
of all this terror, the prudence against which all the plans
of the nations were vain, the force against which their arms
were powerless, the brutality that wiped out in blood and
fire every hope of freedom, Nineveh was simply the concrete
expression.

For practically a century, the great city thus dominated
men's minds, making an impression, indelible as only the

impressions of unspeakable hatred can be; and then, exhausted by the gigantic efforts of her own ambition, she collapsed almost as swiftly as she had arisen. Scarcely twenty years after the close of the brilliant reign of Ashurbani-pal, the grandson of Sennacherib, the hosts of the Medes, or perhaps of the Scythians, allied with the Babylonian armies under Nabopolassar, the founder of the New Babylonian Empire, took vengeance upon Assyria for generations of cruelty and oppression; and Sin-sharishkun, the last king of Assyria, hopelessly defeated in the field, perished in the blazing ruins of his royal palace, and Nineveh was given over to the doom which she had imposed upon so many other cities. For a moment the world held its breath. Accustomed for so long to regard Assyria as inevitable and invincible, men could scarcely credit the good news of her fall. Then one universal shout of joy went up from all the nations. You can still feel the living fury of fierce delight, the reaction from generations of abject terror, in the grim verses of Nahum—"Draw thee waters for the siege, fortify thy strongholds; go into clay, and tread the mortar, make strong the brick-kiln. There shall the fire devour thee; the sword shall cut thee off, it shall eat thee up like the cankerworm. . . . Thou hast multiplied thy merchants above the stars of heaven; the cankerworm spoileth, and fleeth away. Thy crowned are as the locusts, and as the great grasshoppers which camp in the hedges in the cold day, but when the sun ariseth they flee away, and their places are not known where they are. Thy shepherds slumber, O King of Assyria, thy nobles shall dwell in the dust; thy people are scattered upon the mountains, and no man gathereth them. There is no healing of thy bruise; thy wound is grievous; all that hear the report of thee shall clap the hands at thee; for upon whom hath not thy wickedness passed continually?" The whole world said "Amen."

Then came down oblivion. Assyria speedily became merely a memory of unspeakable cruelty, and the ruins of her great cities formed the cores of great mounds of dust and rubbish, round which the idle fancy of the wandering tribes of the desert wove wild and fantastic legends. Erelong the very memory of their true names was lost. Two hundred years after the fall of the great city, Xenophon led his Ten Thousand past the site of Nineveh, and makes no mention of its name. A vague but persistent local tradition identified the two great mounds of Kouyunjik and Neby Yunus, on the east side of the Tigris, opposite to Mosul, with the city, and with the story of Jonah's mission to it; and various travellers, from Benjamin of Tudela, in the twelfth century, down to Carsten Niebuhr in 1766, have recorded their opinion that the tradition was well-founded. In the first quarter of the nineteenth century, Claudius James Rich made the first attempt at measurement and survey of the mounds in question, and gathered a few inscriptions, which found their way in the end, along with other relics collected from the mound of Nimrud (Kalah), to the British Museum. But no real exploration had been done, and no certainty reached as to the true site of Nineveh, till about the middle of the century, and the great city had lain practically unknown for more than 2500 years when its sudden resurrection amazed the whole world.

Up to the year 1842, Layard's words as to our knowledge on these matters were literally true—"A case scarcely three feet square enclosed all that remained, not only of the great city Nineveh, but of Babylon itself." How all this was changed in a few years, the site of Nineveh and other ancient cities of Assyria identified, her palaces traced out, her libraries ransacked, her literature made an open book to all who care to read it, and the story of her conquests and cruelties revealed, we must now try to tell.

In the year 1842, Paul Emil Botta was appointed French Consul at Mosul,—a most fortunate appointment from the point of view of science. He was then 37 years of age, and was well equipped, both by education and experience, for dealing with Orientals; while in addition he was an intelligent and careful observer. Acting on the advice of Julius Mohl, secretary to the French Asiatic Society, he began exploration in December, 1842, at the mound of Kouyunjik, the northern of the two mounds opposite Mosul. At first his labours met with little encouragement. Many fragments of bas-reliefs came to light, but no finds in perfect condition, or of large objects, were obtained. In spite of this discouraging start, however, he continued his excavations till March, 1843. At the very beginning of his work, an Arab dyer from Khorsabad, a village several miles to the north, happened to pass by the mound, and stopped to ask the meaning of the operations, wondering, no doubt, why Allah ever made such fools as these Franks. On being informed that the workmen were digging for inscribed stones, he declared that such things were to be found in abundance near his village, and offered to bring Botta as many as he wished. For the time Botta paid little heed to the offer, though the Arab even brought two bricks with arrow-headed inscriptions to Mosul. But when he was about to abandon the work at Kouyunjik in disappointment, he remembered his Arab dyer, and on March 20, 1843, he sent several of his workmen to Khorsabad, to make a trial exploration of the mound. Almost at once they began to find evidence of the truth of the dyer's statement, in the shape of two walls covered with reliefs and inscriptions, and on receiving specimens of their finds, Botta hastened to Khorsabad. He was only able to remain on the spot for a single day, but the evidence before his eyes was sufficiently convincing to induce him to sit down at once and send to Paris an account of his success, accompanied with sketches of the most important finds.

On April 5, 1843, Botta wrote to Julius Mohl the first of the series of letters which announced the beginnings of the resurrection of the Ancient East. "I believe myself," he said, "to be the first who has discovered sculptures which with some reason can be referred to the period when Nineveh was flourishing," and the modest statement, when read before the Asiatic Society, roused remarkable enthusiasm in France. The government at once made a grant towards the continuance of the excavations and the transport of the objects recovered, and as soon as possible dispatched a skilled artist, M. E. Flandin, to sketch such objects as could not be brought to Europe.   Meanwhile Botta was fighting at Khorsabad against the climate, sickness, the opposition of the inhabitants, and all the obstacles which Turkish officials have always known so well how to put in the way of intruding unbelievers.   His tact and perseverance triumphed at last even over the avarice and ignorant prejudice of the governor of Mosul, and when Flandin, in May, 1844, brought the firman authorising the resumption and extension of the excavations, he was allowed to proceed without further hindrance.   Three hundred Christian refugees were employed to excavate the untouched part of the mound, while Botta and Flandin devoted themselves to the copying of inscriptions and sketching of sculptures.

In November of the same year, Flandin returned to Paris with a large collection of fine drawings, and French interest, already roused by these, was a hundredfold increased by the arrival in 1846 of the original sculptures.   "When these gigantic winged bulls, with their serene expression of dignified strength and intellectual power, and these fine reliefs illustrating the different scenes of peace and war of a bygone race before which the nations of Asia had trembled, stood there again before the eyes of the whole world, as a powerful witness to the beginning of a resurrection of an almost forgotten empire, the enthusiasm of France knew no bounds." The results of the work of the two explorers were published in 1849-50, in five splendid volumes, illustrated with 400 plates, and in 1851 another expedition was sent out, under Victor Place, to complete the work at Khorsabad.   Unfortunately a large part of the objects discovered by Place was lost in the Tigris on the way to France; but the explorer's drawings and measurements enabled him to put before the world a fairly complete plan and restoration of the great palace and royal city which had lain so long beneath the mound of Khorsabad. Meanwhile the efforts of Rawlinson and others had gradually been furnishing the key to the interpretation of the inscriptions discovered, and it was found that Botta had disclosed, not Nineveh, as he had imagined, but the royal city of Sargon, the conqueror of Samaria (722 B. C.).

Dur-Sharrukin, "Sargon-Burgh," as the place was called, formed a great parallelogram, covering a space of 741 acres, and providing for a population of perhaps 80,000. Its wall was pierced by eight great gates, and was interrupted on its northwest side by the royal palace, which projected like a huge bastion into the plain. "The royal residence," says Hilprecht, "was erected on a lofty terrace, nearly 45 feet high and built of unbaked bricks cased with a wall of large square stones. At the northern corner of this raised platform, covering an area of nearly 25 acres of land, was an open place; near the western corner stood a temple, and at the centre of the southwest side rose the stage-tower belonging to it, and used also for astronomical observations; the rest was occupied by the palace itself. This latter was divided into three sections, the seraglio, occupying the centre of the terrace and extending towards the plain; the harem, with only two entrances, situated at the southern corner; and the domestic quarters at the eastern corner, connected with the store and provision rooms, the stables, kitchen, and bakery, at the centre of the southeast side. The seraglio, inhabited by the king and his large retinue of military and civil officers, like the other two sections of the extensive building, consisted of a great many larger and smaller rooms grouped around several open courts. The northwest wing contained the public reception rooms, —wide halls elaborately decorated with winged bulls, magnificent sculptures and historical inscriptions, glorifying the king in his actions of peace and war. We see him hunting wild animals, doing homage to the gods, sitting at the table and listening to the singers and musicians, or attacking strong cities and castles, subduing foreign nations, punishing rebels, and leading back thousands of captives and innumerable spoil of every description. The private apartments of the monarch, which were much smaller and simpler, occupied the southeast wing, close to the harem or women's quarter. The latter was entirely separated from the other two sections, even its single rooms, as the traces of discovered hinges indicate, being closed by folding doors, while everywhere else the entrances appear to have been covered with curtains."

Botta's discoveries had thus taught the modern world to realise that at a time when Europe was only beginning to emerge from barbarism, there were nations in the Ancient East which had reached a very high level of civilisation; and the interest in this old-world culture, so suddenly brought to light, was for the time intense. "There have been made other and even greater discoveries in Assyrian and Babylonian ruins since Botta's far-reaching exploration of the mounds of Khorsabad, but there never has been aroused again such a deep and general interest in the excavation of distant Oriental sites as towards the middle of last century, when Sargon's palace rose suddenly out of the ground, and furnished the first faithful picture of a great epoch of art which had vanished completely from human sight."

True in the main, this statement requires qualification as regards the English-speaking races, whose interest was roused, not so much by the discoveries of Botta as by those of his English fellow-labourer and friend, Austen Henry Layard. From early youth Layard was possessed by the craving after adventure and exploration in the East. In 1839-40 he travelled to Mosul and Baghdad, and visited several of the mounds of Mesopotamia, and in 1842 he met with Botta at Mosul. The French explorer, then at the beginning of his work, found in the young Englishman a kindred spirit, and their intercourse was never tainted by the international jealousy which so often disfigured the record of early Eastern exploration. From the first, Botta communicated his results to Layard, and his inspiration did much to feed the flame in the Englishman's mind. His journey completed, Layard settled for a time at Constantinople as unpaid assistant to the British Ambassador, Sir Stratford Canning, afterwards Lord Stratford de Redcliffe. The reports which reached him of Botta's brilliant success spurred his eagerness to be himself in the field, and finally his chief offered to advance £60 towards the expense of excavation. With such scanty means, Layard set out, in

October, 1845, to explore the ruins of Nineveh.  Burning
with eagerness to be on the spot, he "crossed the mountains
of Pontus and the great steppes of the Usun Yilak as fast
as post-horses would carry him, descended the high lands
into the valley of the Tigris, galloped over the vast plains
of Assyria, and reached Mosul in 12 days."

He had already decided to make the mound of Nimrud,
five hours down the Tigris from Mosul, the scene of his
first attempt; but he had first to reckon with Mohammed
Pasha, governor of the province, a characteristic specimen
of the old school of Turkish official.  This amiable individual, who had signalised his appointment by taxing the
inhabitants of the villages through which he passed for the
wear and tear caused to his teeth in consuming the food
with which they were forced to provide him, was gloating
when Layard saw him, over the success of a pleasant trick
which he had newly played upon his subjects.  He had
caused a report of his death to be circulated in the town,
and when the joy of the citizens had sufficiently declared
itself, had come to life again, and was now grimly amusing
himself by stripping of their property those whose rejoicing
had been most pronounced.  So enlightened a ruler could,
of course, conceive of no object in exploration but the
finding of treasure, and, equally of course, was of no mind
to see any one enriched but himself; so the problem of
evading his friendly curiosity was no easy one.

Layard was obliged to give out that he was going on a
hunting expedition, and, well provided with guns, boar-
spears, and other weapons, he set out, on November 8, 1845,

accompanied by Mr. Ross, a British merchant of Mosul, and two servants, to drift down the Tigris on a raft to the scene of his operations. Arrived at Nimrud, he quickly made friends with Awad, the sheikh of the Arab tribe whose camp lay near the mound, and this worthy volunteered to find workmen for him. Layard has described, in his own inimitable way, his sensations during the hours of darkness which lay between him and the fruition or disappointment of his hopes. "Hopes, long cherished, were now to be realised, or were to end in disappointment. Visions of palaces under-ground, of gigantic monsters, of sculptured figures, and endless inscriptions, floated before me. After forming plan after plan for removing the earth, and extricating these treasures, I fancied myself wandering in a maze of chambers from which I could find no outlet. Then again, all was reburied, and I was standing on the grass-covered mound. Exhausted, I was at length sinking into sleep, when hearing the voice of Awad, I rose from my carpet, and joined him outside the hovel. The day already dawned; he had returned with six Arabs, who agreed for a small sum to work under my direction."

Almost immediately it became manifest that his faith was justified. Before the forenoon was over, the ruins of a chamber lined with inscribed slabs had been uncovered, and setting three of his men to continue the excavation at this western side of the mound, he put the others to work at the southwest corner. Ere nightfall, the two gangs had partially excavated two chambers lined with inscribed alabaster slabs, those on the west side in fine preservation, those on the southwest calcined by fierce heat. "Night interrupted our labours," says Layard, "I returned to the village well satisfied with their result."

His satisfaction was well-warranted. One day's digging with six Arab workmen had resulted, as subsequent investigation showed, in the discovery of two Assyrian palaces! For a few days the work went on, with varying results, and on November 28 the first reliefs were discovered; but there were continual hindrances from the Turkish officials, and even Layard's Arab friends added to his troubles by their persistent belief that he was seeking for treasure. Awad came to him one day with a few fragments of gold leaf, found among the rubbish. "O Bey," said he, "Wallah your books are right, and the Franks know that which is hid from the true believer. Here is the gold, sure enough, and please God, we shall find it all in a few days. Only don't say anything about it to those Arabs, for they are asses and cannot hold their tongues. The matter will come to the ears of the Pasha." Great was his surprise to be told that he might keep all the gold he might find, and his opinion of the wisdom of the Frank suffered a considerable strain. The discovery of the reliefs brought obstruction to a head, and an order came from the amiable ogre at Mosul that the excavations were to be closed down at once, as they were disturbing the graves of true believers. Layard knew that this was a mere pretext, for no graves had been violated, and the officer in command of the irregular troops in the neighbourhood admitted to him that he had been ordered to make graves on the mound, and that his men had been employed for two nights in bringing tomb-stones from distant villages for that purpose. "We have destroyed more real tombs of the true Believers," said he, "in making sham ones, than you could have defiled between the Zab and Selamiyah. We have killed our horses and ourselves in carrying those accursed stones." Before long, however, the tyrant of Mosul exceeded even the fairly wide bounds allowed to a Turkish Pasha, and was superseded; and his successor proved more reasonable.

In February, 1846, sculptured figures of kings, courtiers, and soldiers began to come to light in abundance; and their appearance was speedily followed by one of the most dramatic incidents of the excavation—the discovery of the first winged human-headed lion. Again it will be best to allow Layard to tell his own story. "On the morning following these discoveries," he says, "I rode to the camp of Sheikh Abd-ur-rahman, and was returning to the mound when I saw two Arabs of his tribe urging their mares to the top of their speed. On approaching me they stopped. 'Hasten, O Bey,' exclaimed one of them, 'hasten to the diggers, for they have found Nimrod himself. Wallah, it is wonderful, but it is true! we have seen him with our eyes. There is no God but God'; and both joining in the pious exclamation, they galloped off, without further words, in the direction of their tents.

"On reaching the ruins I descended into the new trench, and found the workmen, who had already seen me, as I approached, standing near a heap of baskets and cloaks. Whilst Awad advanced, and asked for a present to celebrate

the occasion, the Arabs withdrew the screen they had hastily
constructed, and disclosed an enormous human head sculptured in full out of the alabaster of the country. They had
uncovered the upper part of a figure, the remainder of which
was still buried in the earth. I saw at once that the head
must belong to a winged lion or bull, similar to those of
Khorsabad and Persepolis. It was in admirable preservation. The expression was calm, yet majestic, and the outline
of the features showed a freedom and knowledge of art,
scarcely to be looked for in the works of so remote a period.
. . . I was not surprised that the Arabs had been amazed
and terrified at this apparition. It required no stretch of
imagination to conjure up the most strange fancies. This
gigantic head, blanched with age, thus rising from the
bowels of the earth, might well have belonged to one of
those fearful beings which are pictured in the traditions of
the country, as appearing to mortals, slowly ascending from
the regions below."

Always a master of the art of picturesque narrative,
Layard is nowhere more vivacious than in his description of
the bewilderment of Turk and Arab over the strange monster which had thus been revealed. The new pasha, doubtful whether Nimrod was a true-believing prophet or an
infidel, gave orders that his remains were to be treated with
all respect, and by no means to be further disturbed, and
intimated that the excavations had better cease. On various pretexts Layard managed to evade this order, and proceeded with his work, discovering many interesting reliefs,
among them the hunting scenes, now in the British Museum,

PLATE XXIII

WINGED MAN-HEADED LION

From the sculpture in the British Museum

and notable, even among Assyrian sculptures, for the vigour and spirit of their execution. The appointment of a new governor, Tahyar Pasha, "a perfect specimen of the Turkish gentleman of the old school," considerably eased the situation, and the explorer's path was further smoothed by the arrival of a firman authorising the continuance of the excavations. The pasha at length came in person to inspect the works, accompanied by all the dignitaries of the province, and protected against the demons of the mound by a large body of regular and irregular troops and three guns. The comments of the great men of Mosul were more curious than enlightening. "These are the idols of the infidels," said one, as they stood before the human-headed lion, "I saw many such when I was in Italia with Reshid Pasha, the ambassador. Wallah, they have them in all the churches, and the Papas [priests] kneel and burn candles before them." "No, my lamb," said a more experienced traveller, "these are the works of the Jin whom the holy Solomon, peace be upon him, reduced to obedience and imprisoned under his seal." The final judgment of Turkish officialdom was expressed by the deputy of the Cadi. "May God curse all infidels and their works! what comes from their hands is of Satan: it has pleased the Almighty to let them be more powerful and ingenious than the true believers in this world, that their punishment and the reward of the faithful may be greater in the next."

Hampered though he was, and continued to be to the last, by the meagreness of the funds at his disposal, Layard continued his work with indomitable courage and faith.

Turning for awhile from Nimrud, he drove trial trenches into the great mound of Kouyunjik, opposite Mosul, and was rewarded by the discovery of sculptures which he rightly judged to be of later date than those found at Nimrud, and probably contemporary with the reliefs of Khorsabad. Returning to Nimrud, he resumed his work in the northwest palace, which so far had yielded the best-preserved sculptures. His good fortune was as remarkable as ever; and even his untaught workmen began to catch the same enthusiasm which possessed their master. "The Arabs marvelled at these strange figures. As each head was uncovered, they showed their amazement by extravagant gestures, or exclamations of surprise. If it was a bearded man, they concluded at once that it was an idol or a Jin, and cursed or spat upon it. If an eunuch, they declared that it was the likeness of a beautiful female, and kissed or patted the cheek. They soon felt as much interest as I did in the objects discovered, and worked with renewed ardour when their curiosity was excited by the appearance of a fresh sculpture. On such occasions they would strip themselves almost naked, throw the kerchief from their heads, and letting their matted hair stream in the wind, rush like madmen into the trenches, to carry off the baskets of earth, shouting, at the same time, the war cry of the tribe."

By July, 1846, Layard had accumulated so many reliefs and inscriptions that he deemed it advisable to dispatch a number of them to London, where they were presented by Sir Stratford Canning to the British Museum. The result was that the authorities of the Museum secured from government a grant for the prosecution of the excavations, though unfortunately it was totally inadequate in amount. Layard, however, resolved to do his best with the means at his disposal, and continued the work. In judging his methods, unsatisfactory as they appear in the light of modern experience, we have to remember that he wrought throughout with means which, compared with those of later excavators, were ludicrously insufficient. The only wonder is that he succeeded in accomplishing so much.

By November he recommenced his task. In the north-west palace, which proved to be that of King Ashur-natsir-pal (885-860 B. C.), a series of very beautiful slabs was brought to light, representing the glories of the king in war and peace, the whole business of Assyrian warfare and hunting being pictured with extraordinary vivacity. The central palace of the mound was discovered to have belonged to Ashur-natsir-pal's son and successor, Shalmaneser II (860-825 B. C.). Layard's trench had reached a length of 50 feet without yielding anything of importance, and he was about to abandon it as fruitless, when the diggers unearthed an obelisk of black marble, nearly seven feet high, and in admirable preservation. It proved to be the triumphal stele of King Shalmaneser, who had recorded on it the leading events of his reign. On its four sides it bears twenty bas-reliefs, and 210 lines of cuneiform inscription, which contain the first direct reference in any Assyrian record to a person known to us from Scripture. "I received the tribute of Jehu, son of Omri, silver, gold, etc." Layard at once recognised the priceless value of his find. It was placed under strict guard, and on Christmas, 1846, it was sent, with 22 other cases of antiquities, to England, where Rawlinson shortly afterwards published a first attempt at a translation of its record.

April, 1847 found the work so far advanced that 28 halls of Ashur-natsir-pal's palace had been explored, and Layard turned his mind to the very difficult task of the transport of a couple of the winged lions and bulls, thirteen pairs of which had by this time been found.

The story of the making of the famous cart, which was a nine days' wonder to Mosul, of the way in which patience and skill triumphed over the wretched material with which a big engineering task had to be faced, and of how at last, spite of cables of rubbishy palm-fibre, which broke at the critical moment, bullocks which would not pull, and Arabs who pulled with more zeal than discretion, the huge monsters found themselves rafted to Basra, transshipped to England, and installed in the British Museum, is one of the epics of exploration. Rossetti has immortalised the advent of the "wingéd beast from Nineveh" in noble verse; but after all the best memorial of the feat is Layard's own brilliant narrative. The world learned, for the first time, from his sparkling pages, that the dry-as-dust record of archæological research might be transformed into a story as fascinating as any romance of hidden treasure.

The city which had thus been revealed at Nimrud was not Nineveh, but Kalah, for 220 years (885-668 B. C.)

the capital of Assyria, before the rise of Nineveh to pre-eminence under Sennacherib. Before leaving the scene of his labours, Layard devoted a short time to a preliminary exploration at Kalat Sherkat, the site of Asshur, the most ancient capital of Assyria, and at Kouyunjik, the true Nineveh. His work here was virtually only a tentative opening of the ground, yet, even so, his good fortune was still in the ascendant, and his trial trenches revealed the first traces, sorely marred by fire, of Sennacherib's great palace. In June, 1847, Layard returned to England for a time. The result of his two years' toil had been amazing. He had identified the sites of two Assyrian capitals, Kalah and Nineveh. At the former, he had discovered and partly explored the palace of Ashur-natsir-pal (885-860 B. C.), the palace of Shalmaneser II (860-825 B. C.), re-occupied and rebuilt by Tiglath-Pileser III (745-727 B. C.), the palace of Adad-nirari (882-873 B. C.), that of Esarhaddon (681-668 B. C.), and the poor remains of the palace of Ashur-etil-ilani (626- ? ), one of the last kings of the decaying empire. At Nineveh he had discovered the palace of the mighty Sennacherib (705-681 B. C.). Such a record no other explorer has ever been able to show for such a period. It adds a touch of irony to the story to read of the splendid reward with which the British government of the day repaid services so brilliant, services which will be remembered when the government which so acknowledged them is long since forgotten. "As a reward for my various services and discoveries," says Layard, with a simplicity beyond all satire, "I was appointed an unpaid attaché of her Majesty's Embassy at Constantinople."

Erelong, however, Layard was called to work more important and congenial than that of his lucrative post at Constantinople. He was requested by the British Museum to take charge of a new expedition to Nineveh, and in 1849 the work was resumed at Kouyunjik. The chief object of his labours was the excavation of the southwest palace at Kouyunjik erected by Sennacherib. It had been largely destroyed by fire in the great siege when the Median armies captured and sacked Nineveh, and many of the sculptured slabs were cracked and broken, or almost entirely calcined by the heat. Nevertheless a most wonderful series of pictures was secured, giving the record of Sennacherib's warfare in Babylonia, in Syria and other lands. "Without the knowledge of a single cuneiform character, we learned the principal events of Sennacherib's government, and from a mere study of those sculptured walls we got familiar with the customs and habits of the ancient Assyrians, at the same time obtaining a first clear glance of the whole civilisation of Western Asia." In particular a fine series of 13 slabs recorded the story of part of that famous campaign in southern Palestine, in which Lachish was captured, the Jerusalem of Isaiah and Hezekiah threatened, and the invader's power broken by that mysterious disaster when "the angel of the Lord went out, and smote in the camp of the Assyrians an hundred fourscore and five thousand." In addition, the investigation of the seventy halls and galleries of the great palace accomplished by the expedition revealed the fact that much of the building had been renewed and adorned by Sennacherib's grandson, Ashur-bani-pal, the last great ruler of the Empire.

It was in two of the chambers of this monarch that Layard made a discovery by no means so spectacular as that of the winged bulls, but of infinitely greater importance. In the process of clearing out these rooms he found that "to the height of a foot or more from the floor they were entirely filled with inscribed tablets; some entire, but the greater part broken into many fragments, probably by the falling in of the upper part of the building. They were of different sizes; the largest tablets were flat, and measured about 9 inches by 6½ inches; the smaller were slightly convex, and some were not more than an inch long, with but one or two lines of writing. The cuneiform characters on most of them were singularly sharp and well-defined, but so minute in some instances as to be almost illegible without a magnifying glass." What he had done was to discover part of the Royal Library of Nineveh, gathered by its later kings, and especially by Ashur-bani-pal; and the other half of it was found later by his assistant, Hormuzd Rassam, in Ashur-bani-pal's north palace at Kouyunjik. The value of such a discovery it is impossible to overrate. At once students were placed in possession of original documents, historical, scientific, legal, grammatical, and religious, to which the progress of the study of cuneiform had now given the key, and which provided the materials for the placing on the surest of bases of our knowledge on all the subjects with which they dealt. Nor was the boon thus conferred upon science limited to our knowledge of Assyria, for Ashur-bani-pal proved to have been a diligent collector of the literature of the sister kingdom of Babylonia, and many of the tablets were copies of far more ancient Babylonian writings, and grammatical manuals with bilingual texts, in which the Babylonian text is accompanied by its equivalent in the most ancient language of the land. These texts at once provided the foundation for the study of Sumerian, the language of the first civilisation of Babylonia. Had Layard's second expedition yielded no other results than this, it would still have been abundantly justified.

With this crowning triumph we may leave the great explorer's work, which he finally relinquished in April, 1851. His task was taken up by Rassam, his able assistant, whose efforts met with remarkable success. At Kouyunjik this explorer found, in December, 1853, the great palace of Ashur-bani-pal, the Sardanapalus of the Greeks. Apart from the importance of the discovery of the second half of the Royal Library, made in this building, the greatest interest attached to the wonderful series of sculptured slabs representing the king's lion-hunting. For the comparative study of Assyrian art, these slabs afford a most effective contrast with the earlier Nimrud series of Ashur-natsir-pal; and, while the earlier works are in some respects the stronger, it is difficult to imagine anything finer than the execution of some of the later ones. No animal sculptor, ancient or modern, has ever made more faithful or more realistic studies of the noblest of wild creatures than the Assyrian artist of 650 B. C. "The furious lion, foiled in

PLATE XXIV

W. A. Mansell & Co.

1. DYING LION          2. DYING LIONESS

From the slabs in the British Museum

his revenge, burying his teeth in the chariot wheels; the wounded lioness with her outstretched head, suffering agony, and vainly endeavouring to drag her paralysed lower limbs after her; or the king on his spirited horse with wild excitement in his face, and in hot pursuit of the swift wild ass of the desert,—all these scenes are so realistic in their conception, and at the same time so beautifully portrayed, that from the beginning they have found a most deserved admiration."

Even more important, however, was the discovery, already alluded to, of the second half of Ashur-bani-pal's library. From the centre of the hall in which the hunting scenes were found, Rassam excavated several thousand tablets, among them a number containing the Assyrian story of the Deluge; and these, in the hands of the able school of interpreters which had been growing up in Europe, proved invaluable for the reconstruction of the Assyrian and Babylonian mythology. Rassam was succeeded in the work at Kouyunjik by Loftus, whose most striking success was the discovery of the famous relief of Ashur-bani-pal and his queen feasting in a garden; but the funds at his disposal were lamentably insufficient, and the excavation of the great palace had to be abandoned.

Meanwhile the work of interpreting the records thus discovered had proceeded apace, and the European school of Assyriologists, headed by Rawlinson, Oppert, Hincks and Pinches, had succeeded in placing the study of cuneiform on a thoroughly sound basis. Their work received a wonderful impetus from the efforts of Rawlinson's assistant, George

Smith. Trained originally as an engraver, and employed by his chief only to sort out the fragments of the library of Ashur-bani-pal, and to piece together those which seemed to him to belong to one another, Smith soon developed an extraordinary talent for grasping the thread of the narratives with which he was dealing. One day, in the autumn of 1872, he came upon a large fragment containing the story of a great flood, and a huge ship, which rested upon the mountain of Nisir, and from which a dove, a swallow, and a raven were successively sent out to see if the waters had abated. Struck with its resemblance to the Biblical account of the Deluge, he persevered in his researches, and with infinite toil at last succeeded in piecing together a great part of the Babylonian legend of the hero Gilgamesh, of which the Deluge narrative formed a part. His account of the discovery created a profound sensation, and the *Daily Telegraph* voiced the public feeling by its offer of a thousand guineas for a new expedition to Assyria, under the charge of Smith, to search for other tablets of the legend. The offer was accepted, and by April, 1873, Smith was at work on the mound of Nimrud, which, however, yielded nothing of outstanding importance.

By the beginning of May, he gave up Nimrud, and moved to Kouyunjik, which he found a "vast picture of utter confusion and destruction." Many of Layard's underground galleries had collapsed, and the destruction thus wrought had been multiplied by the builders of the Mosul bridge, who had found in the mound a convenient quarry for material. The only course open to him was to clear once more the library rooms of the palace, and subject their contents to a thorough examination. His success was startlingly swift. On the fourteenth of May, he was inspecting the fragments of clay which had been the results of the day's digging, when he was amazed to find that one of them contained a portion of the story of the Deluge which fitted into the only place where there was a serious gap in the British Museum set. At once he cabled the news to London in the expectation that success so remarkable would result in the continuance and extension of the excavations; but the proprietors of the *Daily Telegraph* apparently considered that enough had been done "pour chauffer la gloire," and replied that as the object of the expedition had been attained, it was now to be abandoned. Disappointed and disgusted, Smith had no alternative but to obey; but he was scarcely back in London, when the trustees of the British Museum woke up, somewhat tardily, to the value of the opportunity in their hands, set aside a sum of £1000 for a new expedition, and directed Smith to return at once to Nineveh, and resume his search. By the beginning of 1874, he was once more at Kouyunjik; only to find, however, that the months lost in useless travelling had been worse than wasted. A change of governor had taken place during his absence, and every possible obstacle was put in his way by the new authority. One can imagine his private opinion of the muddling which had kept him running to London and back again on a fool's errand, while the priceless months of his firman were slipping away; but nothing remained save to make the most of the little time that remained.   For three months he worked at high pressure, employing as many as 600 men on the mound; then in April, 1874, he closed his trenches, and returned to England.   He had accomplished nothing spectacular; but the results of his labours, carried through in face of hindrances of all sorts that might well have seemed insuperable, can scarcely be over-estimated.   In his three months he had discovered 3000 tablets, covering almost every department of Assyrian literature, science, and mythology; and the value of his finds was ten-fold increased by the fact that in many cases the new tablets proved to complete or to extend the materials which were already in the possession of his museum.   The record of early Assyrian excavation is rich in instances of great work accomplished with small means, and difficulties overcome by patience and stubborn resolution; but seldom have these qualities been more conspicuously shown than by George Smith, whose work, in the eyes of the general public, was more or less of a failure.

In spite of the fact that he could point to no great sculptures as the fruit of his labours, the two books in which he published the account of his two expeditions ("Assyrian Discoveries," and "The Chaldæan Account of Genesis") achieved a great popularity, and awoke a renewed interest in their subject,—an interest destined to prove fatal to their author.   Smith was commissioned to go out to Nineveh on a third expedition, and the spring of 1876 found him once more in Mesopotamia.   But the fates had ordained that his last journey should be only to the grave.   He found on his arrival that cholera and plague were raging through the land; the terrified Arabs were beyond control, and the work for which he had come was an impossibility. For several months he fought despairingly against his evil star; but disease and panic proved an overmatch for even his indomitable courage. Broken down by overwork, insufficient nourishment, and exposure, he dragged himself at last, a dying man, to the house of the British Consul at Aleppo, and died there, a martyr in the cause of the science to which his life had been devoted.

Two years after the death of George Smith, Rassam resumed work in Assyria for the Trustees of the British Museum. His sphere was supposed to be Nineveh; but Rassam had a soul quite above the limitations of instructions or a firman where the question of the big game of archæology was concerned. Before he came out to Assyria, a friend had sent him some fragments of a bronze door-panel with figures and cuneiform inscriptions, and he had set his heart on tracking these out to their source. Erelong he found that his fragments had come from a mound called Balawat, about 15 miles east of Mosul. The place was beyond the limits of his firman, and the situation was complicated by the fact that the site had been used as a burying-place by the Moslems of the neighbourhood; but he took the double risk of the hostility of the Turkish government and the indignation of the local population, and began the excavation of Balawat. He had better luck than perhaps he deserved, for before long he succeeded in unearthing the remains of the great gates from which the fragments which had excited his curiosity had come. The

Gates of Balawat proved to have been set up by Shalmaneser II (860-825 B. C.), the successor of Ashur-natsirpal, and the maker of the famous Black Obelisk, already mentioned, on which occurs the first mention of Assyria's contact with Israel. The bronze gates were the chief fruit of Rassam's labours, though he also discovered a small temple, and a marble coffer, containing two tablets of Ashur-natsir-pal. At Nineveh, he also discovered a number of clay tablets, the most important among them being a ten-sided baked clay prism with the annals of Ashur-bani-pal inscribed upon it, and four barrel-shaped cylinders with accounts of the campaigns of Sennacherib.

Since the close of Rassam's excavations, the chief work done in Assyria has been that of the German expedition at Kalat-Sherkat, the site of Asshur, the most ancient capital of the land. The German excavations, which began in 1903, resulted in the discovery of many of the most ancient remains of the old city, going back as far as the reign of Ushpia, one of the earliest of Assyrian rulers; but the most remarkable result of the work was the unearthing of the remains of the Anu-Adad temple founded by Ashur-resh-ishi about 1140 B. C., with its double ziggurat corresponding to its double ownership,—a temple which remains the most complete example of Assyrian temple architecture. The great temple of Ashur, the patron god of Assyria, was also excavated, together with the remains of several palaces, and a great number of burials of no less than seven different types.

Before we go on to consider the light which all these

labours have cast upon the civilisation of the great robber-nation of the Ancient East, it may be worth while to glance briefly at the course of the national history which culminated in the brief splendour of Nineveh, and ended in her downfall probably about 606 B. C. The earlier days in which the Assyrian nation was growing to maturity do not bring it very prominently on the world-stage. Even up to the time of the Tell-el-Amarna letters (c. 1400 B. C.), Assyria has no dominant position in the Eastern world, though she appears as a power to be reckoned with. She ranks much on the same level with Mitanni under Dushratta, or Babylonia under Kassite rule and Ashur-uballit of Assyria writes to Amenhotep IV (Akhenaten) in much the same tone as the other northern potentates who in the latter days of the XVIIIth Dynasty grovelled before Pharaoh, and begged for subsidies. He has sent, he says, a royal chariot with a pair of horses, two white horses, a chariot without horses, and a seal of blue stone; and he asks for gold for a new palace which he is building. His ancestor Ashur-nadin-akhi sent to Egypt, and received 20 talents of gold, and the king of Khanigalbat got the same. Ashur-uballit would like as much. These were the last of the days when Egypt was unquestioned master of the ancient world; and times were to change before long.

For another century Assyria was still only proving her strength, and her ancient capital of Asshur was still sufficient for her kings; but with Shalmaneser I (c. 1300 B. C.), the extension of Assyrian conquest towards the west necessitated a shift of the centre of government, and the king builds a palace at Kalah, and begins the creation of a great city there. Tukulti-Ninib, who succeeded Shalmaneser, has left full annals of his reign, and of his conquest of Babylonia. He was building a new city to be called after his own name, Kar-Tukulti-Ninib, when he, like so many of his successors, fell by the hand of an assassin. His own son, Ashur-natsir-pal and the notables of the land rebelled against him, besieged him in his new palace, and slew him there. Thereafter for nearly two centuries the land plays a comparatively insignificant part in the struggle of the nations, and was, perhaps, passing through one of those periodic stages of exhaustion which, fortunately for the ancient world, were interpolated every now and then between the furious outbursts of lust for blood and plunder which were Assyria's chief contributions to history. But about 1100 B. C. the sceptre passes to Tiglath-Pileser I, a ruler of a type with which the surrounding countries were to become fatally familiar during the next five centuries, and Assyria definitely emerges as a claimant for world-power. Tiglath-Pileser's great prism-inscription, which, in the early days of Assyriology, was used as the test of a scholar's ability to read cuneiform, gives the details of his first five campaigns, against the Mushki, the Qummukhi, and other nations of the north and west. By the fifth year of his reign, he tells us, he had subdued 42 lands, and "made them of one tongue." With no less complacency he records on the same prism his exploits as a mighty hunter before the Lord, telling us that he slew 120 lions on foot, to say nothing of the 800 which he killed from his chariot, while he also killed ten mighty bull elephants, and brought four live ones to Asshur.

Tiglath-Pileser's great effort is again succeeded by a period of comparative quiescence, till in 890 another great soldier emerges in the person of Tukulti-Ninib II, of whose campaigns we have unfortunately only a very fragmentary record. He was succeeded by Ashur-natsir-pal III, the mighty captain and most ruthless monster who has left us the records which Layard so patiently unearthed at Kalah. He found Kalah, he tells us, a heap of ruins, and rebuilt it with great splendour. His annals as a conqueror come down to the eighteenth year of his reign, with a campaign in practically every year, and the amount of misery which he inflicted upon the world in that period is incalculable. "War is hell," and always has been, and probably always will be hell; but the Assyrian conquerors, as typified by Ashur-natsir-pal and his successors, made war in a fashion worthy of the very lowest pit of Gehenna. The heart sickens over the brutal record of thousands slain, of countless victims maimed, blinded, flayed, built alive into the triumphal column of the victor. Five years of such warfare left him with no rival from the Tigris to the Lebanon and the Mediterranean. In one of his later expeditions he emulated the feat of one of the greatest of his predecessors, and "washed his weapons in the Great Sea." His achievements were clearly the greatest that any Assyrian king had yet accomplished, and he left to his son Shalmaneser an heritage which it cost that notable soldier thirty-five years of constant warfare to maintain. Indeed the unstable character of Assyrian Empire is seen nowhere so clearly as in the fact that each new king has no sooner got the crown settled upon his head than he has to set out to make over again the conquests which his predecessor had made. Assyria's ruthless cruelty did not even serve its poor purpose of breaking the spirit of the nations on whom it was exercised.   It cowed them for the moment; but it roused in their hearts an unquenchable passion of hatred, and as soon as the first freshness of the impression of slaughter and torture had worn off, the conquered nation flew to arms again and faced the Assyrian tiger with new courage.   In the end it was the unconquerable spirit of freedom which wore down even the brutal might of the robber-nation.

Shalmaneser's famous Black Obelisk records 32 campaigns for the 35 years of his reign, and leaves one wondering how he could have been so remiss as to have neglected his obvious duty for those three peaceful years.   He inflicted on Babylon one of the many humiliations which the old Queen of the Euphrates had to endure at the hands of her younger rival, but from which she always rose again as unsubdued as ever; and he came in contact with Biblical history when at Karkar he defeated the army of the Syrian League, of which Ahab of Israel was a prominent member.

The next outstanding figure is that of Tiglath-Pileser IV (745-727), who is chiefly memorable to us as being the king to whom Ahaz of Judah appealed for help against his enemies, Pekah of Israel and Rezin of Damascus, with the natural result that the powerful ally whom he had called in made himself master of all the countries concerned. By the end of Tiglath-Pileser's reign, Assyria was lord of everything from the Mediterranean to the Persian Gulf and the Red Sea. We can only mention the great conqueror Sargon II, who in 722 B. C. captured Samaria, and reduced Israel to the position of a province of Assyria. The greatest relic of his reign left to us is the royal city and palace of Dur-Sharrukin, "Sargon-Burgh," which was excavated by Botta at the beginning of Assyrian exploration. There, in the magnificent palace which he had reared, he shared the fate which overtook so many Assyrian kings and was murdered. At his death Assyria was clearly the chief power of the ancient world, and its prestige was maintained undiminished by his son the redoubtable Sennacherib. Our conception of Sennacherib is chiefly coloured by the Bible account of the quarrel with Hezekiah of Judah, and the marvellous deliverance of Jerusalem from his overwhelming army. But though evidently the Assyrian king suffered a check in one of his Syrian campaigns, probably through an outbreak of plague among his troops, the set-back was only a momentary one, and in his later years he reached the very summit of his glory by the conquest and the destruction, final as he fondly thought it, of Babylon. He razed the ancient city to the ground, destroying all its temples and palaces as well as its fortifications, and turned the waters of the Arakhtu canal over its site. But Babylon was endowed with a vitality too great to be permanently eclipsed even by Sennacherib's fury, and under his son Esarhaddon she began to rise again from her ruins, and erelong was greater and stronger than ever. It was Sennacherib who made Nineveh that wonder of the world which so impressed the minds of all who saw the city during her brief period of supremacy. He found it "a wretched poor place," as he says, though we need not take his words literally, for the city had been mentioned as long before as the times of Hammurabi; and he left it the most splendid of capitals. Diverting to right and left the small river Khusur which now runs directly through the mounds of Nineveh, he led it into the moat which formed the outer defence of the vast walls of the city. These walls were 100 feet high, as Diodorus tells us, at no point less than 50 feet thick, and excavation has shown that near the gates this thickness was increased to 100 feet. These huge defences girdled an irregular parallelogram whose complete circuit was about seven miles. To secure a plentiful water supply, eighteen mountain streams were led into an aqueduct which brought their waters within the walls to fill the tanks and cisterns of the city. On the northern platform, where the junction of the Khusur and the Tigris formed an angle, the king reared his great palace. Its exploration, already referred to, has revealed over seventy chambers, though the work is only partially accomplished; and the palace must, to all appearance, have been the greatest ever built by an Assyrian monarch. Especially notable is the wonderful series of reliefs with which the walls of the huge building were adorned. "No series of bas-reliefs hitherto executed in Assyria, or even in the ancient world," says Goodspeed, "reaches the height of artistic excellence attained by those of Sennacherib. In variety of subject-matter, strength and accuracy of portraiture, simplicity and breadth of composition, they are among the most remarkable productions of antiquity." Along with this development of artistic power went a growth of literary activity. "The clear, pointed, but dry annals are enlivened by many little touches of humour, and a real gift for writing prose is developed. For pure dramatic power and vivid word painting the description of the battle of Khalule would be difficult to surpass in any early literature." It was Sennacherib who made the beginning of the great library of Nineveh which was completed by his grandson Ashur-bani-pal.

Sennacherib's brilliant reign of a quarter of a century was brought to a close by his assassination in 680 B. C. The chief events of the milder (for an Assyrian king) reign of his son and successor Esarhaddon were the restoration of Babylon and the conquest of Lower Egypt, where he stormed Memphis, and took the titles of "King of the kings of Egypt," and "King of Egypt and Kush." Times were changed from the days when Ashur-uballit wrote humbly begging Amenhotep III to send him twenty talents to help to build his new palace. But the glory of Assyria was only to endure for a brief space after its brilliant culmination. For a few years, under Ashur-bani-pal, the star of Nineveh shone brighter than ever. The last desperate effort of the Ethiopian Dynasty of Egypt under Tanutamen was crushed with ease by the merciless Assyrian soldiery, and even Thebes, the emblem to the ancient world of all that was most glorious and stable in human power, was ruthlessly sacked. The power of those old rivals of Assyria, the

Elamites, was broken at the battle of Tulliz, and their king Te-umman was slain and his head brought to dangle from the trees under the shade of which Ashur-bani-pal and his queen feasted. Even the last rebellion of Babylon under the king's own brother was swiftly put down, and in his later days Ashur-bani-pal reigned in Babylon as "Kandal-anu," as well as in Nineveh. Never had Assyrian art and literature reached greater heights than they did in the great series of reliefs with which Ashur-bani-pal rivalled those of Sennacherib, and the library which he gathered to complete the foundation of his grandfather. But Ashur-bani-pal was the last of the great kings of the robber-nation. For five centuries of bloodshed and cruelty it had thrown its blight-ing shadow across all the lands of the Ancient East; and now the great spoiler was to learn what it meant to be spoiled.

Two brief and inglorious reigns, those of Ashur-etil-ilani, and Sin-shar-ishkun, the sons of Ashur-bani-pal, bring the story to a close. When, somewhere about 606 B. C. the Babylonians and the Medes, or perhaps the Scythians, com-bined against the slackening rule of an overlord whose power was exhausted by his own ceaseless efforts to extend his empire, the end was not long in coming. For three years, the legend says, the mighty walls of Nineveh held out against all assaults, and then Sin-shar-ishkun, in de-spair, heaped all the treasures of his palace together into a vast funeral pyre four hundred feet high, and threw him-self and his wives into the flames. Few empires have ever fallen with less sympathy for the overthrow of ancient greatness; few empires have ever so justly earned the fury of hatred with which the Assyrian Empire was regarded, or the fierce exultation with which its downfall was welcomed.

We turn now in conclusion to consider the type of civilisation which has been revealed to us by the discoveries whose story has been told in this chapter. What manner of man was the Assyrian, what were his leading characteristics, and what was his contribution to the art, the culture, and the literature of the world? Perhaps no ancient race, with the exception of the Egyptian, has left us a fuller or more complete picture of the things in which it delighted than the Assyrian; and it may safely be said that no race, ancient or modern, has left us a more complete justification of the hatred and loathing with which its dominion was regarded by all the other peoples which were subjected to its tyranny. The great Hebrew prophet and statesman Isaiah has left in a single verse his judgment on the Assyrian conqueror at the height of his pride—a judgment to which, it may safely be said, all the other nations of the ancient world would have subscribed with the most perfect unanimity and satisfaction. "Woe to thee that spoilest, and thou wast not spoiled; and dealest treacherously, and they dealt not treacherously with thee! when thou shalt cease to spoil, thou shalt be spoiled; and when thou shalt make an end to deal treacherously, they shall deal treacherously with thee!" Assyria, alone of all the great empires of the world, woke no sympathy in any human heart outside of her own national boundaries, and wakes no sympathy still. Wonder, admiration, interest, if you like; but never the touch of nature which makes even the sternest judge relent for a moment as he surveys the ruin of greatness.  Egypt's hand had often been laid heavily enough upon the little Hebrew state; but even for Egypt in her overthrow the bitter Hebrew can feel regret; Tyre was to him the type of all that pride of life which was hateful in the sight of his God; yet even for Tyre he can mourn as he contemplates the downfall of so much magnificence.  But when Assyria reaps as she had sown for centuries, and Nineveh is laid low in the dust, the only utterance of Hebrew prophecy is a shout of savage joy—"At last!"  "All that hear the report of thee shall clap the hands over thee: for upon whom hath not thy wickedness passed continually?"

Such exultation seems to our minds almost indecent; and yet no one can deny that the Assyrian had given cause, and more, for it all.  We need not turn for our evidence to the prejudiced witness of the enemies of Nineveh; her own sculptured slabs and endless inscriptions have risen out of the dust of ages to bear witness against her, and to tell us, beyond the shadow of a doubt, of the things in which she delighted, and by which she lived.  In the face of the actual records which have been left, not by one king alone, but by king after king, for century after century, there can be no question as to what the verdict upon Assyria must be. It is this,—that never in the history of the world has there been another race, so brutally and senselessly cruel, so utterly devoid of that quality of mercy, without which no race can be really great, so entirely infertile in anything that makes for the real and permanent uplift of the human race, or in which supreme ability has been used for ages for one of the paltriest of ends—the mere attainment of mastery over other nations. A sweeping judgment, certainly; but one from which no one who has any knowledge of Assyrian records or Assyrian art will feel inclined to dissent.

No doubt there must have been times when even Sennacherib or Ashur-bani-pal unbent, and felt the power of softer emotions; but so far as the evidence goes by which they deliberately chose to be judged, they had hearts harder than the nether millstone, minds intent solely on the one narrow aim of self-aggrandisement, and ideals which never reached higher than the glorification of brute force. Take the art with which every Assyrian king delighted to adorn the palace in which he lived; and you can have no surer index of character than is given by the things which a man chooses as those on which his eyes shall rest, and in which he shall find pleasure day by day. The magnificent series of bas-reliefs that has come from the palaces of Ashur-natsir-pal, Sennacherib, and Ashur-bani-pal fills the mind with amazement and admiration. The human figure and face, it is true, are not portrayed on these reliefs with quite the same suppleness and vividness with which the sculptor depicts the various animals represented in the chase or in battle; but with this one qualification, it may be said that no work of such astonishing vitality was turned out by any nation of the ancient world. Compared with the swing and vigour of the reliefs of Assyria, even the finest work of Ancient Egypt seems stiff and conventional, though it has its own charm, which the Assyrian sculptor cannot rival, in other directions. It may be questioned whether any age has ever excelled the representations of animal form which are given in some of the reliefs of these Assyrian palaces. The dying lion, pierced by many arrows, and vomiting blood, the lioness stricken through the spine, and painfully trying to drag her paralysed hind legs, the lion and lioness taking their ease in the royal park, the hunting dogs straining on the leash, and the lion majestically stalking forth from his cage, or the scene in which the wild asses are being pursued and captured, these and many other reliefs show Assyrian art at its best, and form a series which can scarcely be paralleled in the artistic achievement of any other land. Even in the battle scenes, with the limitation already mentioned, the Assyrian sculptor shows a spirit of realism, and a grasp of the essentially pictorial aspects of his theme, which puts his work far above the conventional representations, beyond which, with one or two notable exceptions, the Egyptian artist never reached in his glorification of the deeds of the Pharaohs.

But when this has been said, one has said all that can safely be said in praise of the art of Ancient Assyria. Behind it all there lies the question of the spirit which inspires these remarkable achievements of the sculptor's art; and there is no other word to describe this than "devilish." An Egyptian Pharaoh could be cruel enough on occasion, and in the sculptures with which he adorned the outer walls of the temples of his gods, could show himself pitilessly trampling upon his foes, or clubbing helpless prisoners before Amen; but when he sought adornment for the chambers of his palace, he chose scenes of harmless enjoyment, or pictures of pastoral beauty, the calf gambolling in the meadow, or the wild duck fluttering among the reeds of the marsh; a Minoan monarch might have his brutal sport of bull-grappling, with its dreadful risks to the youths and girls who played their part in it; but he chose for the decoration of his walls the dancer whirling in her pirouette, the Cup-bearer carrying his wine-strainer, or the Blue Boy gathering white crocuses. Sennacherib or Ashur-bani-pal deliberately chose to brutalise the finest art at their command by making the walls of their palaces a shambles. What can have been the nature of kings who delighted to have continually beneath their eyes such scenes of horror as those in which their miserable captives are flayed alive, have their eyes put out, or are impaled, or in which the heads of the vanquished are slowly sawed off with a short dagger, to be borne in triumph before the victor, and hung up before him in the garden where he feasts with his wife? Cruelty was never lacking in these fierce early days; but the Assyrian was the only race which seems to have deliberately delighted in cruelty for its own sake, and to have found a diabolical satisfaction in the contemplation of scenes of human misery.

The story which is told us by the royal records is in entire accordance with the evidence derived from the national art. War, of course, was the business of kings in those days, and the phrase of the Hebrew historian, "the return of the year, when kings go out to battle," tells of a time when the spring campaign came as regularly as the spring flowers. In the case of a nation like the Assyrian, which lived on the proceeds of robbery with violence, we need not wonder that warfare was pretty continuous, though 32 campaigns in 35 years does seem a fairly liberal allowance of the sport of kings, even for a Shalmaneser; but there are ways and ways of making warfare. This was war, as made by a typical Assyrian conquerer—"I drew near to the city of Tela," says Ashur-natsir-pal. "The city was very strong; three walls surrounded it. The inhabitants trusted to their strong walls and numerous soldiers; they did not come down or embrace my feet. With battle and slaughter I assaulted and took the city. Three thousand warriors I slew in battle. Their booty and possessions, cattle, sheep, I carried away; many captives I burned with fire. Many of their soldiers I took alive; of some I cut off hands and limbs; of others, the noses, ears, and arms; of many soldiers I put out the eyes. I reared a column of the living and a column of heads. I hung up on high their heads on trees in the vicinity of their city. Their boys and girls I burned up in the flame. I devastated the city, dug it up, in fire burned it; I annihilated it."

At the city of Suru, which had revolted from this gentle rule, Ashur-natsir-pal gave another example of his tender mercies. "He flayed all the chief men who had revolted, and built a pillar at the city gate, which he covered with their skins. Some he walled up within the pillar, and some he impaled on stakes about it. Some he carried back to Assyria, and flayed them there, as he did Akhiababa, and

PLATE XXV

ASHUR-NATSIR-PAL ATTACKING A CITY

spread his skin upon the wall of Nineveh." Nor was the amiable practice of Ashur-natsir-pal in any way exceptional.

Every Assyrian king followed the example so enticingly set before him; the only question was one of his greater or less ability to imitate the laudable pattern which his ancestors had left him. If he did this with success, he might look for a happy reign; if he failed, or showed signs of a peaceful disposition, he was murdered to make room for some one who would show the merciless Assyrian troopers the sport in which they delighted. Try to form a picture of war as Ashur-natsir-pal has described it, with all its devilish cruelty of torture and devastation, and realise that this kind of thing went on, with greater or less intensity, for five centuries, during which the Assyrian robber-colossus bestrode the ancient world, and all the other nations cowered in his blighting shadow, waiting the time when their turn to be devoured would come; and you may come to understand, and to sympathise with that furious passion of hatred with which Assyria was regarded by the nations which she had robbed, slaughtered, and tortured for so long.

Yet there was another side to the shield, and it would be a mistake to regard the Assyrian as merely a devouring brute whose rule was simply one of blood and iron. On the other side of his being the Assyrian monarch was often a brilliant and lordly gentleman, with a notable, if a trifle bloodthirsty, taste in the fine arts, a passion for literature and history, and a piety which was perhaps all the more real because it was of a cast so sombre. We have heard Ashur-natsir-pal telling of his deeds in war; let us listen to him as he tells of his tastes in peace. "A palace for my royal dwelling-place, for the glorious seat of my royalty, I founded for ever, and splendidly planned it. I surrounded it with a cornice of copper. Sculptures of the creatures of land and sea carved in alabaster I made and placed them at the doors. Lofty door-posts of cedar-wood I made, and sheathed them with copper, and set them up in the gates. Thrones of costly woods, dishes of ivory containing silver, gold, lead, copper, and iron, the spoil of my hand, taken from conquered lands, I deposited therein." Or we may hear Tiglath-Pileser, as he tells of the piety with which he adorned the Temple of Anu and Adad. "I built it from foundation to roof larger and grander than before, and erected also two great temple-towers, fitting ornaments of their great divinities. The splendid temple, a brilliant and magnificent dwelling, the habitation of their joys, the house for their delight, shining as bright as the stars on heaven's firmament and richly decorated with ornaments through the skill of my artists, I planned, devised, thought out, built, and completed. I made its interior brilliant like the dome of the heavens; decorated its walls like the splendour of the rising stars, and made it grand with resplendent brilliancy. I reared its temple-towers to heaven, and completed its roof with burned brick; located therein the upper terrace containing the chamber of their great divinities; and led into the interior Anu and Adad, the great gods, and made them to dwell in their lofty house, thus gladdening the heart of their great divinities."

We may feel that such glowing descriptions have a

thoroughly Semitic flavour, in their delight in gaudiness and glitter; but at least the men who thought and planned in such a fashion cannot have been merely the ravening brute-beasts that one would fancy from the records of their warfare. Indeed the Assyrian presents one of the most extraordinary compounds that the world has ever seen of the natural brute and the cultured product of ages of civilisation. On the one side, a fiend incarnate, with a heart as merciless as an Indian brave, or a Bengal tiger; on the other a cultured and enlightened patron of art and literature. Yet on the whole it must be said of him, as of few of the races of the world, that the evil which he wrought heavily outweighs any good that he did. He has contributed next to nothing, save in his wonderfully vivid art, to the sum of the world's culture. He was totally lacking in originality and initiative, and all that he practised, save his own fiendish cruelty, he borrowed from the more ancient and more humane culture of Babylonia, which he so often wasted with fire and sword. Humanity owes a heavy debt to the great city of the Euphrates, which first gave to the world the conception of law and order, and the rudiments of science; but its debt to Babylon's great rival of the Tigris is more easily reckoned. It is little more than the lesson that force and fraud are the poorest of foundations for the building of an empire upon, and that in the end a nation gets the fate which it has deserved.

# CHAPTER X

In the year 1822, there was born, at Neu-Buckow, in Mecklenburg-Schwerin, a boy who was destined to be the pioneer of a revolution in knowledge which has changed all our ideas of the early civilisation of the Ægean, and has pushed back, by many centuries, the accepted date of the beginnings of civilised life in Eastern Europe. Heinrich Schliemann was the son of a clergyman, who, like many of his class, was richer in classical lore than in the world's goods. By his vivid narration of the great story of the Trojan War, the worthy pastor early inspired in his son's mind a passionate love of the splendid romance of Greek history, and the flame was fed by a Christmas gift which the boy received when he was seven years old. It was a child's history of the world, and its picture of Troy in flames, with Æneas fleeing out of the Skaian Gate, his father Anchises on his shoulders, and his son Ascanius led by the hand, made a deep impression on him, and filled him with a keen longing to visit the scenes of these ancient heroisms, and see what might still remain of their old-time splendours. At this tender age, he had already settled with a girl-playmate that some day they would marry, and together discover Troy. The vision was to be splendidly

realised, though not in the company of his early sweetheart.

The boy's education had progressed so far that by his
tenth year he was able to send to his father a Latin essay
on the Trojan War; but, soon after, it began to become
apparent that to educate adequately a family of seven on
a country pastor's income was beyond the bounds of possibility. Accordingly Heinrich had to sacrifice his classical
tastes on the altar of hard necessity, and in 1836, at the
age of fourteen, he was apprenticed to a country grocer,
and was obliged to devote the mind which longed to be
wandering on the plains of Troy with Hector and Achilles,
to the selling of herring and potato-brandy, and the sweeping out of a dingy little shop. Yet even in such unfavor-
able circumstances, his appetite for the classics survived, and
found the quaintest means of gratification. One of the
visitors to the shop was a miller's carter, who had once been
in good circumstances, and had been well educated, but
had fallen in the world, and taken to drink. Even in his
degradation, however, he had not quite forgotten his Homer,
and the little grocer's shop witnessed a curious scene, which
Schliemann must be allowed to describe in his own words.
"That evening he recited to us about a hundred lines of the
poet, observing the rhythmic cadence of the verses. Although I did not understand a syllable, the melodious sound
of the words made a deep impression upon me, and I wept
bitter tears over my unhappy fate. Three times over did
I get him to repeat to me those divine verses, rewarding his
trouble with three glasses of whiskey, which I bought with

the few pence which made up my whole wealth. From that moment I never ceased to pray God that by His grace I might yet have the happiness of learning Greek."

The young apprentice was transferred to Amsterdam, where he had to run errands all day long; and as the task imposed no great strain on his mind, he used the mental leisure for the purpose of carrying on his education. In his first half-year at Amsterdam he made himself master of English, and in the next, of French, managing, incidentally, to save for intellectual purposes the half of his salary of 800 francs. Fired by his success, the third half-year saw Dutch, Spanish, Italian, and Portuguese added to the list of his linguistic attainments. To such fiery energy, nothing could be denied. The young grocer made his mark in business as rapidly as in study, and by the time he was 41, he had amassed a large fortune, and was able to retire, and to devote himself to the true aim of his life.

The first six years of his leisure were spent in travel, chiefly among the scenes of his boyish enthusiasms, and in the publication of the account of his journeys. In April, 1870, he cut the first sod of the excavation of which he had dreamed as a boy of seven, and stood committed to the task of revealing the site and remains of the ancient capital of King Priam. The spot which he chose as the scene of his excavations was itself an evidence of his independence of mind, and the tenacity with which he held his convictions. For he chose Hissarlik, three miles from the Dardanelles, the site of the New Ilion of Græco-Roman times, and that favoured by all ancient tradition as the position of the mighty fortress which the Greeks besieged for ten long years. In thus adhering to ancient authority, he was going against practically the whole weight of more modern Continental opinion, which had deserted Hissarlik and fixed upon Bunarbashi, some considerable distance inland, as the true site of the city. Schliemann, however, was not the man to be frightened out of his convictions even by such names as those of Moltke, Kiepert or Curtius. He was convinced that Hissarlik was not only the most natural site for such a city as Homer describes, but that ancient tradition, unless it asserts a manifest impossibility, is to be regarded with respect; and he was ready to stake his money and his reputation upon his faith.

The earlier stages of the work were not marked by any noteworthy success. Though a trial cutting was made early in the season, it was not till the end of September, 1870, that the excavations were authorised by the Turkish Government, and systematic work did not begin till October 11. Even then, the number of workmen was quite insufficient, and their equipment was hopelessly inadequate. When work ceased for the season on November 24, there was nothing to show for the effort but a Hellenistic building in the upper stratum of ruin, and, at a depth of 33 feet, in the great trench which had been cut in the north side of the hill, a few rough brick walls and stone implements. In March, 1872, the excavations were resumed with somewhat better equipment. The digging was carried on till the middle of August; but the results were completely disappointing, and Schliemann's faith in his theory must have been sorely tried. Nevertheless he returned to Hissarlik with unabated enthusiasm in 1873, beginning work so early as February 1. The severity of the early Ægean spring, with its chilly winds whistling through the chinks in the thin wooden shed in which the explorers lived, severely tried Schliemann and his young Greek wife, who shared her husband's labours and enthusiasms. During the day, when they were busy with the excavations, the cold was bearable; "but of an evening," says the explorer, "we had nothing to keep us warm except our enthusiasm for the great work of discovering Troy."

Patience and endurance were, however, now to reap their first reward. Bit by bit the walls of a fortified town began to disclose themselves. On the southwest of the hill three great gates were revealed. The roadway of the largest of these passed through a huge tower, 130 feet by 59, projecting 59 feet beyond the city wall. To Schliemann it seemed certain that this was the "great tower of Ilios" mentioned by Homer as guarding the Skaian Gate. When the Goddess Iris brings Helen from her chamber to view the duel between Menelaos and Paris, "they came straightway to the place of the Skaian Gates. And they that were with Priam and Panthoos . . . being elders of the people, sat on the Skaian Gates." To the second gate a massive ramp of approach led up, 26 feet broad, and paved with large slabs of stone. Schliemann was now confident that he had succeeded in the object of his search, and discovered the very walls around which the strife between Greek and Trojan surged for so long; and he was confirmed in this belief by the discovery of a treasure of golden diadems, bracelets, earrings, and weapons of wrought copper, spear-heads, axes, and daggers, which seemed not unworthy to have belonged to a great king.

This discovery was made in May, 1873, in the fortification-wall near the second gate. Again Schliemann must be allowed to describe it in his own words. "While following up the circuit wall, and bringing more and more of it to light," he says, "I struck, at a point slightly north-west of the gate, on a large copper article of the most remarkable form, which attracted my attention all the more as I thought I saw gold glimmering behind it. On the top was a layer of reddish and brown calcined ruins from 4 to 5 feet thick, as hard as stone, and above this again the wall of fortification (5 feet broad and 20 feet high), which must have been erected shortly after the destruction of Troy. In order to secure the treasure from my workmen and save it for archæology, it was necessary to lose no time; so, although it was not yet the hour for breakfast, I immediately had the *paidos* (interval for rest) called, and while the men were eating and resting I cut out the treasure with a large knife. This involved risk, as the fortification wall, beneath which I had to dig, threatened every moment to fall on my head. And indeed I should not have succeeded in getting possession of the treasure without the help of my wife, who stood at my side, ready to pack the things I cut out in her shawl and to carry them away. As I found all these articles together, packed into one another in the form of a rectangular mass, it seems certain that they were placed inside a wooden chest."

To a man of Schliemann's Homeric enthusiasm, there could, of course, be only one interpretation of such a find. The treasure was "Priam's Treasure," and the diadems might have been worn by Hecuba or Andromache. Indeed the workmanship and design of the articles of adornment, and of the gold and silver cups and dishes with which they were accompanied, were sufficiently remarkable to render such an assumption not impossible. The further fact that the whole city whose remains were thus coming to light had obviously been destroyed by fire, and succeeded by an entirely new creation whose walls rested on the debris of the older settlement, seemed to confirm the supposition that the Homeric Troy had indeed been discovered. Accordingly, when after this third campaign Schliemann published the results of his excavations in "Trojan Antiquities," this view was maintained and the largest building discovered within the city wall was named "Priam's Palace," to keep company with "Priam's Treasure," and "the Skaian Gate." For the moment the romance of the discoveries, and of the idea that the actual scene of the events of Homer's immortal song had been brought to light, stirred the world out of its usual apathy with regard to such matters, and in England, at all events, under the enthusiastic championship of Mr. Gladstone, there was a disposition to believe that the explorer had made his theories good.

Scholars, however, were doubtful. They could not accept the small citadel, only 320 feet across, with its masonry of small stones and clay, as the mighty fortress whose walls were reared for King Laomedon by Poseidon and Apollo. Moreover the articles of adornment and the weapons found were much more primitive than could have been expected of a civilisation so advanced as that depicted by Homer, the copper weapons, especially, appearing a poor substitute for the bronze and iron of which the poet sings. In the end these criticisms proved to be soundly based. Schliemann had not discovered, as he believed, the actual Troy of the Iliad, though he was right as to its position. What he had done was a far bigger thing. He had revealed the first traces known to the world of a civilisation far older than the Homeric, and given the first impetus, though on Asiatic soil, to that search for the origins of European civilisation which has resulted in the establishment of its right to be equated, in point alike of date and quality, with the immemorial cultures of the Nile and Euphrates Valleys. He went to his grave before the actual discovery of the unmistakable Homeric Troy was communicated to the world by his colleague, Dr. Dörpfeld; but he would have been more than compensated for the disappointment had he foreseen the wonderful harvest which has been reaped from the seed which he first sowed.

Meanwhile the Turkish Government, aggrieved by the division of the spoils of the third campaign, began to put obstacles in the explorer's way, and started a lawsuit against him which resulted in a fine of 10,000 francs being imposed upon him. With characteristic impetuosity, Schliemann sent 50,000 francs, instead of 10,000, to the Ministry at

Constantinople, hoping to gain the goodwill of the Government for his work; but for several years his position with regard to Turkish officialdom was a difficult one. When, in April, 1876, he resumed work at Hissarlik, he was subjected to continual annoyance by the governor of the Troad, and found that excavation in such circumstances was an impossibility. Accordingly, in July of that year, he crossed to Greek soil, and began at Mycenæ a series of excavations which proved amazingly fruitful. The work at Mycenæ and Tiryns, however, must be dealt with by itself; we therefore return with the explorer to the earlier scene of his labours.

Successive campaigns in 1878-1879, led only to comparatively insignificant results, though this period was marked by the publication in 1880 of his great work "Ilios," in which he summed up the conclusions of his labours, modifying somewhat the confidence of his earlier certainty as to the Homeric origin of his finds. In March, 1882, he began to work again on the old site, in the company of Dr. W. Dörpfeld, a trained and skilful archæologist, whose collaboration was of great service to him. The result of their work was to establish the fact that on the site there had stood at various periods no fewer than nine successive cities (seven as Schliemann reckoned them). Of these the oldest and smallest was a fortress built on the virgin rock, and covering an area only 150 feet in breadth. Upon its debris, which formed a new level from 11 to 20 feet higher, rose the Second City, which Schliemann had identified, wrongly, with the Homeric Troy. Its walls were built of brick on stone substructures, and while the Great Treasure (if it be not a relic of later date which has got misplaced) is a witness to a certain degree of opulence and culture, the rude and often grotesque pottery points to a period considerably earlier than that of the fine Mycenæan work which belongs to the true Homeric period. This city had perished in a vast conflagration, like Homer's Troy; but its fate had befallen it many centuries before the siege of Priam's capital.

Above the Second City, came three successive village settlements, of small importance, then a fortified town, the Sixth City, to which we shall have to return, then a small unfortified settlement, which carries on the history of the site to the time of Alexander, then the Hellenistic Ilios, which was destroyed by the Roman general Fimbria in the Mithridatic War; and lastly a Græco-Roman city, belonging to the earlier centuries of our era, with the remains of a theatre, gateway, and other buildings. Thus the mound of Hissarlik is seen to have had a sufficiently chequered history, lasting for at least 3500 years.

It was with regard to the Sixth City that the later important work of Schliemann and Dörpfeld was accomplished. In 1890, they began excavating a mound of debris outside the Southwest Gate of the Second City, but within the area of the Græco-Roman citadel. Schliemann hoped to find here the graves of the ancient kings of Troy, as he had found the Royal Graves at Mycenæ; instead, he only missed, by the narrowest chance, the discovery, which he could scarcely have failed to recognise, of

the Homeric Troy of his dreams.  In this mound were found
the remains of a great circuit wall, and of several important
buildings, with pottery of the type which was now recognised
as Mycenæan.  Dörpfeld at once saw that this discovery
put the Second City out of court as a claimant for Homeric
honours.  "The second stratum," he says, "must be older
than this stratum with the Mycenæan vases,—how much
older it is impossible to say, but the interval cannot have
been a short one, as between the two lie three other strata
of poor settlements."

Even at this stage Schliemann and his colleague would
probably have gone on to draw the conclusion that now at
last they had discovered the unquestionable Homeric Troy,
but for the fact that the extent of the ruins which they had
uncovered was not sufficient to warrant them in saying that
they had found a city at all.  Unfortunately the unhealthy
summer heat obliged Schliemann to suspend operations,
with the intention of resuming them the following year.
Had he been able to carry out his intention, there can be
no doubt that to him would have fallen the glory and satisfaction of proving that his early dreams had been true
inspirations.  It would have fittingly crowned the splendid
labour of a devoted life, if this had been granted; but it
was not to be.  The great explorer died suddenly at Naples,
on December 26, 1890, and it was left to his colleague to
complete the demonstration that Schliemann's life-work
rested on indestructible foundations.

The fact that the remains of the Sixth City were not
sooner recognised was due to the almost total destruction

of the central portion of it by the builders of the Græco-Roman Ilios. Like all other Mycenæan cities, Troy was a terraced city, rising in the centre to a point at least 7 metres higher than the lowest level within the walls. Naturally the most important buildings, such as the palace, stood on the highest point of the hill, as at Mycenæ. After the destruction of the city, the people of the Seventh and Eighth settlements reared their small houses upon the rounded mound of debris; but the Romans were not content with such a hampered site for their New Ilium. They peeled away the whole summit of the mound, and used the materials thus obtained to level up the lower slopes of the hill, in order to secure a broad platform for their great buildings; and thus their solid foundations go down in many instances to the layer of debris of the Fifth City. In the result there only remains of the Homeric Troy a portion of the lower stages of the circuit wall, and a narrow band of buildings, about 40 metres wide, within the enceinte. Thus Schliemann, working almost entirely on the inner portion of the mound, failed to come across the Homeric buildings until he began to dig outside the southwest gate of the Second City,—too late in his life for him to gain the crowning triumph which his twenty years of patient toil had so well earned—the sight of the actual walls which Hector defended, and from which Andromache saw the body of her gallant husband dragged at the chariot wheels of Achilles.

And now as to the poor remnants of Priam's stately citadel, which Dörpfeld has unearthed. The circuit wall still stands on the east, south, and west to a length of about

300 metres; but on the north it has been destroyed, probably by Archæanax of Mitylene, who used the stones, as Strabo tells us, to build Sigeion,—an act of vandalism for which one can only hope that he is haunted by the shades of all the heroes who fell on "the ringing plains of windy Troy." Even when the circuit was complete, the area enclosed by the wall was comparatively small, and we must dismiss from our minds all idea of a great and populous city, and substitute for it that of a crowded citadel crowning a low mound, formidable enough, indeed, for the strength of its defences, but by no means imposing in size, even when compared with other fortresses of ancient times. The area enclosed by the walls of the Second City, which had a circuit of 350 metres, was only 8000 square metres. That of the Homeric City, with a circuit of 500 metres, was considerably larger—about 20,000 square metres. Thus it is almost exactly as large as the citadel of Tiryns, 5000 square metres smaller than the Acropolis of Athens, and 10,000 smaller than Mycenæ. In fact an ordinary city-square would hold the whole of Homer's Troy, with something to spare,—a curious instance, when we think of the place which Troy has held, and the influence which it has exerted on men's minds for two and a half millenniums, of the fact that size and importance are two very different things.

The remains consist of a great circuit wall, pierced by three gates, and strengthened by three flanking towers. Within the wall, and on a somewhat higher level, was a ring of buildings, dwelling-houses, to all appearance, which rose from a wide terrace which ran round the whole city in-

PLATE XXVI

WALLS OF TROY—SIXTH CITY

side the wall. As we have seen, the central portion of the city, higher and containing the most important buildings, has entirely disappeared, having been swept away by the Romans, during their levelling operations, to secure a wider basis for the buildings of New Ilium. Homeric Troy, therefore, presents somewhat the appearance of a cocoanut with an outer shell and a layer of material within, and a central void. The best preserved section of the wall is on the eastern side, where it still stands to a height of about 20 feet. It is built of squared blocks of first-rate workmanship, and like the wall of the Second City, it has an inward slope as it rises, the lowest course projecting about 6 feet in advance of the course at the 20-foot level. Its thickness at the present top is about 16 feet, and, of course, it is correspondingly thicker below, though the actual measurement has not been ascertained. Sufficiently imposing as this massive rampart is, however, it was only the base of the true wall, which rose vertically above this substructure, and was originally built of crude brick, with a thickness the same as that of the foundation on which it rested. Later, this wall was superseded by a parapet of hewn stone, fragments of which still remain to a height of 6 or 7 feet. It was possible to make this rampart thinner, as its materials were so much stronger than the crude brick; accordingly its thickness was only 6 to 6½ feet, and a 10-foot gallery thus ran round inside the parapet, on the level of the top of the substructure. The wall is built in straight sections of about 30 feet long, and at each angle where these join it has a shallow set-back whose projection, nowhere so much as a foot, is not sufficient to be of use for flanking purposes, and can only have served the purely ornamental purpose of giving relief and shadow to the appearance of the wall from without.

Dörpfeld is of opinion that the masonry, alike in its workmanship, and in the slope of the lower part, finds its true analogy in Egyptian building practice, and suggests that there may have been a distinct connection between Troy and Egypt. May the old tradition that the walls of Troy were not built by native effort, but by Poseidon and Apollo, perhaps preserve a glorified version of an actual fact—that the builders, or at least the architects, were men of an alien, and even more ancient culture, coming over the Ægean, Poseidon's realm, in the galleys which make so picturesque an element in many an Egyptian picture and relief?

The existing portion of the wall was pierced by three great gates. Of these, one, on the southwest side, was not in use when the siege ended in the sack of the city. It had been closed by a cross-wall, very probably during the siege, and with the obvious idea of lessening by one the number of weak points which needed to be strongly held. On the south lay the second gate. Probably, from the fact that it is in the natural line of approach from the plateau beyond the walls, and is practically in line with the great gate of the Second City, and with the main entrance of the sacred precinct of the Ninth City, it was the chief gate of Troy. It was flanked by one of the towers, and was further protected by two sacred stone pillars, which stood as guardians, like Jachin and Boaz before Solomon's Temple.

The third gate, on the east, is formed in an overlap where

PLATE XXVII

WALL AND POSTERN-STAIR, TROY

the northern wall meets the southern. The two do not actually meet, but run parallel to one another for a short space, and the gate, in the northern end of this overlap, is thus approached by a right-angled turn along a narrow passage which forces the assailant to expose his right or unshielded side to the archery of the defenders. This plan became the regular rule in all subsequent Greek fortresses. It is probable that there may have been a fourth gate on the northwest side; but here the wall has never been bared, and, as we have seen, the greater part of the north wall was destroyed and removed in ancient times.

Of the three towers whose remains survive, the most important is the Water-Tower, which stands at the northeast angle of the fortress. It still rises to a height of nearly 30 feet, and is close on 60 feet broad. In the centre of it is a great well more then 12 feet square, going down to a depth of over 30 feet. This, no doubt, was the chief water supply of the garrison and populace, and its strong defences show the importance attached to it. Four steps lead down to the well-mouth, and another staircase led up from it to the streets of the city. One may imagine the daily traffic on the old well-stairway during the long months of the great siege, and the anxious watch that was kept on the Water-Tower lest the very life-blood of the city should be cut off by the capture of its main defence. Two other wells were found within the circuit wall, so that Troy was fairly well provided with the supply without which all her mighty walls would have been useless.

Within the walls are the remains of a few houses, nearly

all built on one simple plan—that of a large hall with a projecting porch in front.    Whether or not the houses were so simple in arrangement as their foundations would seem to indicate, cannot be determined; but their simplicity of plan forms a strong contrast to the complexity of the contemporary Minoan houses and palaces at Knossos and elsewhere.    No central hearth has been found, such as was the rule at Tiryns and Mycenæ.    The houses are built radially, the passages between them running up towards the summit of the mound like the spokes of a wheel.    The ancient stronghold of Priam was completely destroyed by an enemy—in whom we may with little hesitation recognise Agamemnon and his "well-greaved Achæans."    The spoilers did their work thoroughly, for the Sixth City is remarkably poor in objects of value.    Nothing in any way approaching to the richness of the great treasure of the Second City rewarded the explorer's search, but the pottery found was sufficient to establish, beyond the possibility of question, that the city belonged to the Mycenæan period, and to its latest years.    A part of the ware is imported Mycenæan, while the rest is native work such as is found from the very beginning of the settlement, though with some attempt at an adoption of Mycenæan adornment. "We may therefore say with confidence," says Dr. Leaf, "that the Sixth Stratum flourished during the second half of the second millennium, say from 1500 to 1200 or 1100 B. C."

Such, then, was the structure of the greatest City of Romance that the world has ever known, so far as its remains have been revealed by the spade, and such was the result of the life-work of the man who began as the little grocer's apprentice, dreaming of the splendours of Ilion and its palaces. In one way it may seem as if Schliemann had little to show for a lifelong devotion, and twenty years' hard work—a few hundred yards of crumbling wall, and the weathered foundations of a handful of ruined houses; and even so the inexorable call of death before the actual triumph, such as it was, was reached. Troy, as we now know it, is a poor substitute for the stately towers and palaces, the teeming throngs and the great bronze-clad hosts of Homer's dream-picture. A mean little place that you could hide away in an obscure corner of one of our modern cities, and forget all about it!

Yet the greatness of a city is not measured by the circuit of its walls or the magnificence of its palaces and temples, but by the heroism of the men and women who made and fought for it, and of the deeds which were done within and around it. Judged by that standard, Troy's greatness is unquestioned and secure. The city which bred the knightly valour and generosity of Hector, and the wifely devotion of Andromache, will still be great when half of our vast modern Babylons are tumbled heaps of unremembered ruin; and its name will forever be linked, not only with the name of the mighty minstrel who sang its glories and its woes, but with that also of the man whose boyish soul was inspired by the immortal song to recover for the world the scene of the noblest story of human endurance and courage that our race has known.

# CHAPTER XI

WHEN we attempt to form some idea of the life and civilisation of Greece in those early days which go before the
beginnings of her history, and are only commemorated in
their later stages by the brilliant pictures of an advanced
and splendid culture presented in the Iliad and Odyssey,
we must dismiss from our minds all that we have been
accustomed to call *Greek* from our acquaintance with the
later story of Hellas. The very race with which we are
dealing is different; its dress, its habit of life, its culture, and
its art, all are different, though elements from all of them
may have been mingled with others, derived from very
different sources, to compose that wonderful alloy which
we know as the civilisation of Historic Greece. Probably
the thing which would strike us most forcibly, as it would
strike us first, were we able to transport ourselves to the
Greece of the pre-historic period, would be the total disappearance from the picture of the one feature without
which "the glory that was Greece" would be shorn of half
its radiance—the City-State, with its complex life, and its
splendid adornment of architecture and art. Nowhere in
this most ancient Greece would you see anything even

remotely reminding you of the historic Greek city, such as Athens, with its temple-crowned Acropolis, crowded with immortal wonders of human genius and craftsmanship, and the busy city spread beneath in the shadow of the sacred rock,—the fairest sight, of all in which man's handiwork has part, on which the sun ever shone.

In place of that fair scene you have to substitute the picture of a thinly-peopled land, with narrow strips of poor cultivation where the hills fall towards the sea or to a river bed, with rough trade-tracks winding up the valleys, along which the wares of the traders whose little galleys are beached in the sandy bay find their way from one petty hamlet to another. Here and there on the line of the trade-route rises a forbidding hill or rock, crowned with a grim stronghold, and here, like an eagle in his eyrie, dwells the overlord of the district, Basileus, or King, as he calls himself, with a kingdom which may extend for a few miles round his hold, till it meets the sphere of influence of a brother robber, perched also on his rocky height. These nests of the robber-barons, where each gathered round him as many retainers as he could lodge and feed within the fortress walls, were the only cities of which Greece could boast in these prehistoric days; and their very position, almost invariably within comparatively easy distance of the sea, and commanding one or more of the tracks by which the merchantmen found their way up into the country, sufficiently shows the purpose for which they were built, and the business of their masters. The Basileus may have been, like Agamemnon, the "leader of men"; but he was also the "devourer of men," and found his living on "the simple plan

> That they should take who have the power,
> And they should keep who can."

"In an age which looked on war as the only liberal profession," say Drs. Tsountas and Manatt, "the fenced city must have been the prime concern. So the hilltops of Hellas, often forbidding enough by nature, were turned into frowning castles, each the seat of a Basileus lording it over a realm sometimes as wide as he could readily watch with his own eyes, sometimes—as in Argolis—with two or three rival royal perches within the range of vision. Of these ancient hill-forts, the Acrocorinthus and the Athenian Acropolis are perhaps the noblest examples—the first, with its beetling brow a thousand feet in air, standing sentinel at the gates of the Peloponnese; the second hardly half as lofty, but with a matchless distinction in its free and queenly relief above the Attic plain."

It is not, however, to such strongholds as these, whose earlier glories have been completely eclipsed and overlaid by their later splendours, enduring throughout the whole of the historic period, that we must turn for the evidence of the character of the prehistoric culture of Greece; but rather to sites whose fame waned with the coming of the New Greece, and which have remained more or less in the condition which was theirs in their time of power. And of these, we find the supreme examples in two of the rock-eyries which dominated the Plain of Argos between 2000 and 1000 B. C.

The conditions which determined the position of such fortresses were these: First, security, attained by placing the castle on a hill or rocky eminence; second, the existence in the neighbourhood of a stretch of cornland sufficient to supply the needs of the garrison, in so far as these were not met by robbery; third, comparative nearness to the sea, so that the movements of the traders could be watched, while yet the castle was not so near to the shore but that any raid of pirates could be prepared against; lastly, command of one or more of the tracks by which traffic passed from the coast inland, or from one bay overland to another. A glance at the map of the Peloponnese will show how admirably these desirable conditions (for a robber-chieftain) were fulfilled by several sites in the Argolid.

The Gulf of Argos runs deep into the land, inviting the seafarer to the sheltered bay at its head. From the shore, the valley of the Inachos runs up towards the northern hills, widening towards its southern end into a sunny plain, girdled on either side with mountains, and looking to the south and the sea. Up the valley and over the mountain-pass at its head runs the way to the sister Gulf of Corinth, and the Isthmus. Everything was here which the most exacting highwayman could desire. It was here, as Herodotus tells us, that the Phœnicians, coming to trade with the Argives, wound up a week's business by kidnapping Io, the daughter of King Inachos, so that, for once in a way, the spoiler was spoiled. The Argive Plain was dotted with rock strongholds from the sea to the hills. Almost at the head of the gulf lies the rock of Palamedes, the modern Nauplia;

across the bay from the foot of the western hills frowns
the Larissa of Argos; and midway between these two Tiryns
rises on its low hillock, crowned with ramparts as enduring
as the hill.  Halfway up the plain, a little towards its
eastern side, stands Mideia; and at the head of the valley,
on a spur of the hills 912 feet high, and backed by mountains which tower above it to 2600 feet, lies the most
famous of them all,—"well-built," "broad-wayed,"
"golden" Mycenæ.  Of these we have to deal with Tiryns
and Mycenæ, which have preserved to the present day,
almost unchanged, the main features which characterised
the Greek Fortress-Palace in the palmy days when robbery
by land and piracy by sea were the natural occupations for
an enterprising gentleman of birth and courage.

History began for the Argolid, according to one theory,
by the incursion of a warrior race, the Perseids, who came
by sea, and established themselves at Nauplia and Tiryns,
thereafter advancing through the plain, first to Mideia, and
then to Mycenæ at the head of the plain.  Later came a
second wave of immigrants, the Pelopids, Asiatics, who
came into the plain overland, by Macedonia and the Isthmus, seized the old Perseid fort at Mycenæ and made it
their headquarters.  It is under Agamemnon of the Pelopid
line that Homer tells us of the glory of Mycenæ.  Small
though the kingship of the "Ruler of Men" would seem to
modern ideas (for only 9 miles away Diomed, another
Basileus, reigned in Argos), it yet carried with it a kind of
suzerainty over all the tribes of Hellas, and Agamemnon
is recognised leader of all the kinglets who gathered for the

siege of Troy, though he is foremost neither in power nor in prowess.

Agamemnon comes home, however, from his triumph at Troy, to find a dreadful doom at the hands of his guilty wife Klytemnestra, and her lover Aigisthos; and with his death, the glory of Mycenæ begins to fade. Erelong the Dorians, pressing ceaselessly southwards, besiege the old rock-fortress, and after a siege of unknown duration the eyrie of the Achæan chieftains falls, and its splendour perishes in the flames, or is swept away by the hands of spoilers, as that of Troy had been two generations before. And with that sack, Mycenæ disappears, as a serious factor, from the page of history. For the Dorian conquerors recognised that the key position of the Argolid was not remote Mycenæ, still less insignificant Tiryns, but Diomed's Argos with its impregnable Larissa, and there they made their capital, while the old strongholds of the Achæans gradually dwindled and withered.

Once, indeed, the two old nests of heroes reappear with honour on the immortal record of the Greek struggle against the tide of Eastern invasion. When the Persian poured his myriads upon Greece, the Dorians of Argos, to their shame, held aloof from the muster of Hellas; but 80 men of Mycenæ stood with Dorian Leonidas at Thermopylæ, and when Pausanias broke the whole might of Persia, a year later, at Platæa, Tiryns and Mycenæ sent 400 men to swell his ranks. Their names can still be read on the serpent-column in the Hippodrome at Constantinople, which once supported the golden tripod dedicated at Delphi in honour of the Grecian victory.  The honour of the little townships, however, proved their doom.  Argos, shameful herself, could not endure that her ancient neighbours should reap the glory which she had been too cowardly to claim for herself.  In 468 B. C., barely 10 years after Platæa, the Argives captured Mycenæ, and drove the inhabitants into exile.  Later they planted a colony of their own citizens within the deserted walls; but though we have first-hand evidence for this fact in the shape of inscriptions found on the site, the glory of the ancient stronghold had so utterly departed that Strabo, Diodorus, and Pausanias all agree in stating that Mycenæ remained a desolation from the time of the Argive sack.

Accordingly we have at Tiryns and Mycenæ what it is very rare to find—two sites which have remained almost entirely untouched from the time of their early glory.  At Tiryns we have the perfect type of the simple Fortress-Palace, with no elaboration of dependencies around it; at Mycenæ, though a Doric temple was built on the highest part of the palace site in the sixth century B. C., and remained there till Roman days, the rest of the palace area remains intact, and the wonders of its ancient sepulchres lay in fortunate obscurity till time brought the man who could appreciate their value and at least part of their significance.  Other sites in Hellas had retained a busy life throughout the historic period, and had been occupied and re-occupied till almost all traces of the most ancient chapters of their story had been swept away by the hands of successive restorers; Tiryns and Mycenæ had dreamed away the centuries in enchanted slumber, waiting the appointed time. It came for Mycenæ in 1876, and for Tiryns a few years later.

In 1874, as we have seen in the story of Troy, the Turkish Government, aggrieved by the distribution of "Priam's Treasure," began a lawsuit against Schliemann, and even after its settlement still showed hostility to the resumption of work at Hissarlik by the great explorer. When therefore, in 1876, he found his work in the Troad made almost impossible by the meddling of the Turkish pasha, he at once transferred his operations to Mycenæ, where he had already in 1874 sunk some trial shafts. His work at the old stronghold of Agamemnon proved so amazingly successful that it was continued for three successive seasons; while in 1884 he returned again to the Argolid, and worked on the site of Tiryns, entrusting the operations the following season to Dr. Dörpfeld. Though Mycenæ has thus the priority in respect of the date of its exploration, it will be better to begin with the older and smaller stronghold, for the reason that Tiryns is the simpler site, consisting of nothing but the Palace-Fortress, pure and simple, while at Mycenæ the interests involved are much more complex.

Tiryns stands upon a limestone ridge which stretches across the marshy plain at the head of the Gulf of Argos, less than a mile from the sea. The ridge itself is comparatively insignificant, measuring only 328 yards in length, and 129 in width, while its greatest height is only 59 feet above the plain and 72 above sea-level. Despite its smallness, however, the old fortress is singularly impressive. "In

reality so small," says Mr. H. R. Hall, "that a few big
trees of the English kind would hide it effectually (and even
the Greek cypresses do mask it), it yet gives the impression
of a Gibraltar." The impression is due, not to the site,
but to the enormous defences with which it was girdled by
its ancient lords. Legend said that Proitos, the founder of
Tiryns, brought the Cyclopes from Lycia to rear his fortress
walls; and indeed after so many centuries have done their
work of destruction, the mighty walls seem still not unworthy of the hands of giant builders. Pausanias, the
father of all makers of guide books, was so amazed at the
size of the limestone blocks as to declare that a yoke of
mules could not move the smallest of them. His enthusiasm carried him a little away, but not very far; for some
of the blocks measure 10 feet in length, by 3 in breadth
and height.

Composed of such massive materials, the wall encloses
three terraces at different levels, the Upper, Middle, and
Lower Citadels. Around the Lower Citadel, the wall varies
in thickness from 23 to 26 feet, and still rises to a height of
over 24 feet. About the Upper Citadel, however, the varia-
tion in the thickness of the wall is much greater. In some
places only 16 feet thick, in others the huge structure reaches
the amazing figure of 57 feet. "It has been impossible,"
says Mr. Hall again, "to destroy Tiryns. Its galleries are
simply built of these boulders piled up to form a rude
arch. If they are displaced they merely come to rest in a
new combination; they are almost indestructible, even by
earthquake."

PLATE XXVIII

THE LION GATE, MYCENÆ

The most remarkable feature of this enormous fortification is the system of galleries shaped in the thickness of the wall. There are two sets of these galleries, one in the southern, the other in the southeastern section of the wall. The southern system, which is the more complete, is reached from the Upper Citadel by a staircase which ends in a narrow corridor about 50 feet long, and 5 feet broad, from which open five chambers varying in length from 17 feet to 14½, and of a uniform breadth of 10¾ feet. In the southeastern system the six chambers are smaller, and the corridor is not so well preserved. Both corridors, and the chambers which open off them, are roughly vaulted with pointed arches, the vault, however, being not a true arch, but formed simply by the projection of each successive layer of blocks beyond the one below it, until at last the roof is closed. The obvious purpose of the galleries is to serve as storehouses for grain, oil and munitions of war against a siege. They form a remarkable parallel with the cellular construction of the wall of the citadel of Ancient Carthage, and we may suppose that the Lycian builders of Proitos and the Phœnician founders of Carthage were alike borrowing from a still earlier Asiatic race of fortress-builders.

The approach to the gate of this formidable stronghold was by an ascending ramp, nearly 20 feet broad, which led the assailant, always exposing his unshielded side, parallel with the wall, till he reached the level of the Upper Citadel. There the passage turned at right angles and pierced the wall, then turning again to the left, brought him along a narrow alley commanded on both sides by the defenders on the wall, till he was brought up by the outer gate. The great stone threshold, 4¾ feet broad, and 10⅓ feet long, and the stone gateposts, 10½ feet high, are still in position, while the sockets in the jambs, 16 inches deep, and 6½ inches square, show where the great bar was driven home to close the gate against any unwelcome visitor.

Once past the outer gate, the approach leads, still between walls, to an open court, and, turning to the right, the Great Gate of the Palace-Fortress is before you. It was this inner structure, of later date than the great encircling wall, which was revealed by the excavations of Schliemann and Dörpfeld, while later work has disclosed the traces of a palace of much earlier date. Schliemann's palace must have been built when lengthened familiarity with mainland conditions and intermixture with mainland races had modified the ideas of house-building which the original colonists or conquerors had brought with them from their (probably Cretan) home. The result was a house of typically Homeric form. Entering by the Great Gate, which is a regular Propylæum, the type of all such gateways in Greece down to the magnificent culmination of the series in the Propylæum of the Acropolis at Athens, you are faced by the main courtyard of the palace, 52 feet by 66, with an altar midway along its southern side. From this court a pillared vestibule leads through a triple folding-door into the antechamber, from which the great Hall, the Megaron, is reached. Thus we have in succession all the regular features of the Homeric house, the *aithousa*, the *prodomos*, and the *megaron*. The Megaron probably had only one storey, and its roof was supported by beams which rested on four columns grouped round a central hearth. Here we have a feature unknown to the great Cretan palaces with their warmer climate, and thoroughly characteristic of the more Northern type of house. The smoke from the open hearth found its way out, or at least a part of it did, through a great hole in the roof, which may possibly have had a louvre over it to guard against the rain. Behind the Men's Court and Megaron, lay a second court, and group of rooms of a similar type, though smaller, which was, no doubt, sacred to the women of the palace. Around these chief suites of rooms lay a number of smaller chambers whose grouping, or lack of grouping, reminds one more of the labyrinthine corridors and passages of Knossos.

Tiryns, therefore, presents us with a curious mixture of Northern and Southern elements in its structure. "Certainly," says Mr. H. R. Hall, "however un-Cretan the plan of the two *megara* at Tiryns, with their halls, may be, the whole style of construction is thoroughly Cretan, with its gypsum wall-lining, its fine stone paving, and so forth. The Cretans taught the Northern Greeks how to build palaces, though the Northerners liked their own plan to be followed." Perhaps we may rather say that the Cretans, coming to the sterner weather conditions of a more northerly home, learned to adapt their southern style of building, with its open light-wells and wide open spaces, to their new environment. The decoration of the palace, however, is thoroughly Cretan, though Cretan of the decadence. Schliemann's finds in this direction were somewhat limited, though they were of considerable significance, especially in the light of later discoveries. In the vestibule of the Megaron he found the remains of a fine alabaster frieze, inlaid with blue glass paste. This was at once recognised as furnishing an apt illustration of Homer's description of the decoration of the Palace of Alkinoös. "Brazen were the walls, which ran this way and that from the threshold to the inmost chamber, and round them was a frieze of blue." The blue paste of Tiryns was obviously the *kyanos* of the poet. The most notable piece of the fresco-work in which the Cretans took such delight was a fragment on which was depicted a bull galloping at full speed, with a toreador, such as we have become familiar with from the Knossian frescoes, swinging himself over the brute's back. Apart from this significant find, one or two fragments of conventional ornament, spirals, and figure-8 bucklers, summed up the artistic discoveries.

Later excavations on the site, however, have yielded the remains of a very much completer piece of work, in the shape of a fresco representing a boar-hunt. Groups of attendants, wearing sleeved tunics girt at the waist, carry boar-spears, or hold in leash the great hounds destined for the chase. Two of the palace ladies drive out in their chariot along an avenue of highly conventionalised trees, to view the sport,—Mycenæan prototypes of Atalanta. They are dressed in long sleeved gowns with dark borders to neck and sleeves, a type of costume strikingly different from the flounces and tight-lacing of the Knossian dames, and their dark hair falls in long curls on their shoulders.

The actual scene of the boar and his pursuers has been fairly well preserved, so that it has been possible to reconstruct the picture with certainty. The mighty boar dashes along in the flying gallop with which Minoan art has familiarised us, literally *ventre à terre*. In front of him, close to the grim snout with its fierce tusks, are seen the hands of two of his enemies, holding boar-spears which they thrust against his shoulder and his eye. On either side, and behind the rushing monster, gallop the fierce hounds, big and powerful animals with long hairy tails. The detail of the coats, both of the hounds and their quarry, is highly conventionalised. The boar is clad in zones of brown along which his bristles stand out with perfect regularity in a darker brown. The dogs are of a pinkish white colour, and are dappled with very conventional spots in red, black and blue. Altogether the picture is one of astonishingly vivid and effective style, reminding one forcibly of Pisanello's great "Venator Intrepidus" medal. All the same it is a style which has left behind it the great days of Minoan art, and is far on the down-grade. "Full of 'go' as the boar-hunt is, it is crude and primitive in execution when compared with the flying-fish fresco at Phylakopi. And the colours of the Tirynthian decadence are poor in comparison with those of the earlier age." Had such frescoes been found in Crete, they would unhesitatingly have been described as Late Minoan III, and that, no doubt, is the true place to which to refer them. The later palace which Schliemann unearthed is of still later date, probably of the thirteenth century B. C.

We turn back now to the year 1876, when Schliemann, disgusted by Turkish opposition, left the Troad, and sought a new field for his energies at Mycenæ. The lure which drew him to the old stronghold at the head of the Argolid was, quite characteristically, again Homeric. It was offered to him by a passage in the writings of Pausanias, the second century Baedeker of the Greek world. "Some remains of the circuit wall [of Mycenæ] are still to be seen," he says, "and the gate which has lions over it. These were built, they say, by the Cyclopes who made the wall at Tiryns for Proitos. Among the ruins at Mycenæ is the fountain caled Perseia, and some subterranean buildings belonging to Atreus and his children, where their treasures were kept. There is the tomb of Atreus, and of those whom Aigisthos slew at the banquet on their return from Ilion with Agamemnon. . . . There is also the tomb of Agamemnon, and that of Eurymedon the charioteer, and the joint tomb of Teledamos and Pelops, the twin children of Kassandra, whom Aigisthos slew with their parents while still mere babes. . . . Klytemnestra and Aigisthos were buried a little way outside the wall, for they were not thought worthy to be within, where Agamemnon lay and those who fell with him."

The walls which Pausanias describes remained in practically the same condition as when he saw them down to the time when the exploration of the site was begun—an almost triangular fortification, partly of Cyclopean, partly of rectangular, and partly of polygonal masonry, the last being the contribution of the later Mycenæans of the period immediately preceding the sack by the Argives in 468 B. C. The chief feature of the enceinte was "the gate which has lions over it," a monument of ancient skill and art which has never failed to excite wonder and admiration. The Lion Gate is approached by a rising roadway about 20 feet wide, hemmed in on either side by walls, from which the garrison could overwhelm with their missiles any assailant. The gate itself is 10⅓ feet in height, with a width at the foot of 9 feet 10 inches, and at the top of 9 feet. The posts, the threshold, and the lintel are huge single blocks of breccia, still bearing the marks of the saw by which they were shaped. In the threshold and lintel can still be seen the sockets in which the pivots of the great doors turned, while the jambs bear the marks of the holes in which the beam used to fasten the doors was driven home. Above the great lintel block—15 feet by 7, and 3½—is a triangular space, designed to relieve the pressure of the stonework above. This space is not left blank, however, but is closed in front by a slab of limestone, 12 feet long, 10 feet high, and only 2 feet thick. On this slab are sculptured in relief two lions standing heraldically opposed, with their forepaws planted upon an altar-like pedestal. Between them rises a pillar with the curious downward taper characteristic of Mycenæan and Minoan architecture, crowned with a capital and entablature which apparently represent the ends of the roofing-beams of a Mycenæan house or temple. Altogether the gate is a very remarkable piece of ancient art, and though no longer regarded as the most ancient piece of sculpture in Greece, it still remains one of the most striking. It was not, however, with the walls, nor even with the wonderful "Treasury of Atreus," still visible in the Lower City outside the walls, that Schliemann meant to deal, at least until he had satisfied himself on other points. His mind was full of the statement of Pausanias about the tombs of Agamemnon and his companions, and he wished to prove or disprove it by personal search. Fixing, more by chance than by any certain clue, upon a site about 40 feet inside the Lion Gate, he began to dig a great trial pit 113 feet square. It was as if his good genius had led him to the spot, for his pit almost exactly covered the area beneath which lay that which he was seeking. At a depth of from 12 to 14 feet the diggers came upon a rude altar of circular form, and several sculptured steles, of very rude workmanship. At a little above the same level the digging as it widened revealed a circle of stone slabs, 87 feet in diameter, all standing on edge, in two concentric rings. Schliemann at once concluded that he had found the council-chamber of Agamemnon, the "well-polished circle of stones," where the Greek chieftain sat with his advisers to plan the Trojan expedition; but the Homeric heroes must have been of gigantic stature, if that had been the case, for the lowest slabs were 3 feet, and the highest 5 feet in height. The circle was rather a *temenos*, or sacred enclosure within which sacrificial rites might be offered in memory of the great dead who slept below. In any case Schliemann was determined to go down to virgin soil or rock; and his perseverance was not long of meeting with its reward.

At a depth of 7½ feet below one of the steles, and 21

feet below the surface of the ground, he came upon a number of skeletons of men lying on the slope of the rock, —skeletons, no doubt, of slaves who had been slain or buried alive to keep their lord company and to serve him in the underworld. Nine feet deeper still, 30 feet from the surface, the explorer reached a great rock-hewn tomb, 16⅔ feet long by 10¼ broad, lined with a slanting wall of schist, 5 feet high and 2¼ broad. Within this first grave, afterwards known as Grave III, were "the mortal remains of three persons who, to judge by the smallness of the bones, and particularly of the teeth, and by the masses of female ornaments, must have been women." There were also indications that two children had been buried with the women. Less than 5 feet from this grave the diggers came upon a still larger tomb, measuring 24 by 18½ feet, and containing five bodies, all those of men. Further excavation revealed three more graves, all of the same type, though varying in size, and in the number of their occupants. In every case the bodies rested upon a bed of pebbles, not in the usual extended posture, but in a half-sitting position, with their heads supported by high pillows. Later a sixth grave was discovered by Stamatakes, which has been reproduced in the National Museum at Athens, where "its occupants,—two men,—lie outstretched on their pebble bed, with their drinking cups at hand and their armoury in reach, while great vases are ranged about their feet."

The amazing thing about the Circle-Graves, however, was not their construction, but the wealth and the artistic and technical skill of the civilisation of which the men and women whose poor shrivelled bodies lay there before the explorer's eyes had been the representatives. There had been buried with them such a store of treasure as never greeted an excavator, save in the pages of romantic fiction. "Gold," says Dr. Hogarth, "appeared in abundance never before seen in Greek tombs, . . . beaten into face-masks, head-bands, breast-pieces, and innumerable stamped plaques, into bracelets, necklaces, rings, baldrics, trinkets, and dagger and sword hilts. Ivory, silver, bronze, alabaster were there as well and in profusion, the whole treasure in mere money value being worth thousands sterling." The enumeration of the objects found in the two graves first discovered alone occupies over 115 pages of Schliemann's "Mycenæ." "Three of the dead had golden masks still on their faces, and two of the three had their breasts covered with large golden breastplates. Near the head of another lay a large golden crown, and there were also two smaller diadems. There were two signet-rings with intaglios of a chariot hunt and a battle scene (hand to hand), and a massive gold bracelet of enormous size; and the knee-bone of one of the men was still encircled by the ornate gold clasp which had fastened on the greave. Of other golden ornaments there were some 600, such as hairpins, ribbons, axes, rings, buttons, flowers, cuttle-fish, etc.; and to complete the heroic outfit there were the dragon-pommel and part of the gold sheath of a sceptre, with a second smaller sceptre-sheath; a gold lion-mask; a great silver ox-head with golden horns, and 56 little replicas of the same in gold; three gold models of a temple with Aphrodite's doves perching on the roof; 10 splendid golden vessels; and 19 silver vessels,— goblets, flagons, bowls, vases, etc. Further there were objects in alabaster, bronze, terra-cotta, and by two of the dead in two heaps lay 800 amber beads varying from the size of a pea to the size of a silver dollar, while the whole sepulchre was strewn with small gold leaves, of which more than half a pound were gathered up." (Tsountas and Manatt.)

No such find had, up to that time, rewarded the archæ-ologist, though there have been many since which have rivalled or surpassed it; but the mere profusion of the precious metals in the Circle-Graves was the least of the business. Schliemann imagined and proclaimed with un-bounded enthusiasm that he had found Agamemnon and all his comrades, hastily buried, with all their splendour about them, after their treacherous slaughter by Aigisthos and Klytemnestra. It seemed to him certain that all the bodies had been buried at once. "The identity of the mode of burial in all the tombs, the similar style and decoration of the ornaments," all seemed to justify the conclusion that no interval of time had elapsed between the various inter-ments. Further, to his mind the state in which the bodies were found seemed to point in the direction of their identi-fication with the victims of Klytemnestra's perfidy. "Cer-tain unmistakable signs of disorder, the position of one body whose head was squeezed down on to the breast, and similar observations, were all proof of a hurried and care-less burial." Above all, there was the most remarkable and undeniable coincidence between what Schliemann had found and what Pausanias described 17 centuries before; for though Schliemann misread Pausanias, and thought that he only spoke of five graves, and therefore ceased to search for any more after the fifth had been discovered, the Sixth Grave, necessary to complete the correspondence with the statement of the old topographer, was found, as already mentioned, by Stamatakes.

Schliemann's enthusiasm woke a loud echo, especially in Britain, where "Mr. Gladstone, writing a preface to the narrative of discovery, quoted approvingly Schliemann's inferences drawn from the 'hasty character' of the burials and the 'half-shut eye' of one male corpse, *videlicet*, the murdered king's, denied by Clytemnestra the last sad rites of piety." Erelong, however, opinion began to change. Scholars pointed out that the burial furniture was not all of the one period, that the supposed disorder of the burials was simply the result of the collapse of the tomb-roofs upon the bodies, and that neither the number of persons nor their sex would fit the story of Pausanias. Then followed a period of incredulity and angry scepticism, mixed with a good deal of undeserved ridicule. "Wonder turned to laughter," says Dr. Hogarth, "laughter which Schliemann's fanaticism, issuing in headlong joyous discovery of trivial realities in the Homeric story, was always in danger of rousing. But there is less laughter to-day. Twenty years [40 now] have brought opinion almost round to him again. The majority of critics now admit the extreme probability that what Schliemann found was at least what Pausanias intended to denote. . . . Whether these graves contained the real Atreus and Agamemnon and their house we are not, and shall probably never be, able to say; but little doubt remains that what were believed to be their remains 17 centuries ago have now been brought to light."

The mere question of Agamemnon or not Agamemnon, however, was an infinitely small matter, however interesting it might be. Schliemann had done a far bigger thing than he imagined. Whether he had found the "king of men" or not, he had proved once and for all that the old Greek tradition of an Heroic Age, going far back beyond the beginnings of Historic Greece, was no dream, but a solid fact. It is difficult for us to-day, with the results of excavation before us, to realise how utterly sceptical was the attitude of the great mass of European scholarship 50 years ago towards all tradition and legend which suggested the existence of a civilisation at all, to say nothing of an Heroic Age, before the First Olympiad. Grote's attitude may be taken as typical of by no means the least sympathetic judgment on the Legendary Age of Hellas. "To analyse the fables," he says, "and to elicit from them any trustworthy particular facts appears to me a fruitless attempt. . . . For the farther we travel back into the past, the more do we recede from the clear day of positive history, and the deeper do we plunge into the unsteady twilight and gorgeous clouds of fancy and feeling." Grote was moderate compared to many scholars. "To talk of the Heroic Age was to invite a smile in the days when every legend was deemed a sun-myth." Schliemann's discovery had dealt the death-blow to all that arrogant and intolerant spirit which denied reality to the myths, while forcing upon them an interpretation far more baseless and airy than anything in themselves.

What the great explorer had done, though even he himself never thoroughly realised the greatness of his achievement, was to prove once and for all that the beginnings of European civilisation must be thrust back many centuries from the then accepted date. It was as yet not possible to foresee that this was only the first stage of a process which would not cease till it had equated the origins of Mediterranean culture with those of the Nile and Euphrates Valleys; but that was the real meaning of the finds of the Circle-Graves at Mycenæ.

"Brave men lived before Agamemnon," and in the Circle-Graves Schliemann had revealed the last resting-place of these prehistoric heroes,—the men to whom the heroes who fought on "the ringing plains of windy Troy" looked back with reverence, and in comparison with whose times, those of Diomede, Achilles, Ajax, seemed only "degenerate days." Since the discoveries at Knossos and Phaistos, we have learned that the civilisation of Mycenæ was already decadent when the great dead of the Circle-Graves were laid to rest beside the Lion Gate; yet even in its decay it spoke of a culture and an artistic sense whose results were not unworthy to be compared with the best of either Egypt or Mesopotamia, and in naturalness and freedom were beyond either. The inlaid daggers of Grave IV and V, with their scenes of the lion hunt and the cat hunting in the papyrus-swamp not only show Egyptian influence, but

also a technique equal to anything which Egypt ever produced, and a suppleness which she can rarely parallel.  One
of the most interesting things about them was the complete
justification which they afforded to what many people considered the sheer romancing of Homer, in his descriptions
of the metal-working of the period of the Trojan War.
"There were plenty of discerning people," says Schuchhardt, "who held that the Homeric shields decorated with
marvellous art, the splendid cups, the palaces of magical
beauty, had not been all evolved out of nothing, but must
have been suggested by things that actually existed.  On
the other hand there were the faint-hearted, who held all
this for idle phantasy and fable, because not supported by
actual finds.  Now we have the great civilisation of the
Mycenæan period before our eyes, and can no longer doubt
that this is the civilisation which underlay those Homeric
descriptions, where every detail is so fondly dwelt upon."
Take, for instance, the Shield of Achilles, so often discussed
and reconstructed.  "Also he set therein a vineyard teeming
plenteously with clusters, wrought fair in gold; black were
the grapes, but the vines hung throughout on silver poles.
And around it he ran a ditch of blue, and round that a fence
of tin. . . . Also he wrought therein a herd of kine with
upright horns, and the kine were fashioned of gold and
tin."  Compare this with the technique of the Hunting-Cat
dagger from Grave V.  "The cats, the plants, and the bodies
of the ducks are inlaid with gold, the wings of the ducks
and the river are silver, and the fish are given in some dark
substance.  On the neck of one of the ducks is a red

drop of blood, probably given by coloured, i.e. alloyed gold." Homer, in a word, knew perfectly what he was writing about, and had, no doubt, in his memory the stories of men who had seen with their own eyes some of the relics of the splendour of the Heroic Age, even though his own lot had fallen upon a day of small things and men.

Among the ruins of a house outside the Grave-Circle, there was found, along with fine gold cups, and signet-rings, the famous fragment of a Warrior-Vase, on which are depicted the somewhat grotesque figures of five warriors going out to battle, arrayed in full Greek panoply, which forms a remarkable contrast to the equipment of the regular Mycenæan warrior, with its figure-8 shield, skull-cap and spear. This is by far the earliest representation of the Greek panoply, and it has been supposed that its presence brings down the date of the other things found along with it to almost the dawn of the Historic Period; but it does not seem beyond the range of possibility that the vase belongs to the period of the articles with which it was found, which, in any other company, would have been referred, quite naturally, to the height of the Mycenæan period, and that it teaches us, that, just as the Minoan colonists of Tiryns and Mycenæ found themselves obliged to adapt their Cretan ideas of house-building to the needs of the more rigorous climate of Greece, as stern necessity early taught them the need of fortifications on a scale unknown to the great palaces of Crete, so they learned to discard the light equipment of their native land in favour of heavy body-armour more suited to the ruder struggles they had to wage on the mainland.

The palace of Mycenæ stood on the highest point of the hill, within the wall; but, as already mentioned, a Doric temple was built on the summit as early as the sixth century B. C., and in consequence the existing remains are by no means so complete as those of Tiryns, to which they conform in general type, so that we need not delay over them. We turn to the Bee-Hive Tombs of the Lower City.

The Lower City of Mycenæ occupies a ridge which runs down from the citadel between the two streams of the Chavos and the Kokoretza, and the two most famous tombs out of those which have been found look out from the slope over the ravine. Pausanias mentions them as "underground structures of Atreus and his sons, where they kept their treasures," and, in referring to the similar tomb at Orchomenos, which he names the Treasury of Minyas, he expresses his astonishment at the indifference of his countrymen to such marvellous works. "The Greeks are great hands at admiring things abroad in preference to those at home: thus eminent writers have seen fit to describe minutely the Pyramids of Egypt, while they have not a word to say of the Treasury of Minyas and the Walls at Tiryns, *though these are not a whit less wonderful.*" Most may think that the old Greek has allowed his patriotism to run away with his judgment in such an assertion; but Mr. H. R. Hall, with no national prejudice to obscure his vision, is even more emphatic than Pausanias. "The interior [of the Treasury of Atreus], though only 50 feet in height, is more impressive than anything Egypt has to show, and far more impressive, in my opinion, than the interior chamber of the Great Pyramid.   For here we have an art of building more developed than that of Egypt."

Be that as it may, the two so-called Treasuries, of Atreus and Klytemnestra, are beyond doubt most impressive buildings, which speak of a civilisation far advanced alike in its ideas, and in the technical and artistic skill needed to carry them into execution.   Of these the first, the Treasury of Atreus, has always been known and open, though its final clearance was due to Schliemann; the second was discovered in the course of the excavations, and was cleared at the expense of Mrs. Schliemann, whose name it often bears. The Treasury of Atreus may be taken as the type of such tombs, which at one time must have been fashionable, as more than 25 are known to exist in Greece and Crete.   A *dromos* or entrance passage, 115 feet long and 20 feet wide, runs back into the face of the hill, its sides, which of course rise higher and higher as the passage recedes, being revetted with great blocks of hewn stone.   At the end of the *dromos* rises a vertical façade, 46 feet high, built of finely hewn blocks of stone, which were formerly adorned with bronze rosettes.   This imposing front is pierced by a doorway 17¾ feet high, 8¾ feet broad at the base, and 8 feet 1 inch at the top.   Originally this noble door was framed by two monolith columns of dark grey alabaster, tapering, in the curious Mycenæan fashion, from the capital downwards.   These have been missing since the beginning of the nineteenth century, when they, or the greater portions of them, were

PLATE XXIX

BEEHIVE TOMB—TREASURY OF ATREUS, MYCENÆ

transported to the seat of the Marquess of Sligo in Ireland. They were then lost sight of and forgotten till about a dozen years ago, when, their true character being at last recognised, they were presented to the British Museum, where they now stand against a background representing to scale the doorway which they once adorned. The lintel of this great doorway is gigantic. It consists of two great monoliths, each reaching right across the space of the door- way, and between them bridging the whole depth of the entrance. The inner block, which projects far beyond the door on both sides, is 29½ feet long, 16½ feet broad, and 3 feet deep, its weight being approximately 120 tons. Egyp- tian builders were, of course, familiar enough with such blocks, though even they reserved them for special occa- sions. The sepulchral chamber of the pyramid of Amenem- hat III, at Hawara, consists, for example, of one single block of yellow quartzite, weighing about 110 tons—a block fairly comparable with the lintel of the Mycenæan Treasury. In the case of the obelisks and colossal statues, the Egyptian builders handled still larger blocks, ranging from the 300 tons of Hatshepsut's obelisk at Karnak to the 1000 tons of the colossi of Ramses II at Tanis and the Ramesseum; but apart from these and the huge blocks of Baalbec, this stone of the Treasury of Atreus represents one of the greatest engineering and constructional feats of the old world.

Even to such a mighty lintel, however, the Mycenæan builders did not venture to entrust the huge weight of the rest of the façade above the portal. Accordingly, as in the case of the Lion Gate, they introduced above the lintel-block a relieving space, triangular in shape, and closed by a comparatively thin slab of red porphyry carved with spiral ornaments. This filling has now disappeared, and parts of the porphyry slab are in the Museum at Athens and in the British Museum. Altogether, with its finely hewn ashlar, decorated with bronze, its columns and frieze of grey alabaster, adorned with spirals and chevrons, and its red porphyry relieving slabs, the façade of the Treasury of Atreus must have presented an appearance of dignified richness hardly to be surpassed.

Passing through the portal, the visitor finds himself in a spacious chamber about 50 feet in diameter, whose apparently domed roof rises about the same height above his head. In this case, however, we have not to deal with true vaulting. The vault is formed of 33 horizontal courses, each course projecting a little beyond the one below it, until at the apex the opening becomes so small that it can be closed by a single slab. The stones were then carefully trimmed to the uniform curve of the vault, and polished. Holes, still to be seen in the blocks of the dome, show where the stonework was adorned with bronze rosettes, probably arranged in groups of five according to a regular pattern, while the lower courses of the dome show traces of the fixing of a bronze frieze.

From the circular-domed chamber, a smaller door, still bearing traces of rich decoration, leads into a side chamber, 27 feet square by 19 feet high, whose rock-hewn sides had once been cased with alabaster. Fragments of the casing are now scattered through various European museums. Here, in all probability, were the actual interments, while the domed chamber may have been the scene of the rites of the cult of the great dead. In this, the Treasury of Atreus is exceptional, as the other vaulted tombs, except at Orchomenos, have no side chamber, and the rites of the dead must have been performed in the actual chamber where they lay.

On the same slope as the Treasury of Atreus, but a little further to the north, lies another bee-hive tomb known as the Treasury of Klytemnestra, or Mrs. Schliemann's Treasury. It is not in such perfect condition as its neighbour, for the upper courses of the dome have long since fallen; but it must have been of a splendour scarcely less striking. Its columns were also of alabaster, bearing a regular Doric fluting instead of the chevrons of the Treasury of Atreus; its lintel is formed of three great blocks of leek-green marble, and its relieving-slab of red porphyry. It has no side-chamber, and, curiously enough, it has a separate pit-grave sunk in the middle of the *dromos*, about 18 feet from the façade. This grave had contained a woman, probably a slave of the great man buried in the vaulted tomb, who had been slain to keep her master company in the underworld. If so, she had been a favourite, and highly prized, for, though as a rule there are no offerings found with those who have been thus immolated, her grave yielded two bronze mirrors with carved ivory handles, and several golden ornaments.

Of the other bee-hive tombs at Mycenæ, one was fairly

comparable to the two chief tombs in size and material. Outside Mycenæ, the chief rival to the Treasuries of Atreus and Klytemnestra is at Orchomenos in Bœotia—a city which, insignificant in the historic period, had yet been made so splendid by the legendary dynasty of the Minyæ, as to be coupled in the Iliad with the great world-capital of Ancient Egypt, "hundred-gated Thebes." That the legend of the greatness of Orchomenos had something behind it, was shown by the magnificence of the great tomb which Schliemann opened in 1880. This building had been from time immemorial considered one of the wonders of Greece. Pausanias, in the passage in which he rebuked the Greeks of his time for their neglect of the glories of their own land, speaks of it as "a round stone building, ending in a blunt conical point; it is said that the topmost stone acts as a keystone to the whole building." In this, judging from the analogy of the tombs of Mycenæ, he is probably wrong; but the fact that the dome fell in long ago makes it impossible to determine the point with absolute certainty.

"The Treasury of Minyas," as Pausanias calls it, consisted of a *dromos* 16¾ feet wide, and of unknown length,— unknown because in 1862 the local demarch destroyed it, all but one solitary stone, to build a third quite unnecessary church in the neighbouring village of Skripou. The main domed building has been almost identical in dimensions and in style of decoration, down to the bronze rosettes, with the Mycenæan Treasuries; but the point of special interest in the Treasury of Minyas is the side-chamber,—a room 12⅓ feet by 9. It is entered, as in the case of the Treasury of

Atreus, by a door from the large chamber; but the method of its construction is quite different. Instead of being hewn out from the level of the great chamber, it was formed by a shaft sunk independently from the surface of the hill above. Eight feet above its floor, a magnificent ceiling was formed by slabs of green schist, profusely adorned with a beautiful pattern of spirals and rosettes; then, above this, comes a relieving chamber to take the weight off the ceiling, and the shaft above was filled with earth. This device had served its purpose so well, that it was not until 1870, according to the statement of the villagers, that the roof fell in, creating a deep hole in the ground above the chamber. The exquisite spiral and rosette design of the slate ceiling remains one of the most characteristic and remarkable pieces of Mycenæan work.

Though the idea of Pausanias that these great vaulted structures were treasuries has long since been dismissed, there can be no doubt that the monarchs or chiefs who were buried in such splendid tombs must have carried with them to the grave an equipment not less gorgeous and valuable than their predecessors of the Circle-Graves. Probably the very conspicuousness and magnificence of their monuments, as in the case of the Pyramids of Egypt, proved an irresistible temptation to the plunderer, and hindered the preservation of treasures which would have been priceless, not from their material, but from their evidence as to the civilisation which produced them. The treasuries of Mycenæ and Orchomenos had already been rifled in antiquity, very probably by the Dorian conquerors, who have left traces of their presence, in the shape of fragments of pottery of the debased Dipylon style, which followed the Mycenæan, before the doorways of two of the tombs at Mycenæ. Veli Pasha, the Turkish governor of the Morea, is said to have cut down into the *dromos* of the Treasury of Atreus in 1808, and to have plundered the tomb; but while the action was quite in accordance with Turkish tradition, the chances are that, as he deserved, he had his labour for nothing.

Among the other tombs, however, two at least yielded results of great value. In 1872, a tomb at Menidi in Attica was excavated, yielding a variety of articles of adornment, chiefly in glass paste, ivory, and engraved gems. In 1889, M. Tsountas excavated the bee-hive tomb at Vaphio in Laconia, with results which created almost as much interest as the finds of the Circle-Graves, and which have only been surpassed in artistic value by the Cretan work of the period when the Bronze Age civilisation of the Ægean was at its zenith. "On the floor of the round chamber at Vaphio," says the explorer, "were found 13 engraved gems, two gold rings, silver and bronze needles, some smaller gold ornaments, and a few leaves of gold." But the main treasure was in the grave which was sunk in the middle of the rotunda, and which had never been disturbed. "Near where the head had lain were two bronze vessels (one of them a sort of skillet, possibly for sacrificial uses); a bronze sword, three feet long; two spear-heads; seven bronze knives; a bronze sceptre-sheath; a large bronze spoon; a mirror disk; ten smaller disks of five different sizes, probably making up five pairs of balances; five leaden disks; two stone basins;

two alabaster vases, with a little silver spoon in one of them; two terracotta vessels; and three other terracottas which look like lamps. . . . Where the neck and breast must have lain, we found some 80 amethyst beads, with two engraved gems, apparently forming a necklace of two chains. On the left lay a gold-plated dagger, and in the middle of the grave a silver cup with a gold-plated rim. At either hand lay two more cups, one (pair) of silver and one of gold. . . . So at either hand lay a heap of 12 engraved gems,—the two heaps obviously forming once a pair of bracelets,—with three more silver objects, including an ear-pick, and three rings, one of gold, one of bronze, and one of iron. At the foot lay a bronze knife, two bronze axes, and four more lead disks."

The two cups mentioned above were the famous Vaphio Cups, still the most remarkable work of the Mycenæan, or rather the Minoan, goldsmith which we possess. They were a pair of small cups, $3\frac{1}{4}$ inches in height, and 9 ounces in weight, and formed each of two plates of pure gold. The outer plate bore the design in repoussé work, and was bent to a cylindrical shape and riveted end to end at the handle; the inner gave a smooth lining, and was rolled over the outer to form a rim. The design in either case was one of those scenes of bull and hunter in which the Minoan artist so much delighted. In the one instance the hunt is in actual progress; one bull is caught in a net fastened between two trees, another has cleared the trap at a bound, while a third has shaken off one hunter, and is tossing another on his horns. On the second cup, on the other hand, all is quietness. Two bulls stand side by side in a meadow, tranquilly rubbing their heads together; another quietly grazes behind them, while on the other side a fourth bull is being led away, bellowing as he goes. Problems of perspective and foreshortening have, of course, been a little too much for the primitive Benvenuto Cellini who beat the cups in what we may pretty certainly call Late Minoan I (c. 1600-1500 B. C.); but all the same the designs have wonderful swing and go in them, and the craftsmanship is admirable. The Cretan excavations have shown us, in such work as the Harvester and Chieftain Vases of Hagia Triada, that the Minoan stone carver, who no doubt imitated in his gilded steatite the costlier work of the goldsmith, could produce work even more brilliant than that of the Vaphio Cups; but the dearth of vessels in the previous metals on Cretan sites leaves these still unrivalled in their own kind. There can be no doubt that they are really imported Cretan work; and if Crete sent across the Ægean to the lesser palaces of her mainland colonies such splendid art, how much more splendid must have been the treasures which she kept for the great mansions of her native kings,—treasures, alas! now lost forever.

We have wandered somewhat from Tiryns and Mycenæ in discussing the Vaphio treasure; but all these discoveries of what used to be called Mycenæan art on Greek soil only emphasise the importance of the work which Schliemann began when he opened the Circle-Graves at Mycenæ. In one word, Schliemann's discoveries and their sequel forced upon the world an entirely new conception of the origins of European civilisation, and particularly of their date. More than 20 years ago, Hogarth summed up the position, as it then appeared, in words which may have seemed exaggerated to many, but are now seen to have been a modest statement of literal truth. "The result," he said, "rounded in a paragraph, is this: that before the epoch at which we are used to place the beginnings of Greek civilisation, that is, the opening centuries of the last millennial period B. C., we must allow for an immensely long record of human artistic productivity, going back into the neolithic age, and culminating towards the close of the age of bronze in a culture more fecund and more refined than any we are to find again in the same lands till the age of iron was far advanced. Man in Hellas was more highly civilised before history than when history begins to record his state; and there existed human society in the Hellenic area, organised and productive, to a period so remote that its origins were more distant from the age of Pericles than that age is from our own. *We have probably to deal with a total period of civilisation in the Ægean not much shorter than in the Nile valley.*"

Fifty years ago, such a statement would have seemed the wildest and most incredible of ravings. Twenty-five years ago, it would probably have been regarded as an intelligent anticipation, with a good deal of probability in it, but without any very certain foundation. To-day it is a proved fact, which no man who knows anything about the evidence would ever dream of questioning. No longer do we regard the prehistoric period as a vast illimitable inane of outer darkness, through which there shone dimly the two jealously guarded lights of Mesopotamian and Nilotic civilisation. We have learned that for at least 3000 years before the beginning of our era, the whole Ægean area was at least as intensely alive as the Valleys of the Euphrates or the Nile, and that if the great ancient civilisations of these valleys were giving light to the peoples, they were in turn receiving light from a race not less gifted, though differently gifted, than themselves. We know now that we must abandon the idea, long cherished by many students of Ancient Egypt, that the Nilotic civilisation was a thing apart, shut up in water-tight compartments from contact with the rest of the world, and substitute for it that of a world in which the great civilisations, Nilotic, Mesopotamian, and Minoan, were in touch with one another as closely, though with less rapidity in their inter-play, as the national cultures of to-day, and far more closely than those of the early historic period, when Greek and Roman had slowly to build up again all that had been ruined when the great civilisation of the Minoan and Mycenæan periods collapsed. Something of what the splendour of Minoan civilisation was in its great days, the days of which the glories of Tiryns and Mycenæ were but a dying reflection, we may see in the story of the work of Sir Arthur Evans at Knossos.

Since the war, British excavators, under Dr. A. J. B. Wace, have resumed work at Mycenæ, and have reached results of considerable importance. On the site of the palace, traces were discovered of occupation from the time of the Early Helladic Period (c. 2200-1800 B. C.). Above them were relics of the Middle Helladic Period (c. 1800-1600), and, a little later, at the beginning of the Late Helladic Age, the kings of the Shaft or Circle-Graves built their palace, which, though it has almost entirely vanished, has left abundance of debris, fragments of fresco, pottery, and disconnected walls. The later palace, however, was a much more important building, "with a large court lighting the rooms and corridors looking on to it, two entrances, a large hall with columns, storerooms, staircases, and at least two storeys." The planning of the building shows great architectural skill; and indeed the relics of occupation at Mycenæ reveal much of the same outlook on matters concerning the comforts and decencies of life, e.g. with regard to drainage, as is found at Knossos. In one of the chambers were found the remains of a stepped tank lined with red stucco, probably a bath, as a drain runs by its side. "When one reflects that according to tradition Agamemnon on his return from Troy was slain in his bath by his wife, red is a most suggestive colour!"

The search for further tombs was rewarded by the discovery of several, and among them one very important chamber-tomb, 20 feet square by 20 feet high. The great domed tomb found by Tsountas, and named the Tomb of Ægisthus, was cleared and preserved from the danger of further ruin. The excavators find that the domed tombs may be ranged in three groups, the Tomb of Ægisthus falling in the first of these, in which the construction is still somewhat primitive, and large blocks are not handled with the same facility as later. The second group shows increase of skill in this respect, large blocks and hard stone being handled with considerable skill, while the architects of this period have discovered the principle of the relieving triangle above the doors of the tombs. In the last group, which includes the Treasury of Atreus and the Tomb of Klytemnestra, the skill of the Mycenæan designer and workman is at its height. "Big blocks like the gigantic lintel stones are handled with surprising ease, and the tombs will always remain as amazing examples of bold and imaginative calculation in planning, and of marvellous mechanical skill in construction."

The kings who were laid in these noble sepulchres reigned later than those of the Shaft-Graves. We may say that Mycenæ was ruled from about 1600 to 1500 B. C. by the Shaft-Grave Dynasty. The kings of this line were then succeeded by those of the Domed-Tomb Dynasty, who ruled, at all events, till the thirteenth century B. C. Agamemnon and his house were the successors, or perhaps rather the latest branch of this dynasty.

Evidence was found of the existence of a system of writing, not Cretan, but more akin to an Asia Minor type, though belonging to no known alphabet. With regard to the town, the conclusion of the excavators was that "Homeric Mycenæ was not a walled town like Chester, but a fortified Royal and official residence like Edinburgh Castle. The ordinary people lived in open villages scattered here and there about the countryside, and this was probably the case with Troy as well. The fortified city excavated by Schliemann is quite small, and could not contain a large population. This would account for the fact that in Homer the Trojans and their allies defended the city not from its walls, but in battle line on the plain before them, much as can be seen on the famous silver vase from the Royal tombs of Mycenæ."

Dr. Wace's results may be roughly summed up thus. Mycenæ was first settled in the beginning of the Bronze Age; but only attained importance in the Middle Helladic Age, 1800 to 1600 B. C. Towards the end of this period, Cretan influence was strong, and by the First Late Helladic Period, the city was rich and powerful. In the succeeding age its products are found influencing even Crete. In the fourteenth century, after the downfall of Knossos, Mycenæ supplanted Crete as the chief centre of power and civilisation. "The clever apprentice took the master's place." This was the time when Mycenæ reached the zenith of its power and skill, and though its best is not so fine in artistic quality as the best of the preceding age, yet in technical skill the products of this period are in advance of anything previously attained. "The massive Cyclopean walls, the domestic luxury, the splendid palaces, and the technical perfection—as shown, for instance, in the Treasury of Atreus and in the other complete domed tomb at Mycenæ . . . bear witness that the Mycenæans of the Third Late Helladic Period (1400-1100 B. C.) were craftsmen of no mean skill and the worthy heirs of a long line of human effort. All research in this period helps us not merely to write the earliest history of Greece, but to fill out little by little the material background of Homer. We now realise that Homer does not give us the first struggles of a rising Hellas, but the climax, or rather an epitome, of the wonderful pre-Homeric Greece, of which even Athens in its prime knew little.  Yet it was in the pre-Homeric days of the Bronze Age that the broad foundations of the glory of Greece were laid."

# CHAPTER XII

"Less than a generation back," says Sir Arthur Evans, in that brilliant article which first gave to the general public the results of his excavations at Knossos, "the origin of Greek civilisation, and with it the sources of all great culture that has ever been, were wrapped in an impenetrable mist. That ancient world was still girt round within its narrow confines by the circling 'Stream of Ocean.' Was there anything beyond? The fabled kings and heroes of the Homeric Age, with their palaces and strongholds, were they aught, after all, but more or less humanised sun-myths?"

The answer to this question was partly given, as we have seen, by the remarkable work of Dr. Schliemann and his successors, at Troy, Mycenæ, Tiryns and elsewhere. It was shown that many generations before that First Olympiad (776 B. C.), from which Greek History, as we have known it, begins, there lived on Greek soil a race not only civilised, but much further advanced in the refinements of civilisation that the historic Greeks who succeeded them. We learned that the products of Mycenæan art and manufacture had already, by the end of the sixteenth century B. C., found their way throughout the Levant and Syria, into the Nile Valley, to Sicily and Southern Italy, and even as far as the coasts of Spain.

There was one spot of the Greek world, however, which so far had not contributed anything to the evidence of this ancient splendour, though its situation and its traditions alike pointed to the probability that it had taken its place, and that no unimportant one, in the great story of those bygone days. "Crete, the central island—a half-way house between three Continents—flanked by the great Libyan promontory and linked by smaller island stepping stones to the Peloponnese and the mainland of Anatolia, was called upon by Nature to play a leading part in the development of the early Ægean culture." Nor were the indications of Nature contradicted by the evidence of tradition,—rather they were corroborated by it. It is true that in the Classical period of Greek history Crete occupies a comparatively insignificant place, and has sorely declined from the great days when she sent 80 ships to the siege of Troy, and reckoned 100 cities within her borders; but no land holds a larger place in Greek legend, and of none are the legends more significant.

It was to Crete that Rhea, the wife of Kronos, the father of the gods, fled to bear her son, Zeus; and in the Dictæan Cave the future ruler of gods and men was nourished with honey and goat's milk by the nymph Amaltheia, till the time was ripe for his vengeance on his unnatural father. It was in the Dictæan Cave, also, that Zeus was united to Europa, the daughter of man, in that union from which sprang Minos, the supreme legendary figure of Crete. And

THRONE ROOM, KNOSSOS

it was to the land of his birth that the island god returned
to close his life. His tomb, it was said, was on the conical
peak of Mt. Juktas, which overlooks the city of Minos, his
son, his priest, and his friend. Round the figure of Minos
gathers a wealth of legend, almost Biblical in its character.
He is not only the son, but the "gossip" of Zeus, like
Abraham, "the friend of God." Like Moses, he receives
on the mountain-top from the hand of God the code of laws
which is to form the basis of all subsequent legislation,
and once in every nine years he goes up to the Dictæan
Cave, "to converse with Zeus," to give account of his
stewardship, and to receive new commandments. Finally,
at his death, he is transferred to the underworld, and the
great human lawgiver becomes the judge of the dead in
Hades.

This sacred aspect of the great Cretan king represents
perhaps the most ancient stratum of legend; but along with
it, and often so inconsistent with it as to suggest that in the
word "Minos" we have, not the name of a single man, but
the title of a race of kings, there goes a wealth of legend of
a more secular type. The Minos with whom we are most
familiar in Greek story is not the righteous lawgiver and
friend of God, but a very mundane ruler indeed. He is the
great tyrant of the Ægean, sending out his fleets, and exacting his dreadful tribute from all lands; he is the patron of
Dædalus, the father of all artificers and inventors, who
made for his master the gruesome brazen man Talos, and
who built the dancing-ground of Ariadne in Knossos, and
reared the famous Labyrinth where dwelt the man-devour-

ing Minotaur.  In the inmost maze of the labyrinth the monster, half-man, half-bull, was fed daily with human flesh, the flesh of the youths and maidens whom the king exacted as his tribute from the cities and lands which he had conquered; until at last Theseus, the young Athenian prince, offered his own life to rid the world of such an infamy, and, guided by Ariadne's clue, penetrated to the depths of the maze and slew the Minotaur.  Or, again, Bacchylides tells us how Theseus at the court of Minos went down to the palace of Amphitrite beneath the sea, and brought up the ring, "the splendour of gold," which the king had flung into the deep.  Such stories seem to have little enough touch with any possible reality; and indeed the Greeks themselves grew to be somewhat incredulous of the claims of Crete.  In particular the story of the burial of Zeus on Mt. Juktas excited their scorn, and the poet Kallimachus expressed his opinion of Cretan veracity in a verse which has become familiar to us all because St. Paul has quoted it in his Epistle to Titus.  "The Cretans are alway liars, evil beasts, idle gluttons."

Nevertheless there still remained in the Greek mind a tradition of the empire of Minos, and the means by which it was created and maintained.  Both Herodotus and Thucydides have preserved the record of the belief that a Cretan king called Minos was the first Sea-king known to history. "Polykrates," says Herodotus, "is the first of the Grecians of whom we know who formed a design to make himself master of the sea, except Minos the Knossian."  The testimony of Thucydides is still clearer.  "The first person known to us as having established a navy, is Minos. He made himself master of what is now called the Hellenic sea, and ruled over the Cyclades, into most of which he sent the first colonists, expelling the Karians, and appointing his own sons governors; and thus did his best to put down piracy in those waters, a necessary step to secure the revenues for his own use." More conclusive than any merely literary evidence is the frequency with which the name Minoa appears on the coasts of the Mediterranean from Sicily on the west to Gaza on the east, each instance marking the spot where the king or kings who bore the name of Minos once held a fortress or a trading station. One other legend, perhaps the most romantic of all, preserved by the greatest of Greek philosophers, has only found its interpretation since the excavations in Crete have taught us the character of the Minoan civilisation. In the Timæus, Plato tells how Solon, when in Egypt, was told by a priest of Sais that there was once an island in the western sea, where a great central power held sway, not only over its own territory, but over other islands and even over parts of the continent. In the pride of power this state was overwhelmed by the sea as a judgment of the gods, leaving only a range of mud banks to mark its place. Plato enters with considerable detail into the account of this island state, the "Lost Atlantis," which has been the subject of so many romances, and his details are such as to leave practically no doubt that the Egyptian priest was actually describing what he had heard of the port and palace of Minos at Knossos.

Thus a great body of Greek legend pointed to Crete as one of the fountain-heads of the earliest European civilisation, and, wild as some of the legends may seem, one of the most pointed lessons of excavation has just been that no legend is so wild that it may not have some point of contact with reality, and that behind what seems mere romance there always lies some substratum of fact, if you can discover it. So it has proved, in the most wonderful fashion, with these stories of Ancient Crete.

It was not till the closing year of the nineteenth century that any serious work of excavation was undertaken in Crete. The site of the capital of the Minoan Empire had never been forgotten, and had been frequently visited by travellers; but the remains apparent were not imposing enough to tempt to further investigation. In 1834, Pashley found that "All the now existing vestiges of the ancient metropolis of Crete are some rude masses of Roman brickwork," and Spratt, in 1851, saw little more. Cornaro, in the time of the Venetian occupation, speaks of "a very large quantity of ruins, and in particular a wall, many paces long and very thick"; but the probability is that most of what he saw perished in the long interval of Turkish misrule. Schliemann had marked the Knossos site for future exploration, and the attention of the American Stillman had been drawn to the hill called "Kephala," overlooking the site of Knossos, by the report of ruined walls of gypsum blocks engraved with curious characters; but all efforts at exploration were thwarted by the obstacles raised by the native proprietors. In 1878, a native Cretan, who bore, curiously enough, the name of the great Cretan monarch, Minos Kalochærinos, made some small excavations, and found a few of the huge jars which are characteristic of Minoan sites, and some fragments of Mycenæan pottery; but it was not till Dr. A. J. Evans (now Sir Arthur Evans) came upon the scene in 1895 that the prospect of any real work began to dawn.

The attention of Dr. Evans had been drawn to Crete by his purchase at Athens of some Cretan seal-stones, and in 1894 he began a series of explorations in Central and Eastern Crete, with the hope of discovering evidence of a Cretan system of writing. In this he was successful, a libation-table, in particular, being found in the Dictæan Cave, inscribed with a dedication in the unknown writing. In 1895, he purchased part of the hill of Kephala, and though delayed by the political troubles of the island, he was at last enabled to secure the remainder of the site in 1900, and on March 23 of that year he began the excavations which have had results even more important than those of Schliemann, and have revealed to us a forgotten world of ancient days.

Seldom has an explorer been so speedily or so completely rewarded for his faith. His first campaign lasted for nine weeks, a staff of from 80 to 150 men being employed, and during that short time about two acres of a huge prehistoric building had been unearthed. Already by the end of the first season, the palace of Knossos could be seen to have been far larger and more splendid than the mainland palaces of Tiryns or Mycenæ, and successive campaigns have revealed a vast complex of building, unparalleled on any ancient site.

The Palace was approached on the southwest side by a portico with a double doorway, whose lintel had once been supported by a massive column of wood. On the wall flanking the entrance were the remains of a fresco, part of which represented one of the favourite subjects of Mycenæan and Minoan art—a galloping bull. The walls of the corridor leading away from the portico were adorned with a painting of a procession of life-sized figures. The most prominent figure was that of a woman, probably a queen or priestess, clothed in magnificent robes, and there were also remains of the figures of two young men, wearing loin-cloths, and tight silver-edged belts, one of whom bore a fluted marble vase with a silver base. This corridor,— "the Corridor of the Procession,"—led round at its southern extremity to another great portico with double columns, and behind this portico there came to light in a passage-way the most complete picture yet found of a member of the great prehistoric race which had created the civilisation of Knossos and Mycenæ. The picture was that of the upper part of a youth, bearing in his uplifted hands a silver wine-strainer with gold mountings. He was clothed in a loin-cloth, decorated with a beautiful foliated pattern, girt in at the waist with the usual tight silver-edged belt; while he wore on the neck and upper arm silver rings, and on the wrist a silver bracelet set with an agate signet. "The colours," says Sir Arthur Evans, "were almost as brilliant as when laid down over three thousand years before. For the first time the true portraiture of a man of this mysterious Mycenæan race rises before us. The flesh tint, following perhaps an Egyptian precedent, is of a deep reddish-brown. The limbs are finely moulded, though the waist, as usual in Mycenæan fashion, is tightly drawn in by a silver-mounted girdle, giving great relief to the hips. The profile of the face is pure and almost classically Greek. . . . The lips are somewhat full, but the physiognomy has certainly no Semitic cast. The profile rendering of the eye shows an advance in human portraiture foreign to Egyptian art, and only achieved by the artists of classical Greece in the early fine-art period of the fifth century B. C.—after some eight centuries, that is, of barbaric decadence and slow revival."

Those who have seen the fresco of the Cup-bearer will not wonder at the amazement with which the discovery of this vision of prehistoric youth was greeted. "There was something very impressive," says Evans again, "in this vision of brilliant youth and of male beauty, recalled after so long an interval to our upper air from what had been till yesterday a forgotten world. Even our untutored Cretan workmen felt the spell and fascination. They, indeed, regarded the discovery of such a painting in the bosom of the earth as nothing less than miraculous, and saw in it the 'icon' of a saint! The removal of the fresco required a delicate and laborious process of under-plastering, which necessitated its being watched at night, and old Manolis, one of the most trustworthy of our gang, was told off for the purpose. Somehow or other he fell asleep, but the wrathful Saint appeared to him in a dream. Waking with a start, he was conscious of a mysterious presence; the animals round began to low and neigh, and 'there were visions about'; '$\phi a\nu\tau a\zeta\epsilon\iota$' he said, in summing up his experiences next morning. 'The whole place spooks!' "

The southern Portico gave access to a great court which turned out to have been the Central Court of the Palace—the most magnificent court ever discovered in any ancient palace and the focus of all the life of the vast building. Parallel with it there ran for 160 feet a gallery paved with blocks of gypsum, and about 11 feet in breadth. The space between this gallery and the outer wall of the palace on the western side was occupied by rows of narrow chambers which had obviously been magazines for the storage of oil and corn. Their furniture consisted of double ranges of huge earthenware jars or "pithoi," twenty of which were found in one chamber alone. These jars were all ornamented, some of them very elaborately, with spiral and rope-work patterns, and they were of a size amply sufficient to have accommodated the Forty Thieves. One of the most beautifully adorned stood almost five feet in height. Such jars had already been found, both on the Knossos site, and by Schliemann at Troy, in one instance with a quantity of pease still stored in them; but the larders of Knossos were on a scale proportioned to the magnificence of the whole building. Down the centre of each chamber, between the rows of jars, ran a row of square openings in the pavement, which had evidently been the safes for the storing of more valuable articles. They were carefully lined with lead, and so elaborately covered with stone slabs that in

some cases they could not be opened without removing the
whole pavement. All the same they had been thoroughly
rifled in ancient days, and there was little left to tell of what
they once held. Humble as was the function of this section
of the great palace, its scale, its solidity, and its finish were
such as to convey a very lively impression of the splendour
of a building whose very domestic offices were of such a type.
Fine stone-work in the doorways, careful plaster-work on
the walls, enlivened by horizontal bands of red and blue,
and the elaboration of the store-jars, all bore evidence to a
life of thoroughly organised luxury and refinement.

It was in the rooms between the Long Gallery and the
Central Court that the progress of the excavations began
to reveal some of the most interesting features of the palace.
About halfway along the court, on its western side, two
small rooms were excavated, in the centre of each of which
stood a column of four gypsum blocks, each block marked
with a single sign, the sign of the Double Axe. At once a
connection with the ancient traditions about Minos and his
works was suggested to the explorer. Already many specimens of such a weapon had been found associated with the
worship of the Cretan Zeus, and they have been found in
abundance in the cave-sanctuary of Dikté, the fabled birth-
place of the god. Now the name of the Double Axe is
"Labrys," a name found also in the title of Zeus of Karia,—
"Zeus of Labraunda." But romance has always associated
Minos and Knossos with the great structure of Dædalus
which went by the name of the Labyrinth, and in which the
Minotaur and his wretched victims were kept; and the

presence of these signs on the sacred pillars of the house of Minos linked the old tradition with the great palace which was slowly revealing itself under the spade. "There can be little doubt," said Sir Arthur Evans, "that this vast edifice, which in a broad historic sense we are justified in calling the 'Palace of Minos,' is one and the same as the traditional 'Labyrinth.'" In spite of some criticism, the identification thus suggested by the first season's excavations has grown more and more probable in the light of subsequent investigation, and is now generally accepted. Thus we have already a link between the wildly romantic legends of Ancient Greece and the solid results of modern investigation. The Labyrinth is found, and we shall see, as we go on, if not the finding of the Minotaur, at least the explanation and the evidence of how there arose in Greece the gruesome stories of the man-devouring monster—"the Bull of Minos."

A little to the north of the Pillar Rooms, access was gained to a comparatively small room, which proved of surpassing interest from the character of its appointments. Its walls were decorated with frescoes of flowering plants and running water, while on either side of the doorway leading to a small inner room there stood, in a similar flowery landscape, guardian gryphons adorned with peacock's plumes. Round the wall ran low stone benches, and on the north side there stood on a stone base a gypsum throne, its high back adorned with a curiously carved arch, with crocketed mouldings. Opposite the throne was a finely wrought tank of stone slabs, approached by a flight of steps, and originally surrounded by columns of cypress-wood supporting a kind of impluvium. Among the rubbish on the floor were many relics of former splendour; fragments of gold-foil, crystal, and lapis lazuli, and crystal plaques with painting on the back, one of them bearing an exceedingly fine miniature of a galloping bull on a blue ground, while one agate plaque, with a relief of a dagger laid upon a folded belt, almost equalled cameo work in delicacy. "Here truly was the council chamber of a Mycenæan King or Sovereign Lady." Probably Sir Arthur Evans never hoped, in his wildest dreams, to find the actual throne of Minos; yet we may fairly say that he has done so, and no more fitting or dramatic recompense could have been given to his skill and perseverance. At the least this is the oldest throne in the world, and 3500 years have passed since a king sat in it.

The main entrance of the palace lay on the north side, where the road from the harbour, 3½ miles distant, ran up to the gates. The entrance passage was a stone gangway, on the northwest side of which stood a solid bastion, with guard-room and sally-port,—the one and only trace of fortification found in the whole building. And here at once we see the difference between Knossos and the mainland palaces of the Mycenæan Age. Tiryns and Mycenæ are almost smothered in fortifications. Their imposing walls, 57 feet thick at Tiryns, 46 feet at Mycenæ, rising still, after so many centuries of ruin, to a height of 24 feet in the smaller citadel, and of 56 feet in the great fortress of Agamemnon; their stupendous gateways, and the various devices by which the assailant was forced to expose his

unshielded side to the fire of the defenders, all point to a
time of war and insecurity.  But at Knossos a palace, far
greater and richer than either, is left practically unguarded,
with its spacious courts and porticoes open on every side;
its only defence capable, perhaps, of containing a score of
guards.  It is manifest that the Minoan kings ruled a land
where peace was the rule, and where the advent of an enemy
was the last thing in the world to be expected.  And the
reason is plain when we remember the statements of Herodotus and Thucydides.  The Minoan Empire, like the
British, rested upon sea-power, and the true fortifications
of the palace of the Sea-Kings were the wooden walls of the
black, crimson-bowed galleys, which lay off the mouth of
the Kairatos River, or cruised round the island, keeping the
Minoan Peace of the Ægean.  So long as Minos had "a
fleet in being," Knossos needed no other defences; once the
fleet failed, no other defences would avail.  All the evidence
goes to show that the fleet did fail at last.  Everywhere
throughout the palace are the marks of a great conflagration,
perhaps repeated more then once during its long history.
Many of the inscribed tablets are baked as hard as stone by
the flaring of the oil in the great jars; on a site so huge,
scarcely any vessels of metal are to be found, save in one
room where the roof of the room above had fallen in blazing
ruin before the plunderers could enter; of the precious
metals there is hardly a trace, except for scattered fragments of gold foil.  All these witnesses combine to indicate
that destruction, sudden and overwhelming, fell upon the
splendour of Knossos.  Either the later Minoan sovereigns

failed to maintain the weapon which created and defended their empire, or the Minoan navy met at last with a stronger fleet or abler captains. Sea-power was lost, and with it went everything.

One of the most curious and surprising revelations of the site was that of the fashion in dress affected by the ladies of the Minoan court 1500 years before Christ. With the Minoan male garb, the fresco of the Cupbearer, and other representations, had made us familiar; and it was pretty much what would have been expected of the land and period, the only distinctive peculiarity being the excessive wasp-waistedness produced by the tight belt. But the ladies were as elaborate as their male companions were simple. Near the northern portico there came to light a series of miniature frescoes, valuable in the highest degree as contemporary documents for the appearance and dress of the period. The attire of the ladies was staggeringly modern. Anything more unlike the flowing robes of the Greek dames of the classical period it is impossible to imagine. Evening dress, extremely low-cut, puffed sleeves, skirts elaborately flounced from hem to waist, hair wonderfully frizzed and curled,—the whole effect was as far as possible removed from our preconceived ideas of the attire of Ariadne and her maids of honour. In fact, the Minoan court ladies looked as if they had stepped out of a Mid-Victorian fashion-plate. "Mais," said a French savant who came to Knossos, and was shown the portraits of these tight-laced and fur-belowed dames, "Mais, ce sont des Parisiennes!" Subsequent discoveries, such as those of the Snake-Goddesses, and

that of the marvellous little ivory and gold statuette from
an unknown site which is now in the Art Museum at Boston,
show that the court fresco-painter of Knossos in no way
exaggerated the peculiarities of Minoan feminine garb. The
men of Knossos seem to belong to their period; but the
ladies of the court of Minos are of the mid-nineteenth
century.

One of the great artistic finds of the season's work, valuable intrinsically, was yet more precious because of the
emphasis which it laid on a feature of Minoan life of which
evidence had already been forthcoming, both at Knossos,
and in the mainland excavations at Tiryns and Vaphio.
This was the plaster relief of a great bull's head, which had
once formed part of a complete figure. As a work of art it
is superb in its realism and vigour. "No figure of a bull,"
says Evans, "at once so powerful and so true, was produced
by later classical art." Indeed to match this magnificent
monster, one must go, not to Greece, but to Egypt, where
his parallels are to be found in the Old Empire tomb-reliefs,
or the splendid Eighteenth Dynasty statue of the Hathor-
Cow unearthed in 1906 by Naville from the Eleventh Dynasty Temple at Der-el-Bahri. The bull-relief, however,
has another importance, not inferior to that of its artistic
quality, in the evidence which it gives of the stress which
was laid on the bull as an object either of sport or religion,
or, more probably, of both combined. The bull of Tiryns,
the bull of the western corridor fresco, and the bull-relief,
all emphasise the place which this animal held in the
Minoan scheme of things, and the grim significance of that

place was revealed by the later discovery of a fresco which gave the key to all the previous finds, and to the origin of the legend of the man-devouring Minotaur.

The fresco in question was a picture of the sport in which the Minoan monarchs took delight. It was found among the debris which had fallen from a room overlooking one of the courts of the palace, known as the Court of the Olive-Spout. It represented a group of three toreadors, a youth and two girls, with a single bull. The girls are dressed like their male companion, but are distinguished by their white skins, their more highly coloured costumes, their curlier hair, and their diadems of blue and red. In the centre, the great bull is in full charge. The youth has grasped the horn of the monster, and is turning a clean somersault over the brute's back, and one of the girls holds out her hands to catch him as he leaps to the ground. The other girl, standing in front of the galloping bull, is just at the critical moment of the cruel game. The great horns are almost passing under her arms, and a moment will decide whether she succeeds in catching them and following her companions in their daring leap, or misses her grip, and is tossed and trampled in the dust of the arena. Such was the sport on which the kings of the House of Minos delighted to look,—a sport where life or death hung on a moment, and in which the slightest failure of nerve, or miscalculation of distance, meant instant and horrible death. In such a game, we may be sure that the tragedies of the Knossian bull-ring were many and ghastly, and we need not wonder that the nations whose captives perished

to make sport for the Minoan court wove tales of super-
natural horror around the scene of their death.  The Bull
of Minos was a man-devouring monster sure enough, even
though he was not the half-man, half-brute of the old
legend.

A suggestion of how the captives were kept till the time
came for their ordeal was given by the discovery of two
pits, which went down beneath the palace floor for 25 feet
to the solid rock.  They were lined with masonry faced
with smooth cement, and were perhaps the dungeons of the
palace, where the human tribute paid by the conquered
states dragged out a miserable existence until the time came
for training in the dreadful sport, and the stern alternative
of life or death in the bull-ring.  Curiously enough, the
room beneath which one of these dark pits was found was
itself decorated with one of the daintiest evidences of Minoan artistic taste,—the figure of a Minoan Blue-Boy, gathering white crocuses, and placing them in a vase.  Cruelty
and beauty went often hand in hand in many of the civilisations of the Ancient East; but it is not often that the two
things are found so close as in that room at Knossos, with
its innocent picture of the Crocus-Gatherer on the wall, and
its grim pit beneath.

In another room of the palace, a small obscure chamber,
which had apparently served as a treasury, there came to
light further evidence of the place which this cruel sport
of Bull-grappling held in the Minoan scheme of things.
This was a deposit of ivory figurines of exquisite workmanship.  The best preserved specimen measures about 11½

PLATE XXXI

PALACE OF MINOS, KNOSSOS—GENERAL VIEW

inches in height. It is that of a man hurling himself forth
in a violent leap, legs and arms at full stretch. The straining muscles are indicated with perfect faithfulness, and
the veins of the tiny hand, and the diminutive finger nails
are clearly marked. Originally the head had been covered
with curling locks of hair in gold wire, the insertions of
which were still visible. Doubtless these figures once
formed part of a model representation of the sport of the
Knossian Bull-ring, and were suspended by thin gold wires
over the backs of ivory bulls. Such multiplication of representations of a single theme suggests the grasp which this
sport had upon the Cretan mind, and the probability that
its universality was the result of the important place which
the bull appears to have held in the Minoan religion.

Further evidence of the Minoan love of sport was forthcoming in 1903, in the discovery of what Sir Arthur Evans
has called the Theatral Area of the palace. At the northwest angle of the building, close to the western court, there
was revealed a paved area, measuring about 40 by 30 feet,
and divided up the middle by a gangway. Its eastern and
southern sides were lined with rows of steps, arranged in
a manner suggesting that they may have been used as seats.
At the meeting-point of the two sets of rows, in the southeastern angle, there stood a bastion of solid masonry. In
the view of the discoverer this was a primitive theatre, where
the inhabitants of the palace gathered to witness sports
of some kind, the rows of steps answering to the benches
of the Roman Circus, while the bastion may have been the
royal box, where the throne was placed. The steps would

give accommodation for something like four or five hundred spectators. If we may assume that this is the true explanation of the building, it is obvious that the sport of the bull-ring cannot have taken place here, for the area is far too small, while the undefended position of the spectators would have ensured that the audience ran as much risk as the actors. We know from the great vase found at Hagia Triada, and from many other sources, that boxing was a favourite sport with the Minoans, and the Theatral Area may conceivably have been the first recorded boxing-ring, in which the champions of the Minoan Fancy contended for the championship belt of the Ægean. On the other hand, it may have been the scene of less brutal exhibitions. Dancing played a great part in the life, both secular and religious, of these old days, and Homer has told us of "The Dancing-ground which Dædalus wrought in broad Knossos for fair-haired Ariadne." It is quite possible that the Theatral Area may have been the very "Choros" of which the old minstrel sang.

One of the most amazing revelations of the excavations at Knossos was that of the artistic quality of the race of the Sea-Kings. The Minoan race, spite of the cruel twist which is revealed by the bull-fighting pictures and reliefs, was one possessed, almost more than any ancient people, by a passionate love of the beautiful. We have already seen the evidence of this in the fresco-painting which was everywhere in evidence throughout the palace. But the passion for beauty went into every department and aspect of life. Even the great earthenware pots of the palace storehouses were of fine shape and tasteful decoration, and the smaller articles of pottery, especially the vessels of the fine polychrome ware, known as "Kamares" ware, are exquisite alike in shape, colour, and workmanship. Some of the cups of this ware are of extreme fineness and delicacy, approaching to that of the finest egg-shell china. One can scarcely imagine anything more beautiful than the dainty conventionalism of the famous "Water-Lily Cup," with its ground of lustrous black, and its design of conventionalised water-lilies whose white petals start from a centre at the foot of the cup, and enfold its body.

Among the most convincing evidences of Minoan artistic skill were the steatite vases found, not at Knossos, but at Hagia Triada, with their decoration in low relief. On one of these is represented a procession, which has been variously interpreted as a band of soldiers returning in triumph from a victory, or as a group of harvesters celebrating the harvest-festival. Apart from all questions of its meaning, the artistic quality of the group is very remarkable. It has been truly said of this little vase that "not until the fifth century B. C. should we find a sculptor capable of representing, with such absolute truth, a party of men in motion." On another of these vases, the "Chieftain Vase," the artist has modelled on one side a body of soldiers, with their great shields locked together, and their heads and feet showing above and below the shield-wall. On the other side stands a chieftain, with long flowing hair, and a staff of office, apparently giving orders to a captain who stands before him in an attitude of attention, his long heavy sword sloped over his shoulder. The modelling of these two figures, and the way in which their muscular development is indicated, is marvellous, especially when the diminutive scale is considered, for the vase measures only four inches in height. "The ideal grace and dignity of these two figures," says Professor Burrows, "the pose with which they throw head and body back, is beyond any representation of the human figure hitherto known before the best period of Archaic Hellenic art."

Little of the work of Minoan artists in metal was forthcoming from the excavations at Knossos, for obvious reasons. Metal-work, especially in the precious metals, was too tempting for the plunderers who sacked the great palace to leave much of it behind. The golden cups found at Vaphio in Greece, and considered by all competent authorities to be of Cretan workmanship, gave evidence that the Minoan goldsmith was possessed of a skill which would not have disgraced the best artists of the Renaissance, and their witness was supplemented by the discovery at Knossos, in a room where the floor of the room above had fallen in before the plunderers had time to do their work, of four splendid bronze basins and a single-handled ewer. These proved to be of fine design and workmanship, the largest basin, 39 centimetres in diameter, being exquisitely wrought with a foliated margin and handle, while another has a beautiful design of conventionalised lilies on its border.

The passion for beauty went even into the sports of the Minoan court, as was proved by the discovery of the splendid "King's Gaming-Board." This was a board of over a yard in length, and more than half a yard in breadth. Its frame was of ivory, originally overlaid with thin gold plate, and it was covered with a mosaic of strips and discs of rock-crystal, backed with silver and blue enamel. Round its margin ran a border of marguerites, whose central bosses were discs of rock-crystal, set originally in blue enamel. At the top were four fine reliefs of nautilus shells, set round with crystal plaques, and bossed with crystal, and below them four large medallions, set among crystal bars, backed with silver plate, while the rest of the ornament consisted of bars of gold-plated ivory alternating with bars of crystal on a setting of blue enamel. Mere detail of its decoration can convey no idea of the splendour of a piece of work which "defies description, with its blaze of gold and silver, ivory and crystal."

Curiously enough, with the exception of the large frescoes, which are often somewhat inferior in artistic merit to the smaller efforts of the Knossian artist, little or no work on a large scale was found; above all no large sculpture in the round. Minoan art was almost entirely small art, so far as scale goes, a fact which points to a distinct limitation in the artistic outlook of the race. It is remarkable that a people which was in constant touch, throughout its great period, with the Egypt of the Eighteenth Dynasty, and its magnificent works of sculpture on the grand scale, should never have been inspired by them to emulation. Along with this goes the strange inequality in the artistic merit of the work which the Minoan monarchs accepted, apparently with equanimity, for the decoration of their palace. In the same building you have work of the very highest quality, side by side with work which is crude and elementary in design and execution. Mr. Hall's explanation is probably the true one. "The love of life and beauty dominated the Cretan artists; they were bound by no trammels of convention, and to this was due the inequality of their work. . . . The highly trained hands of the Egyptian craftsman, an artist rather from education than in spirit, would have been incapable of such unequal work. The Cretan, however, a true artist, did what pleased him."

It is perhaps this fact which gives the curious feeling of modernity which is characteristic of Minoan work. Before the great art of Mesopotamia, and perhaps even more before that of Egypt, one feels that here is something which, however splendid, has said all that it has to say; but Minoan art, with all its crudities and imperfections, is seminal, and has the promise of something greater in it. What that something greater was, the world was to see with wonder that has never ceased to grow, when to the swifter, subtler, and more beauty-loving genius of the conquered Minoan race was wedded the stronger, sterner, and more restrained spirit of the conquering Achæans and Dorians, in that union which bore as its fruit the wonders of fifth century Hellenic Art.

Altogether the impression left upon the mind by the relics of Minoan art is that of a people of astonishing mental agility, extraordinarily alert and sensitive to original ideas, and sometimes overflowing, in the very fulness of its life, into the crudity and gaudiness which not uncommonly char-

acterise an art which is superabundant in strength, but has
not yet learned how to curb its energy. Side by side with
this occasional lapse into what can only be called bad taste,
there goes the revelation, not only in the great frescoes, but
even more in such work as the seal-impressions from Zakro
and elsewhere, of a strange, weird, unpleasant twist in the
Minoan nature. There was something perverted and unhealthy in the fancy which designed some of the nightmare figures on these seals, whether their significance was
religious or merely fantastic. Yet, when all is said, the fact
remains that to turn from the reliefs of an Assyrian palace
to the frescoes of Knossos is like turning from a shambles to
a green meadow in spring-time. The Assyrian was a
magnificent and cultured brute, a primitive savage, for all
his surface splendour; the Minoan was a true artist, essentially modern in his love of beauty for its own sake.

Perhaps the most surprising evidence of his modernity
was that given in the most commonplace aspect of his life
by the discovery of the amazingly complete system of drainage with which the palace of Knossos was provided,—a
discovery supplemented by that of similar systems, on a
smaller scale, in other places. The position of the palace, on
the side of a hill, enabled the architect to carry out a
drainage-system on a scale of completeness which it would
be difficult to parallel, not only in any ancient building, but
in any European house or city, until the middle of the nineteenth century. The main drain of the palace was a well-
built stone conduit, 1 metre by ½ metre, lined with smooth
cement, and provided with an ample supply of ventilators

and manholes for inspection.   Into this main artery led a number of stone shafts, descending from the upper floors, and leading into the great conduit the surface water from the palace roofs, so that the periodical flushing of the drain was secured.   Some of the terra-cotta pipes which served as connections to the main drain have been found in perfect preservation.   They are actually faucet-jointed pipes of the most modern type, each section 2 feet in length and 6 inches in diameter, tapering to 4 inches.   "Jamming was carefully prevented by a stop-ridge that ran round the outside of each narrow end a few inches from the mouth, while the inside of the butt, or broader end, was provided with a raised collar that enabled it to bear the pressure of the next pipe's stop-ridge, and gave an extra hold for the cement that bound the two pipes together."   In connection with this system of conduits and pipes, there was elaborated a system of latrines and other contrivances of a sanitary nature, which, as Sir Arthur Evans says, are "staggeringly modern" in their appointments.   Nothing gives a clearer idea of the essentially civilised character of Minoan life, 14 centuries B. C., than this humble adjunct to the splendours of the great palace.   It took the European world more than three thousand years to regain the sanitary knowledge which was lost when the Minoan Empire collapsed.

One of the questions which Evans hoped to solve by his excavations at Knossos was that of the existence or non-existence of a system of writing among the Mediterranean race.   As late as 1894, M. Perrot wrote with perfect correctness, so far as the existing evidence went, "Nowhere, neither in the Peloponnese nor in Greece proper, . . . has there anything been discovered which resembled any kind of writing." Plainly, however, it was only lack of evidence that made such a statement possible. It was quite un-thinkable, that while the Egyptians and the Mesopotamian races had their fully-developed scripts, a race capable of building the palaces and tombs of Mycenæ and Tiryns, and of executing such works of art as the diadems of the Shaft-Graves, or the Vaphio Cups, should have been so rude in one of the essentials of progress as to have possessed no means of written communication. The first season's work at Knossos confirmed the explorer in his faith that "that great early civilisation was not dumb." By the end of the first month's work the finding of one inscribed clay tablet had solved the problem, and before work closed for the season upwards of a thousand such tablets had been dis-covered. Since then the material has been rapidly accumu-lating, till now the number of articles, tablets, labels, and other things, inscribed with one or other of the various forms of Minoan writing, may be reckoned by thousands.

Unfortunately all this mass of material has so far proved indecipherable. We can trace a gradual development from the earliest rude pictographs, though a hieroglyphic system, apparently somewhat akin to that of the Hittites, to a definitely linear script, which exists in two distinct forms; but beyond this it has been impossible to advance. The chief ground for hope would seem to lie in the possibility that there may come to light a bilingual inscription, giving a Minoan version of some treaty or other document, side by

side with an Egyptian version of the same text.  In view of
the long-continued connection between the two empires, it
seems fairly certain that such documents must have existed,
and it is not beyond the bounds of possibility that future
excavation may provide the key to the earliest of European
scripts, which antedates the earliest Phœnician writing by
at least five centuries.

In 1908 there was found at Phæstos, the site of the
other large Cretan palace, the largest inscribed tablet which
has yet been discovered.  It was a disc of terra-cotta, 6.67
inches in diameter, covered on both sides with an inscription
which coils round from the centre outwards.  "It contains
241 signs, and 64 sign-groups, and it exhibits the remarkable
peculiarity that every sign has been separately impressed
on the clay while in a soft state by a stamp or punch.  It
is, in fact, a printed inscription."  Sir Arthur Evans, in his
"Scripta Minoa," has advanced the theory that this inscription is not Cretan, but Lycian, and may represent a script
used in the coast-lands of Asia Minor.  Various attempts
at an interpretation of the disc have been put forward; but
it is stating the matter mildly to say that none of these has
yet won any conviction.  The Phæstos disc, along with the
tablets of Knossos, remains an enigma, which may, and
doubtless will, be solved, but which so far has found no
solution worth considering.

Excavation has been resumed by Sir Arthur Evans at
Knossos in 1922, with results which seem to suggest that
the site is almost inexhaustible.  Perhaps the most interesting of the fruits of the last campaign was the discovery

in the South-East angle of the palace of a feature which seemed to suggest that, as the explorer puts it—"Fables certainly seemed to be coming true." "The excavation of the neighbouring vault within the Palace angle—dangerous work, which had to be conducted slowly—had brought us to a floor-level about thirty feet down. Here were no signs of earlier human occupation, but on the southeast side appeared the opening of an artificial cave with three roughly-cut steps leading down to what can only be described as a lair adapted for some great beast. . . . Is it possible that lions—already, as we know, frequent subjects of Minoan engravers before the date of the foundation of the Palace—were kept for show in the precincts of the more ancient Residency that seems to have existed on the hill of Knossos? The traditions of such an usage—doubtless with other accretions—may well have contributed to the origin of the later tales of the Minotaur that haunted the site in historic times." It is perhaps too much to say, as has been said, that the actual lair of the Minotaur has been discovered, and the excavator himself is notably cautious in his use of the discovery; yet it would only be in accordance with the extraordinary developments yielded by recent exploration in the Ægean area, that while Dr. Wace at Mycenæ is finding the red-stuccoed bath which suggests the slaughter of Agamemnon, Sir Arthur Evans, at Knossos, should be finding the lair in which, if not the Minotaur, yet at all events the creature which gave its origin to the old fable, found its abode.

So far, our attention has been mainly confined to the

results of the excavations at Knossos, because these have illustrated in the most remarkable manner the legendary history of Crete.   Other work, only less important than that at Knossos, has, however, been carried on at various other sites in the island.   At Phæstos, the Italian Expedition, under Professor Halbherr and Signor Pernier, has excavated the remains of another great palace, similar to, though somewhat smaller than, that of Knossos.   Like the larger palace, that of Phæstos has its central court, its Theatral Area, and its treasure of beautiful Kamares ware; while its main glory is the magnificent flight of steps, 45 feet in width, which formed the State Entrance—perhaps the most splendid staircase that ever a royal palace had.   Apart from its Kamares vases, Phæstos proved extraordinarily poor in articles of artistic value; but this disappointment was atoned for by the discovery, on the hill of Hagia Triada, about two miles northwest of the palace, of a Royal Villa, which proved as rich in objects of art as Phæstos had been poor.   Here were discovered the Harvester and Chieftain Vases, already described, together with a larger vessel of less artistic merit, representing boxing scenes.   One of the frescoes, a picture of a cat hunting a red pheasant, is of extraordinary vivacity, and has been pronounced by Professor Burrows superior to the famous Egyptian tomb-picture of the marsh fowler with his trained cat.   This is a hard saying; and yet the Minoan work is of astonishing quality.

The Royal Villa showed the same careful attention to the details of sanitation which characterised Knossos, and

an Italian observer has noted a curious circumstance, showing the honesty with which the old work had been
performed. "One day," says Dr. Mosso, describing a visit
to Hagia Triada, "after a heavy downpour of rain, I was
interested to find that all the drains acted perfectly, and I
saw the water flow from sewers through which a man could
walk upright. I doubt if there is another instance of a
drainage system acting after 4000 years."

The results of excavation in Crete have not been confined
to royal palaces. At Gournia, on the northeastern side of
the island, an American lady, Miss Harriet Boyd (now
Mrs. Boyd-Hawes) unearthed a complete little town with
its modest palace for the local magnate, its shrine, and its
cluster of burgher's houses. The narrow roadways of the
little town—only 5 feet broad, and neatly paved—give
proof that wheeled vehicles were seldom used. The average house suggests a considerable amount of comfort, and a
fairly high standard of life. The houses of common craftsmen have from 6 to 8 rooms, while those of the better-off
townsmen have sometimes twice as many. That the citizens
could read and write was evidenced by the tablet bearing
an inscription in the script of Knossos, and that they, like
their superiors in the great palaces, were not deficient in
taste for art was shown by the beauty of their painted pottery. The little town, its discoverer thinks, was sacked
and burned about 1500 B. C. Similar evidence as to the
standard of common life under the Minoan Sea-Kings came
from Palaikastro, while at Zakro, on the eastern coast, Mr.
Hogarth excavated the remains of an important trading-

station.  Here were found those clay seal-impressions of weird design, 500 of them in a single house, to which allusion has already been made.  Among other sites must be mentioned the tiny island of Mokhlos, which yielded to another American explorer, Mr. Seager, evidence, so conspicuously lacking on the great palace sites, of the skill with which the Minoan craftsman wrought in the precious metals. Some of the gold chains found here would not have disgraced the best workmen of any period.  "As beautifully wrought," says Sir A. Evans, "as the best Alexandrian fabrics of the beginning of our era."

Thus, then, we have seen some of the evidence which has been yielded by excavation of the existence of a great civilisation which must have played a conspicuous part in the history of human development; which yet had passed entirely, save for a few fragments of romantic legend, from the memory of man.  There remain two questions, inevitably suggested by the facts which we have been considering, to which we must endeavour to find some kind of an answer. These are—first—Where, in the framework of ancient history as it is known to us, are we to place this forgotten Empire of the Minoan Sea-Kings? and—second—How was it that a state apparently so powerful, and certainly so remarkably advanced in civilisation, fell from its high estate and passed away so utterly?

The answer to the first question is rendered more difficult by the absence of any intelligible records.  Could we read the inscribed tablets of Knossos, it is possible, though by no means certain, that we might find evidence which would

enable us to establish synchronisms with one or other of the
great civilisations of the Ancient East, most probably with
that of Egypt, which might help to fix the various periods
of Minoan chronology on a sure basis. Meanwhile this is
impossible, and our only guide is that of the artistic development of the race as it can be traced in the various strata
of the excavated remains, and emphasised by finds in Egypt
which link its stages with one or other of the definitely
established periods of Egyptian history.

Working on these lines, Evans has framed a scheme of
Minoan development which agrees with the known facts,
and which at certain points is buttressed by Egyptian evi-
dence in such a manner as to leave no doubt of its general
accuracy. He divides Minoan development into three great
periods, each in its turn subdivided into three sub-periods.
Before the rise of the first of these periods, we have the
Neolithic Age, going back in Crete, according to his estimate,
to about 10,000 B. C., and continuing till about 3000 B. C.
From 3000 to 2200 B. C., we have the Early Minoan
Period, divided, as already indicated, into three sub-periods.
At the beginning of this period, the links with the Egypt of
the earliest dynasties are few and a little uncertain. Vases
of primitive hand-burnished ware, found by Professor Petrie
in some of the First Dynasty graves at Abydos, are certainly
not of native Egyptian origin, and closely resemble the
primitive ware found in the stratum immediately overlying
the Neolithic deposit at Knossos, while at Knossos in turn
have been found vessels of hard stone exquisitely wrought.
The taste for these vessels is a marked characteristic of the

Egypt of the earliest dynasties, and their presence at
Knossos would seem to indicate, if not direct importation,
at least the influence of Egyptian taste on the Cretan craftsmen of the period. By the time of the Sixth Dynasty, the
evidence for intercourse is unmistakable. Egyptian stone
vases of the period are copied by Cretan craftsmen, while in
one instance, discovered by Mr. Seager at Mokhlos, an
Egyptian vase of this time has been imported. Artists, both
in the Nile Valley and in Crete, are borrowing each other's
motives and using them on native materials, in a manner
which makes frequent intercourse unquestionable. We
may say, then, that the earliest stage of Minoan culture
roughly equates with the earliest Dynastic culture of Egypt.

With Middle Minoan (c. 2200-1600 B. C.), in its first
division, we have the beginnings of the earlier palaces at
Knossos and Phæstos, and in its second, the development
of the beautiful polychrome Kamares ware, and, towards
the end, the first destruction of Knossos, while Third Middle
Minoan witnesses the beginning of the later palace of
Knossos, and the first villa of Hagia Triada. The occur-
rence, in Twelfth Dynasty tombs in Egypt, of specimens of
Kamares ware, shows that Middle Minoan was contemporary with this Golden Age of Egypt, the age of the Amen-
emhats, while Third Middle Minoan has given us from
Knossos an Egyptian statuette, bearing a name characteristic
of the Thirteenth Egyptian Dynasty, and an alabastron
inscribed with the name of Khyan, one of the most famous
kings of the Hyksos, whose usurpation follows, and continues up to the rise of the Seventeenth and Eighteenth

Dynasties. We may say with some confidence then, that Middle Minoan, the period which has left some of the most exquisite examples of Cretan ceramic art, is to be equated with the Middle Kingdom of Egypt, and the subsequent period of confusion under the Hyksos invaders.

Late Minoan (c. 1600-1400 B. C.) brings us upon sure ground. For in the tombs of Sen-mut and Rekh-ma-ra, the famous viziers of Hatshepsut and Thothmes III, there are depicted, under the name of "Keftiu," "the Men from Beyond," manifest Minoans, bearing vessels which are equally manifest products of First Late Minoan art. The Third Late Minoan period began before the end of Egypt's Eighteenth Dynasty, for Minoan pottery of this period has been found in the ruins of the palace of the unfortunate Akhenaten at Tell-el-Amarna. So that we may safely place this last great division of Cretan culture, which witnesses the splendours and the destruction of the later palaces at Knossos and Phæstos, in the same two centuries which saw Egypt establish herself as a world-empire, and then collapse under the misguided zeal of the first great religious innovator.

The Minoan Empire comes to a close with the fall of Knossos (c. 1400 B. C.), but the Third Late Minoan art lasts much longer, continuing in Greece, to which the overlordship of the Ægean passed after the fall of the Sea-Kings, probably till somewhere round about 1200 B. C.

The evidence, then, of Knossos, Phæstos, and the other Cretan sites is absolutely conclusive on the point that the origins of European civilisation are not the comparatively modern things which they were esteemed to be, not so long ago, in comparison with the hoary antiquity of the cultures of the Nile and Euphrates Valleys, and that still less can they be assumed to have been derived from these. Civilisation was beginning to find itself in Crete practically at the same time when it began to dawn upon the Nile Valley, and its development in the Island Kingdom kept step, pace for pace, with the very different development of the Egyptian genius. In some respects the Cretan was the inferior of his Egyptian contemporary; Crete has nothing to show even remotely approaching the magnificence of the great Egyptian temples; in others he was the superior (speaking of Knossos, Mr. H. R. Hall has risked the opinion that "in comparison with this wonderful building the palaces of Egyptian Pharaohs were but elaborate hovels of painted mud"); but always he was thoroughly original, owing inspiration to nothing but his own amazingly alert and fresh mind.

"In material civilisation," says Mr. Hall again, "the Minoan Cretans were at least as highly developed as the Egyptians or Mesopotamians, in some ways more highly developed, at any rate as regards the amenities of life. Their sense of beauty and mental freedom seem to have been untrammelled by Semitic asceticism or Egyptian religious conventionality. They lived cruelly, perhaps, and possibly (according to our ideas) wickedly, but certainly beautifully."

There remains our second question—How a civilisation so great and splendid should have collapsed so suddenly and passed away so utterly as that of the Minoans, to all appearance, did. Here, again, the absence of any intelligible record bars the way to any certain conclusion, and we are reduced to inference. We know that fire and sword was no uncommon end to the splendours and comforts of Ægean life in those wild days, when piracy was the natural and gentlemanly resource for young scions of noble houses without visible means of support. A seafaring stranger was possibly an honest trader, but quite as likely a pirate, and it was no insult, but the natural thing, to ask him to which category he belonged. "Who are you?" says Nestor to Telemachus. "Whence do you come? Are you engaged in trade, or do you rove at adventure as sea-robbers who wander at hazard of their lives, bringing bane to strangers?" The palace of Knossos had already been destroyed, at the end of the Second Middle Minoan Period, perhaps by some of these sea-rovers, perhaps by the rival lords of Phæstos. The little trading towns of Gournia and Pseira were found, by Miss Boyd and Mr. Seager, to have been sacked and burned; and no doubt such disasters were frequent enough.

But the second catastrophe of Knossos was something more overwhelming and conclusive than could have been caused by any mere raid of pirates. It was a disaster which completely broke the power and spirit of the race of the Sea-kings. Knossos rose from its first burning greater and more splendid than ever; but from the second there was no recovery. A period of re-occupation there was indeed, in which some of the old stock who had escaped the slaughter of the sack crept back to the ruins of their holy and beautiful house, and dwelt in it, dividing its stately halls by flimsy partitions into smaller rooms suited to their fallen state. But from this time the headship of the Ægean passes to the mainland of Greece, and the Minoan civilisation becomes Mycenæan.

That fact may suggest to us how the end came, and by whose hands. Dr. Mackenzie has put forward the theory that the destruction of the Palace of Knossos, and the break-up of Minoan power, was the work of the Mycenæans of Tiryns and Mycenæ. Already, towards the close of the Minoan period, the pressure of the invading northern tribes, Achæans, and Danaoi, was beginning to be felt by the mainland cities, and it became necessary for the Mycenæans to find new homes for themselves. Naturally they turned, in their need, to the land from which their forefathers had come, hoping that the Cretans would be willing to welcome immigrants of their own race. But this expectation was disappointed. The Minoan rulers were not prepared to receive the new-comers, and the homeless Mycenæans, under the spur of a stern necessity, took by force what was denied to their supplication.

Mr. H. R. Hall has modified this theory to some extent. In his view, the sack of Knossos was the work of Mycenæans who were still masters in their own mainland realm, and had succeeded, so far, in holding in subjection the first waves of Achæan immigration, and in using their power for their own ends. The conquerors who destroyed Knossos and brought the Minoan Empire to an end "were, it may be, the descendants of those Cretans who had gone forth to colonise Pylos, Mycenæ and Orchomenos, and had sent the yearly tribute of Athenian youth to be sacrificed to the deity of Knossos. And with them marched their subjects, the Achæans or Danaoi of the North." The difference is small, and in either case the result was the same. The Empire of the Sea-Kings of the Ægean fell by the hands of its own children, and fell never to rise again.

The traces of the ruined civilisation did not disappear all at once. After all, the mainland destroyers were men of the same stock as the race which they dispossessed, and the products of Cretan culture are still found filtering into Egypt for a matter of two centuries more; but the spirit of the race had been broken by the great disaster, and its art is no longer living, but dragging out an existence from which the soul has departed. "For Crete," says Professor Burrows, "the sack is Ægospotami, Late Minoan III, the long months that culminate in the surrender of Athens; the sack is Leipzig, Late Minoan III, the slow closing in on Paris that leads up to the abdication of Napoleon." The destruction of the sea-power of Knossos must have involved anarchy in the Ægean, and with it the disappearance of the commerce on which the great island depended for the support of its teeming population. Lycian pirates and other wolves of the sea would quickly drive the defenceless Minoan merchant fleet from the seas. With it would vanish the purple fisheries and the oil-trade, and the land would no longer be able to maintain its people.

Doubtless the Cretans, in their need, did to others what

had been done to them; and it is probably to a piece of forcible colonising on their part that we may refer the sudden appearance, in the midst of the sluggish Bronze Age Culture of Cyprus, of a Cypriote version of Late Minoan III art. Another trace of their influence is seen in the great invasion of the Sea-Peoples, which caused such trouble and anxiety to the Egypt of Ramses III. In the eighth year of the reign of this king, the eastern Mediterranean was swept by the incursion of a cluster of allied tribes. "The isles were restless, disturbed among themselves," says Ramses in his inscription at Medinet Habu. The invading island host landed in Northern Syria, absorbed the fragments of the once formidable Hittite confederacy, and pressed southwards by the coast route, their war-fleet keeping pace with the march of the land-army. Somewhere on the coast of Palestine the invaders were met by the fleet and army of Egypt, and the double battle which ensued ended in their complete overthrow. Of the invading tribes, three have been identified, more or less probably, with the fragments of the old Minoan Empire. Of these the Zakkaru have been associated with the town of Zakro in Crete, and the Uashasha with Axos. The third tribe, the Pulesti, are of supreme interest; for, practically beyond question, they are the Philistines, who disputed so long with the rising Hebrew state the dominion of Palestine, and though defeated in the end, yet have left the impress of their might in the name of the land which they came so near mastering.

Hebrew tradition brought the Philistines from Kaphtor, which is the Egyptian Kefti, "the Land at the Back of

Beyond," from which the Minoan ambassadors came to the court of Queen Hatshepsut and Thothmes III. Further, in the district of the Philistine League, and especially at Tell-es-Safi (Gath), many specimens of Late Minoan III pottery have been discovered.

It is surely one of the romances of history that the nation which has been so familiar to us all as the dreaded enemy of the Hebrew kingdom should turn out to have been the last remnant of the vanished empire of the Sea-Kings of Knossos. It gives a new perspective to think of Samson making sport for his captors in a Minoan Theatral Area, like the one at Knossos, while Cretan ladies, in their strangely modern garb, look on, as their ancestresses had looked upon the feats and agonies of their captives from Athens or Megara; while the pulling down of the pillars of the portico becomes intelligible when you realise that the Hebrew champion was dealing, not with a built column, but with one of cedar or cypress-wood, set on a stone base. Goliath, too, was no rude barbaric figure, such as we used to picture, but one of these Greeks before the Greeks, wearing the bronze panoply and the feather-crested helmet which his people had adopted in their later days instead of the leather cap and figure-8 shield of earlier times.

Strangest of all is the fact that we have to revise completely our conception of the character of a whole race, and of the relative position of East and West. To us, from time immemorial, the Philistine has stood for the type of the outer barbarian, intellectually and artistically; he was actually the descendant of what was perhaps the most naturally gifted and artistic race that the world has ever known. To us, also, the East has been the type of all that is ancient in civilisation, and the West, with its rude strength, comes in to dispossess the inheritor of an ancient culture which it could never have created. But the actual facts of the case, when East and West, in the persons of Hebrew and Philistine, first met in conflict, were exactly the opposite of our pre-conceived opinion. "When West first met East on the shores of the Holy Land," says Dr. Macalister, "it was the former which represented the magnificent tradition of the past, and the latter which looked forward to the future. The Philistines were of the remnant of the dying glories of Crete; the Hebrews had no past to speak of, but were entering on the heritage they regarded as theirs, by right of a recently ratified divine covenant."

Further, and most important of all, is the fact that it seems not improbable that it is to the Philistines, and through them to the old culture of the Sea-Kings, that we owe our Bible. More than likely the Hebrews learned from their great enemies the use of the alphabet, with all that this implies. It used to be believed that the Phœnicians gave to the world the use of the alphabet, as distinct from Egyptian picture-writing, or Mesopotamian cuneiform. But we now know that, centuries before the Phœnicians dreamed of writing, the Minoans were using a linear script far in advance of anything attained by either Egypt or Babylonia. The Philistines brought their linear writing with them to Palestine, and it was from the example of their old enemies that the Hebrews learned to form an alphabet of their own.

And thus, by the most curious chain of interwoven national destinies, the West has provided the means for the transmission of that precious spiritual heritage which it has been the glory of the East to give to the world, and the wonderful art of expression which reached its first development in the clay tablets of the Palace of Knossos has its own share in the great book which is the treasure of every Christian nation to-day, and has influenced so profoundly the course of world-civilisation.

# CHAPTER XIII

### GEZER: A CITY OF MANY RACES

FROM one point of view, and that the point which most appeals to the average intelligent person of the present day, the story of excavation in Palestine has been, on the whole, one of disappointment.  Half a century has now passed since Captain Warren began the work of seeking in Bible lands the material which should elucidate the existing records of the nation which has had a greater influence on the spiritual history of the world than any other race.  At that time the hopes of those who supported the new enterprise were high, —as we now know, unreasonably high.  "When Captain Warren began his work," says Dr. R. A. S. Macalister, "it was expected by many that a few strokes of the spade would settle the questionings on Biblical subjects that were then being asked with ever increasing persistence.  The dreams of the subscribers centred round records of David's wars and of Solomon's glory; the Ark of the Covenant and the idols of Manasseh; some, perhaps, hoped for a letter or two written by one privileged to hear the words of Him who spake as never man spake.  Nothing of the kind has come to light, however, with the single exception of the Moabite Stone— and that was not discovered by a professed explorer, but

[410]

lighted upon by accident by a travelling missionary who had no idea of the value of his 'find'!"

The reasons for the disappointment are sufficiently manifest to us now, and it is comparatively easy to be wise after the event, and to point out causes which should have been taken into consideration, and which were sufficient to render the meagre result of so much labour practically inevitable; but it was not so easy for men whose eyes were dazzled by the brilliant results of the work of Botta and Layard in Mesopotamia, and Mariette in Egypt, to see that the conditions in Palestine were so entirely different as almost to preclude the possibility of any similar success being attained there. We have to remember that in Palestine, throughout its history, there never existed any such great organised and long-enduring state as that which created the vast palaces of Nineveh, Khorsabad, and Babylon, or the yet vaster temples of Thebes. The domination of a single central power in Palestine only began about 1000 B. C., at a time when Egypt was already far advanced towards decadence; and it only endured for what, in the ancient history of the East, is nothing more than a day. There was nothing in the known history of Palestine to encourage the hope that there could be any survival even of the most fragmentary ruins of such great works as marked the dominion of the great empires of Mesopotamia and the Nile Valley. Great works were, no doubt, carried out during the brief splendour of the reign of Solomon; but the subsequent history of the land was such that little of these could be expected to have survived.

For we have to remember that Palestine was for many centuries the cockpit of the Ancient East, just as the Low Countries were the cockpit of Europe. Her Maritime Plain was the old war road, the bridge by which the armies of the Egyptian Pharaohs passed up for generations into Syria, and by which the fiercer hordes of the Assyrian Empire passed down into Egypt on their errand of revenge. The tide of war has surged up and down over Palestine within the time of actually written history, from the day when Thothmes III scattered the army of the Syrian League at Megiddo till yesterday when Allenby routed the Turk on practically the same ground. The soil of Palestine has been more continuously fought over than that of any other land in the world; and the chance of the survival, on any great scale, of any important relics, either in the shape of inscriptions or buildings or works of art, is correspondingly smaller. There are probably no sites in Palestine which have not been ruined to their foundations, not once only, but again and again, by the blast of war.

Moreover, the race which, throughout the greater part of the history of the land, was the dominant one, was a race which, in all its branches, whether the Canaanite, which displaced the earlier inhabitants, or the Hebrew, who displaced the Canaanite, has always shown itself singularly infertile in great works either of art or architecture. There was, indeed, a race in the land which, in virtue of its origin and its traditions, might have altered the whole course of the development of Palestine. "The Philistines," as Dr. Macalister says, "were the only cultured or artistic race who

ever occupied the soil of Palestine, at least until the time
when the influence of classical Greece asserted itself too
strongly to be withstood.  Whatsoever things raised life in
the country above the dull animal existence of fellahin were
due to this people." But the Philistines were too few, and
their dominion was too brief, to have left any lasting
material impression on the land, though they succeeded in
impressing the imagination of the other races to such an
extent that the country still bears their name, and not
that of their conquerors.  The Palestinian Semite, Canaanite
or Hebrew, was neither a builder nor an artist.  When he
wanted great works in either sense, he had to seek for foreign
workmen and artists to carry them out; and, with characteristic bad taste, he turned, not to pure sources, but to the
corrupt and vulgar parodies on art of the great middlemen
of the ancient world—the Phœnicians.  Solomon's temple
was, no doubt, very gorgeous; but there can be little doubt
that it was also very bad architecture and worse art; for it
was the work of Phœnician architects and artists.  The
artistic barrenness of the Palestinian Semite is a very valid
reason for the limitation of hopes from excavation, so far
as regards works of large scale or of artistic value.

One more reason for the absence of the dramatic finds
which have rewarded excavation in other eastern lands is
found in the character of the soil and the climate.  In a land
like Egypt, with its almost rainless climate and its dry soil,
the most delicate objects, papyri, ivories, gold filigree work,
are preserved sometimes in a condition and for a length of
time which borders on the miraculous.  Professor Petrie

dug from one of the Royal Tombs at Abydos an ivory figurine of a pre-historic king whose condition after 6000 years was still such that the details of the features and even of the chequered robe were perfectly preserved. Papyri are found in which not only the writing but the colours of the vignettes with which the roll is illustrated are still amazingly fresh, in spite of their having been buried for more than 3000 years. Such a thing would be impossible in Palestine, with its variable climate and the frequent dampness of the soil. Accordingly the nearest approach to the fulfilment of that hope to which Dr. Macalister referred, of finding a letter or two from one who had heard the living words of Jesus, has come, not from Palestine, but from Egypt, where the excavations at Oxyrrhynchus have yielded the Logia of Jesus, containing sayings of our Lord unrecorded in the Gospels.

For these and other reasons, excavation in Palestine has been comparatively unproductive of results such as were once hoped for; but that is not to say that it has been fruitless and unprofitable. On the contrary, work which has produced scarcely a single object to which the casual visitor to a museum would give a second glance has sometimes done more to advance our knowledge of history and of the life of the race concerned than the discovery of the finest specimens of winged bulls or carved slabs of alabaster would do. In the early days of excavation, it was such material that was sought for almost exclusively, and not unnaturally, for only the discovery of such big and conspicuous objects could keep alive the public enthusiasm on which the explorers depended for the provision of their generally miserably scanty funds. Nowadays we have learned that the biggest and finest objects often tell us far less of real moment about the life of the race than the trifling objects which a people used in the common routine of daily life,—in fact that a potsherd may be more important than a pyramid, so far as the increase of our knowledge is concerned. This change in our estimate of the relative values of the prizes of excavation applies even to the finding of historical inscriptions. To-day an Egyptologist would scarcely thank you for the discovery of another of the vainglorious vauntings of Ramses II; but the smallest object which would help him to realise the life of the people in one of the obscure periods of Egyptian history would be welcomed with unbounded gratitude. "It is a disastrous mistake," says Dr. Macalister again, "to imagine that the aim of excavation is the discovery of contemporary written documents. They are most important, but it is very easy to exaggerate their value, especially when we are dealing with the ancient East. The monument of a vainglorious oriental king is not less fulsome, and not more convincing, than is a modern patent-medicine advertisement. . . . When (as has notoriously been the case in explorations in Assyria and Babylonia) tablets and bas-reliefs are made the chief purpose of the work, the humbler utensils that speak of the life and civilisation of the country are apt to be neglected, and their essential value lost for ever by the destructive processes of the excavation itself."

It has been in the discovery of these nominally humbler

objects, really more vital for the reconstruction of the civilisation of the race in question than the big game which lured on the early Mesopotamian explorers, that exploration in Palestine has been most fruitful, so that "we now look back through vistas of history undreamt of forty years ago, and our way is illumined by strange lights breaking through from unexpected quarters." And of such work as Dr. Macalister has blessed in the above-quoted passage, none has been more thorough nor crowned with more remarkable success than the excavations which he himself conducted from 1902 to 1905, and from 1907 to 1909 at the mound of Gezer.

Gezer has been chosen as our representative Palestinian site, not because of the greatness of the town in its historic days, nor because of any very remarkable chain of events in its story. As a matter of fact, it was never more than a comparatively insignificant town, and the main events of the current of Palestinian history mostly passed it by. It is for that very reason that it has been possible for the excavator to trace out what it is next to impossible to trace on the greater sites—the whole course of the town's development for a period of three thousand years. The site of supreme interest in the land is, of course, Jerusalem; but the levels at which the remains of the unique story of Jerusalem lie are buried beneath anything from fifty to a hundred and twenty feet of debris, the accumulation of nineteen centuries of growth and destruction, with a comparatively modern city on the top, which renders excavation, on any great and adequate scale, a practical impossibility in the

meantime, whatever may happen in the future. But at
Gezer we have a site which was occupied from Neolithic
times, which was inhabited during the historic period from
2500 B. C. onwards to the Maccabæan era by a succession
of races who have left the evidences of their culture, such as
it was, in the various strata of the mound, and where there
is, if not a series of great events, at all events a sufficiency
of historic notices to enable us to link up the story of the
town with the great movements which were happening in
the wider world. And in Gezer we have, what is comparatively rare in Palestine,—a site which has been explored and recorded with some approach to thoroughness.
The very fact that Gezer is no longer a living town, but has
been deserted for many centuries, has given to the explorer
an opportunity such as is rarely forthcoming. Save for one
modern house, and the *wely* of a Moslem saint on the northwest corner of the mound, the site is unoccupied, and the
explorer has a free hand.

The traveller from Jaffa to Jerusalem, as he crosses the
Philistian Plain, and begins to draw near to the Judæan
foothills, notices a conspicuous mound about 16¾ miles
southeast of Jaffa, which remains in sight till he enters the
hill-country. The mound is about half a mile long, and
from 450 to 600 feet broad, and rises to a height of 756
feet above sea-level, and 200 to 300 feet above the plain.
At the eastern and western ends it forms two knolls, sinking
between these to a saddle. The lower part of the mound is
of limestone rock, like the low hills to the south of it; the
upper part consists of the accumulated debris of 3000 years

of human occupation. The rock which forms the foundation of the mound is honeycombed with caves, and is itself of a soft and friable character, and is easily worked; and the neighbourhood possesses what few other sites in South Palestine possess to anything like the same extent—an abundant supply of water.

Moreover the position has unusual advantages in other respects, which in the troubled days of the early history of man in Palestine were of considerable importance. The slope of the mound, while easy enough to render its ascent by the inhabitants no very difficult task, was yet such as to render the task of an assailant no easy one in the face of opposition; while from the summit of the rock an uninterrupted view can be obtained of the whole Maritime Plain to the west and north as far as the sea and Carmel; and though the view to the south and east is restricted by the foothills and the Judæan range, a little eminence near at hand, which could readily be occupied as an outpost, gives an outlook in these directions also. Whether for honest or dishonest purposes, therefore, for watching one's enemies as they approached across the plain, or for marking from afar the caravans as they wound along the trade routes from Egypt to Mesopotamia or from Jerusalem to the sea, and swooping down upon them to take toll of their wealth, the position was admirable. You could build your city on the low hill-top, with plenty of water, the most vital of necessities, at hand; your enemies could not approach without giving you ample warning, if you kept a decent watch; and your good friends the merchants, who contributed so kindly, if involuntarily, to your well-being, were kept well under observation till such time as it was most convenient to you to relieve them of their burdens. Altogether a most desirable site in days when men lived as most men did when the world was young, either in fear themselves, or by putting fear into the hearts of others.

How it came to be known that a city of old renown had once stood upon the mound, what men they were who inhabited it, and what they call their robber's nest is a rather curious and interesting story. In 1869 Professor Clermont-Ganneau happened to be reading in the chronicle of Mujir-ed-Din the story of a Bedawin raid, in attempting to repel which the governor of Jerusalem and his subordinate of Ramleh got rather roughly handled. In the story a certain Tell-el-Jezar is mentioned more than once, and was, in fact, the place where the Arab pursuit of the discomfited governor stopped. M. Clermont-Ganneau was struck with the likeness between the name of this Tell, and that of an ancient and once famous city, which had vanished from human ken for centuries,—the city of Gezer, mentioned more than once in Egyptian records, in the historical books of the Bible, in the First Book of Maccabees, and by Josephus; and he laid down the conditions which the story of the Arab raid afforded for establishing the position of this unknown mound.

Two years later, when in Palestine, he succeeded in finding a mound which fulfilled the conditions, and which bore a name, Tell-el-Jazari, sufficiently near to that of the chronicler; but his proposal to identify Tell-el-Jazari with

Gezer was rather coldly received because he was unable to support it with positive evidence in the shape of an inscription of any sort. It seemed sufficiently unlikely that such evidence would ever be forthcoming from a site so long wrapped in oblivion, and in a country like Palestine; but the chain of coincidence, or the hand of his good genius, which had led M. Clermont-Ganneau so far, was to lead him further still, till the problem was completely solved. Two years later again the famous scholar was in Jerusalem; and a fellah brought him a rough copy of a rock-cut inscription, which he had found not far from the perennial spring of water at the foot of the mound of Tell-el-Jazari. Not very much could be made of the fellah's rude attempt at copying; but when M. Clermont-Ganneau reached the site himself, he recognised the inscription as a boundary inscription marking out one of the limits of the ancient Gezer. The extraordinary good fortune which had thus led him to the very evidence which was needed has been maintained by the subsequent discovery of four other inscriptions marking out the bounds of the city property. Few sites in the Ancient East, save those of which the tradition has never been lost, or which have been continuously occupied down to modern times, are identified so absolutely beyond the possibility of doubt as the site of Gezer.

The known history of the town thus recovered after so many centuries of oblivion may be briefly told; for there is little of outstanding interest in it. Gezer makes its earliest appearance on the page of history in the Tell-el-Amarna Tablets, where nine of these Egyptian Foreign Office letters refer to the city. From these, and especially from the letters of Abd-Khiba, governor of Jerusalem, it appears that in 1400 B. C. the loyalty of Gezer to its overlord in Egypt, like that of a good many of the Palestinian cities at the same time, was a rather more than doubtful quantity. The people of Gezer were evidently worshippers of the rising sun, not of the solar disc whose cult Akhenaten was so devoutly fostering at Tell-el-Amarna; and the rising sun was to them the invading Habiru. Later, in the XIXth Egyptian Dynasty, we find the place mentioned on the famous Merenptah Stele—"Gezer, too, is taken," while Merenptah regarded the capture of the city as an event of sufficient importance to warrant him in taking a new title from it, and called himself "the Binder of Gezer."

After Egypt, comes Israel, unless perhaps Israel has already made an appearance in the shape of the Habiru. Gezer, however, proved evidently a tougher morsel to the men of Ephraim than she had proved to Merenptah's trained soldiers, for "Ephraim drave not out the Canaanites that dwelt in Gezer." While the city proved strong enough to hold off the invaders, ill-luck attended the attempt of its kinglet to help his brother sheikh of Lachish in the hour of need. "Horam king of Gezer came up to help Lachish, and Joshua smote him and his people, till he had left him none remaining." We are to imagine the strong little city remaining as a Canaanite *enclave* in the midst of the Ephraimite occupation, though it is allotted to the Levites as one of the sacred cities.

Later, the place seems to have fallen into the hands of

Israel's stubborn enemy, the Philistine; for mention is made that David's pursuit of the routed Philistines stops at Gezer. Evidently the king did not venture to press the chase past a stronghold held by an enemy garrison. And we find David again fighting with his old enemies at Gezer, where one of his champions has to deal with one of the big men over whom the king won the victory which gave him his first fame.

Then Egypt comes into the picture once more in the days of Solomon. The magnificent king has made an alliance, which, even in the days when Egypt's fortunes had sunk low, was a splendid one for the king of the little Palestinian hill-state; and as a dowry with his Egyptian princess he got Gezer. "Pharaoh, king of Egypt, had gone up, and taken Gezer, and burnt it with fire, and slain the Canaanites that dwelt in the city, and given it for a portion unto his daughter, Solomon's wife." Curiously enough, the tradition of the city's ancient connection with the wise king and his father-in-law still survives in the neighbourhood, though the men who have preserved it have no idea of the identity of the mound with the city to which it refers. "There is an old watercourse called *Kanaet Bint-el-Kafir*— 'the conduit of the infidel's daughter'—running west of the mound in the direction of Ramleh. One day the foreman of the works asked an old man of the village, 'Who was this infidel's daughter?' 'I do not know,' said the old man, 'unless it be Pharaoh's daughter, whom our lord Solomon took to wife. For Pharaoh was an infidel. And when Solomon married her, a gift came to her from the sea, and came as far as Jazer, but we know not where Jazer may be.' "

Infidel or not, however, Pharaoh was evidently too shrewd a man to let a fortress standing close to one of his main trade routes out of his hands, even though it were to his son-in-law. The gift to the princess gave him a fine opportunity for breaking up a nest of robbers, and no doubt Solomon's wife got the revenues derived from the town as her pin-money; but Pharaoh kept a tight hand over Gezer all the same, as is shown by the abundant traces of Egyptian influence.

After the time of Solomon, the Old Testament is silent with regard to Gezer. The town continues to show evidence of Egyptian suzerainty, and there are unmistakable traces of an Hebrew element among the population; but Gezer never was really within the Hebrew kingdom, though it might be within the sphere of influence of the Jew. Then, after the fall of the Northern kingdom a more sinister figure appears for a little upon the scene, and there is evidence of an Assyrian garrison and Assyrian forms of government. Then for five hundred years there is silence again till we see the little city in the midst of the storm of the Maccabæan wars,—a bone of contention between the Syrians, and Judas and his heroic brethren. It was at Gezer that the pursuit was stayed after Judas had routed the great army of Ptolemy, Nicanor, and Gorgias at Emmaus Nicopolis, five miles away; and Gezer was again the halting place after the great Jewish captain had beaten Nicanor once more at Adasa. Then came the disastrous battle of Elasa in which Judas fell, and Bacchides the Syrian commander took possession of Gezer, and strengthened its fortifications.  They were soon tested, for erelong Simon, the last survivor of the brilliant band of brothers, laid siege to the old stronghold, battered down a part of the walls, and captured the town, building new fortifications to take the place of those which he had destroyed, and placing his son John in command of the garrison, after he had expelled the Syrian population.  We get one or two other glimpses of the place during the rest of the Maccabæan wars, and the last historical reference to it, in Josephus, shows that it had once more fallen into the hands of the Syrians, for the Jewish ambassadors sent to Rome in 128 B. C. ask that "Gazara and its springs . . . which Antiochus had taken from them in the war, contrary to the decree of the senate, might be restored to them."

Apparently the claim was allowed, and the old fortress given back to the Maccabees; and with this appeal the place vanishes from the page of history.  Before long the strong hand of Roman government rendered such strongholds useless, or perhaps put them down as undesirable. The inhabitants, no longer needing to perch within their walls on the hill-top for safety, and no longer permitted to exercise their immemorial trade of caravan-robbing, moved from the cramped site on the mound to opener quarters in the surrounding plains; and Gezer, after its three thousand years of chequered and troubled history, settled down to two thousand years more of unbroken slumber, till it was wakened, in June, 1902, by the spades and picks of Dr.

PLATE XXXII

*Palestine Exploration Fund*

EXCAVATING THE CITY OF GEZER

Macalister's workmen, and compelled to yield up line by line the story of its past.

It is, of course, quite impossible to tell within the limits of a single chapter the story of the lengthy and complicated work by which Dr. Macalister succeeded in disentangling the record of the city's growth, and of the changes which swept over it during its three thousand years of variegated life. The details of the work must be sought in the three great volumes in which the explorer has given his results to the world. To attempt to tell the story even in the order in which Dr. Macalister puzzled it out during years of hard labour would only result in hopeless confusion. For, by the very nature of the case, an excavator must begin, in all but the most exceptional cases, at the last sentence of the last chapter of the tale which he wishes to read,—in other words at the top of his mound; whereas the reader naturally wants his story to begin, as well-conducted stories should, at the beginning. Even this, however, does not sufficiently express the difficulty of taking the narrative in the order in which it revealed itself to the discoverer. You have to imagine a story in which bits of some of the chapters have disappeared altogether, and where bits of narrative lie alongside of bits of others, with which they have in reality no connection. Cutting down through the strata of an ancient city has been compared to cutting through the coats of an onion, and the simile is in some respects not inapt; but the stratification of your onion is uniform, while that of your city is not,—is indeed, anything but that. At Gezer, there were found in all eight strata, representing different periods of the city's history; but in some parts of the town six of these were missing, leaving only two chapters to be read, and in other places bits of chapters were interpolated where in the natural course of the narrative they would not have occurred. In other words, at some points the clearing away of debris before rebuilding had been so complete that there were no relics of the preceding stratum, and at others building had taken place on open spaces which had been unoccupied before, and the houses so built were therefore at a different level from those of the period to which they really belonged.

Had the town simply been ruined and rebuilt time after time, the case would have been that of our imaginary onion; but there was never a complete destruction and subsequent reconstruction. Rebuilding took place gradually and partially, and even the sack by Pharaoh did not involve a complete wreck of the town. Consequently Dr. Macalister's great onion had a skin varying greatly in thickness in different parts, and consisting in one place of quite a different number of layers from what it had in another. At one point, for example, the soil of accumulation above the rock was 16 to 17 feet thick, and contained from 3 to 6 strata of debris; at another, it varied from 5 to 23 feet, with 3 to 7 strata involved; while at a third the depth was 40 feet and 8 strata of building showed themselves.

How are we to account for the gradual rising to such a height of the successive towns occupying such a site as that of Gezer? With Western and modern customs and ideas, the thing would be impossible; but under Eastern conditions

it is very simple. To begin with, it was nobody's business
to clear away refuse and garbage, any more than to attend
to other sanitary matters. All refuse was simply thrown out
into the narrow street, there to fester and rot at its leisure,
and so the level of the streets gradually rose year by year.
Then the houses themselves were not built with mortar,
but with rough stones laid in clay. The winter rains gradually washed out the clay, and it added its contribution to
the rising level. When enough of it had been washed out,
the house naturally fell down, sometimes with deadly
suddenness; and when that happened, the house-owner, if
he survived, did not trouble to clear the ruins away before
rebuilding; he simply smoothed down the excrescences a
little, and built on the top of the rest. An instance of the
callousness of the early Oriental in this respect was found
by the Austrian excavators at Taanach. A house had fallen,
crushing to death a Canaanite mother and her five children.
The knife was still in the woman's hand when her skeleton
was discovered, and it was manifest that she had been
preparing a meal for her children when the tragedy took
place. "On her skeleton were her ornaments and amulets
still in their places, and on the wall was fixed the image of
the goddess whom the ill-fated family had regarded as their
patron." No attempt at rescue or recovery of the bodies had
been made. It was nobody's business. They were dead and
gone, and the site would do for some other person's house.
Why should anybody trouble over a few dead bodies lying
under the floor? Such considerations sufficiently explain
the phenomenon, otherwise so strange to Western minds,

of a city gradually piling itself up on the dust of its predecessors, until its last ruins are many feet above the
stratum which represents its first youth.

The story of Gezer, then, begins, so far as we are
concerned, with a race of cave-dwellers who are found in
occupation, perhaps about 3000 B. C., of the caves on the
hill-top. We are to imagine the hill stripped of all the
accumulations which subsequent ages added to its height,—
a bare limestone ridge, pierced here and there with caves of
various sizes, some wholly natural, some partly enlarged
by their occupants, others wholly artificial. The caves are
irregular chambers, or groups of chambers, varying in number, and connected by narrow winding passages and doors;
and they vary in breadth from 12 to 30 feet or
even more. The height of the roofs is so small as to suggest
that the race which used them cannot have been of lofty
stature, though in most cases a man of average height can
stand upright in them. Access to these rude dwellings is
gained by a doorway which is generally in the roof, and
opens on a rock-cut flight of steps which leads down to the
floor of the cave. The only lighting comes from the doorway, and the appointments of the caves must have been of
the rudest description, pointing to their use by a race whose
civilisation, if you can give it such a name, was of the most
elementary type. Scarcely a trace can be found of what
would have been thought one of the prime necessities of such
a dwelling,—a channel round the doorway to carry off the
water from the rock above, and prevent it from streaming
down into the house. Apparently the Troglodyte inhabi-

tants of the primitive Gezer did not bother about such trifles as a little water more or less. During the rainy season the water must have run unchecked into the mouth of the stair-way and lain in pools upon the floor below, with the pleasantest results, in the shape of rheumatism and other evils, to the inhabitants. In one case the tenant, evidently a man of advanced views, had cut a cistern in the floor of his cave to collect and store the incoming water; but obviously he was too far in advance of his time, and his rash attempt to interfere with the normal course of nature was not imitated by his neighbours.

Naturally under such conditions, and in such a climate as that of Palestine, next to nothing has survived of the furniture of these primitive homes. The pottery of the Troglodytes, here as elsewhere the most enduring memorial of a race, is of the rudest description imaginable, hand-moulded, and occasionally decorated with rudely painted cross-lines in red or white. Of the use of metal they appar-ently knew nothing, and even their flint tools, though some-times of fair workmanship, are generally only roughly flaked—a strong contrast to the exquisitely flaked tools and weapons which the neolithic inhabitants of Egypt had been turning out for centuries before. Of any attempt at art in the shape of decoration on the walls of the caves, there is hardly a trace. In one cave there are sets of rude scratch-ings, forming a kind of frieze on a band of smoother rock about four feet above the floor, and with painful effort one can distinguish attempts at the figures of animals among a maze of meaningless lines; but the figures are pathetic in their crudeness, and infinitely worse than the worst scribble of a lazy school-boy on the margin of his lesson-book. The bison of the Altamira Cave, or the rude paintings of the pre-dynastic Egyptian at Hierakonpolis are the products of a finished art compared with the crude scratchings of the Gezer artist.

Here and there in the caves were found stores of stones, some of which had been used for various purposes, artistic or domestic, and some probably stored as a handy means of defence against any intruder, man or beast. One imagines a race very little removed in culture or intelligence from the brutes with whom they contested the right to their rude homes, living a starved, comfortless, danger-haunted life on their bleak hill-top, at a time when the more highly endowed races to the north and south of them were already developing all the essentials of an advanced culture,—a people with no future, destined to be swept out of existence by the first inroad of a stronger race.

Such as they were, they still had their own primitive religion, and they have left the traces of it in the shape of a rock-cut Place of Sacrifice, where the rock surface is covered with over eighty saucer-shaped holes. Beneath this rock lie two large caves, in which, no doubt, the medicine-men of the tribe performed part of their rites to whatever god they worshipped. One of the caves has a funnel-shaped opening leading through to the surface of the rock above, in which there is cut a broad shallow channel sloping to the mouth of the funnel. Probably the sacrificed animal was laid in this channel, and its blood trickled down through the opening into the cave beneath, a pleasing offering to the Earth-God of the Troglodytes. What the sacrificial animal was may be gathered from the fact that in the cave the explorers found a number of pig bones; and it has been suggested that in this use of the pig as a sacred animal by this primitive race, which their successors no doubt regarded as everything that was vile and unclean, we may trace the origin of that aversion which has all along characterised the Semitic race which drove them out or exterminated them. "A people," says the second Isaiah, "which remain among the graves, and lodge in the monuments; which eat swine's flesh, and broth of abominable things is in their vessels." We seem to catch, after so many centuries, an echo of the horror with which the earliest Semitic invaders, no very innocent people themselves, as we shall see, regarded a race which dwelt underground, and sacrificed pigs to their dark god of the underworld. To add to the horror with which the incomers regarded the native race, the Troglodytes burned their dead,—a custom which to this day is abhorrent to the Semitic mind. Their crematorium was found by the excavators, with its layer of bone ash, its unburnt, or partially-burnt bones, and its rude pottery.

As to the race itself which we thus catch a glimpse of for a moment through the mists of the past before it is swept from the face of the world, next to nothing can ever be known. All that can be said is that they were a people of small stature, averaging not much more than an inch or two over five feet, with fair muscular development, low foreheads, and probably small intellectual capacity. It has been suggested that we may trace in them a branch of that mysterious race, the Horites, who flit like shadows for a moment across the early chapters of the Bible story, mentioned only in the record of their destruction. That may be, or may not be; we know so little, either of the Horites or of the Troglodytes of Gezer, that any assured identification of the one race with the other is impossible.

So the first chapter of the story of Gezer opens and closes. We see for a moment the rude settlement in the limestone rock, with the little skin-clad figures gathering about the doors of their homes, or clustered on the High-Place to sacrifice the sacred swine to the Earth-God in the cave below,—"a feeble folk," like the conies, who "make their houses in the rock." And then the mist comes down on the hill, and for awhile we can see nothing. When it lifts, the cave-men have vanished from the rock, and bigger and fiercer men have taken their place. How the Troglodytes vanished we cannot tell with certainty; but as we come to grasp some of the amiable characteristics of the people who succeeded them, we may form our own opinion, which probably will not be very far from the truth. When you were in the way in those days, and stood between a strong man or a strong clan and something desirable, such as the rock of Gezer with its water-springs and its outlook on the trade-routes, you were liable to be removed with swiftness and thoroughness, unless you had the heavier hand,—above all if you were a barbarous idolater who burned the dead, and used pigs for sacrifice.

The invading Semite, pious man, preferred costlier sacrifices, and has left the evidence of his taste in that direction for our edification.  It is such as to convince us that the wiping out of the little Horite settlement would be to him a trifle not worth mentioning, save as a righteous deed, well-pleasing to his god.

How and when the earliest Semitic invaders, call them Amorites, or whatever else you may choose, came to sweep away the original inhabitants of Gezer, it is impossible to say.  Roughly speaking, by perhaps 2500 B. C., or from that to 2000, the Semite had established himself upon the mound, and the town of the cave-dwellers was a thing of the past.  About 2000 B. C., let us say, the cloud lifts, and we can see the city on the hill again.  A great change has come over it, since we saw the Horites clustering on the High-Place for the sacrifice to the Earth-God.  The whole top of the hill, about half a mile in length, is surrounded by a great wall, strongly built of big stones, roughly dressed with the hammer, and bedded in mud.  The wall is from 20 to 30 feet high and 13 feet thick.  On the top of it is a parapet from which the defenders can throw down missiles upon any enemy; and at intervals the curtain is broken by shallow projecting towers, about 40 feet long and 24 feet thick.  As we come up the hill from the south, we find that this massive bulwark is pierced by a gate about 9 feet broad, leading to a narrow passage between two solid towers of brickwork. The gate is open during the day; but at sunset it will be closed by two heavy portcullises of wood, which are dropped between the six great stone slabs, which stand, three on either side of the gate, and are then jammed tight by baulks of timber. Already, before you reach the gate, your nostrils have been saluted by the aroma of Gezer, and once within the wall you are almost stifled with it; the overpowering stench of a crowded Oriental town, where such a thing as sanitation is undreamt of, and where all the garbage and filth of the tightly packed population is cast out into the narrow streets or upon the nearest open space, there to rot and fester, and breed disease. One would think that the mighty wall was a useless waste of labour, for the smell of Gezer is solid enough to repel the most daring enemy; but the inhabitants are quite careless of the horror which they breathe every day and all day, though it has left its marks, plainly enough to be seen, on their unhealthy complexions, and their disease-marked frames. Over the sea, in Crete, the Minoan of this time is rearing stately palaces, whose drainage-systems make us open our eyes with wonder at the present day, so modern are they; but the Semite of Gezer in those days was as indifferent as his successor of to-day to what the ordinary civilised man regards as a first essential of decency in life. If you were to examine the cisterns from which they draw the water-supply for their cooking, or for their infrequent ablutions, you would very likely find at the bottom of several of them all that remains of one of the family, or of the family next door, who unfortunately over-balanced himself or herself in stooping to draw up the water-pot, and found a watery grave. Literally so; for again it was nobody's business to clean out the cistern, and the mourners were at least saved the trouble of providing a funeral. Whether they went on drinking essence of ancestor or not, one cannnot say positively. "We can but hope," says Dr. Macalister, "that the water was never used again: certainly the bodies were never taken out." On the one side you have a hope; on the other a certainty.

Passing through the narrow crooked streets, paved with cobblestones worn smooth by the tread of innumerable bare feet, we notice among the dirty mud-plastered houses one considerably larger than its fellows, with a courtyard around it. Hold your breath as you pass it, for this is the palace of the sheikh,—King of Gezer, as he calls himself, who holds the power of life and death over every one within the walls, except when the Egyptian resident sees fit to interfere. For these are days when the arm of Egypt, under the Senuserts and Amenemhats of the XIIth Dynasty, is both long and strong, and the king of Gezer, big man as he is within his own walls, is as the dust under the sandals of the Good God who rules by the Nile. If you enter the court-yard, you may see the workmen busy upon the most remark-able piece of engineering that ever was carried out in Gezer, or, for the matter of that, anywhere else in Palestine, save in later Jerusalem; so much the most remarkable, that one wonders if the Amorite really had much to do with the planning of it at all events, or if that was not rather the work of one of Senusert's military engineers.

This is the great water-tunnel of Gezer. You enter it by a key-hole-shaped entrance, and find yourself in a huge arched passage, 12 feet across, and 23 feet high, whose

walls the workmen are busily finishing off with their
flint tools. The passage slopes downwards at an angle
of about 30 degrees, and you follow it down a staircase of
80 steps, hewn, like the rest of the work, out of the solid
rock, till you are 90 feet below the level of the courtyard
above. Here the passage ends in a great natural cave, 80
feet by 28, in which rises a strong spring of water. One
thing is sure,—that with such a spring in the very heart of
the town, Gezer will never suffer from thirst in time of
siege. Even if the plan of the work was due to Egyptian
influence, the execution of it is at least a testimony to the
industry of the Amorite workmen who carried it out with
their rude stone tools.

Further on in the town you come upon another trace
of Egyptian influence, in the shape of a small temple to one
of the Egyptian gods, inscribed all over with the picture-
writing of the Nile, like its huge sister which Senusert has
been rearing to Ra at Heliopolis. But though Egyptian
religion has thus its place in the town, the inhabitants have
their own High-Place on an open piece of ground near the
centre of the town. It is an irregularly shaped area, about
150 feet by 120, and in the middle of it stands a row of ten
great unhewn stones set upright, such stones as Jacob set
up for a pillar at Bethel, anointing them with oil, after his
vision of the heavenly ladder. The seventh stone is different from the others, and has been brought from a distance,
for no such rock is found in the neighbourhood. If you
examine it, you will see that a groove runs round the middle
of it, where a rope has been fastened to drag it along, or to

hold it steady on a sledge; and you remember how in later days Mesha, king of Moab, records how he dragged the "Ariel of Dodah" from Ataroth, and set it up before Chemosh, his god, in Kerioth. No doubt this seventh stone (the lucky number), is the record of some successful raid on another town, perhaps on Jerusalem, for the stone is of a kind found there, in which the king of Gezer carried off one of the sacred pillars of the Jebusite High-Place to adorn his sanctuary. As to the rites which go on under the shadow of the standing-stones of Gezer, perhaps the less said the better. To the Amorite mind of that day there may have been something very sacred about them; to the Western mind of to-day they can be summed up in two words,—beastliness and blood. As to the first part of this description, the evidence of the type of votive offering found on the high place is too clear to be misunderstood; as to the second, it is enough to say that "the whole area of the High Place was found on excavation to be a cemetery of new-born infants." How deep in the Semitic mind the idea of the need of sacrificing the first-born to the Lord lay is shown by the fact that even a man like Abraham was obsessed by it till the vampire thought was driven from his mind by the incident on Moriah. Manifestly the Gezerites regularly sacrificed their first-born to whatever god or demon they adored, and the little skeletons, crushed into large two-handled jars, and buried under the shadow of the sacred stones, are the witnesses to their devotion to a faith surely the most horrible and degrading which has ever possessed the human mind. Indications were not wanting that adults, as well as infants, were sometimes offered on this place of abominations; and indeed the whole city gave evidence of what Dr. Macalister calls "an Aztec-like disregard of the value of human life."

As you go through the streets you are stopped by the crowd gathered to watch the ceremony at the foundation of a new house. No house can be lucky unless it is reared upon a sacrificed life, and so the builder of this one is going to ensure good fortune by the offering of one of his dependants. Being a thrifty man, he chooses one who is crippled with disease and comparatively useless; and so a poor old woman, bent double with spinal curvature, is dragged along, bound, and thrown into a hole in the ground, with a jar of food and a bowl of water beside her to nourish her spirit in the shades; and the stones of the new house are piled above the poor tortured body. A little further along they sacrificed a man recently; but he had lost his left hand in a fight anyway, and so was not of much use. If you could dig down in another spot, not far away, you would come upon three bodies, or rather two bodies and a half, disposed in a way that suggests an even ghastlier horror. Two skeletons are lying side by side, and above them lies the upper half of the body of a youth about 18 years of age, who has been sawn asunder at the waist. Around the bones lie vessels for food and drink; and the grimmest horror of all is that the skeleton fingers of the left hand of one of the figures are dipping into one of the bowls. You picture the poor wretch groping in the stifling darkness of his living grave for a last morsel of food; and when you have seen the "weird charnel-house," as the excavator justly calls the ghastly cistern where fourteen men and a young girl of sixteen, this last sawn asunder at the waist also, had been cast, and wondered what horrible tragedy could account for their presence in such a place, you have probably had about enough of "the iniquity of the Amorite," and wonder, not at the command of extermination which went forth against the race, but rather that it was allowed to curse the earth for so long.

We turn from these horrors to see if the craftsmen of Gezer are doing any work of such quality as that by which even a race so brutal as the Assyrian has succeeded in asserting its claim to the interest of the civilised world, if not to its affection; but the Amorite is as infertile in art as he is fertile in cruelty. Up in the streets above the abominations we have been talking about, and in such air as Gezer may call fresh, you find her craftsmen working in their little booths,—potters, metal-workers, joiners and weavers. Not one of them apparently has an idea of his own; before them they all have some Egyptian model or another, and they are all feebly and bunglingly imitating the products of a civilisation that they have not the wit really to understand or appreciate. "From first to last," says Dr. Macalister, "there was not a native potter in Palestine who could so much as invent a new design to paint on his waterpots. There was not an armourer who could invent a new pattern of sword or arrowhead." The native Canaanite was never more than an imitator, and a feeble one at that, of the handicraft of better men. Yet in this land, so cursed from the beginning by unoriginality, and from the same stock as

this Amorite race, so helpless without the prop of other
men's ideas, and so revoltingly brutal in its religious conceptions, there rose at last a conception of God and of
human duty, the purest, the most spiritual, and the stateliest which the world has ever known! It is one of the
standing mysteries of human history.

It is a matter of four centuries before the cloud lifts from
the hill again so that we can get another glimpse of what is
happening in Gezer. When we see the little city again,
the Amorite is still there, and as much indebted to outside
influences as ever; but meanwhile great changes have taken
place in the wider world, and these are reflected in the city's
attitude towards its old suzerain, Egypt. In a rash moment
the king of Gezer had joined the Syrian League, which
dreamed of holding back the great conqueror, Thothmes III,
from his career of conquest in Syria. The army of the
League was scattered like chaff at Megiddo by the first
whirlwind charge of the Egyptian chariots, and Gezer, like
the other cities of the ill-fated coalition, had to pay the price
of its folly. For many a day the strong hand of the
XVIIIth Dynasty Egyptian Empire held the old hill
fortress in a grip of iron. Then came evil days for the
Empire. Amenhotep III, last of the great kings of the
dynasty, passed away, and his son, Amenhotep IV or
Akhenaten, one of the most remarkable men of history, sat
upon the throne of the Pharaohs,—a saint, no doubt, but,
like another saintly royalty, "a sair sanct for the crown."
Under his rule, which was concerned more with religious
reformations than with the guarding of the empire which

his ancestors had won, Syria slipped bit by bit from the slackening grasp of its overlord, till scarcely a city was left to Egypt.

Gezer shared in the general scuttle from under the shadow of Egypt to the protection of what seemed the stronger, at all events the nearer and more active power. The Amorite king of the town is a certain Yapahi, and he has left us the written record of some of his troubles and perplexities. His first letter to his overlord shows him still loyal, in words, at all events, but very uncomfortable. His brother has deserted him to join the enemies of Pharaoh, and doubtless Yapahi only holds to his allegiance because he is not yet quite sure which way the cat is going to jump. We may listen to his first letter, as a specimen of the grovelling of these little local kinglets before a real king. "To the king my lord, my gods, my sun, the sun of heaven, thus hath spoken Yapahi the Man of Gezer, the dust of thy two feet, the groom of thy horse. At the two feet of the king my lord, the sun of heaven, have I bowed me down seven and seven times with breast and back. All that the king saith to me, well, well do I hear. A servant of the king am I, and the dust of thy two feet. Let the king my lord learn that my youngest brother hath deserted me, and hath entered Makkedah, and his two hands have submitted to the *Sa-Gaz*. And lo, the land . . . is hostile to me. Therefore care for thy land. Let my lord write to his lieutenant regarding this event."

Yapahi's somewhat tremulous loyalty was not above suspicion, if we may believe another of the letter-writers

of the time, Abd-Khiba, governor of Jerusalem, who has
much to say of the disloyalty of Gezer; and in any case,
loyalty was of little avail in the general landslide of the
Egyptian possessions in Syria.  Gezer finally passed from
Yapahi's feeble grasp into rebel hands; and no doubt paid
for its defection when Merenptah invaded the land, and
added to his titles the epithet, "Binder of Gezer."  One
ivory pectoral bearing the cartouche of Merenptah is the sole
record of his conquest which the excavations have brought
to light.

The exploration of the mound has added nothing to the
story which the Books of Joshua and Judges give of the
city's relation to the Hebrew conquest.  We can figure King
Horam and his fighting men setting out on their ill-fated
expedition for the relief of Lachish, never to return; and
then we see the little robber's nest rallying after its disaster,
and facing the enemy so boldly that the Ephraimites do not
venture to risk a siege, but simply people the country around,
leaving the Gezerites, who, after all, were their not very far-
removed cousins, to the enjoyment of their amiable rites on
the hill-top—a source of future corruption for the Israel
that was to be.

What the Hebrews were not able to do, the Philistines
had apparently succeeded in doing by the time of David.
The references to Gezer in the accounts of the wars of the
Hebrew champion indicate that the town was then a Philistine stronghold, past which David did not venture to press
his victorious pursuit of his routed foes; and that later in
his reign the king attacked his old enemies there with some

success, though there is no claim to the capture of the city. The richest graves which were found during the excavations belong to this period, and the articles found in them, particularly those of wrought silver, are such as elsewhere would be called Late Mycenæan. That is to say, they correspond to what we know of the origin and culture of the Philistines, who were, in all probability, a fragment of the Dispersal of the great Minoan Empire. Specially interesting is the fact that one of the rare occurrences of iron in the city of this time is in one of these Philistine tombs,—a fact which lends an added probability to the interpretation of the obscure passage in I Samuel xiii, which suggests that the Philistines alone had the use of iron weapons at this time, and by their control of the coast trade hindered their enemies the Hebrews from gaining possession of the superior metal, only King Saul and his son Jonathan being able to secure the coveted iron equipment.

The traces of the occupation of the city and the strengthening of its fortifications by Solomon, after its capture by his father-in-law, the Egyptian Pharaoh, are probably to be found in the solid towers of squared masonry which appear to have been added to the outer wall at this period, and in the section of wall of the same character which seems to have taken the place of a part of the wall which had been breached, no doubt by the siege-engines of the Egyptian king when he captured the town. These towers were added to and strengthened by rougher masonry in later days, probably at the time when the Syrian general Bacchides refortified the city; but the Solomonic work is of infinitely better character than the hasty patching of the Syrian bastions which mask it.

Of the Assyrian domination of Gezer, about the time of Manasseh, the only evidence which survives is in the shape of two tablets bearing cuneiform inscriptions, one of which relates to the sale of certain slaves, and guarantees them against sickness and physical defects, and the other gives details of the sale of a field by a Hebrew named Nethaniah. Even at this time, though Assyrian influence is strong enough to render the transaction of business according to Assyrian forms necessary, the town was still apparently under Egyptian officials, for one of the witnesses to the first document is the governor, who bears a name, Huruasi, of regular Egyptian form.

From this time, about 649 B. C., the story of Gezer is a blank, till we see it once more as a centre of strife in the troubled days of the Maccabæan revolt. In the earlier days of the War of Independence, Gezer appears in its old rôle of the stronghold of the foes of Israel, a thorn in the flesh of the champions of Hebrew freedom, and, as in old days, the spot where their victorious pursuit of their enemies is checked.   But in 143 B. C., there comes the last, and one of the most dramatic chapters of the history of the old fortress. For "in those days, he [Simon Maccabæus] encamped against Gazara, and compassed it round about with armies; and he made an engine of siege, and brought it up to the city and smote a tower, and took it.   And they that were in the engine leaped forth into the city; and there was a great uproar in the city; and they of the city rent their clothes, and went upon the walls with their wives and children, and cried with a loud voice, making request to Simon to give them his right hand. And they said, 'Deal not with us according to our wickedness, but according to thy mercy.' And Simon was reconciled unto them, and did not fight against them: and he put them out of the city, and cleansed the houses wherein the idols were, and so entered into it with singing and giving praise. And he put all uncleanness out of it, and placed in it such men as would keep the law, and made it stronger than it was before, and built therein a dwelling-place for himself." (I Macc. xiii 43-48.)

The story of the discovery of the actual relics of this old chapter of victory and clemency is one of the curiosities of the excavation of Gezer. Dr. Macalister, as he tells us, had found it necessary to establish a standard punishment for those of his workmen who were found to be playing tricks with any of the antiquities which they discovered. Men who held back any of their finds were placed on a "penal settlement"—that is to say, they were set to trace the course of the city wall—a piece of work with few possibilities of interesting finds, and therefore with correspondingly few possibilities of the consequent "bakhshish." One day these culprits, in their monotonous work of tracing the line of the wall, found that it came to a sudden stop. They were transferred to the opposite side of the wall, and bidden to trace it backwards towards the place where the gap occurred; and again they lost track of it, so that there was a space of about 300 feet in which no wall could be found. Trenches were cut at right angles to the line of the wall to find out if it bent inwards at this point, with the quite unexpected result that instead of a wall there came to light the remains of two gates and a large castellated structure, which was proved, by the pottery associated with it, to be of the Maccabæan period. Gradually Dr. Macalister began to form the hope that what he had discovered was the Maccabæan Castle, the "dwelling-place" which Simon had built in Gezer for himself.

So far, however, this was no more than a probability; but then the good genius who had led M. Clermont-Ganneau in the beginning to the identification of the site, evidently took the matter in hand again, and put the conjecture beyond the reach of doubt. One day one of the basket-girls who carried away the earth dug out by the regular diggers spied some marks on a fragment of stone lying by the wall. She at once brought the stone to the excavator, and the marks proved to be a Greek inscription, roughly scratched in an almost illegible hand. Patient study was required for the decipherment of the hurriedly scratched letters; but the toil brought its own reward, in the shape of the quaintest possible evidence, absolutely unquestionable, that the enigmatic building was indeed the castle of the victorious Simon Maccabæus. The inscription, when deciphered, was seen to run thus: "Says Pampras; may fire pursue Simon's palace!"

The little scrap of lettered stone brings the whole story of more than two thousand years ago to light again. You see the triumphant Maccabæan in his mercy giving life to his Syrian foes, but inexorably driving them out of the town to make room for "such men as would keep the law," and perhaps keeping enough of his conquered enemies about for a while to rear the castle by which he meant to close the breach which his battering-ram had made in the wall. And then you see Pampras, one of these Syrian labourers, sore at being dispossessed of his home, and sorer still at being put to forced labour for his conquerer, casting about in his mind for a mode of revenging himself. Simon had showed him mercy indeed; but what was a mercy which drove you from your home, and forced you to toil at the rearing of a standing memorial of your loss and shame! Force was impossible against the conquering Maccabæan; but to get a blasting curse built into the very walls of his insolent castle,—that would be a revenge worth while! So Pampras hurriedly scratched his curse on the block of stone which he was handling, taking care that no Jewish overseer noticed what he was doing, and in due course the stone was built into the wall, and Pampras felt that he had at least got a little of his own back. But "the best-laid schemes" have a proverbial habit of failing, and that of poor Pampras was no exception. Surely it would have doubled his bitterness of soul could he have foreseen the result of his curse, and realised that his device to blast his enemy would be the one thing needed to give the credit for the Maccabæan castle to the hated conqueror.

So, with this sad miscarriage of a well-planned scheme, the story of Gezer comes to a close, for the later fragments of history relating to the old site are not of importance sufficient for us to linger over them. Roughly we may

estimate the life of the old hill-fortress at from 3000 to
3500 years, and the glimpses we have had of it during that
period show us a sufficiently chequered story. Horite,
Amorite, Hebrew, Egyptian, Philistine, Assyrian, Macedonian, and Hebrew again, come and go through the thirty-
odd centuries, each leaving his impress on the mound for our
time to read—a city of many races, indeed! And if we
have seen little to admire, and much to disgust in the record
of the peoples who reared the walls and crowded the close-
packed homes of Gezer, we can at least be thankful that
the record closes with a true hero, in the person of Simon
Maccabæus, and (shall we say?) with a touch of genuine
human nature, which we should be sorry to miss, in the
Curse of Pampras.

# BIBLIOGRAPHY

The following short list of books contains those which will be found most useful for the further study of the subjects dealt with in the preceding pages. It makes no claim to be exhaustive, but mentions the bulk of the volumes which are both authoritative and accessible.

*Chapters II to VI:*
MASPERO: Histoire Ancienne des Peuples de l'Orient Classique.
MASPERO: Les Momies Royales de Deir-el-Bahari.
PETRIE: History of Egypt.
PETRIE: Syria and Egypt.
PETRIE: Royal Tombs of the First Dynasty.
PETRIE: Abydos.
PETRIE: Tell el Amarna.
BREASTED: History of Egypt.
BREASTED: Ancient Records.
BREASTED: Development of Religion and Thought in Ancient Egypt.
HALL: Ancient History of the Near East.
PEET: The Cemeteries of Abydos.
AMÉLINEAU: Les Nouvelles Fouilles d'Abydos.
J. DE MORGAN: Recherches sur les origines de l'Égypte.
ERMAN: Life in Ancient Egypt.
ERMAN: Handbook of Egyptian Religion.
WEIGALL: The Treasury of Ancient Egypt.
WEIGALL: Akhnaton, Pharaoh of Egypt.
WIEDEMANN: Religion of the Ancient Egyptians.
NAVILLE: Deir-el-Bahari.
DAVIES, N. DE G.: The Rock Tombs of El Amarna.
BELZONI: Narrative of the Operations and Recent Discoveries
KING and HALL: Egypt and Western Asia.
DAVIS, T. M.: The Tomb of Iouiya and Touiyou.
DAVIS, T. M.: The Tomb of Hatshopsouitou.
DAVIS, T. M.: The Tomb of Harmhabi and Touatankhamanou.
DAVIS, T. M.: The Tomb of Siphtah.

DAVIS, T. M.: The Tomb of Thoutmes IV.
BAEDEKER: Guide-Book—Egypt.
HAMMERTON: The Wonders of the Past.
BAIKIE: The Story of the Pharaohs.
ELLIOT SMITH: Tutankhamen and the Discovery of his Tomb.
BUDGE: Tutankhamen, Amenism, Atenism, and Egyptian Monotheism.
PETRIE: Social Life in Ancient Egypt.
CAMBRIDGE ANCIENT HISTORY, THE, Vol. I, Egypt and Babylonia to 1580 B. C.—various authors.

*Chapters VII to IX:*
DE SARZEC and HEUZEY: Découvertes en Chaldée.
HILPRECHT: Recent Explorations in Bible Lands.
HALL: Ancient History, and Egypt and Western Asia.
KING, L. W.: History of Sumer and Akkad.
KING, L. W.: History of Babylon.
MASPERO: Histoire Ancienne.
SAYCE: Babylonians and Assyrians.
JASTROW: Religion of Babylonia and Assyria.
JASTROW: History of Babylonia and Assyria.
GOODSPEED: History of the Babylonians and Assyrians.
WINCKLER: History of Babylonia and Assyria.
HANDCOCK: Mesopotamian Archæology.
KOLDEWEY: The Excavations at Babylon.
LAYARD: Nineveh and Its Remains.
LAYARD: Nineveh and Babylon.
CAMBRIDGE ANCIENT HISTORY, THE, Vol. I, Egypt and Babylonia to 1580 B. C.—various authors.

*Chapters X to XII:*
EVANS: The Palace of Minos at Knossos.
EVANS: Essai de Classification des Époques de la Civilisation Minoenne.
EVANS: Reports in the Annual of the British School at Athens, Vol. VI, *et seq.*
DUSSAUD: Les Civilisations pré-Helléniques dans le Bassin de la Mer Egée.
BURROWS: The Discoveries in Crete.
HALL: Ægean Archæology.
HAWES: Crete, the Forerunner of Greece.

HAWES, H. B.: Gournia, Vasiliki, and Other Prehistoric Sites.
HOGARTH: Authority and Archæology.
HOGARTH: Ionia and the East.
LANG: Homer and His Age.
LEAF: Troy.
RIDGEWAY: The Early Age of Greece.
TSOUNTAS and MANATT: The Mycenæan Age.
MOSSO: The Palaces of Crete.
SCHUCHHARDT: Schliemann's Excavations.
GLASGOW: The Minoans.
BAIKIE: The Sea-Kings of Crete.

*Chapter XIII:*

MACALISTER: The Excavation of Gezer.
MACALISTER: Bible Side-Lights from the Mound of Gezer.
MACALISTER: Civilization in Palestine.
DRIVER: Modern Research as Illustrating the Bible.
Reports of the Palestine Exploration Fund.

# INDEX

## A

Aahmes, 93, 123
Aahmes Nefertari, 132
Aah-hotep II, 132
Abbott Papyrus, 148
Abdashirta, 72-74
Abd-er-Rassoul Ahmed, 131
  Mohammed, 130, 131
Abd-khiba, 73, 74, 421, 442
Abimilki, 54, 73, 81
Abu-Shahrain, 183
Abydos, 19 et seq.
  List of Kings, 31, 32
  Royal Tombs, 32 et seq.
Abzu-banda, 215
Achæans, 4, 404, 405
Achilles, 348; Shield of, 349
Acrocorinthus, 328
Acropolis, 328
Adad-nirari, 281
Adasa, 423
Agamemnon, 327, 330, 331, 340-
  45-47, 363
Ahab, 294
Ahaz, 294
Aigisthos, 331, 340, 345, 363
Aithousa, 336
Ajax, 348
Akhenaten, 50 et seq. 127, 141 et
  seq. 440-1
  Burial of, 76 et seq.
Akhetaten, 50 et seq.
Akhiababa, 304.
Akkad, 184 et seq.
  Dynasty of, 217
  Akhush, 215
Alexander, 95, 227, 242
Alkinoös, 338

Amanus, Mt., 221
Amarna, Tell el, 49 et seq.
  Palace of, 65
  Temple, 66
  Art of, 68-70
  Tablets of, 71 et seq., 291, 420
Amélineau, 23, 29, 34-37
Amelu, 257
Amen, 29, 55
Amenemhat, 92
  III, 92, 99, 355
Amenhotep I, 132
  Temple of, 111
  Mummy of, 134
  III, 53, 55-57, 96, 97, 105, 107-
  109, 123
  Temple of, 111 et seq.
  Mummy of, 134
Amentet, 31
Amherst Papyrus, 148
Ammiditana, 243
Amorites (Amurru), 221, 433 et
  seq.
Anastasi, 85
Ankh. s. en. Amen, 179-181
Ankh. s. en. pa. Aten, 77, 163
Anshan, 218
Antasurra, 215
Antefs, 92
Antiochus, 424
Anu, 250
Anu-Adad Temple, 290, 306
Anubis, 160
Annunaki, 250
Arakhtu Canal, 295
Archæanax, 320
Archæology, methods of, 9-18
Argolis, 328-330
Argos, 330-332